Gender and Diversity Studies

Ingrid Jungwirth
Carola Bauschke-Urban (eds.)

Gender and Diversity Studies

European Perspectives

Verlag Barbara Budrich
Opladen • Berlin • Toronto 2019

A CIP catalogue record for this book is available from
Die Deutsche Bibliothek (The German Library)

ISBN 978-3-8474-0549-8 (Paperback)
eISBN 978-3-8474-0948-9 (eBook)

Die Deutsche Bibliothek – CIP-Einheitsaufnahme
Ein Titeldatensatz für die Publikation ist bei der Deutschen Bibliothek erhältlich.

Verlag Barbara Budrich GmbH
Stauffenbergstr. 7. D-51379 Leverkusen Opladen, Germany

86 Delma Drive. Toronto, ON M8W 4P6 Canada
www.barbara-budrich.net

Jacket illustration by Bettina Lehfeldt, Kleinmachnow, Germany – www.lehfeldtgraphic.de
Picture credits: Florian Losch, Germany
Typesetting: Beate Glaubitz, Leverkusen, Germany
Printed in Europe on acid-free paper by
paper&tinta, Warsaw

Content

Ilse Lenz

Foreword: Diversity and Transnational Exchange

How can diversity studies develop its own reflexive diversity, and its own vivid internal and international exchanges? There is a trend towards 'diversity speech' in public which tends to repeat ideas and formulas along the same lines of diversity and economic efficiency: the same people in diverse locations circulating the same concepts.

In contrast, this book about *Gender and Diversity Studies in European Perspectives* shows the potential and meaning of fresh transnational approaches: it showcases process perspectives on 'diversity on the move' – particularly relevant since the EU legally incorporated gender equality and anti-discrimination into its policies, which has stimulated diversity research and practice. The book reflects these processes from both inside the EU and outside it, creating a conversation about gender equality and anti-discrimination between Germany, the United Kingdom, Turkey, Tunisia and Russia. Thus, perspectives on EU Gender Equality Policies in times of crisis are exchanged. The section on *Gender and Diversity Studies: Concepts and Methods* is especially promising for exchange and mutual conceptual development in these fields.

Gender and Diversity Studies in European Perspectives also focuses on global power relationships and the processes of drawing boundaries around 'fortress EU' in the entangled developments between, for example, Europe and North Africa. External boundaries are being enforced in these regions at the same time as gender equality and anti-discrimination policies are being promoted in the European Union. In order to be inclusive, the discussion on diversity must analyse these power relations and their shifts.

What would transnational and interdisciplinary gender and diversity studies look like? They would not be limited to an assemblage of national reports or speakers from the Global North. Rather, they would include diverse speakers from diverse regions, reflect on power relationships as well as shared goals of gender/intersectional justice, and promote intensive exchange and conversation.

These exchanges and interconnections are especially important for students. This book can be widely used for teaching on both disciplinary and interdisciplinary courses. It covers the fields of *Gender and Diversity Studies: practices, methods and concepts*, *Equal Opportunities and Human Rights*, and *Changing Inequalities: work and organizations*. It will be relevant not only for diversity and gender studies, but for legal and labour studies as well.

This volume is so promising for diversity studies, reflecting diversity and its changing contexts – I am really looking forward to reading and discussing it!

Ingrid Jungwirth

Introduction: Gender and Diversity Studies – European perspectives

Gender and diversity studies as a developing field of research is approached in this volume by drawing a connection to a broader political context, and by arguing that the process of Europeanization, and particularly its equal opportunity policies, have also contributed to the formation of gender and diversity studies. In this book we emphasize the link between equal opportunity policies and the development of an academic field of gender and diversity studies. The starting point for our textbook is the implementation of anti-discrimination laws and policies promoted by the European Union on the basis of treaties and directives binding on the member states. With the Amsterdam treaty of 1997, gender mainstreaming became obligatory and EU-directives (2000 to 2004) required the integration of anti-discrimination principles and activities by national law. These legally binding conditions have had an impact on theoretical, methodological and practical challenges faced by gender and diversity studies. We argue that universities and the sciences have had to incorporate these requirements into the curricula in research and teaching to align with the objectives of anti-discrimination and gender mainstreaming. Consequently, the book examines the current state of gender and diversity studies taking into account that the path to establishing gender and diversity studies at universities and in research has been paved by these policies – be it by the establishment of research issues or be it by the determination of equal opportunity requirements for the organization of research. Roughly 30 years after the definition of 'gender mainstreaming', by the EU-commission in 1988, may be a good point in time for such an assessment.

The intention of this book is to present a variety of approaches to gender and diversity studies in different regions in Europe as an important basis for the future development of the field. Starting with a German-Dutch cross-border cooperation, we extended the scope to other parts of Europe and beyond. Dealing with rights has two sides to it: on the one side, a homogenization is pursued including, in the case of the EU, its members to equal opportunity policies and anti-discrimination law. On the other side, these policies and laws are exclusive to non-members. Put differently, while certain rights and antidiscrimination policies are strengthened within the EU and internal borders between member states are successively being dissolved, external borders are enforced – be it South European /African or East European. Taking processes of European homogenization into consideration: What does this mean for the definition of 'European perspectives' on gender and diversity? Which regional inequalities are reproduced and what kind of impact do these have on European gender and diversity studies? How inclusive is a European gender and diversity discussion itself?

The book includes articles from different regions in Europe and beyond in the fields of gender and diversity studies. We take a critical perspective on the effects of the integration policy of the EU and the exclusions it produces. The book is conceptualized as a textbook for students of gender and diversity studies, introducing issues and objectives as well as theoretical approaches, methods and recent research findings.

1 Gender and Diversity Studies

Diversity studies as a developing field has been defined in connection to the concept of 'difference' taking up political discourses that were initiated decades ago by social movements, such as the women's movements, gay, lesbian and queer, anti-racism as well as disability rights movements. 'Difference' is brought up and emphasized in political discourses and theory formation in the context of globalization processes and increased societal differentiation, particularly in post-industrial economies. The recognition of difference is a central focus, referring to social categories, for example, those that are mentioned in the recently implemented laws such as the German General Act on Equal Treatment (*Allgemeines Gleichbehandlungsgesetz*) include gender, race, ethnicity, sexuality, disability, age, religion and beliefs. Building up on EU directives, nation states that are members of the European Union were to come up with laws that address anti-discrimination more concretely and as such beyond existing laws in the member states which included equal rights in a general sense, an example being the Basic Law (*Grundgesetz*) in Germany. One of the core issues promoted in the context of the emerging field of diversity studies are claims to recognize differences, plurality, inclusion, amongst others, and the challenging of norms and norm setting, for example, amongst the dominant groups in organizations (Krell, Riedmüller, Sieben and Vinz 2006:8).

In this regard, diversity studies link to human rights discourses that are identified in the context of globalization and migration studies, often opposing nationalist or re-nationalization tendencies and political agendas (Steger 2017;

Portes and DeWind 2007; Castles and Miller 2009; Pries 2004). The public discourse on diversity seems to be connected to the normative claim that "'difference' is OK" (Vertovec 2015:3), in the sense of difference from the dominant norm. One of the observations that we could locate, while writing this book, is that the ideal of diversity as being different from a dominant norm, seems to have gained legitimacy in the public discourse in many societies.

Diversity studies as a scientific field can be distinguished from the public discourse. From the perspective of the social sciences, a distance between scientific concepts and analysis, on the one hand, and everyday experience of diversity and/or difference, on the other hand, is required, in order to not only reproduce commonplace knowledge – what we have known already. Diversity studies needs to come up with scientific concepts and theoretical approaches that are specific and can be examined through empirical research. This principle of the social sciences is put forward by Brubaker in an investigation among social sciences and humanities scholars carried through by Vertovec (2015:4). Other positions and notions of diversity from these interviews, summarized by Vertovec, include the expectation that new opportunities are created to deal with difference in more advanced ways (according to Brubaker, Landau and Wimmer, cited in Vertovec 2015:9) and their social organization (according to Appadurai, cited in Vertovec 2015:9) as well as with their interrelations, comprise intersectionality and multidimensionality in particular (Glick-Schiller, Beck, Eriksen and Eade, cited in Vertovec 2015:9). Moreover, issues of differentiation as a core topic of the social sciences can be addressed (according to Brubaker and Koenig, cited in Vertovec 2015:9).

In an attempt to define topics in diversity studies, Vertovec includes topics of social differentiation and questions on how "categories of difference" are constructed and reproduced (ibid.:10), distinguishing these processes from the study of "complex social environments" (ibid.) in which these processes evolve. In the social sciences, several theoretical approaches have been developed to deal with these processes of reproduction of 'differences', which have been analyzed as 'social inequalities' in sociology. This leads us to social inequality as a further central concept of diversity in diversity studies which refers to the systematic access (or lack of access) to socially validated assets and resources, based on belonging to a social group determined by categorizations of gender, class, ethnicity or race, sexuality, religion or disability. Diversity studies can draw on these theoretical foundations for the design and realization of empirical research and successive theory building, which should give further insights into how these processes of reproducing social inequalities happen in an increasingly complex and faster changing social world. Moreover, the question of the interrelation between the reproduction of social inequalities and societal changes leading to an increased differentiation can be addressed.

Krell et al. (2006) emphasize the significance of gender studies when defining the scope of diversity studies by linking gender studies and diversity studies. Gender studies has contributed influential theoretical approaches (see Bührmann 2015), for example, the approach of 'doing gender' by West and Zimmerman (1987) that explains the relevance of the interactional level for the reproduction of 'differences' or inequalities of gender in relation to the level of societal institutions. This approach has been extended to other social categories such as the construction of race, ethnicity and class under the term of 'doing difference' (West and Fenstermaker 1995). Similarly, migration and racism studies have come up with concepts to analyze the construction of ethnicity and race in interactions in relation to societal institutions (for example, Omi and Winant 1994; Brubaker 2004; Miles and Brown 2008; Wimmer 2013). In disability studies the central social model of disability has been coined (Oliver 1990; Bury 1996; Barnes 1997). This research and theory development is built on theoretical approaches in sociology which focus specifically on interactions and everyday life as a most relevant site in which society and social inequalities are reproduced through the interrelatedness of social actions, social institutions and social structures (Goffman 1959; Berger and Luckmann 1966; Garfinkel 1967)[1]. Class, as a social category of achieved inequality ranges on a different level than the categories of ascribed inequalities, for example, gender. The extent to which the interactional level is significant in the reproduction of social inequality based on social origin related to class or social milieu has been shown most prominently by Bourdieu's study *Distinction* (1979/1984) and has engendered a broad range of research. Consequently, we can point out three levels of interest for diversity studies – structures, institutions and interactions, or, in reference to Vertovec' formulation: configurations, representations and 'encounters' (2015:17).

What seems to come increasingly to the forefront in the context of emerging diversity studies is the intersectionality and multidimensionality of social relations and social inequalities (Lutz 2015; Faist 2015). The focus on one social category alone and, specifically, determining hierarchies between dimensions of social inequality is rejected under the umbrella of diversity studies (Krell et al. 2006:13; Vertovec 2015:10). From a sociological perspective, we address differences and diversity as dimensions of social inequality, since it is a systematic access or lack of access to opportunities related to belonging to social groups that is one of the core interests of research and theory formation in sociology and several other social sciences. Moreover, these inequalities are in sharp contrast to features of societies that are characterized by increasing functional dif-

1 For an analysis of public discourse and social movements discourse on inequalities based on the construction of gender and race since the 1950s in the US and how this interrelates with the social science discourse, see Jungwirth (2007).

ferentiation and individualization. Consequently, further insights in the continuing co-existence of functional differentiation, on the one hand, and the significance of membership in social groups in the reproduction of society, on the other, are crucial. The focus on organizations in research and publications of diversity studies is based on the relevance and pivotal contribution of organizations in highly differentiated societies (see the contribution by Jungwirth as well as the contributions by Vader and Showunmi in this volume).

2 Interdisciplinarity/Transdisciplinarity

Diversity studies, similar to gender studies, claims to pursue an approach that goes beyond disciplinary boundaries and to integrate the perspectives of different disciplines with regard to methodologies to address the identified issues and research topics. Krell et al. (2006:13f.) argue for a 'multi-disciplinary' approach under the roof of diversity studies, explicitly naming business administration, as a discipline in which diversity management has been developed, along with educational science, political science and law – or 'diversity politics', ethnology and anthropology, womens' and gender studies, migration studies, health studies and gerontology. Vertovec goes beyond this position by determining diversity studies as 'interdisciplinary' in the legacy of migration studies, gender studies and sexuality studies (Vertovec 2015:9f.), while relating diversity studies to the social sciences and the humanities. The argument for an interdisciplinary approach is that we can gain further insights about questions raised, if findings from different disciplines are 'integrated' and linked to each other, for example, about gender relations in a specific neighbourhood or the relations of dominant and dominated groups in certain organizations (Krell et al. 2006:14; Vertovec 2015:9f.). Consequently, an interdisciplinary approach requires that the specificities of each research project have to be defined distinctly, including different disciplinary approaches, and that research fields link these different disciplinary approaches.

Beyond this position, gender studies have been defined as interdisciplinary and transdisciplinary with a critical stance towards disciplines and modes of knowledge formation within the context of university. Hark and Wetterer (2010:280) point out the extent to which gender studies represent both approaches, on the one hand, challenging existing orders of knowledge and the means for their formation in academia, and the possibility of being co-opted by an economic usability logic and requirements for flexibility, on the other. In relation to this, the concept of interdisciplinarity has been identified as a buzz word that is often used for funding applications or the evaluation of study programs in the context of the university reforms in the EU members states, also known as 'Bologna reforms' since the new millennium. Working as a 'magical sign' that is not too clearly determined, it may represent even two opposing approaches (ibid.). According to Hark and Wetterer, from the perspective of the history of science, these endeavors can be seen as an attempt to define an 'uncharted space' in academia and determine a border line in relation to other disciplines (ibid.:284f.). An interdisciplinary or transdisciplinary approach in gender and diversity studies, can create the space for developing new concepts and theoretical approaches. Moreover, the concept of linking not only disciplines but sciences and every day life experiences and politics in transdisciplinary research, is presented in this book (see the contribution by Vinz).

All in all, the question about the extent of gender and diversity studies serving as critical science and the provisions it offers, still remains, which promotes a critical reflection of knowledge production in academia. At the same time, the aim of achieving more encompassing insights in research through an interdisciplinary or transdisciplinary approach is pertinent to gender and diversity studies. We argue that a critical stance against an economic usability logic and flexibility claims can be provided by taking into account societal power relations. In order to include these in the research in gender and diversity studies, resorting to the sociology of social inequality and sociology of organizations in which core concepts of analysis have been coined for the issues and questions raised in gender and diversity studies would be an important contribution. Moreover, social theories such as the ones named above can build a theoretical foundation for gender and diversity studies, in an attempt to include the examination of power relations and to come up with explanations for experiences of difference and diversity on these grounds (see the contribution by Jungwirth as well as the contributions by Vader and by Showunmi in this volume).

3 Gender and Diversity Studies as a Profession

The question of the extent to which gender and diversity studies operate as a profession is linked to the establishment of a field of research and teaching or of a discipline. This issue is raised by gender studies which already has undergone a process of establishment in academia to a certain level. The ATGENDER network, which was founded by three key players in gender studies in Europe, WISE, AOIFE and ATHENA in 2009, currently counts 51 members of gender studies institutes and centers located at universities all over European member states.[2] Diversity studies has not been established in the same manner but has of-

2 https://atgender.eu/about/background/, retrieved February 28, 2019. It has to be mentioned that only a certain number of gender study institutes and gender study programmes are organized in this network. This number can be estimated to be much higher, if we take only

ten emerged within the context of gender studies as gender and diversity studies. More than gender studies, diversity studies has been linked to an orientation of application by some (Krell et al. 2006:14), particularly if one takes into account issues of diversity management, which have been developed in the context of organization studies and business administration (e.g. Loden and Rosener 1991; Cox and Blake 1991; Kirton and Greene 2010). In education sciences, in addition to approaches of diversity and inclusion (e.g. Terzi 2005; Gonzalez-Mena and Bhavnagri 2000; Prengel 2010), diversity trainings have evolved (Adams and Bell 2016; Czollek, Perko and Weinbach 2012; see also Weinbach's as well as Schwärzer-Dutta's contributions in this volume). Consequently, on the grounds of new legal requirements in EU member states, on the one hand, and emerging concepts for organization analysis, trainings and other instruments to enable participation of diverse members of an organization, on the other, have led to developments towards a research and teaching field of gender and diversity studies as a profession.

With the focus on gender studies, an encompassing comparative study was done to analyze the institutionalization of womens's studies in Europe in nine countries, as well as on the careers of women's and gender studies graduates' (Griffin 2005; 2010). Griffin points out two characteristics of the professionalization of gender studies (2010:247), firstly, gender studies contents have been spread within academia since contents of gender studies have been included in study programmes in social sciences and the humanities and secondly, pedagogical innovations, such as participatory teaching, which is related to women's studies by Griffin, are meanwhile taken up in other disciplines to a certain extent (ibid.). Moreover, a widespread infrastructure of institutes, publication opportunities and the establishment of professional associations, are seen to be indicators for professionalization (ibid.).

According to this European study in nine countries the fields of work in which the graduates of gender studies are employed are research and education, equal opportunity offices in public services, civil society organizations, "journalism and information" and the social and health sector (Silius 2005: 118). The findings revealed the employment of women's studies graduates in jobs as women's officer or equality officer, work in rape crisis centers, working with women refugees as well as for women's helplines (Griffin 2010:247). Research and education is aspired by a high share of the graduates (ibid.:119). This finding is confirmed by a study on the work situation of graduates of gender studies at Humboldt-Universität zu Berlin, based on a complete survey

---

the number of the previously active ATHENA network into account which comprised more than 100 institutional members (ibid.). The diminishing of the number of independent gender studies institutes and centers can also be the result of a successful institutionalization in the form of a study programme integrated in an institution.

of the graduates. According to this survey, one third of the graduates are working in the field of research (Kriszio 2012:32). The study analyzed media and culture and the private sector to be the other two fields, in addition to research. Silius found that, depending on the level of institutionalization of equal opportunity measures in the different countries, the number of jobs in a "strictly defined" equal opportunities sector was comparatively low (2005:122). The encompassing European study showed that employment opportunities, for gender study graduates were comparable or better than those for other social science and humanities graduates (Griffin 2010:246). This finding was confirmed in the research on the gender studies graduates from Humboldt-Universität zu Berlin, according to which two thirds were employed, self-employed or did an internship (Kriszio 2012:18), while others continued with further study programmes (15%) or did their PhD (22%) or fulfilled caring duties (5%). When the survey was carried through 6.8% of the graduates were unemployed (ibid.).

To sum up, the establishment of binding guidelines for EU member states to establish effective anti-discrimination and equal opportunities laws and policies determine new requirements. Gender and diversity studies can form the foundation for training of these newly required professionals. This includes certain competencies, which have been named by women's and gender studies' graduates in the European study (Silius 2005:127), such as critical thinking, analytical abilities and innovative working methods, specific gender expertise and analytical tools to work with "diversity, power and differences" (ibid.). The graduates also referred to "practical tools concerning the work place and work place culture" including "working in solidarity with other women" (ibid.). Moreover, gender studies endowed the graduates with a higher self-confidence (ibid.). These skills can certainly be acquired in other study progammes, too. But the specific issues, theories and methods of gender and diversity studies can be regarded as a foundation on which competencies in dealing with an increasing complex social world and world of labor can be developed.

4 EU Policies: between economization, demography and equal opportunities

Equal opportunities policies of the European Union have contributed to the implementation of specific national laws in the member states with an aim of determining more concretely the legal conditions for the realization of equal opportunities (see the contribution by Liebscher in this volume). At the same time, this approach towards equal opportunities is closely linked to the European Union's aim of strengthening the economy of EU member states through trade and, amongst other, the opportunity of free movement for EU-citizens.

The increase in the number of women in the workforce, as well as minority group members, is seen to be one prerequisite to this end. Moreover, demographic change poses a sufficiently present and threatening development for many EU member states such that women's and minority group members' access to the labor force is at stake. As a consequence, equal opportunity and human rights endeavors in the European Union go together – or rather *only* go together, as some authors have pointed out – with economic reasoning (see the contribution by Streckeisen and the contribution by Ahrens and van der Vleuten in this volume).

For example, findings of the encompassing Europe wide research on gender equality policies, QUING, reveals that policies that are based on a solely economic argumentation do not only limit but may even deteriorate gender equality policies (Verloo 2010). If equal opportunity policies related to gender are framed only as an issue of women's participation in the labour market or with regard to labour power shortage and economic disadvantages that follow, dominant norms and ideals of gender and gender relations are not challenged (Verloo 2010:54ff.). These policies do not sufficiently question a stereotypical division of paid and unpaid work between men and women (or genders) and gender based power relations. On the contrary, in certain states of the EU, gender policies were linked to political agendas, promoting nationalistic politics by connecting gender equality policies to demographic change and family related policies (ibid.:62ff.).

The orientation of EU policies towards market requirements is challenged in a more general sense, for example by Streeck (2015). He argues that, within the context of global developments through which the nation state and capitalist economies are linked differently, the EU – specifically the European Monetary Union (EMU) – works towards strengthening the market orientation of nation states. While the (former) type of the 'debt state' is seen to be based on conflicting interests between the constituency (*Staatsvolk*) and the creditors of a national economy (*Marktvolk*), in the emerging 'consolidation state' (ibid.:11), the conviction is that the commercial debts have priority over other debts of the nation state and the welfare state towards their citizens. Streeck is describing a worldwide development in wealthy capitalist economies and nation states. In the European Union, he argues, the EMU is most influential in shaping this "political-economic regime" of the "consolidation state" (ibid.:16). This finally leads to "a far-reaching rationalization, or 'economization', of politics and society" in Europe (ibid.:20).

These tendencies of economization of politics and society as well as the described co-optation of gender related equal opportunity policies through nationalist political agendas in the context of the European Union stand in contrast to the ideals and values that are often related to Europe. Ideals of the human rights and equal opportunities policies as well as democracy are, consequently, not the only discourse of Europe. Instead, the two-sidedness of the discourse of Europe is pointed out by several authors. For example, Griffin and Braidotti (2002) refer to Europe's history of colonialism and fascism. Similarly, women and migrants are, according to Griffin and Braidotti (2002: 10), "an antidote to the notion of democracy".

Against this background, what can be 'European perspectives' of gender and diversity studies? Griffin and Braidotti emphatically argue that, in the wake of Europeanization in the sense of post-nationalism (ibid.:12), gender studies can work as a model for the process of 'dis-identification' from dominant and essentialist forms of identification with the nation and a step towards a more process-related as well as in-between conception of identification that would be necessary. Moreover, 'European perspectives' refer to geographical locatedness, taking into account a dynamic conception of Europe (Griffin and Braidotti 2002:9), characterized by 'shifting boundaries', including and excluding geopolitical spaces and peoples at its borders. Different from other continents, Europe is characterized by diversity with regard to the spoken languages and cultures (ibid.:10). Similarly, Bauman points out an open and dynamic character of 'Europe' (Bauman 2004:129). A combination of values of rationality, justice and democracy, can be seen to be 'European', Bauman insists.

Taking critical perspectives on values such as rationality into account, rationality would include reflexivity of its geographical and historical location, while claiming universalism and incorporating all humans in these values (ibid.:125). Consequently, justifying actions "in the court of reason" (ibid.: 126) as well as "criticism and disaffection" (ibid.) are put forward as important in this regard. Justice and the continuous endeavor towards a just society refers to guarding a "common good" instead of "egoistic self-promotion" (ibid.:127), being the foundation for solidarity and society (ibid.). Democracy should enable political participation of different groups. At the same time, the contribution of citizens is a necessary requirement which can be ensured through granting citizens individual liberty and responsibility (ibid.:129). Based on these values, Bauman argues that it would be the "function" of European institutions to work against the undermining of the political power of nation states through economic actors: "arresting the capital assets that have escaped from the cages of the nation state inside the continental stockade and keep it there" (ibid.:136).

Finally, we focus on the link between anti-discrimination, equal opportunities policies and the institutions of the European Union which have furthered and supported these policies. At the same time, we investigate the consequences of these policies. This requires self-reflexivity with regard to the limits and boundaries that are drawn through these policies as well as to the consequences of politics that are not necessarily intended, emerging when several actors are interacting on an increasingly global scale. In this context, gender and diversity studies can provide theoretical and methodological approaches for a critical investigation of the production of knowledge and its conditions.

5 The Contributions

The book examines the development of gender and diversity studies in the fields of equal opportunities and human rights (1), practices, concepts and methods of gender and diversity studies (2) and changing social inequalities: work and organizations (3). In the first section *Equal Opportunities and Human Rights* are examined from different disciplinary and geographical perspectives. Petra Ahrens and Anna van der Vleuten introduce in their chapter, *EU Gender Equality Policies in Times of Crisis: Different Instruments, Different Actors, Different Outcomes,* EU policies promoting gender equality giving an overview of the development of these programs. They argue that a multi-level setup in EU gender equality policies including supra-national and intergovernmental actors as well as civil society organizations and experts have furthered gender equality in a considerable manner. Nonetheless, more recent developments have replaced 'hard law' by 'soft' new public management measures and moreover restricting the access of actors to policy making in this regard. This is a consequence of the weakening of EU gender policy programmes since 2006, on the one hand, and changes in responsibilities for gender equality policy within EU institutions, on the other. Ahrens and van der Vleuten argue that, under the conditions of the financial crisis, the influence of new member states in the European Union since 2004 and conservative populist parties, the "variety of tools" of EU gender equality policy have come under pressure and claim a "revised feminist utopia" of a "more gender equal European society" (p. 54).

The following chapters discuss legal regulations and policies referring to antidiscrimination and equal opportunities in different European states enabling cross-national European perspectives. Two examples of legal regulations referring to antidiscrimination and equal opportunities, in Germany and in Great Britain, are presented and discussed. They are transnational to the extent that antidiscrimination and equal opportunities policies have led to the establishment of, not only norms and laws in this regard, but also ideals which hold true for these societies. Doris Liebscher introduces in her article, *Opening Doors: how the German Act on Equal Treatment advaces racial equality,* the German *Allgemeines Gleichbehandlungsgesetz* (AGG, General Act on Equal Treatment) which was passed in 2006. The law was implemented after an extensive public debate during which the planned law was criticized by "the business community" as well as the "mainstream legal field" (p. 52). Meanwhile research has been carried through on the AGG, jurisprudence according to the AGG and institutionalization exists. Liebscher argues that the opportunity for legal claims established by this law specifically in cases of discrimination, goes beyond the German Basic Law that includes the prohibition of discrimination in "the traditional understanding" as "not directly applicable to the horizontal relationship between individuals" but rather to a "vertical" relationship between the state and the individual (p. 56). Consequently, the private sector including companies as employers, for example, is now covered which was not the case previous to the establishment of the AGG. Deficits in the law are related to the different responsibilities at the national level and the level of the federal states. Nonetheless, Liebscher points out the empowering effects of the law (p. 69) for persons with experiences of discrimination.

A different case of equal opportunities legislation in the UK is presented by Hazel Conley in the chapter, *Gender Equality in the UK Public Sector: is reflexive legislation the way forward?* Here, equality law is "underpinned" by European directives without being "prompted" by these (p. 71). For example, gender mainstreaming principles as part of the Equality Act (2010) included additionally age, sexual orientation, gender reassignment, religious belief as well as pregnancy and maternity. Critique against existing regulations was that equality law was "fragmented" in several regulations and was, moreover, not working well by the end of the 1990s (ibid.). Conley argues that, in order to overcome limitations of "traditional anti-discrimination legislative approaches", the involvement of "women's and other civil society groups seeking equality" is required (ibid.). With reference to concepts of 'responsive and reflexive legislation' by Nonet and Selznik (1978/2001) as well as 'reflexive legislation' by Teubner (1983), she examines the implementation of the equality law in the UK regarding gender equality in the public services in form of the 'gender equality duty'. This approach towards equal opportunities legislation is specifically interesting, since it can be regarded as a response to the critique of the European Union's policy to be too bureaucratic or not considering sufficiently its constituency in the member states, and has opened up the perspective for the involvement of civil society organizations, such as women's lobby or feminist organizations, in the legislative process and the impact they can exert.

Hülya Şimga and Zeynep Oya Usal, in their contribution, *A Case of Collateral Damage: widows of religious weddings in Turkey*, focus on a further European institution, the European Convention on Human Rights, and the question to which extent it can be, in connection with the Convention on the Elimination of Discrimination Against Women (CEDAW), a foundation for the protection of women against discrimination. They examine this question by referring to the specific case of women in Turkey being married solely on the basis of religious marriage. They argue that these women can suffer indirect discrimination by taking up the case of Şerife Ygit, a widow who was declined retirement benefits because of a solely religious marriage. Şimga and Usal show how the ambiguous position of the Turkish authorities towards religious marriage and secular laws led to indirect discrimination for these women. While secular law is in place in Turkey, and as a corollary religious marriage alone not legally binding, it is not enforced sufficiently, to the detriment of women who are denied social benefits such as the pension.

They base their argumentation on the concept of 'hermeneutical injustice' by Miranda Fricker (2007), arguing that specifically women lacking resources like education can become objects of discrimination because they cannot "make sense of their experience" (p. 89) and are unable to claim certain rights and justice. At the same time, their social reality of *de facto* partnerships is disregarded by Turkish courts and the European Court of Human Rights, ECHR, where the case was decided in favour of the Turkish state and against Şerife Yigit. Şimga and Usal argue that the justification of the ECHR as well as the Turkish courts based solely on formal argumentation is neglecting the social reality of Turkish women who live in families based on religious marriages. The case exemplifies contradictions which may be connected to Human Rights, if factual realities are disregarded, as in the case of women in religious marriages in Turkey discussed in this article. The European Convention on Human Rights is, moreover, an example for the institutionalization of such general rights as the human rights, which are binding to the member states of the Council of Europe, Turkey being one of them.

Amel Grami's chapter, *The Parity Law: Tunisian women's next battle*, adds a case study of equal opportunities law and its impacts on women's political participation in Tunisia at the border of Europe, in Tunisia. Referring to the 'Revolution of 14 January 2011', which was the start for a number of social and political upheavals of the so called 'Arab Spring', the article gives insight into a highly topical instance of political change of our time. While focusing on the political participation of women, she examines related ambiguous developments in Tunisia. Moreover, the chapter provides an overview of the considerable engagement of feminist activists at different levels.

Tunisia being a precursor for women's rights in the Middle East and North Africa since the 1950s, the ideal of gender equality was linked to the state's policies. At the same time, the 'woman question' was instrumentalized by authoritarian regimes and dictatorships such as Ben Ali's in Tunisia (p. 113). After the revolution of 2011, a new law was introduced with the intention to improve women's access to active political participation in the parliament. The ideal of women's equal political participation as a motor for gender equality was pursued by feminist activists, following "the success story of Nordic gender equality" (p. 115). Grami describes the political processes under which the new 'Parity

Law' was implemented and the political discourses accompanying the elections of 2011. According to this law, every other name on an electoral list should be a woman's. The elections to the NCA (National Constituent Assembly) had a result of a women's share of 24%, falling below expectations. According to Grami, this is a consequence of "the divide between laws and cultures at all levels of practice, social structures or even institutions" (p. 126). While some women were encouraged to run for elections, they were not given favourable positions at the top of electoral lists. In connection to "religious norms and patriarchal ways of interpreting religious texts" (ibid.), Grami argues that women's participation was restricted by the political parties. As a consequence, by far most of the elected women were from the relatively popular Islamist party *Ennahda* that gained many votes. She concludes with the claim for continuous political engagement of women activists and members of civil society.

The following section, *Gender and Diversity Studies: practices, concepts and methods*, gathers articles on gender and diversity studies, its implementation as well as specific concepts and methods. The chapter, *Adventures of Gender Studies in the Russian Political Context – From Discovery to Politicization: the trajectory of Russian gender studies*, by Anna Temkina and Elena Zdravomyslova gives insight into the development of gender studies in Russia, its interrelatedness to political conditions, such as the *perestroika* at the beginning of the 1990s. The establishment of gender studies in Russia was informed by the interrelations to gender studies on an international scale, on the one hand, and civil society engagement as well as feminist activism in Russia, on the other hand. Moreover, the authors describe how the institutionalization of gender studies was connected to both, sociology and its theories and empirical methods, and international financial support.

The political and social changes at the beginning of the 1990s created opportunities for new scientific and institutional developments on the grounds of which a critical reflection of gender relations in the Soviet era as well as the post-Soviet era was enabled. More recently, gender studies have been again challenged to come up with the analysis of "new cultural conservatism" and "gender ideology" connected to that (p. 132). Interestingly, the concept of gender was also used by anti-feminist standpoints in the 1990s. Gender had developed into an "umbrella category" containing "both critical and opportunist positions" (p. 139). Gender expertise was now demanded also by a coalition of conservative actors in politics and religion, such as the Russian Orthodox Church, promoting a "conservative turn" in Russia (p. 142). This inversion of the concept of gender links to the findings of the European wide research on gender equality policies QUING, cited above, which also came up with the result that the concept of gender was used by nationalistic political agendas as well (Verloo 2010).

In Russia, since the years of 2000s international institutions, which had formerly supported gender studies, increasingly withdrew funding leading to several centers of women's studies shutting down. As a consequence, gender studies in Russia had a smaller financial basis. At the same time, as Temkina and Zdravomyslova argue, they became "more critical" and enjoy increasing support in civil society (p. 146). The case of gender studies in Russia shows, just as the other case studies presented in this book, to which extent social and political debates and changes are relevant and taken up in gender and diversity studies and how in turn they can have an impact on society.

The following chapters deal with concepts and methods that have been developed in the context of gender and diversity studies. Martina Tißberger addresses in her text, *At the Intersection of Gender and Racism: critical whiteness as a method of hegemonial self-reflection,* the interrelations between racism and sexism, and by this complying with the claims of feminists and gender studies scholars for intersectionality, instead of making one form of discrimination, for example based on gender, to the one that counts more. Focusing on the subject's experiences of sexism and racism, Tißberger draws on critical whiteness studies and their endeavor to put "the signifying rather than the signified of race" at the center of interest (p. 149). In this context, "whiteness as a method and didactics of self-reflection" is sketched (p. 150.). Referring to psychoanalytic theory, the text points out how processes of becoming a subject are not only based on gendered differences and their "inscription […] into the 'nature' of individual psyche", as analyzed by Judith Butler and Gayle Rubin, for example, but "how psychoanalysis is an example for the inscription of racism, evolutionism and the normativity of whiteness into the theories of the social sciences" (p. 157). In this process Tißberger analyses "ontologization" as an essential mechanism that makes the social construction of differences of gender and racism invisible (p. 158). The objective of gender and diversity studies as "critical scholarship" is (p. 159), consequently, to uncover these mechanisms.

Additionally to an overview on critical whiteness studies in the Anglo-American context, the contributions to critical whiteness studies in the German speaking discourse are outlined. Critical whiteness studies may inform self-reflexivity with regard to constructions of race, for example in professional environments, such as counseling, and in our everyday life, the author concludes.

In the chapter, *Social Justice Trainings: a dialogic approach to diversity education*, Heike Weinbach describes characteristics of the training. Diversity trainings – as a general term for trainings concerned with education on anti-discrimination issues and attitudes – have been one outcome of the establishment of gender and diversity approaches also outside academia. Often developed in certain professional contexts, such as educational institutions and development policy, in connection to activism, diversity trainings make up a field that is directly connected to putting into practice insights of gender and diversity studies. Approaches such as the social justice and diversity training and the anti-bias training, which are covered in this volume, refer to ethical and political questions. They relate to human rights and have the objective to overcome discrimination in educational organizations, work organizations, political and civil rights organizations, profit and non-profit organizations, by coming up with educational means to address individuals.

The social justice and diversity training which was taken up by Czollek, Perko and Weinbach, has been transformed by the inclusion of a different method, compared to the foundations created by Adams, Bell and Griffin (2007) at the University of Massachusetts, the "dialogic concept of *Mahloquet*" (p. 176). Dialogic exchange is emphasized in this approach which is described in detail in the article. The specificity of this approach is the emphasis put on the development of empathy as well as understanding which includes a "metacognitive reflection" (p. 183).

In gender and diversity studies, which is not confined to the limits of one discipline, the question of methods is crucial. Dagmar Vinz discusses in her contribution, *Transdisciplinarity with 'Science & Fiction'*, the concept of transdisciplinarity as an approach that spans not only different disciplines but also academia and the social world. The concept of transdisciplinarity presented in the chapter has been developed in environment studies as well as in gender studies and gender and diversity studies in the German-speaking context. Drawing on her experiences of teaching in Gender and Diversity studies, Vinz presents an approach of 'science & fiction' with the intention to bridge "the gap between academic feminism and popular culture" (p. 187). She addresses change agents in organizations by linking theoretical contents with fiction, in order "to engender transformations in organizations" (ibid.). She states that by use of this approach, the participation of a broader public in the political as well as scientific debates in the context of gender and diversity studies should be promoted.

After sketching in a first part concepts and models of transdisciplinarity (TR), she distinguishes between a first approach of "TR as Super-Interdisciplinarity" as it is being discussed, for example, in gender studies, a second approach of "TR as Participation", going back to ideas of empowerment and action research. The third approach is Vinz' approach of 'Science & Fiction' (p. 195). Vinz links this to ideas that have been developed earlier by Donna Harraway (1991). The second part of the chapter is dedicated to the discussion of several novels and how they can be included in the work with students on equal opportunities and change in organizations. The novels have been published in German, some of them have been translated into English, and the author gives suggestions on how to apply them in teaching gender and diversity studies.

Another type of diversity training is presented by Constanze Schwärzer-Dutta in her article *Unlearning Discrimination: experiences with the anti-bias approach in adult-education in Germany*. She describes the development of the approach in early childhood education in the United States and how it has been adapted for adult-education in South-Africa in the post-Apartheid era. The concept has been transferred to the German context in the 1990s, when the divide between East and West Germany was becoming a widely recognized issue, shortly after the fall of the wall in 1989. Apart from that, violent racist attacks in this period made apparent that dealing with racism on an individual level is a requirement, which was launched together with policy programmes at that time. The specificity of the anti-bias approach is, according to Schwärzer-Dutta, to start with the participants' individual experiences of holding biases and to make them aware of how they can be suffering discrimination and exerting discrimination in certain situations. Power relations and the link between individual experiences and structural conditions are emphasized with this approach, similar to the social justice and diversity training. In fact, this distinguishes these types of trainings from many other diversity trainings in which power relations may be left out with more short-term and superficial aims for trainings. An additional distinguishing factor is the inclusion of exercises in which future action is planned, making changes of existing structures and discriminating attitudes concrete and palpable.

The text gives an overview on the political discourse on racism in Germany and describes the specificities of the history of racism. In addition to the Nazi-regime, Germany has a history of colonialism, the genocide of Herero and Nama of this time contributes to this history, as well as the holocaust of Jews and Roma and Sinti (p. 218). After sketching key concepts and procedures in anti-bias trainings, Schwärzer-Dutta presents a revised model on the connection between power structures and attitudes and behaviour on the individual level (p. 226). The chapter reveals ongoing conceptual developments and open questions, such as the assumption that individuals have one or more identities at their disposal in the sense of set entities that have to be taken into account and made compatible. This line of thought has been challenged by poststructuralist, queer, feminist, postcolonial and social theories, while it remains a challenge to transfer this into practice.

The third section of the book presents recent research on *Labour Markets and Organizations: changing social inequalities in Europe*. Peter Streckeisen's contribution, *The Business Case for Diversity: Europe 2020, the economic approach and antidiscrimination policy*, examines the labour-market policy of the European Union which sets norms and requirements for the EU member states. He critically assesses how these policies are not only in line with social movements' claims for equal opportunities but also create "new forms of social exclusion and social control" (p. 239). Streckeisen argues that "EU labour market policy embodies a rising form of power that rests on the individual responsibility of every person able to participate in the labour market" (ibid.). Equal opportunity policies, he points out, "go hand in hand with economic reasoning" (ibid.). The chapter contains a description of the Europe 2020 policy framework and an analysis of interrelations between diversity management and antidiscriminiation policy and a "new conception of full employment" (ibid.). Analyzing governance instruments, such as the Open Method of Coordination and the European Semester, Streckeisen argues that these are "quite evocative of what Foucault calls the economic tribunal" (ibid.). In this regard, the labour market integration of groups that were marginalized under the Fordist regime, such as women and members of minority groups, remain ambivalent. If the Fordist model of employment was based on the male breadwinner model, restricting the scope of action, specifically for women, the question put forth, is the extent to which the current regime aiming at full employment restricts our scope of action similarly to the model, according to which "both parents maximiz[ing] labour market participation" becomes the only rationale (p. 256). This argument follows concerns raised in feminist and critical social science literature with regard to the subordination of action to economic reasoning.

The article *Boundaries that Matter: workforce diversity in the STEM field in Germany* presents findings in research on highly qualified migrant women in the technological branch in Germany, 'STEM' standing for science, technology, engineering and mathematics. It offers an approach to diversity studies by considering multiple dimensions of social inequality, namely gender and migration in their interrelations. Moreover, Bourdieu's concept of the social field is taken up, going beyond organizational studies and taking into account the reproduction of norms and standards in a certain professional context, not only within organizations but also in interaction between actors in different organizations in the field. A relational perspective on migrant women's experiences in the world of labour is enabled by relating them to other social actors, the social groups and positions they inhabit in the social field.

In the chapter Ingrid Jungwirth gives an overview of the technical field in Germany which is less accessible for women than in several other countries, for example some new member states in the European Union. Bourdieu's concept of 'distinction' is applied in regard to the exclusionary mechanisms women may experience in the STEM field.

The empirical research, which included highly qualified migrant women in the STEM field, having immigrated from post-socialist countries, reveals normative constructions of gender that make it difficult for many migrant women to be occupied according to their qualification. Moreover, exclusionary mechanisms in interactions within the workplace and other encounters, such as the employment agency, were experienced. Based on qualitative, in-depth interviews, several forms of direct and indirect forms of devaluation of qualifications were analyzed. In addition to gender being used as a sign of distinction, high proficiency of German language, amongst other, was used to marginalize highly qualified migrant women. To sum up, a relational perspective on experiences in the labour market and the work place, reveals how barriers in the career of highly qualified migrant women are related to advantages of the dominant group.

Another professional field is analyzed in the article *Female Physicians in the Medical Profession: a case study in a German hospital* by Sarah Vader. While women increasingly have entered the medical profession as physicians in Germany, making up a majority in younger age groups (under the age of 35 years), a discourse on the 'feminization of medicine' has evolved within the profession's publications at the same time. On the basis of gender theories, Vader analyzes how, in fact, gender differences are being reproduced in the work sphere in the hospital. This approach is used against the idea of women being "essentially different from men" and will change medicine (p. 283), when they enter the medical profession. The article presents findings from qualitative research on how these changes in numbers and the discourse on 'feminization of medicine' have impacted the work place in the hospital as an organization.

With her chapter, *Leadership and Cultural Identity*, Victoria Showunmi focuses on Black Minority Ethnic (BME) women leaders in the UK, filling a gap in existing research on gender and leadership in organizations. Women leaders belonging to a an ethnic minority have so far not been taken into account sufficiently. She presents insights from an ongoing study about "leadership and constructions of identity" (p. 301). The question of the extent to which constructions of race and constructions of whiteness determine the concept of leadership still needs further exploration. Based on a large number of interviews, important themes in the interviews are sketched in the article. For example, BME women leaders experience ambivalence in considering themselves in the position of a team leader and, similarly, the necessity to "affirm to everybody why they have the right to be in the leadership position and the right to be considered an expert in the field" (p. 308). Other issues are issues of stereotyping; BME women leaders being confronted with difficulties within teams, who perceived them as not being competent (p. 306). All in all, further research is needed on BME women leaders and the question of the extent to which leadership is based not only on constructions of gender but also on constructions of race and ethnicity.

In conclusion, several fields of research and teaching in gender and diversity studies are presented in the chapters. They show the success of institutionalization of equal opportunity policies as well as draw backs in this regard. The influence of political actors in different geographical regions and civil society engagement become visible and to which extent social movements' claims have been co-opted during the process of institutionalization. Continous engagement remains a political demand of equal opportunity policies. The analysis of knowledge production, and self-reflexivity connected with this, and as well as methods of equal opportunities have been identified as important fields of gender and diversity studies. Critical issues of gender and diversity studies are the further development of concepts and theories for the analysis of diversity. In this chapter it has been argued that diversity studies can draw on the sociology of social inequality in connection with the process related approaches in gender studies, queer studies, migration studies, racism studies and disability studies. The focus on the multidimensionality of social inequalities and their interrelations as well as a relational perspective is a common claim of gender and diversity studies. How these diversities are reproduced in the context of an increasing differentiation, is a central concern for an emerging field of gender and diversity studies.

Discussion Questions

1. How are the law and legal regulations in the nation states, on the one hand, and directives and other measures on the EU level, on the other, influential for the development of gender and diversity studies? Give some examples from different countries.
2. Which levels of analysis have been identified for diversity studies?
3. To which extent is self-reflexivity a characteristic of gender and diversity studies? Give some examples.

References

Adams, Maurianne/Bell, Lee Ann et al. (eds.) (2007): Teaching for Diversity and Social Justice. New York: Routledge.

Barnes, Colin (1997): A Legacy of Oppression: a history of disability in western culture. In: Barton, Len/Oliver, Mike (eds.): Disability Studies: Past, Present and Future. Leeds: The Disability Press, pp. 3-24.

Baumann, Zygmunt (2004): Europe: An Unfinished Adventure. Cambridge: Polity Press.

Berger, Peter. L./Luckmann, Thomas (1966): The Social Construction of Reality. New York: Penguin Books.

Bourdieu, Pierre (1979/1984): Distinction: a social critique of judgement. Harvard: Harvard University Press.

Brubaker, Rogers (2004): Ethnicity without groups. Cambridge: Harvard University Press.

Bührmann, Andrea (2015): Gender: A central dimension of diversity studies. In Vertovec, Steven (ed.): Routledge International Handbook of Diversity Studies.. New York: Routledge, pp. 23-32.

Bury, Mike (1996): Defining and Researching Disability: Challenges and Responses. In: Barnes, Colin/Mercer, Geof (eds.): Exploring the Divide: Illness and Disability. Leeds: The Disability Press, pp. 18-38.

Castles, Stephen/Miller, Mark J. (2009): The Age of Migration: International Population Movements in the Modern World. (4th ed.). Hampshire: Palgrave Macmillan.

Cox, Taylor H./Blake, Stacy (1991): Managing Cultural Diversity: Implications for Organizational Competitiveness. In: The Executive 5, 3, pp. 45-56.

Czollek, Lea/Perko , Gudrun/Weinbach, Heike (2012). Praxishandbuch Social Justice und Diversity: Theorien, Training, Methoden, Übungen. Weinheim: Beltz Juventa.

Faist, Thomas (2015): Diversity unpacked: from heterogeneities to inequalities. In: Vertovec, Steve (ed.): Routledge International Handbook of Diversity Studies. New York Routledge, pp. 265-272.

Fricker, Miranda (2007): Epistemic Injustice: Power and the Ethics of Knowing. Oxford: Oxford University Press.

Garfinkel, Harold (1967): Studies in ethnomethodology. New Jersey: Prentice-Hall.

Goffman, Erving (1959): The Presentation of Self in Everday Life. New York: Doubleday.

Gonzalez-Mena, Janet/Bhavnagri, Navaz Peshotan (2000): Diversity and infant/toddler care giving. In: Young Children 55, 5, pp. 31-35.

Griffin, Gabriele (ed.) (2005): Doing Women's Studies: Employment Opportunities, Personal Impacts & Social Consequences. London: Zed Books.

Griffin, Gabriele (2010): Gender Studies as a Profession. In: Riegraf, Birgit/Aulenbacher, Brigitte/Kirsch-Auwätter, Edit/Müller, Ursula (eds.): GenderChange in Academia: Re-Mapping the Fields of Work, Knowledge and Politics from a Gender Perspective. Wiesbaden: VS-Verlag/Springer, pp. 242-251.

Griffin, Gabriele/Braidotti, Rosi (2002): Introduction: Configuring European Womens' Studies. In: Griffin, Gabriele/Braidotti, Rosi (eds.) (2002). London: Zed Books, pp. 1-28.

Haraway, Donna (1991): A Cyborg Manifesto: Science, Technology, and Socialist-Feminism in the Late Twentieth Century. In: Haraway, Donna: Simians, Cyborgs, and Women: the Reinvention of Nature. New York: Routledge, pp. 149-182.

Hark, Sabine/Wetterer, Angelika (2010): Gender Studies in Entrepreneurial Universities. The Case of Inter- and Transdisciplinarity. In Riegraf, Brigitte/Aulenbacher, Brigitte/Kirsch-Auwärter, Edit/Müller, Ursula (eds.): GenderChange in Academia: Re-Mapping the Fields of Work, Knowledge, and Politics from a Gender Perspective. Wiesbaden: VS Verlag/ Springer, pp. 278-317.

Jungwirth, Ingrid (2007): Zum Identitätsdiskurs in den Sozialwissenschaften – eine postkolonial und queer informierte Kritik an George H. Mead, Erik H. Erikson und Erving Goffman. Bielefeld: transcript.

Kirton, Gill/Greene, Anne-Marie (2010): The Dynamics of Managing Diversity: a critical approach. (4th edition) London: Routledge.

Krell, Gertraude/Riedmüller, Barbara/Sieben, Barbara/Vinz, Dagmar (2007): Einleitung: Diversity Studies als integrierende Forschungsrichtung. In: Krell, Gertraude/Riedmüller, Barbara/Sieben, Barbara/Vinz, Dagmar (eds.): Diversity Studies: Grundlagen und disziplinäre Ansätze. Frankfurt: Campus, pp. 7-16.

Kriszio, Marianne (2012): Gender Studies im Beruf: Verbleibstudie zu den Absolvent_innen der Gender Studies an der Humboldt-Universität. Berlin: Humboldt-Universität zu Berlin, Zentrum für Transdisziplinäre Geschlechterstudien.

Loden, Marilyn/Rosener, Judy B. (1991): Workforce America! Managing employee diversity as a vital resource. Illinios: Business One Irwin.

Lutz, Helma (2015): Intersectionality: assembling and disassembling the roads. In: Vertovec, Steve (ed.): Routledge International Handbook of Diversity Studies. New York Routledge, pp. 363-370.

Miles, Robert/Brown, Malcolm (2008): Racism, London: Routledge.

Nonet, Philippe/Selznick, Philip (1978, 2001): Law and Society in Transition. Towards Responsive Law. New York: Harper.

Oliver, Mike (1990): The Politics of Disablement. London: MacMillan.

Omi, Michael/Winant, Howard (1994): Racial formation in the United States: From the 1960s to the 1990s. New York: Routledge.

Portes, Alejandro/DeWind, Josh (2007): Rethinking Migration. New Theoretical and Empirical Perspectives. New York: Berghahn Books.

Prengel, Annedore (2010): Inklusion in der Frühpädagogik. Bildungstheoretische, empirische und pädagogische Grundlagen. München: Deutsches Jugendinstitut.

Pries, Ludger (2004): Determining the Causes and Durability of Transnational Labour Migration between Mexico and the United States: some empirical findings. In: International Migration 42, 2, pp. 3-39.

Silius, Harriet (2005): The Professionalization of Women's Studies Students in Europe: expectations and experiences. In: Griffin, Gabriele (ed.):, Doing Women's Studies: Employment Opportunities, Personal Impacts & Social Consequences. London: Zed Books., pp. 111-140.

Streeck, Wolfgang (2015): The Rise of the European Consolidation State. In: MPIfG Discussion Paper 15, 1, pp. 1-28.

Steger, Manfred (2017): Globalization: A Very Short Introduction. Oxford: Oxford University Press.

Terzi, Lorella (2005): Beyond the Dilemma of Difference: the capability approach to disability and special educational needs. In: Journal of Philosophy of Education 39, pp. 443-459.

Teubner, Gunther (1983): Substantive and Reflexive Elements in Modern Law. In: Law and Society Review 17, 2, pp. 239-285.

Verloo, Mieke (2010): Trojan Horses and the Implications of Strategic Framing. Reflections on Gender Equality Policies, Intimate Citizenship and Demographic Change. In: Kahlert, Heike/Ernst, Waltraud (eds.): Reframing demographic change in Europe: Perspectives on gender and welfare state transformations. Münster: LIT Verlag, pp. 51-73.

Vertovec, Steven (2015): Introduction: formalizing diversity studies. In: Vertovec, Steve (ed.): Routledge International Handbook of Diversity Studies. New York: Routledge, pp. 1-20.

West, Candace/Fenstermaker, Sarah (1995): Doing Difference. In: Gender and Society 9, 1, pp. 8-37.

West, Candace/Zimmerman, Don H. (1987): Doing Gender. In: Gender and Society 1, 2, pp. 125-151.

Wimmer, Andreas (2013): Ethnic Boundary Making: Institutions, Power, Networks. New York: Oxford University Press.

Equal Opportunities and Law

Petra Ahrens and *Anna van der Vleuten*

EU Gender Equality Policies in Times of Crisis: different instruments, different actors, different outcomes

1 Introduction

The financial and banking crisis of the EU and the ensuing austerity policies have resulted in an unprecedented legitimacy crisis of the European project (Borrás and Conzelmann 2007). This triple crisis not only seems to hit women harder than men but has not spared gender equality policy either. For a long time, EU gender equality policy was presented as best practice showing the way for member states, in contrast to its more modest performance in social policy (Beveridge and Velluti 2008). Overviews[1] show how over the past six decades the EU has set up a variety of specific instruments in gender equality policy, which can be roughly divided into legislation, gender mainstreaming and policy programmes. These instruments meet with heterogeneous gender regimes in member states leading to different ways of integrating supranational policies (Liebert 2003; Caporaso and Jupille 2001). As a result, EU policies have promoted change in different countries contributing to more gender equality, but they have not succeeded in creating a single EU-wide gender regime. In this regard it is important to note that the EU is not a state, it is a multi-level polity (Van der Vleuten 2007) or even a 'moving target' (Imig and Tarrow 2001). Policies result from the interplay at the EU-level between supranational and intergovernmental actors, most notably the

1 For overviews please see, for instance, Abels and Mushaben 2012, Jacquot 2015, Kantola 2010, Klein 2013, Van der Vleuten 2007, Wobbe and Biermann 2009.

Commission, the European Parliament and the Council of Ministers, as well as transnational actors such as civil society organisations and expert groups. This interplay in turn is caught in the dynamics of downloading and uploading preferences between national and European politics. Even though this multilevel political system has resulted in an impressive set of gender equality policies in the past, we will argue that the present and the future look less bright. We argue that gender equality policies are facing fundamental changes on three aspects. First, there has been a shift away from 'hard law' to softer new public management instruments such as ranking and benchmarking. Second, there has been a shift as regards soft law instruments making them even softer. Third, and linked to these changes, the access to policy-making for actors that promote gender equality has changed to their disadvantage.

Against the background of the financial and banking crises, we aim to provide an overview of the main changes and their implications for policy making and the variety of actors involved in this policy field. We do so by first discussing the role of hard law and court cases for promoting gender equality at the national level, as well as their fate since 'the crises' broke out and their 'replacement' by new instruments such as the Open Method of Coordination and the European Semester. By discussing gender equality policy programmes as a specific soft law instrument, we then illuminate changes over time with view to policy issues as well as the relationship between supranational and national actors, and the consequences of these changes for EU gender equality policy. Finally, we discuss the role of different key actors in EU gender equality policies, showing how shifts in instruments and institutional venue affect actor constellations and their effectiveness. Overall, we speculate whether the unfortunate coincidence of moving the institutional responsibilities for gender equality further away from the EU institutions responsible for economic and employment policy while 'the crisis' hit hardest, accelerated the downgrading of legislative instruments.

2 The Gender Equality *Acquis*: primary law, secondary law and case law

One of the commonly used categorisations of EU instruments distinguishes between primary law comprising the treaties; secondary law covering directives, regulations and decisions; soft law including instruments such as recommendations, resolutions, Action Programmes and the Open Method of Coordination (OMC); and as a last form, the case law of the European Court of Justice (Hiou-Maniatopoulou 2004). The different categories, however, have not existed all simultaneously since the foundation of the EU but were developed while becoming necessary for different reasons, thereby shaping each period of EU gender equality policy. In this section we focus on 'hard' primary and secondary law and case law. Together these categories form the so-called 'gender equality *acquis*' (Locher 2012). We will now briefly discuss the meaning and content of treaties and directives, as well as recent developments: a further development of such binding standards has become more and more improbable.

The Treaty on European Union is the agreement between the governments of the member states on which the EU is based. It has been renegotiated several times. The original Treaty of Rome (1957), establishing the European Economic Community, contained an article establishing the right to equal pay for equal work, regardless of whether work was performed by a woman or a man. The article was included for economic reasons, in order to prevent distortion of competition between different member states, but it would become the cornerstone for the promotion of gender equality. Only three decades later, in the Treaty of Maastricht (1992), the treaty base for gender equality was extended to include equal treatment and equal opportunity in the labour market. In the Treaty of Amsterdam (1997), an article on the fight against discriminations (sex, race or ethnic origin, religion or belief, disability, age and sexual orientation) as well as the path-breaking provision for gender mainstreaming were included (see Section 4). And, finally, in the Treaty of Lisbon (2007), the fight against human trafficking and sexual exploitation was added as well as a Charter on Fundamental Rights.[2] In addition, Article 2 of the Treaty clearly states that gender equality belongs to the values upon which the EU is founded.

What is the meaning of treaty articles? They offer a basis for legislation and specify which decision making procedure is to be used. In general, however, they do not confer rights directly, as they have to be activated by political or legal activism: turned into legislation, or used for interpretation by the Court if it is given the opportunity to do so.

Based on the Treaties, over the years, ten directives concerning equality between women and men have been adopted as regards access to the labour market, pay and social security, pregnancy and parental leave, self-employed, and access to and provision of goods and services. (see Table 1). They are the outcome of negotiations between the European Parliament and the Council of Ministers, based on proposals by the European Commission. After initial success in the 1970s, which saw the adoption of strong directives, further

2 The Charter states fundamental rights also related to the principle of gender equality, but it operates within the limits of the Treaties. No new rights can be derived from the Charter, and its impact is expected to be limited (Ellis 2010).

progress remained blocked by British vetoes in the Council until treaty reforms enabled the adoption by qualified majority and gave a stronger voice to the European Parliament. In addition, a parallel structure was created which involved the social partners. They could adopt EU-level collective labour agreements, which subsequently should be translated into binding directives, but this procedure has resulted in only three relatively weak directives on part-time work, parental leave and the burden of proof (Van der Vleuten 2007).

Table 1. EU secondary law in the field of gender equality[3]

Directive (year/number)	
Equal pay (75/117) Equal treatment in employment (76/207; amended by 2002/73/EC) Equal treatment in occupational social security schemes (86/378, as amended by 96/97) Burden of proof in the case of discrimination based on sex (97/80/EC)	*Replaced by:* Implementation of the principle of equal opportunities and equal treatment of men and women in matters of employment and occupation (Recast Directive) (2006/54/EC)
Equal treatment in statutory social security schemes (79/7)	
Equal treatment for self-employed women and men (86/613; repealed by 2010/41)	
Pregnant Workers (92/85/EEC)	
Parental Leave (96/34/EC, repealed by 2010/118)	
Part-time Workers (97/81/EC)	
Equal treatment in the access to and the supply of goods and services (2004/113/EC)	

Source: based on Burri and Prechal 2014.

As the term *acquis* indicates, the directives constitute a set of hard provisions. Candidate countries have to show that they have adopted them and translated in national legislation in order to qualify for EU membership. Furthermore, there is a mechanism to hold governments to their obligations, called the infringement procedure. If a government does not implement EU legislation and even a series of written and oral exchanges with the Commission cannot convince it to comply with the rules, the Commission can take it to the European Court of Justice (Court). A judgement by the Court should be complied with and usually national governments do obey the Court because of the rep-

3 In addition, directives have been adopted implementing the principle of equal treatment between persons irrespective of race and ethnic origin (2000/43/EC) and equal treatment in employment and occupation irrespective of religion and belief, handicap, age and sexual orientation (2000/78/EC).

utational damage a ruling entails. This is especially the case when there is simultaneous pressure by civil society in favour of implementation, creating a 'pincer' mechanism which 'squeezes' a government into compliance (Van der Vleuten 2005, 2007). As a result, even unwilling governments have tended to transpose EU legal standards on gender equality in national law. In addition, a second mechanism has further strengthened the provisions contained in the directives. It is the mechanism of preliminary rulings, where a national court asks the Court in Luxembourg for the interpretation of a provision. Starting in the 1970s, this type of request has lead to the Court giving more than 220 rulings on gender equality issues,[4] some of them stretching the meaning and implications of the directives far beyond what governments thought they had agreed on. To cite but three examples, the Court ruled that part-time workers are also entitled to an occupational pension; that positive action measures do not constitute discrimination provided certain conditions are fulfilled; and that equal treatment for women and men also applies to social security entitlements for lesbian and gay couples. This is how the EU became known as a champion of gender equality and was favourably viewed by women's rights groups in member states where national policies continued to discriminate against women, such as in the UK and the Netherlands (Van der Vleuten 2007). Feminist lawyers and activists brought cases for the national courts in order to obtain a decision from the Court which would push reluctant governments to implement EU directives correctly (Cichowski 2007).

Unfortunately, precisely the success of the directives has caused a boomerang effect: governments have become unwilling to commit themselves to new, costly obligations, especially in times of economic crisis when cutting back public spending in the social sphere with negative consequences for gender equality has become a usual practice (Karamessini and Rubery 2013). The latest directives are marginal revisions of existing ones. Two new proposals were tabled since the adoption of the Lisbon Treaty. The first one aims to extend minimum maternity leave. The Commission adopted it in 2008, it was supported and even strengthened by the European Parliament, and then remained blocked at the level of the Council of Ministers for years. In July 2015, struggling with the legitimacy crisis, the Commission withdrew the proposal. The other new proposal aims to achieve 40 percent of women on company boards. In November 2013, it was adopted by the European Parliament, but since then it is blocked in the Council. Against the background of a eurosceptic electorate, governments are not keen on adopting new European regulation, and definitely not on a contentious topic such as quotas for wom-

4 For an overview of ECJ case law in relation to gender equality, see European Commission (2009)

en. As a result, the noble principles contained in the treaties risk to remain dormant especially in times of economic hardship.

Of course, despite their impact, directives also have their limitations. Time and again, feminist actors have questioned the effectiveness of 'hard law' in achieving gender equality. After all, legal instruments establish specific, individual rights, but they do not transform underlying power asymmetries. From the end of the 1990s, a new set of instruments was developed enabling governments to show that they take social issues, including gender equality, seriously without committing themselves to legal obligations. These new type of instruments, however, differs as regards the actors involved and as regards their effectiveness, as we will show in the next section.

3 Ranking & Benchmarking: the open method of coordination and the European semester

In 1997, against the background of the incapacity of the EU to tackle the rise of unemployment and urged by the need to show that the Economic and Monetary Union in the making would entail benefits for 'all Europeans', the European Employment Strategy (EES) was launched. The EES is a multiannual policy programme and strategy which requires member states to coordinate their national employment policies and commit themselves to certain objectives (such as lowering the unemployment rate) (Jacquot 2015). Thanks to the Austrian ministers of women and labour, gender equality was included as a key component of the EES (Rubery 2005). Subsequently, the Lisbon Strategy was formulated in order for the EU 'to become the most competitive and dynamic knowledge-based economy in the world, capable of sustainable economic growth with more and better jobs and greater social cohesion'.[5] For the assessment of progress in realizing the Lisbon ambitions, a new method of policy development was put in place, the Open Method of Coordination (OMC).

The OMC is a semi-voluntary form of coordination. It relies on a mix of 'soft law mechanisms' such as peer review, ranking and identification of best practices. The Spring European Council formulates guidelines based on best practices and sets numerical targets. Each member state develops its own policies to reach the targets and incorporates them in a National Action Plan for Employment. The Commission issues recommendations to individual member states and monitors the implementation of the guidelines in the Joint Em-

5 Cf. presidency Conclusions. Lisbon European Council 23 and 24 March 2000; http://www.consilium.europa.eu/de/uedocs/cms_data/docs/pressdata/en/ec/00100-r1.en0.htm

ployment Report. Discussion in the Council leads to a renewed identification of best practices and to a new round of the OMC cycle. The OMC aims to promote mutual learning, and to foster the generation and diffusion of new ideas and practices across Europe. This postulates the member states as a collective that is eager to learn and committed to finding the 'best' solutions to any of the challenges ahead. These postulations can be questioned on the basis of past performance of states in implementing gender equality directives (Van der Vleuten 2007), and there are fierce debates as to whether or not the OMC is delivering on its promises (Héritier 2003; Trubek and Trubek 2005). How effective is this practice for gender equality?

In general, one could argue that in an increasingly diverse EU, a flexible coordination mechanism enables more progress than a rigid legal instrument. That may be true, but progress seems to be marginal. For gender equality, the most relevant targets of the EES and the ensuing Lisbon Strategy are those concerning the narrowing of the gender gaps in employment, unemployment and pay, as well as the provision of childcare.[6] A basic result is the ongoing production of data and indicators and a yearly ranking of the member states on these issues (Van der Vleuten and Verloo 2012). However, the targets only have 'a general orientation function' (Héritier 2003:118) and member states are pressured but not compelled to meet them. The peer review and the evaluation and recommendations by the Commission constitute a monitoring mechanism without sanctions other than 'naming and shaming' by publishing the performance schedules. Gender equality recommendations were often only selectively picked up or completely ignored by member states (Ahrens 2002), but the Court is not involved and cannot be invoked, so the pincer mechanism cannot work.

Another result is the production of best practices in the field. Member states are 'encouraged to benchmark their performance against the best performer in the Union' (Héritier 2003:117). This so-called Mutual Learning Programme in gender equality may give rise to policy learning, but it has several drawbacks, of which the most problematic one is that an unwilling government cannot be obliged to change a national practice whereas hard legal instruments can force it to do so. For instance, court cases about discrimination in social security schemes (Directive 79/7) required the Dutch and British governments to fundamentally revise their breadwinner-centred systems for pensions and disability benefits which all discriminated directly or indirectly against married women (Van der Vleuten 2007:130-131). The good practice exchange seminars present initiatives on a wide range of topics but

6 The relationship between gender equality and the OMC has been evaluated in detail by Fiona Beveridge and Samantha Velluti (2008).

with no strings attached. Against a background of budgetary constraints the impact is expected to remain limited.

In 2010, the Lisbon Strategy was updated as the Europe 2020 Strategy. Its central aim is to promote an 'intelligent, durable and inclusive' growth (Jacquot 2015:153). It is based on the same coordination mechanism as the OMC and monitors the economic and social reforms which member states conduct, without any possibility for sanctions. Sophie Jacquot argues that, even more alarmingly, gender equality has disappeared almost entirely from the Strategy, as the objectives and indicators of the Europe 2020 Strategy do not refer to gender and even employment indicators are no longer formulated in gender-specific terms but refer to neutral adult workers (2015:154). As a result, the Commission has no tool to include gender (in)equalities in its evaluation of national policies and recommendations for member states.

Not only the Open Method of Coordination is an important EU soft law tool, the strategy for gender mainstreaming and policy programmes also fall into this category. In the next section we will show how, more importantly, they have they been core instruments in EU gender equality policy.

4 Promoting Issues and Actors: gender mainstreaming and gender equality policy programmes

Gender Mainstreaming[7]

The Treaty of Amsterdam (1997) has become famous among feminist scholars and activists alike due to the inclusion of the so-called gender mainstreaming article 3(2).[8] The adoption of the article was not least the result of a coordinated lobbying by the European Women's Lobby and the Women's Rights and Gender Equality Committee in the European Parliament (Helfferich and Kolb 2001) and was broadly perceived as a milestone for gender equality (Walby 2005; Wobbe and Biermann 2009).

Gender mainstreaming is a hybrid instrument: it is a treaty article (see section 2) but without directly enforceable fundament since the ECJ cannot build a case on this obligation; there are no directives based on it, thereby

7 The origin and implementation of gender mainstreaming have been dealt with elsewhere extensively (cf. Frey 2003; Fuhrmann 2005; Jacquot 2015, Lombardo, Meier and Verloo 2009), we focus on its principles and implications only.

8 Article 3(2), Treaty of Amsterdam: „In all the activities referred to in this Article, the Community shall aim to eliminate inequalities, and to promote equality, between men and women."

leaving its implementation to soft law instruments in the end. In some cases gender mainstreaming made it into hard laws such as the regulations for the European Social Fund, but as an approach, gender mainstreaming goes beyond legislation and specific actions. By definition, the full implementation of gender mainstreaming would mean approaching all supranational policies from a gender perspective. Thereby, the policy domains have been – hypothetically – broadened extensively. Also, implementing gender mainstreaming caused the set-up of new actors such as the interinstitutional High Level Group on Gender Mainstreaming, a development we will cover further below.

Gender Equality Policy Programs

The European Commission exploited gender equality policy programmes as a specific soft law tool to deepening and widening gender equality policy when the Council lacked the political will to push forward gender equality issues (Hoskyns 1996; Mazey 1998). The creation of policy programmes was justified in the beginning by references to treaty article 141(2), allowing to launch positive action measures for the underrepresented sex, yet, the policy programmes became institutionalised and an independent soft law tool. Over time, every change in the political environment impacted upon policy programmes and the Commission adjusted the function of policy programmes accordingly thereby making full use of the flexibility of soft law tools.

Based on their long history, policy programmes have become one of the best-institutionalised soft law instruments of EU gender equality policy (Ahrens 2018). A total of eight programmes were adopted with continuous changes regarding time span, topics, approach, scope and actors involved that will be illustrated in more detail below. They can be roughly divided into two groups, with the first one covering the five programmes between 1982 and 2005, and the second group covering the three programmes since then. While the first five programmes were so-called action programmes suggested by the Commission and adopted by the Council of Ministers[9], the Commission adopted the last three without the Council or the EP. The groups also differ regarding their impact on gender equality with the first group being more effective than the second. In particular, the Commission used the first policy programmes as their tool to gain responsibility over policy issues that were previously handled nationally. The last policy programmes indubitably lacked the active inclusion of new aspects and were more a tool maintaining the status quo (Ahrens 2018).

9 The fifth programme was also adopted by the European Parliament.

Creating and Establishing Policy Programmes

In 1982, the Commission proposed the first "Community action programme on the promotion of equal opportunities for women (1982-85)"[10] to the Council. It was set-up at a time when hard law such as the directives (see section 2) were more and more delayed or rejected by member states as a consequence of the neoliberal turn in the 1980s. Unsurprisingly, the formulated programme goal was monitoring the implementation of directives and developing new legislative proposals.

As regards policy issues, the programme went far beyond the policy scope back then (women as workers) and covered innovative actions like women's training networks and promoting the participation of women in information and communication technologies (ICT). Also, the planned actions acknowledged the particularities of female employment and included a section on equal treatment for immigrant women. The title already signalled the specific focus on "the promotion of equal opportunities *for women*" (authors' emphasis), a reference the Commission drew from article 141(2) allowing for positive measures for the underrepresented sex (Ahrens 2002). Thereby the Commission fostered equal opportunities for women with topics not high on the agenda of the member states even though the scope was limited to employed women and blinded out the unpaid (re)productive work women were (and are) responsible for (Ahrens 2007). The programme also supported the set-up of the Advisory Committee on Equal Opportunities bringing together representatives in charge of equal opportunities from member states administrations (Hoskyns 2000). Besides the more formalized Advisory Committee, the policy programme and its successors became generally a tool for creating transnational cooperation between national actors from public administration and from a variety of women's organizations.

The second action programme was labelled "Equal Opportunities for women. Medium-term Community programme 1986-90"[11] and pursued the same goals as the first one, monitoring directives and introducing positive action measures for employed women. Regarding policy issues, as an innovative field of action the portfolio added measures to reconcile professional and private life. With view to actors, it supported establishing the largest umbrel-

10 A new Community action programme on the promotion of equal opportunities for women 1982-85. Commission Communication to the Council. COM (81) 758 final, 9 December 1981. Bulletin of the European Communities, Supplement 1/82.

11 Equal opportunities for women. Medium-term Community programme 1986-90. Commission Communication to the Council. COM (85) 801 final and final/2, 19th December 1985. Bulletin of the European Communities, Supplement 3/86. Second Council Resolution of 24th July 1986 on the promotion of equal opportunities for women, OJ C 203, 12/08/1986.

la organisation of national women's organisations in Europe, the European Women's Lobby (EWL) (Hoskyns 2000).

After this take-off with the first two programmes, the next ones further established them firmly as a soft law tool in gender equality policy. The "Third medium-term Community action programme on equal opportunities for women and men (1991-95)"[12] covered new topics such as women in decision-making and the equal participation of women in economic and social life and thereby extended the programme goals beyond employment policies. It also introduced Commission-led transnational programs[13] and was particularly successful in establishing new transnational cooperation. Another change in the programme was announced in the title with "equal opportunities for *women and men*" (authors' emphasis) signalling a turn from understanding women as a deficient group of workers that need to adjust to a male norm to disadvantaged women that need different support than men (Ahrens 2002). As a consequence, the programmes presented equal opportunity policies including positive action measures as a crucial element of economic and structural policies[14] (Rees 1998, Hoskyns 2000).

Transforming Policy Programmes: transforming gender equality policy

In the "Fourth medium-term Community action programme on equal opportunities for men and women (1996 to 2000)"[15], the Beijing Platform for Action (UN World Conference of Women in 1995) influenced the overall design and gender mainstreaming was introduced as the main organizing principle. As a result, the Commission extended the policy issues to reconciliation and redistribution of paid and unpaid work and to the target group of disadvantaged and marginalized women. On the one hand, the programme put the Commission in the position of a mere moderator of an impressive number of sixty-nine programmes covering a broad diversity of subjects in the member states. On the other hand, the programme introduced a variety of reporting obligations for member states to the Commission, regarding the imple-

12 Council resolution of 21th May 1991 on the third medium- term Community action programme on equal opportunities for women and men (1991 to 1995) (91/C 142/01).

13 The transnational programme was called "New Opportunities for Women" (NOW) and was financed within the framework of the EU structural policy, the European Social Fund. NOW made gender equality policy more visible in EU structural policy, although its narrow focus on women returning to the labour market attracted criticism (Schunter-Kleemann 1999)

14 Also, gender mainstreaming was mentioned on a side-note for the first time in EU policies.

15 95/593/EC: Council Decision of 22th December 1995 on a medium-term Community action programme on equal opportunities for men and women (1996 to 2000)

mentation of gender mainstreaming in the EU structural funds and regarding their best practices; their annual reports were subsequently compiled as the annual "Report on Equality between Women and Men"[16] (Ahrens 2002).

The next policy programme, the "Programme relating to the Community framework strategy on gender equality (2001-2005)"[17], brought a silent revolution, because it was accompanied by the "Community framework strategy on gender equality".[18] This means that the Commission had split up its policy programme into a so-called framework strategy and an (operative) action programme. They became two separate but intertwined entities with the explicit goal of transforming structures and promoting gender equality inside and outside the Commission by means of gender mainstreaming and positive actions. The policy issues were broadened once more to cover gender inequalities *beyond* the labour market, gender equality as an indicator for democracy and gender-based violence. In addition, all topics had to be integrated into external relations policies. The action programme helped launching policy networks for different policy issues and the Commission started developing indicators, benchmarks and monitoring mechanisms. At the end of the intertwined framework strategy and the action programme, a high number of actors far beyond the Commission became involved in gender equality policy programmes, with the trade unions and national women's organizations as main players in funded projects (Ahrens 2018).

The actions taken by the Commission with this policy programme demonstrated a fundamental change and improved gender equality policy considerably compared to the previous programmes. This can already be seen by the switching of title from 'equal opportunities' to 'gender equality' thereby marking a more comprehensive understanding of gendered inequalities and the way gender is constructed in society. Moreover, the framework strategy for the first time also strongly framed gender equality as a question of democracy, a universal right as explained earlier; a question "of all citizens women and men alike to participate and be represented equally in the economy, in decision-making, and in social, cultural and civil life".[19]

16 From 2010 on published as „Report on Progress on Equality between Women and Men".

17 Council Decision 2001/51/EC of 20 December 2000 establishing a Programme relating to the Community framework strategy on gender equality (2001-2005).

18 Hereafter framework strategy. Communication from the Commission to the Council, the European Parliament, the Economic and Social Committee, the Committee of the Regions. Towards a Community Framework Strategy on Gender Equality (2001-2005), 2000/0143 (CNS).

19 Cf. Communication from the Commission to the Council, the European Parliament, the Economic and Social Committee and the Committee of the Regions – Towards a community framework strategy on gender equality (2001-2005), COM/2000/0335 final, p. 2.

In sum, the policy programmes promoted gender equality by supporting harmonization of member states policy on certain topics and by stimulating debates and actions on other topics that were seldom perceived relevant in member states policies. Acknowledging that member states were reluctant to negotiate new directives, the Commission switched to action programmes as one of the main tools in this policy field. By assisting the set-up of a variety of multi-level collaborations, the Commission was also successful in establishing supranational gender equality policy networks via the policy programmes. The Commission created their own network ties, for instance, by closely collaborating with the Women's Rights and Gender Equality Committee (FEMM) in the European Parliament (EP); both aiming to get the most out of the narrow legal possibilities by introducing innovative measures and legislative proposals with each new action programme (Hoskyns 2000). At the end of the fifth policy programme, a large amount of groups with excellent gender expertise existed that could have supported the Commission in designing the next programme; yet, after almost 20 successful years, the nature and function of policy programmes were considerably transformed as will be illustrated in the following chapter.

5 Softening the Soft Law: weakened gender equality policy programmes

The Framework Strategy came to an end at a time when in 2004-2005 the EU experienced its biggest enlargement ever with ten Central and Eastern European Countries and at the same time, faced a serious setback with the failed ratification of the "Treaty establishing a Constitution for Europe". Against this background, the Commission reversed its established approach for policy programmes: the "Roadmap for equality between *women and men* 2006-2010"[20] (authors' emphasis) changed the format and function of this soft law tool; one already visible in the title with switching back from 'gender equality' to 'women and men'.

The certainly most important change was that the Commission gave up on gender equality action programmes with an own budget. The Commission claimed that other Community programmes such as PROGRESS, DAPHNE or the structural funds were providing the necessary resources (Ahrens 2018). Nonetheless, already in 2008 the specific gender branch in PROGRESS only

20 Hereafter roadmap. Cf. Communication from the Commission to the Council, the European Parliament, the European Economic and Social Committee and the Committee of the Regions: A Roadmap for equality between women and men 2006-2010. COM (2006) 92 final.

amounted to nine per cent while the original budget foreseen for gender equality was twelve per cent. The missing three percentage points were spent on the other policy areas and this loss was irreversible as the 2012 analysis of the PROGRESS implementation revealed. Even though the planned share of commitments for gender equality had been raised above 13 percent since 2011, the actual expenditure was alarmingly low. The gap between plans and actual expenditure almost only occurred for gender equality (European Commission 2013:66).

Furthermore, the Commission gave no indication for the overall budget earmarked for gender equality and the FEMM Committee of the EP failed to hold the Commission responsible. Remarkably, the consciousness about the missing roadmap budget disappeared the moment it was decoupled from an action programme (Ahrens 2018), mainly because the FEMM committee was not responsible for the other budget branches which fell under the responsibility of other EP committees.[21] Also, the gender equality unit of DG Employment was not able to control the budget expenditure, because a different Commission unit was in charge of PROGRESS (Ahrens 2018).

In addition, the roadmap was the first gender equality policy programme that did not foresee any new legislative proposals nor – more importantly – any actions with direct outreach to member state level or the social partners. On the contrary, the Commission kept other actors at a distance for the sake of fostering gender mainstreaming implementation in all Directorate Generals (DGs) which boiled down to engaging in an inward-looking time-consuming process (Ahrens 2018).

While some of the issues of the framework strategy (2001-2005) and the roadmap (2006-2010) seemed similar, it is crucial to note that the roadmap reduced broader social justice claims to equal economic independence. A new section in the roadmap on promoting gender equality in external and development policies revealed the shifted focus on exporting the EU gender regime instead of tackling more efficiently remaining gender gaps in the EU (Ahrens 2019).

Further changes can be detected with a view to how topics were framed. The framework strategy featured 'Promoting Equal Participation and Representation', terms linked to descriptive and substantive representation, whereas the roadmap only announced 'Equal Representation in Decision-making', a move that might have limited the scope of actions (Ahrens 2019). Also, the roadmap priority areas of action covered Commission activities *only*. No actions were foreseen with member states, women's organisations and/or trade unions, which was a core element of previous programmes. In addition, the roadmap did not propose new actions, but offered rather a compilation of existing activi-

21 PROGRESS, for instance, fell under the responsibility of the Committee on Employment and Social Affairs.

ties or provided a vague reference to gender mainstreaming and monitoring. It did not contain measures to monitor its implementation progress, but compiled indicators on gender equality progress instead (Ahrens 2018).

The seventh policy programme, “Strategy for equality between women and men 2010-2015“[22] did not bring positive change: the policy issues stagnated as did the scope of accountability and monitoring; the Commission did not set up a new action programme. The policy programme focused on describing the situation of women and men without even mentioning the different impact of the financial and economic crisis on women’s and men’s economic and employment situation (Karamessini and Rubery 2013). The highlighted shift from broad social justice claims to employment and economics as core topics was completed when adopting this latest policy programme.

One of the factors ostensibly explaining the deterioration of the policy programmes might be that in 2010 the responsibility for gender equality policy moved from DG Employment to DG Justice. Since the possibilities of one DG in controlling another DG are rather limited (Hartlapp et al 2013), the Commission officers who drafted the programme in 2010 were not in charge of this policy field anymore and could not support further development. Not only has this moved gender equality policy away from those managing the economic and fiscal crisis, the problem was rather the loss of expertise on gender equality in its original home DG Employment at a time when ‘the crisis’ hit hard.

By the end of 2015 the Commission further downgraded the accountability of gender equality policy programmes when she published its “Strategic engagement for gender equality (2016-2019)”[23] in the form of a commission staff working document; an internal document of lowest status even without approval by the College of Commissioners. With the beginning of 2015 rumours appeared that the Commission was undecided whether to adopt a new gender equality policy programme at all. The Commission’s reluctance helped activating supranational gender equality actors. Since early 2015 the European Women’s Lobby started a European-wide campaign, not only for the continuation of the programmes but for extension and a stronger commitment (European Women’s Lobby 2015). In June 2015, the Commission started a public online consultation ‘Equality between women and men in the EU’ that still left open whether there would be another policy programme. The consultation offered the chance to vote on the relevance of gender equality topics and to select a limited number of specific actions.

---

22 Cf. Communication from the Commission to the European Parliament, the Council, the Economic and Social Committee and the Committee of the Regions. Strategy for equality between women and men 2010-2015, COM (2010) 491 final.

23 Cf. https://ec.europa.eu/anti-trafficking/sites/antitrafficking/files/strategic_engagement_ for _gender_equality_en.pdf (9/9/2016).

This last twist in the history of gender equality policy programmes might become the final criterion for estimating the future role of soft law in EU gender equality policy-making. When approving the Barroso-Commission in 2010, the EP strengthened its role by forcing the Commission to consult the Parliament in certain cases before adopting soft law.[24] The EP insisted on this obligation because of the well-known role of soft law as predecessors of hard law. The FEMM Committee of the EP in an – as the authors would argue – act of deliberative interpretation of Commission consultation obligations, contributed to the debate about the future of gender equality policy programmes by adopting the "Report on the EU Strategy for equality between women and men post-2015" (European Parliament 2015). The report proves the decreasing openness and access to the EP (see section 7) as well as the diverging, not to say contrary ideas about what gender equality actually means. After a heated debate in which nationalist conservative groups tried to prevent its adoption, the report was adopted in plenary. Twenty national gender equality ministers stressed their interest in a renewed Commission policy programme, thereby setting the stage for debates among core supranational gender equality actors (die Standard 2015). Despite this pressure from the EP and from member states, the Commission decided not to proceed with policy programmes in the form of Commission communications and published the staff working document. While this needs further investigation, we assume that this format was an uncomfortable compromise to satisfy the EP and member states by not abandoning the programmes entirely. In the following section we will describe in more detail the key (feminist) gender equality actors, how their role changed over time and which consequences this brings about for EU gender equality policy.

6 Actors Constellations

The previous sections have presented us with an overview of the different policy instruments in the domain of gender equality as well as the changes they have undergone. These changes in instruments cause the entrance of key actors in the political arena or their disappearance from it, and in turn, these (dis)appearances influence the outcome of the policy process. Research indicates that the strength of EU gender equality policies was a result of two characteristics of this policy arena: the presence of velvet triangles and the working of pincers. Velvet triangles are constituted by privileged, personalized links between committed feminist actors at different positions in the pol-

24 Cf. http://www.europarl.europa.eu/sides/getDoc.do?pubRef=-//EP//TEXT+TA+P7-TA-2010-0009+0+DOC+XML+V0//EN (9/0/2016).

icy arena: academics and experts, members of parliament, and administration (Woodward 2004). They have a strong agenda setting function, they help pushing a proposal through the decision making process and critically monitor further developments. The pincer mechanism is at work during the stage of implementation. It refers to the double pressure needed to push unwilling governments and make them adopt as well as implement far-reaching instruments. This pressure is exercised by the Commission, the EP and the Court at the supranational level, as well as women's groups, feminist lawyers and politicians at the (sub)national level, increasing the costs of non-compliance for a reluctant government (Van der Vleuten 2005). In this section, we argue that over the past decade both aspects have changed. We will turn our attention to the actor constellations involved in each policy type and the implications which recent shifts in policy instruments have for the position of feminist actors and the defence of gender equality in times of crisis; how do these changes influence the velvet triangle and the pincers?

The first type of instruments, 'hard law' such as gender equality directives, involves the Commission as agenda setter who formulates the initial proposal, as well as the European Parliament (EP) and the Council of Ministers of Social Affairs (with the acronym EPSCO), who amend and adopt or reject the proposal. A major institutional shift occurred in 2011, when José Manuel Barroso, president of the Commission, moved the portfolio of gender equality from the Commissioner of Social Affairs to the Commissioner of Justice, Consumers and Gender Equality; and at the administrative level, from the Directorate General for Employment and Social Affairs (DG EMPL) to the Directorate General of Justice and Consumers (DG JUST) (Van der Vleuten 2012). This was a major change, because it resulted in a loss of expertise and access, as well as a change in substance. In fact, since the 1970s, the Equal Opportunities Unit (EOU) within DG EMPL had accumulated expertise on gender equality. It had attracted committed 'femocrats', it had established a range of thematic networks with feminist experts in the member states, and it had developed close links with women's groups through the European Women's Lobby, and with the FEMM Committee of the EP. Also, the substance of gender equality policies changed, because gender equality no longer was an objective of economic and social affairs, but it became framed as a human right and part of the broader fight against discrimination. In the EU, Justice and Home Affairs is a relatively new supranational policy domain, as until recently national governments fully controlled policy making. It is not part of the core of EU 'hard law' policy making but has always focused rather on coordination of national policies. Moreover, human rights concerns are mainly 'externally oriented' towards candidate countries and external trade and development partners of the EU, but they do not have a strong treaty base enabling the development of strong binding instruments for 'domestic use' on combating domestic violence, for instance. The Fundamental Rights Agency (FRA), which was set up in order to advise the Commission on human rights issues, takes a legal approach. It considers gender as one of several grounds for discrimination rather than gender equality as a specific aim cross-cutting all policy domains. In short, the velvet triangle has been stretched and weakened by the organizational shift.

Secondly, as we discussed in section three, 'hard law' has been replaced increasingly by other policy instruments such as the social OMC and the European Semester. This shift entails the inclusion of new actors and the exclusion of others, but most of all required and promoted a different public service. In the 1970s and 1980s, DG EMPL and especially the Equal Opportunities Unit (EOU), had a militant approach to gender equality and maintained close personal contacts with women's organizations and feminist experts. The EOU acted as an agenda setter and critical watchdog. The spreading of New Public Management ideas led to a 'professionalization' of the EOU, encouraging mobility of public servants and reducing the autonomy of the Unit. All expert networks were disbanded except for the legal and the labour market networks. In a second wave of reforms, only a single network was maintained (ENEGE, the European Network of Experts on Gender Equality) which no longer was asked to provide the Commission with innovative ideas and critical analyses, but to be a service provider which delivers accurate information. After endless negotiations the European Institute on Gender Equality (EIGE) was set up with the idea to create an independent structure for the coordination and exchange of information and knowledge (Jacquot 2015). This information is needed for the production of rankings, best practices and policy recommendations in the framework of the OMC and the European Semester. In these processes, an increasingly dominant role is played by the member states and their representatives. There is a strong presence of the member states in EIGE, as opposed to their absence from the previous activist networks. In 2001, the High Level Group on Gender Mainstreaming, composed of national civil servants, took over the responsibility for the annual report on gender equality from the EOU. More recently, gender equality has become even less visible. The European Semester requires in-depth analysis of member state policies as to their contribution to competitiveness, employment and the functioning of EMU (Zeitlin and Vanhercke 2014). Accordingly, monitoring is shared by three directorate-generals, namely DG Economic and Financial Affairs (DG ECFIN), DG EMPL and DG TAXUD (responsible for taxation and the customs union) under the coordination of the Secretariat-General (SG) which constitutes the Commission's president staff. They advise member states on a broad range of issues such as real estate prices, pensions and unemployment benefits. This implies that the preeminent DG ECFIN also gives its perspective on labour market issues. In this process, gender equality has been 'mainstreamed away' and been subordinated to fiscal and monetary objectives (Jacquot 2015). Crucially, the EP and the Court are kept outside the process. There is no 'pincer mechanism', because the tools to obtain compliance with the objectives are purely intergovernmental and consensual, such as the discussion of best practices and rankings (Van der Vleuten and Verloo 2012). Litigation, let alone strategic litigation, which has been used in the past as a crowbar to promote implementation of higher standards (Cichowski 2007), simply is not possible when there is no binding legal instrument. In 2014, the EWL and trade unions have joined forces in the European Semester Alliance, with the aim to monitor attention given to social and gender equality issues, but their position is marginalized in the deliberations between ministers and diplomats based on the Commission reports. Also, any recommendation has to match the logic of DG ECFIN, which sits uneasily with the promotion of gender equality.

A third change has resulted from the increase of eurosceptic, populist and conservative political parties in the member states and their presence in the EP, including in the FEMM committee. The FEMM committee used to be an activist promoter of gender equality which became famous for the hearings it organized and its own-initiative reports, but its increasingly mixed composition has contributed to a loss of militancy (see previous section). Also in this respect the velvet triangle has lost some of its mobilizing impact. In addition, the broad support in the EP in general for new far-reaching gender equality policies seems to have waned and the recommendations from the FEMM committee are not taken seriously by other committees (Jacquot 2015).

Table 2. Feminist actors in the European policy arena

Instrument	Key Actors involved at European level	Actors involved w/feminist focus
'Hard law': gender equality directives on socio-economic topics	Commission: DG EMPL Council: EPSCO (Ministers of Social Affairs) European Parliament Court	Femocrats (EOU) in DG EMPL EWL EP FEMM Feminist lawyers network
Social OMC, European Semester/ Europe 2020	DG ECFIN, EMPL, TAXUD ECOFIN (Ministers of Finance) and EPSCO (Ministers of Social Affairs), Council committees	EWL & Trade unions → European Semester Alliance
Gender equality policy programmes	Commission EP EPSCO (Ministers of Social Affairs)	Femocrats (EOU) in DG EMPL EP FEMM EWL
Gender equality policies and human rights	DG JUST JHA (Ministers of Justice) European Parliament	FRA, EIGE EWL EP FEMM

Source: Compilation by authors

Changes in instruments as well as changes in the political climate have disempowered actors promoting gender equality and, as a result, two characteristic mechanisms in this domain, the velvet triangle and the pincer mechanism, have lost importance.

7 Conclusion

In this chapter, we have discussed EU gender equality policy from the angles of instruments and actors, and how they can be understood in the context of European integration over time. The successful adoption of ten directives on gender equality, hard law instruments, involving feminist actors and creating 'pincers', came to a halt each time when in the face of crisis member states did not want to be bound by such far-reaching commitments. However, precisely in times of crisis the EU is expected to show a social face and alleviate conditions of unemployment and precariousness. As a result, we have seen how hard law instruments have been replaced by different types of soft law tools, including the Social OMC, the strategy of gender mainstreaming and gender equality policy programmes. These programmes have undergone profound changes as well. They started as a compromise-driven process between Commission and member states via the adoption in the Council. The European Parliament and civil society (in particular women's organisations) were able to participate in negotiations and the latter also in implementing the policy programmes. The programmes helped harmonizing member states policies through transnational projects and created a common understanding of EU gender equality policy goals. Policy programmes were the Commission's tool to develop innovative policies and their specific gender regime. With the adoption of the roadmap in 2006, gender equality policy programmes lost their innovative potential, their budget, and their role for harmonizing member states policies. They became an ever softer soft law tool, first as Commission communications without Council adoption and ultimately reduced to a Commission staff working document. In the last section we linked these developments to actor constellations and showed how feminist actors have lost access in three respects: because of the replacement of hard law by soft law instruments, which means that no new options for strategic litigation open up; because of the reorganization of the Commission bureaucracy, which has resulted in a loss of access and expertise as well as a shift from feminist to technocratic policymaking; and because of the changes in the composition of the EP.

As a result, nowadays EU gender equality policies cover a wide variety of topics going beyond the labour market, and include a variety of tools with different degrees of effectiveness. However, in times of crisis these policies are under pressure. In addition to the enduring economic and financial crisis, there has been a deepening of the legitimacy crisis because the EU does not seem to be able to deal with the consequences of the ongoing war in Syria and the rise of the so-called Islamic State in the Middle East. The influx of large numbers of refugees and terrorist attacks almost have pushed economic and monetary issues to the second place. Still, in all these debates gender concerns are absent and openings are not self-evident given the actors involved.

In a broader context, it would be necessary to also take into account further urgent gender equality policy issues like reproductive rights, citizen rights for refugees and migrants, and inter/transsexual rights that are not visible on the supranational level. In other words, a revived feminist utopia of what a different, more gender-equal European society should look like is required; an idea that does not deliver an understanding of equality as adjusting females* to white heterosexual males thereby ignoring other social spheres that follow different logics such as the reproductive sphere and 'care' in a broad sense.

Discussion Questions

1. What have been crucial changes in the EU gender equality policy over time?
2. How are these changes influenced by and influencing the triple crisis the EU is facing?
3. How can the EU promote gender equality in the future? Discuss different options with view to legislative instruments and actors available.

References

Abels, Gabriele/Mushaben, Joyce M. (ed.) (2012): Gendering the European Union: new approaches to old democratic deficits. Houndmills, Basingstoke; New York: Palgrave Macmillan.

Ahrens, Petra (2002): Gender Mainstreaming in der Beschäftigungspolitik der Europäischen Union – Im Spannungsfeld feministischer Theorien und politischer Praxis. Diplom.de. ISBN 3-8324-6112-4.

Ahrens, Petra (2007): Gleichstellungspolitik in der Europäischen Union. DIE LINKE (ed.), Berlin.

Ahrens, Petra (2018): Actors, Institutions, and the Making of EU Gender Equality Programs. Basingstoke: Palgrave Macmillan.

Ahrens, Petra (2019): The Birth, Life, and Death of Policy Instruments: 35 years of EU gender equality policy programmes. In: West European Politics, 42, 1, pp. 45-66.

Beveridge, Fiona/Velluti, Samantha (ed.) (2008): Gender and the Open Method of Coordination: Perspectives on Law, Governance and Equality in the EU. Aldershot: Ashgate.

Borrás, Susana/Conzelmann, Thomas (2007): Democracy, Legitimacy and Soft Modes of Governance in the EU: The Empirical Turn. In: *Journal of European Integration,* 29, 5, pp. 531-548.

Burri, Susanne/Prechal, Sacha (2014): EU Gender Equality Law Update 2013. European Commission.

Caporaso, James A./Jupille, Joseph (2001): The Europeanization of Gender Equality Policy and Domestic Structural Change. In: Cowles, Maria G./Caporaso, James A./Risse-Kappen, Thomas (ed.) (2001): Transforming Europe. Ithaca: Cornell Univ. Press, pp. 21-43.

Cichowski, Rachel A. (2007): The European Court and Civil Society: Litigation, Mobilization and Governance. Cambridge, UK: Cambridge University Press.

die Standard (2015): EU lässt bei Frauenpolitik nach. http://diestandard.at/2000017258871/in-der-EU. (5/9/2016)

Ellis, Evelyn (2010): The Impact of the Lisbon Treaty on Gender Equality. In: European Gender Equality Law Review, 1, pp. 7-13.

European Commission (2009): Compilation of case law on the equality of treatment between women and men and on non-discrimination in the European Union, 3rd ed. Directorate-General for Employment, Social Affairs and Equal Opportunities Unit G2, http://ec.europa.eu/justice/gender-equality/files/case-law-compilation_en.pdf (5/9/2016)

European Commission (2013): PROGRESS annual performance monitoring report 2012. Monitoring of the performance of the European Union programme for employment and social solidarity. PROGRESS (2007-13). Luxembourg: Publications Office of the European Union.

European Parliament (2015): Report on the EU Strategy for equality between women and men post 2015, (2014/2152(INI)).

European Women's Lobby (2015): Women's organisations demand a concrete and ambitious European Union's new Strategy for Equality between Women and Men 2016-2020. http://www.womenlobby.org/spip.php?article7186&lang=en (6/2/2015)

Fuhrmann, Nora (2005): Geschlechterpolitik im Prozess der europäischen Integration. Wiesbaden: VS Verlag für Sozialwissenschaften.

Frey, Regina (2003): Gender im Mainstreaming: Geschlechtertheorie und -praxis im internationalen Diskurs. Königstein/Taunus: Helmer.

Hartlapp, Miriam/Metz, Julia/Rauh, Christian (2013): Linking Agenda Setting to Coordination Structures: Bureaucratic Politics Inside the European Commission. In: Journal of European Integration 35, 4, pp. 425-41.

Helfferich, Barbara/Kolb, Felix (2001): Multilevel Action Coordination in European Contentious Politics – the Case of the European Women's Lobby. In: Imig, Douglas R./Tarrow, Sidney G. (ed.) (2001): Contentious Europeans. Lanham: Rowman & Littlefield, pp. 143-162.

Héritier, Adrienne (2003): New Modes of Governance in Europe: Increasing Political Capacity and Policy Effectiveness? In: Börzel, Tanja A./Cichowski, Rachel A. (ed.) (2003): The State of the European Union, Vol. 6. Oxford: Oxford University Press, pp. 105-126.

Hiou-Maniatopoulou, Theodora (2004): Gender equality in the enlarged European Union. In: Revue Hellénique de Droit International 57, 1, pp. 227-39.

Hoskyns, Catherine (1996): Integrating gender: Women, law and politics in the European Union. London: Verso.

Hoskyns, Catherine (2000): A study of four Action Programmes on Equal Opportunities. In: Rossilli, Maria G. (ed.) (2000): Gender policies in the European Union. New York: Lang, pp. 43-59.

Jacquot, Sophie (2015): Transformations in EU Gender Equality: From Emergence to Dismantling. Houndmills/Basingstoke: Palgrave Macmillan.

Imig, Douglas R./Tarrow, Sidney G. (ed.) (2001): Contentious Europeans: Protest and politics in an emerging polity. Lanham: Rowman & Littlefield.

Kantola, Johanna (2010): Gender and the European Union. Houndmills/Basingstoke: Palgrave Macmillan.

Karamessini, Maria/Rubery, Jill (ed.) (2013): Women and austerity: the economic crisis and the future of gender equality. Oxon/New York: Routledge.

Klein, Uta (2013): Geschlechterverhältnisse und Gleichstellungspolitik in der Europäischen Union. Akteure – Themen – Ergebnisse. Wiesbaden: VS Verlag für Sozialwissenschaften.

Liebert, Ulrike (ed.) (2003): Gendering Europeanisation. Bruxelles: PIE Lang.

Locher, Birgit (2012): Gendering the EU Policy Process and Constructing the Gender Acquis. In: Abels, Gabriele/Mushaben, Joyce M. (ed.) (2012): Gendering the European Union. New Approaches to Old Democratic Deficits. Basingstoke: Palgrave Macmillan, pp. 63-84.

Lombardo, Emanuela/Meier, Petra/Verloo, Mieke (ed.) (2009): The Discursive Politics of Gender Equality: Stretching, Bending and Policymaking. London: Routledge.

Mazey, Sonia (1998): The European Union and women's rights: from the Europeanization of national agendas to the nationalization of a European agenda. In: Journal of European public policy 5, 1, pp. 131-52.

Rees, Teresa L. (1998): Mainstreaming equality in the European Union: education, training and labour market policies. London: Routledge.

Rubery, Jill (2005): Gender Mainstreaming and the OMC. Is the Open Method Too Open for Gender Equality Policy? In: Zeitlin, Jonathan/Pochet, Philippe (ed.) (2005): The Open Method of Co-ordination in Action. Bruxelles: Peter Lang, pp. 391-416.

Schunter-Kleemann, Susanne (1999): 'Europäische Geschlechterpolitik – tauglich für das 3. Jahrtausend.' In: Brigitte Stols-Willig and Mechthild Veil (eds.): Es rettet uns kein höh'res Wesen. Hamburg: VSA, 138-167.

Trubek, David M./Trubek, Louise G. (2005): Hard and Soft Law in the Construction of Social Europe: the Role of the Open Method of Co-ordination. In: European Law Journal 11, 3, pp. 343-364.

Van der Vleuten, Anna (2005): Pincers, Prestige and Polarity. Explaining Implementation of EU Gender Equality Legislation. In: Comparative European Politics 3, 4, pp. 464-88.

Van der Vleuten, Anna (2007): The Price of Gender Equality: Member States and Governance in the European Union. Aldershot: Ashgate.

Van der Vleuten, Anna/Verloo, Mieke (2012): Ranking and benchmarking: The political logic of new regulatory instruments in the fields of gender equality and anti-corruption. In: Policy & Politics 40, 1, pp. 71-86.

Walby, Sylvia (2005): Gender Mainstreaming: Productive Tensions in Theory and Practice. In: Social Politics: International Studies in Gender, State and Society 12, 3, pp. 321-43.

Wobbe, Theresa/Biermann, Ingrid (2009): Von Rom nach Amsterdam. Die Metamorphosen des Geschlechts in der Europäischen Union. Wiesbaden: VS Verlag für Sozialwissenschaften.

Woodward, Alison (2004): Building velvet triangles: gender and informal governance. In: Christiansen, Thomas/Piattoni, Simona (2004): Informal Governance in the European Union. Cheltenham: Edward Elgar Publishing.

Zeitlin, Jonathan/Vanhercke, Bart (2014): Socializing the European Semester? Economic Governance and Social Policy Coordination in Europe. Stockholm: SIEPS.

Doris Liebscher

Opening Doors: how the German General Act on Equal Treatment (AGG) advances racial equality

The party was over for 27-year-old Kian before it even began. "Not tonight," said the bouncer of the nightclub in Hanover. Kian intended to go there with some friends, one of whom was celebrating his birthday. Kian´s shirt was white; his sneakers were new. He did not smell of booze, nor look like he was on drugs, but he had a faint idea why he was turned away from the door while his friends were not. It wasn't the first time Kian was not allowed entrance to a club. Sometimes the rejection was blamed on his shoes. Sometimes the bouncers argued that the club was too full. This time the bouncer gave him a surprisingly blatant explanation. "The boss doesn't want too many foreigners to come in," he allegedly said. Kian is German; his parents are Kurdish.

Munich resident Hamado, who is originally from Burkina Faso, had similar experiences in Munich. "You stand there and ask yourself: What have I done wrong? You feel degraded, publicly exposed, injured in your personality. It is a total humiliation that I find hard to take," explains Hamado (O'Sullivan: 2014). He shares this experience with many people of color and migrants in Germany. Turned away so many times and never able to prove that the rejection was based on racist screening, he organized what antidiscrimination organizations call a 'testing'. With a group of friends, he tried to enter several nightclubs in a single night. Shortly after he was rejected – with typical excuses such as "it's a private party" – his white German friends, who also participated in the testing, passed the doors without problems.

Hamado and his friends tried to get into 25 clubs and were turned away at 20. Testings in Leipzig and in Hamburg organized by people of color and of Turkish or Arab origin supported by local anti-discrimination agencies showed similar findings. In all these cases, extrajudicial negotiations with clubs took place to raise awareness for discriminatory practices and change racist door policies, in most of the cases without success.

Can lawsuits based on the AGG help open doors? Can they remedy humiliation? Does the condemnation of racial screening serve as a deterrent, preventing further discrimination in the service sector? To answer these questions, the following sections will introduce the history of the AGG, its material and personal scope, further discussing in which cases differentiations are not discriminatory and finally examine difficulties in the process of the enforcements of civil rights.

1 European Law as Starting Point

Human rights advocates, anti-racist NGOs, organizations for disabled people, feminist scholars and LGBT lawyers celebrated the enactment of the General Act on Equal Treatment (AGG) in August 2006. It had been a long way and not an easy one. The path began in Brussels at the turn of the millennium. On the eve of facing stiff fines from the EU Commission, Germany fulfilled its obligation to enact a comprehensive anti-discrimination act. The AGG incorporated four EU Anti-Discrimination Directives. The business community and their lobby groups reacted quickly against the legislation, claiming that Germany did not have a discrimination problem and warning that the law would be abused. They predicted a flood of lawsuits and the end of the precedence of private autonomy. Their predictions did not come true. Nevertheless, the broader public came to view the AGG as yet another European bureaucratic monster. This view is also held by most of the mainstream legal field.

Ten years later, a number of positive changes have taken place. The AGG has pushed academic research, anti-discrimination jurisprudence and institutionalized anti-discrimination policy forward into areas, which previously covered only issues of gender equality. Before the AGG, discrimination was tangible only by the equality clause in Article 3.2 and 3.3 of the German Basic Law (*Grundgesetz*, GG) and some sections in German labor law prohibiting gender discrimination concerning employment. Since Article 3 GG does not provide legally enforceable claims many cases of discrimination were not covered by the law. This was particularly true in the private sector because German fundamental rights have no direct effect between private law subjects. In the traditional understanding, fundamental rights only have impact on the vertical relationship between individuals and the state. They are not directly applicable to the horizontal relationship between individuals. Civil courts are in fact bound by the fundamental rights and thus have to interpret provisions of private law in conformity with the fundamental rights. But no private party legal claims can result directly from the anti-discriminaltion clause in Article 3.3 Grundgesetz.

But the AGG did more than establishing new legal claims. Anti-discrimination agencies were established on a federal basis, in some *Länder* (federal states) and on a non-governmental level. Legal claims against age discrimination changed collective wage agreements. Through strategic litigation, gay and lesbian spouses' widow's pensions were guaranteed. It was further used to legally clarify that workplace discrimination because of an HIV infection is unlawful under the AGG. Families successfully sued their landlords because they had to pay more rent due to their Turkish or Arabic background.

The impact of doctrinal and philosophical discussions on legal equality must not be underestimated. To counter the attacks on anti-discrimination law in Germany, legal scholars have pointed out that freedom and the freedom of self-determination in contracting with others in particular, should be conceived of as inherently linked with, rather than clashing with, equality and dignity alike (Baer 2009). The whole academic discourse on intersectionality is highly influenced by the anti-discrimination approach. US legal scholar Kimberlè Crenshaw started analyzing anti-discrimination law from a Critical Race and Gender perspective using the term intersectionality. She argues that the experience of Black women cannot be understood in terms of being Black and of being a woman independently, but must consider the specific conjunction of racism and sexism. Intersectionality is more than the sum of race and sex and anti-discrimination law, by attaching rights to well-defined categories, cannot accurately address intersectional experiences of discrimination (Crenshaw 1989). In the German-speaking legal field, feminist and anti-racist scholars have applied the intersectional approach to the European context, examining discriminatory discourse and discriminating treatment of women wearing the Muslim headscarf as well as of young men who were denied access to clubs and discos due to specific culturalized and racialized gender attributions (Lembke and Liebscher 2014).

While such research is important and can help point out the direction in which we should be moving, much still remains to be done. Many scholars and lawyers claim the AGG still does too little, pointing out numerous flaws and loopholes within the law. One example is the so-called 'religious privilege', which allows religious institutions and companies to discriminate against employees or applicants who are not members of their religious communities, even though these institutions and organizations often hold a monopoly in their respective fields of work. Furthermore, they have shown that law enforcement is weak when faced with difficulties in evidencing a claim, biased judges or high legal costs for the plaintiffs. The following chapters describe the scope of the German anti-discrimination law and the challenges to enforce it. To do so it uses claims brought up against racist admission policy in clubs and discos as an example, showing how law, legal practice and public discourse interact.

2 The Substantive Scope of Anti-Discrimination Law

Where does discrimination take place and in which situations does the AGG apply? Raising this question helps us understand what lawyers mean when they speak of the material – or substantive – scope of the law. Discrimination takes place in many contexts, in the workplace, at the university, in the insurance or housing market, in the neighborhood, in contact with public authorities or at an entertainment venue. While the key question for legislators and political activists is: which aspects of life should be covered by legal protection against discrimination, the crucial question for lawyers and judges is always: does the substantive scope of a given provision apply in the specific context of a legal case?

Regarding the former, political convictions and power relations matter as well as questions of legislative power, even more in a multi-level governance system like the European Union and in a federal state like Germany. NGOs in Europe had long pressed for the adoption of such measures. Among the most important organizations was the Starting Line Group, a coalition of non-governmental actors and state organizations based in the United Kingdom and the Netherlands, which had issued a draft for a race directive as early as 1993.

With regard to the scope of non-discrimination legislation, member states' practices have varied considerably in the past. For example, in Germany specific legislation prohibited incitement to hatred on racial or religious grounds, but offered no protection against other manifestations of racial discrimination, except for the equality principle enunciated in Art. 3 par. 3 Constitution that there should be no discrimination on the ground of race. Alternatively, the 1976 British Race Relations Act was considerably broader, forbidding discrimination in employment, training and education, housing and the provision of goods, services and planning. The Starting Line Group's 1993 draft directive went even further, requiring the prohibition of discrimination in employment, social security, health care, welfare, education, vocational training, housing, provision of goods and services and participation in political, economic, social, cultural, religious and public life.

EU anti-discrimination legislation could not go beyond employment discrimination, as this was historically the most developed area of European social policy. A directive against gender discrimination in employment had been passed in 1976. But there was another factor that influenced the decision. When the EU 'Racial Equality Directive' – in the German-speaking context referred to as 'Anti-Racism Directive' – was adopted in 2002, Europe had been facing a wave of racist and anti-Semitic violence. The EU was alarmed by the right-wing populist Freedom Party's (FPÖ) participation in the Austrian government in February 2000 and imposed sanctions against Austria. The political climate was therefore more favorable towards a political project of comprehensive anti-discrimination legislation in the public and private sector. All this led to broadly formulated legal protection against racist discrimination, broader than in any of the following EU directives:

1. The Council Directive 2000/43/EC, implementing the principle of equal treatment between persons irrespective of racial or ethnic origin.
2. The Council Directive 2000/78/EC, establishing a general framework for equal treatment in employment and occupation.
3. The Directive 2002/73/EC of the European Parliament and of the Council, amending Council Directive 76/207/EC on the implementation of the principle of equal treatment for men and women as regarding access to employment, vocational training and promotion and working conditions.
4. The Council Directive 2004/113/EC, implementing the principle of equal treatment between men and women in the access to and supply of goods and services.

The Racial Equality Directive covers employment and occupation, vocational training, membership of employer and employee organizations, social security and health care, education, and access to goods and services available to the public, including housing. All directives must be implemented uniformly regardless of the plurality of national realities. As they set out minimum requirements member states may provide for a higher level of protection in national legislation. Because it implements all four directives, the AGG can be understood as a political compromise both at the European level and at the national level. It protects from discrimination in the fields of:

First, employment and training which includes recruitment and selection, promotion, training, pay and benefits, redundancy and dismissal, terms and conditions of work.

Second, providing goods, facilities, services and housing which includes refusing to provide you with goods, facilities or services or providing any of these things on less favorable terms or conditions.

The substantive scope of the AGG does not include discrimination in advertisement, by public safety authorities, by neighbors and in education. What are the reasons for this legal loophole? The EU directives themselves do not cover discrimination in the areas of advertisement, by public safety authorities, by neighbors, and there was no political will to extend protection. Education is indeed included in the EU Anti-Racism directive. But as Germany is a federal state and education is regulated at the level of the federal states (*Bundesländer*), the national legislature adopting the AGG had no competence in this field. It is still up to the federal states to align their school and higher education legislation with EU law.

The following examples demonstrate the implications of this fragmented legal framework from a lawyer's perspective. Imagine, first, a case of sexual or racist harassment at the workplace. Sexual and racist harassment are forms of discrimination according to Section 3 III, IV AGG. But does the substantive scope of the AGG apply in this context? The AGG covers discrimination in employment in the private and public sector (Sections 6-18 AGG), including conditions of work as defined in Section 2 I no. 2 AGG. Therefore, a person who faces sexual harassment or racist discrimination within the scope of professional activities may rely on his or her right not to suffer discrimination, whether he or she works at a bank, at a workshop or at an university, whether the harassment occurs during the work, at a conference or during a company party, whether the harasser is a superior, a colleague or a client.

In addition, Section 2 II no. 8 AGG provides protection against discrimination related to "access to and supply of goods and services which are available to the public, including housing." Regarding the door policies of discotheques explained above, a lawyer would come to the conclusion that the AGG applies here. A visit to a club is a genuine service available to the public and the denial of access to this service is therefore within the substantial scope of the act.

Now imagine a case of sexual or racist harassment at university or school, but this time a student faces harassment. Even though the behavior is discriminatory according to Section 3 III, IV AGG it does not fall within the scope of the AGG, because public education is not mentioned in the Act. The following step would then be to examine, if the regional school and higher education legislation includes anti-discrimination provisions protecting students against sexual or racist harassment. If it does, these provisions can be used to compensate damages and to prevent further incidents. In case it does not – and this is unfortunately the case in most of the federal states – this lack has to be addressed politically as a legislative issue.

3 The Personal Scope: grounds of discrimination

While the substantive scope of anti-discrimination law is about the spheres where unequal treatment can take place, the personal scope can be understood by asking the following questions: Which person is faced with discrimination? To whom does the AGG apply? When does unequal treatment qualify as discrimination? At first glance these questions are not directly linked to each other. But if we look at the common legal definitions of discrimination, we will quickly see the connection.

Like others, German anti-discrimination law is based on a closed list of grounds for discrimination. Section 1 AGG puts it like this, "The purpose of this Act is to prevent or to stop discrimination on the grounds of race or ethnic origin, gender, religion or belief, disability, age or sexual orientation", and Article 3.3 GG says: "No person shall be favored or disfavored because of sex, parentage, race, language, homeland and origin, faith, or religious or political opinions. No person shall be disfavored because of disability."

Apparently discrimination is linked to certain 'grounds', or categories, and legal protection against unequal, or rather disfavoring treatment is limited to an exhaustive list of grounds. A lawyer therefore checks, whether the disfavoring treatment in question is linked to a legally protected category. A case of sexual harassment is a subset of sex discrimination and therefore linked to gender discrimination. Catherine MacKinnon has explained the link between sexual harassment and gender discrimination in her groundbreaking theoretical and legal analysis of sexual harassment. The link is that a sexually harassing policy or practice integrally contributes to the maintenance of an underclass or deprived position because of gender status (MacKinnon 2013). Susanne Baer adopted this theory to the German context (Baer 1995).

The denial of entrance to a club due to racist stereotypes is a case of racist discrimination and therefore within the scope of the AGG. The wording used in Section 1 AGG, "on grounds of race and ethnic origin," is supposed to indicate that the German legislature does not recognize the existence of different human races, but that it refers to racist behavior. Applied to the club scenario mentioned above, the question is not, what race or ethnic origin does a client belong to, but whether racist attributions lead to his or her unfair treatment. It does not matter if the client is a German or Turkish citizen, if his parents are German or Nigerian, if he speaks German without an accent, or if he is darker or lighter-skinned.

In reality, racist attributions are often linked to physical or cultural markers connected to assumptions concerning the belonging or not belonging of a person to the national community or the majority group. In turn, these racialized assumptions of national affiliation go along with negative attributions of cultural behavior. For example, men of color or male migrants are blamed for being culturally aggressive, misogynist and extraordinarily sexual active. Given this specific convergence of racialized and gender attributions it would be more precise to speak of intersectional discrimination. In fact, the Higher Regional Court of Stuttgart (Oberlandesgericht Stuttgart) classified the denial of access to a club of a young Black men as a multiple discrimination based on the categories of race and gender.

Unlike the sociologically and legally clear cases of racist, gender or disability discrimination there are several experiences of disfavoring treatment, which are not considered discrimination in a legal sense. Smokers may consider themselves to be discriminated against, when their employer does not provide any smoking areas. Holders of fighting dogs often feel exposed to threats and discrimination, due to panic campaigns steered by the media. Obese people who often face unfair treatment at the workplace are not protected by the AGG. Neither are homeless people who are harassed by security staff protected, nor are people whose applications are rejected because of their origin from the former German Democratic Republic (GDR) or because they are ex-convicts.

Regarding the legal definition of discrimination, there are different historical, political and sociological justifications for legal protection against discrimination. Historically evolved and internationally acknowledged principles of non-discrimination are anti-racism and gender equality. Gender was the first discrimination ground in the legal framework of the European Union; race was the first in the Anglo-American context.

Historically, racism has been one of the cruelest forms of discrimination. The equal protection clause in the 14th amendment of the US Constitution from 1868 was a reaction to slavery and the racist Black Codes in the southern states. The Universal Declaration of Human Rights, as well as the equal protection clause in Article 3.3 III of the German Basic Law, responded to the experience of the Shoa, National Socialism and the Second World War. Within the historical framework, the importance of civil rights movements cannot be underestimated. Next to the examples of the women's movement and the anti-racism movement, the disability rights movement and the LGBTI movement have played an important role.

Apart from historical reasons, immutability constitutes a unifying principle for legal protection. Immutability refers either to physical markers, which are not changeable, or to characteristics, which are fundamental to identity, such as sexual orientation and religious believes. Another approach is based on the concept of power relations that structure society such as racism, heterosexism and disability. A similar rationale is the 'suspect class' concept of the US Supreme Court, that refers to social groups that are the likely subject of discrimination.

Critics have been pointing out that all these concepts are not able to provide comprehensive protection. They are not flexible enough to incorporate new forms of discrimination in changing societies. Other critics emphasize the dilemma of difference in anti-discrimination law based on fixed categories such as race or gender. Without question, there is a need to address experiences and acts of discrimination, which are tied to personal features in the context of social stratifications. Race and gender are socially made and meaningful constructions based on racism and heterosexism. By addressing these categories as grounds of discrimination, actors in the field of anti-discrimination law confront substantial risks. Persons who raise claims of discrimination can be essentialized. Heterogeneous intersectional experiences of discrimination can be homogenized. Finally, individuals and social groups who do not fit into any existing category will be excluded from legal protection. The critics of the categorical approach therefore suggest adopting the concept of stigmatization to the legal context. This concept responds to the fact that social stigma leads to exclusion. In addition, stigmata often differ depending on the geopolitical and sociopolitical contexts in distinctive parts of the world.

One possibility allowing for more flexible legal action is an open list of legal anti-discrimination grounds, such as in Article 14 of the European Convention on Human Rights, which provides: "The enjoyment of the rights and freedoms set forth in this European Convention on Human Rights shall be secured without discrimination on any ground such as sex, race, color, language, religion, political or other opinion, national or social origin, association with a national minority, property, birth or other status." The categories are listed as typical grounds of discrimination, but not as an exclusive list.

4 Forms of Discrimination

Discrimination in a legal sense usually includes various elements. First, it refers to treatment, not individually assessing the unique merits, capacities and circumstances of a person, instead making stereotypical assumptions based on a person's presumed traits. Second, it refers to the negative impact of the exclusion of persons, denying them benefits or imposing burdens on them. Many people wrongly think that discrimination does not exist if the impact was not intended. Contrary to this assumption, discrimination does not necessarily require malicious intent. It can lie in the effects of treating certain people in certain ways. The AGG therefore protects persons affected by discrimination, whether or not the discrimination was caused by intentional or unintentional actions or rules. It acknowledges three main forms: direct discrimination, indirect discrimination and harassment.

According to Section 3.1 AGG, 'direct discrimination' refers to less favorable treatment with reference to one or some of the protected categories. An example is the mentioned club scenario, where access is denied only to male people of color or male migrants. In contrast, an indirect act of discrimination is considered to have taken place when apparently neutral rules, regulations, criteria or practices – which do not refer explicitly to a protected ground – have a negative impact on a protected group. One example would be requiring a German language test during the recruitment process for a job as postman or as kitchen assistant. This can be determined as a form of indirect discrimination. First, because although perfect knowledge of German is not important in order to meet the requirements of the job a German language test is set up. Second, this rule affects especially migrants – it discriminates against them indirectly.

In a case decided by the European Court of Justice on 16 July 2015, a Bulgarian municipality had ordered measures that negatively affected a neighborhood largely inhabited by people belonging to the Roma community. The court concluded that this is a case of indirect discrimination under the Bulgarian Anti-Discrimination Act, as the measures were based on negative discrimination assumptions of Roma people. Another case concerning the rights of third parties was related to the parent of a disabled child. This parent was discriminated at the workplace due to her increased care work efforts. She successfully sued the company based on the category of disability, even though she was not disabled herself.

An act of harassment, sexual or otherwise, occurs in the context of the AGG when unwanted conduct harms or hurts a person, especially when causing an atmosphere of intimidation, hostility, humiliation or indignity. Whereas direct and indirect discrimination can be caused both by individual actions and by rules and regulations, harassment always takes place on an interactive level between persons. Sexual harassment can include unwelcome sexual advances, requests for sexual behaviors, e-mails or posters with pornographic content and other verbal, visual or physical conduct with a sexual connotation and an annoying, degrading or abusing effect.

Racist harassment can include incessant racist remarks or verbal abuse by colleagues or superiors in the workplace; criticizing and being intolerant in regards to the victim's differences: his or her accent, clothing, hairdo, customs and beliefs; making jokes, insinuations, humiliating comments or racially oriented remarks; finding excuses for not working with the victim; stereotyping the victim with subordinate tasks or showing comic strips, pictures or images that are racially degrading.

5 Justified Difference of Treatment

Not every unequal treatment is understood to be discriminating. In fact, there are several legal justifications. There is one general exception: harassment on grounds of any of the characteristics cited in the AGG is never admissible.

In the field of employment, difference of treatment on any of the protected grounds is admissible where the characteristics linked to these grounds are genuine and a nearly determining prerequisite for performing the task (Section 8 AGG). A language test for a public relations job is not discriminatory; neither is the employment of solely female staff in a Women's Shelter or in a gynecological practice with predominantly Muslim women patients.

Different treatment with regard to access to and supply of goods and services might also be admissible in cases where there is an objective reason (Section 20 AGG). Price reductions for school children or special opening hours for women in swimming pools are examples of an admissible exception. Separate opening times for women and men in saunas are allowed. It is also admissible for the operator of a club or a dating service to offer price reductions in order to attract female customers, while men are required to pay higher prices. Barring someone from a club because of racist attributions is never an objective reason within the meaning of the law and therefore an unlawful discrimination.

In order to promote groups that have been subject to discrimination, such as women, people of color or people with disabilities, the AGG allows affirmative action measures and thereby goes further than simply prohibiting discrimination. These positive measures (Section 5 AGG) can be adopted by employers in relation to the field of work and by parties for contracts under private law in relation to the access to and supply of goods and services. A law company or a law faculty that wishes to eliminate the underrepresentation of migrant women is allowed to preferentially hire migrant women as long as there is no other person with a better qualification.

6 Legal Claims in Case of Discrimination

Being right is one thing, obtaining justice is often another. The key questions for lawyers are the following: What are the needs and goals of the client? Are there any legal claims meeting the clients' interests? What procedural requirements of litigation have to be met to successfully win the lawsuit?

What Kian from the opening example wanted, when the bouncer turned him away, was an apology and the assurance that the discrimination would not happen again. This is exactly what many people facing discrimination are looking for in the first place. People whose applications for a job or for a flat are rejected based on discriminatory reasons normally wish to get the job or the flat – and an apology. They primarily want fair treatment and access to everyday resources.

The legal entitlements given by the AGG do not necessarily meet these interests. As civil law, the objective of the AGG is less punishing the perpetrator, but compensating the victim for his or her injuries. The AGG provides that victims of unjustified differences of treatment and harassment are entitled to make claims for damages and compensation. The claims must be submitted in writing within two months. It is, however, not possible to make a claim for the job, when an application does not lead to employment or promotion. Section 15.6. AGG states that, "any violation on the part of the employer of the prohibition of discrimination shall not justify a claim to the establishment of an employment relationship, a vocational training relationship or to promotion."

In cases of unjustified discrimination regarding the access to and supply of goods and services, the person involved not only has a claim to damages and compensation. He or she also has the right to demand the elimination of the obstacles (claim of removal) and to apply for an injunction. These claims must also be submitted within two months.

If a client is not allowed entrance to a club due to racism, he can sue the owner for monetary damages, for instance the taxi fares. Also, he can claim compensation for non-pecuniary damage – the harm and humiliation he suffered. Finally, he can apply for an injunction. That means that the court orders an amount payable to the victim in case of repetition of the discriminatory action. If a client's application to job was rejected due to racist ascriptions, he could sue the employer for damages and compensation, but he had no possibility to sue for getting the job.

7 The Enforcement of the Anti-Discrimination Law

One of the biggest challenges is the proof of discrimination when the responsible part, in our case the owner of the discotheque, denies it. Clubs routinely make decisions about whom they let in, which may seem rude and arbitrary. Proving that a club has rejected someone solely for racialized profiling is extremely difficult. Typical excuses or justifications are that the rejected person acted aggressively, that the club contracts Black DJs and that some of bouncers themselves are migrants. Similar difficulties arise in other contexts. It is hard to gather evidence in cases of verbal harassment. It is difficult to prove discrimination in recruitment against an employer or a landlord, especially if the person who feels discriminated against does not know the other applicants.

The AGG responds to these problems with the so-called alleviation of the burden of proof in Section 22: "Where, in case of conflict, one of the parties is able to establish facts from which it may be presumed that there has been discrimination within the personal scope of the act, it shall be for the other party to prove that there has been no breach of the provisions prohibiting discrimination" (Antidiskriminierungsstelle des Bundes 2010). In other words, if one manages to submit documentary or witnessed evidence that suggests that a discriminatory act has taken place, the opposing party must demonstrate that they did not discriminate. Anti-discrimination organizations and lawyers therefore recommend the following behavior in case of being discriminated against. One should remain calm and levelheaded and not allow oneself to be provoked. Apart from that, it is most relevant to ascertain whether there are witnesses and to write down exactly what happened. One should inform the responsible person and/or their superior, preferably in writing, that you do not accept the discrimination and expect compensation.

Testing is a recognized legal method to establish circumstantial evidence. The concept has been developed in the context of the Fair Housing Act in the United States. There, testing refers to the use of individuals who, without any bona fide intent to rent or purchase a home or rent an apartment, pose as prospective buyers or renters of real estate for the purpose of gathering information (U.S. Departement of Justice 2016).This information may indicate whether a housing provider is complying with fair housing laws. The primary focus of the US Fair Housing Testing Program is to identify unlawful housing discrimination based on race, national origin, disability or familial status. But testing is also a tool to proove discrimination in court. For example, in a lawsuit against an owner of a nightclub or a landlord, the testers can be named as witnesses. The outcome of the testing can be used to indicate that discrimination took place.

From the client's perspective the case can still be far from being resolved in a satisfying manner, even though the discrimination can be fully proved in court. Legal enforcement of civil rights is complicated and risky for many reasons (Suk 2012). Besides evidence, time limits for bringing an action may be too short or the plaintiff may consider the risk of the litigation costs too high. An important and often underestimated problem is the risk of facing discrimination in the legal process. The experiences of NGOs and lawyers working with the AGG have shown that the reference to a treatment as discriminatory often leads to defensive reactions instead of reflection, understanding and apologies. To invoke the law means to enter into a demanding and strenuous confrontation, not knowing if the judges, who will decide the case, are sensitive and competent in dealing with discrimination. In the worst case, the painful feeling 'of being the other, and forever staying the other' repeats itself.

Legal demands for the reform of the AGG therefore insist on measures facilitating the enforcement of the law for individuals. One common demand is the possibility of collective enforcement of claims for state and non-state anti-discrimination organizations and for trade unions. Another proposed reform refers to the legal powers of the German Federal Anti-Discrimination Body (Antidiskriminierungsstelle des Bundes, ADS). As the AGG states, this state equality body is only empowered to support persons who have contacted it alleging that they have been the victim of discrimination. It would be an enormous step towards fully implementing the AGG, if the ADS had the competence to initiate investigations and litigate individual cases.

Another key concern is that the compensation awarded to the plaintiff, "must in any event be adequate in relation to the damage sustained," as the European Court of Justice (CJEU) has consistently stated. The CJEU noted that a purely symbolic sanction cannot be regarded as being compatible with the correct and effective implementation of the Anti-Discrimination Directives. Apart from compensation, legal sanctions for discrimination have another important goal: deterrence of future discrimination. The legal reproach – whether it is criminal (fine, imprisonment) or civil (payment of compensation) – will induce the discriminator to refrain from discriminating in the future. A well-functioning regime of anti-discrimination enforcement should deter not only those who have been subject to legal proceedings, but all potential violators, from discriminating.

Average civil compensation awards vary significantly across the Europe Union, ranging from Euro 300 (Germany, Hungary) to Euro 18,000 (United Kingdom). While in the United States or the United Kingdom, plaintiffs in discrimination cases have been awarded upwards of five figures in compensation, in Germany they are often labeled troublemakers and accused of abusing the AGG. The 'discotheque-cases' are most vivid examples about how these assumptions impair effective protection against discrimination. The negative public and legal debate along with the introduction of the AGG together with a limited understanding of the effects of racism leads to very small awards of compensation.

Local courts tend to decisions between zero and five hundred Euro. They argue that what happened to the plaintiffs at the door could happen to anyone; that the harming effect of a rejection is negligible; that explicitly racist insults had to be proved; that there had been other alternatives to go dancing close to the place where the incident took place, etc. Such reasoning reveals a fundamental misunderstanding of first, how racist discrimination works and second, of the requirements of the European Directives. To be fair, the *Oberlandesgericht Stuttgart* (Higher Regional Court, OLG) annulled the local court decision, which regarded such discrimination negligible. In contrast to the zero Euros in the first instance, the OLG ordered a compensation of 900 Euro (OLG Stuttgart 2012). But it was a long, arduous and difficult battle for the plaintiff. It was only possible due to the support of an anti-discrimination organization providing financial and psychological support.

In any event, and whatever the difficulties described, the AGG has had empowering effects on people facing discrimination in everyday life. The mere knowledge about the existence of a law against discrimination has encouraged people to speak up against unfair treatment, exclusion and harassment all over Germany. The AGG has given lawyers, scholars and activists new possibilities. The task for the future is to spread the knowledge of the existence of the anti-discrimination law in Germany, to learn how to use it and to engage in improving its enforcement.

Discussion Questions

1. Discuss the political and legal factors and actors accounted for the implementation of a comprehensive anti-discrimination law in Germany. What are the differences between the United States and Europe regarding the development of the anti-discrimination law? Which other factors can be important in the process of passing a law.
2. What different political, sociological and judicial rationales justify why certain discriminations receive particular attention by the law and others not? Which discrimination grounds do you miss in the AGG? Imagine a legislative initiative for the inclusion of 'lookism' into the AGG, with the aim of protecting people who miss the ideal of beauty against discrimination. List possible arguments for and against the protection of this new ground.
3. The European Anti-Discrimination Directives, as all EU Directives, apply to every member state. As most member states use different languages, the directives are translated into all the languages spoken in the EU. The official English version of the directive 2000/43/EC is Council Directive 2000/43/EC of 29 June 2000 implementing the principle of equal treatment between persons irrespective of racial or ethnic origin. The official German version is Richtlinie 2000/43/EG des Rates vom 29. Juni 2000 zur Anwendung des Gleichbehandlungsgrundsatzes ohne Unterschied der Rasse oder der ethnischen Herkunft. In the public, political and legal discourse the English use is Racial Equality Directive, while in Germany the term Antirassismusrichtlinie is common. What can be possible reasons for these differences? Discuss arguments for and against the use of the term Rasse in Section 1 AGG and in Article 3 III Grundgesetz.
4. Imagine that you or a friend of yours is denied access to a party due to racist attributions. What do you want? How can you respond? Discuss your objectives for obtaining justice and the legal rights you have. What legal and extra-legal tools can you use, 1.) to bring public attention to the problem, 2.) to obtain what you want/your friend wants to achieve. Think of possible challenges you might face in proving discrimination and enforcing

your rights. Think of possible allies. Develop a strategy and discuss it with your colleagues.

5. Do some research. Is there is an existing anti-discrimination regulation protecting all members of the faculty from discrimination? What about students? What about guests? What would you do, to promote an anti-discrimination directive at your university/college? Which problems regarding the enforcement of such regulations can you imagine? Discuss possible solutions.

References

Antidiskriminierungsstelle des Bundes (ed.) (2010): Guide to the General Equal Treatment Act. Explanations and Examples. Berlin. www.agg-ratgeber.de/files/pdf/AGG_en.pdf

Baer, Susanne (2009): Dignity, Liberty, Equality: A Fundamental Rights Triangle Of Constitutionalism. University Of Toronto Law Journal 4, pp. 417-468. https://plone.rewi.hu-berlin.de/de/lf/ls/bae/profdrbaer/publikationen-chronologisch/Baer_Toronto_Journal_2009.pdf

Baer, Susanne (1995): Würde oder Gleichheit? Zur angemessenen grundrechtlichen Konzeption von Recht gegen Diskriminierung am Beispiel sexueller Belästigung am Arbeitsplatz in der Bundesrepublik Deutschland und den USA. Baden-Baden: Nomos.

Catherine MacKinnon (2013): MAKING HISTORY: Catharine MacKinnon Works to Legally Define Sexual Harassment. www.makers.com/blog/making-history-catharine-mackinnon-works-legally-define-sexual-harassment

Crenshaw, Kimberlé (1989): Demarginalizing the intersection of race and sex: a Black feminist critique of antidiscrimination doctrine, feminist theory and antiracist politics". University of Chicago Legal Forum (PhilPapers), pp. 139-167. http://philpapers.org/archive/CREDTI.pdf

Lembke, Ulrike/Liebscher, Doris (2014): Postkategoriales Antidiskriminierungsrecht? – Oder: Wie kommen Konzepte der Intersektionalität in die Rechtsdogmatik?. In: Philipp, Simone/Meiern, Isabella et al. (eds.): Intersektionelle Benachteiligung und Diskriminierung. Baden-Baden, pp. 261-290.

OLG Stuttgart, Urteil vom 02.12.2012, NJW 2012/15, pp. 1085-1087 annoted by Doris Liebscher.

O'Sullivan, Feargus (2014): Germany's Nightclubs Get Called Out for Racism, www.citylab.com/politics/2014/05/insidious-racism-germanys-nightclub-scene/9027/

Suk, Julie C. (2012): Criminal and civil enforcement of antidiscrimination law in Europe, European Anti-Discrimination Law Review 14/june 2012, pp. 11-20. http://ec.europa.eu/justice/discrimination/files/antidiscrimination_lawreview14_en.pdf

U.S. Department of Justice (2016): Fair Housing Testing Program, www.justice.gov/crt/fair-housing-testing-program-1

Hazel Conley

Gender Equality in the UK Public Sector: is reflexive legislation the way forward?

1 Introduction

This chapter examines an experiment with different approaches to the law usually referred to as responsive and reflexive legislation. It outlines the theoretical underpinning of responsive legislation (Nonet and Selznik 1978/2001) and its later development into reflexive legislation (Teubner 1983) before identifying how these theories were implemented in equality law in the UK, particularly in relation to equality between women and men and the production of public services. The chapter provides an example of how the concepts of responsive and reflexive legislation were used to rethink gender equality legislation to overcome the limitations of traditional anti-discrimination legislative approaches by imposing a statutory gender equality duty (GED) on public authorities in 2007. The chapter continues by providing an empirical analysis of the power of responsive and reflexive legislation to facilitate greater participation of civil society groups in bringing about behavioural change in organisations and the political resistance to these changes. The conclusions argue that, whilst responsive legislation does represent a potentially powerful tool for women's and other civil society groups seeking equality, the alignment of legislative innovation and political will identified as necessary for success by Nonet and Selznick (1979/2001) is, as yet, missing in the UK.

The return of a Labour government in 1997 after 18 years out of office marked a turning point in the academic, political and legal debates about the future of equality legislation in the UK. The stimulus for a rethink of the equality legislation was both pragmatic and conceptual. Most of the equality law in the UK is underpinned by European Directives and was first enacted shortly after, or in anticipation of, joining the European Economic Community in 1973. The interpretation and implementation of EU law was often undertaken minimally and half-heartedly in the UK, requiring numerous amendments (Alter and Vargas 2000; Dickens 2007). It is therefore surprising that the GED and subsequent legislation was not prompted by European Directive, but did codify some of the principles of gender mainstreaming policy developed in the European Union. The GED and two other duties covering race and disability were combined in the Equality Act 2010 which was expanded to include age, sexual orientation, gender reassignment, religious belief, pregnancy and maternity to meet the requirements of article 13 of the 1997 Treaty of Amsterdam and the resulting European Directives.

The frequently amended nature of the equality law coupled with the dominance of often quite contradictory case law in British courts meant that by the end of the 1990s the legislation was fragmented across more than 100 pieces of statute. In addition to this complexity, it was evident that the anti-discrimination legislation was not working as well as it could (Hepple et al. 2000). Statistics on the slow progress towards closing the gender pay gap and the explosion of cases reaching the employment courts indicated that the equal pay law had reached the limits of its usefulness[1]. A voluntary approach to gender mainstreaming led to an inconsistent application of the policy in the UK, leading Veitch (2005) to argue that a statutory duty was required. In addition there was growing concern, particularly following the failure to properly investigate the racially motivated murder of Stephen Lawrence[2] that key public bodies were infused with institutional discrimination (Macpherson 1999). Whilst the fragmentation of the law might have been dealt with by a re-codification of the existing statute and assimilation into a single body of law, the failure of the law to penetrate the fabric of British society and root out the most deep seated and insidious forms of discrimination indicated that simple administrative housekeeping would not provide a long-term, 'transformative' solution. A more radical conceptual rethink of equality law was necessary and the need to both consolidate and search for new approaches to equality law was voiced from a wide range of civil society groups, including politicians, employers, trade unions, voluntary organisations, academics and legal practitioners[3].

2 What are Responsive and Reflexive Legislation?

Responsive and reflexive legislation are related concepts that theorise alternative approaches to legal jurisprudence. Responsive legislation was part of a

1 House of Commons Select Committee on Trade and Industry 16th report 22nd March 2005 available at: http://www.publications.parliament.uk/pa/cm200405/cmselect/cmtrdind/300/30002.htm

2 Stephen Lawrence was the victim of a racially motivated murder. His murderers were not sentenced until 19 years later following numerous mistakes and omission by the Metropolitan Police Force (Macpherson, 1999)

3 See 'The Equality Bill: Government response to the consultation', Cm7454, July 2008

theoretical model developed by Nonet and Selznick (1978/2001) who argued that the 'social turbulence' of the 1960s and the growth of civil rights movements were one indication that legal systems had become distanced from the social context in which they operated. They further argued that, to understand this phenomenon, it was necessary to move away from narrowly focussed and abstract legal theory to consider the relationship between legal institutions, the state and society. They compared three conceptual approaches to the law which they termed repressive, autonomous and responsive legislation where the relationship between law, politics and society, in the form of authority and social control, is differently balanced. Although Nonet and Selznick considered that there was a developmental aspect between these different forms of law, in that one led to another, they were keen to stress that it was likely that most legal systems would contain all three forms to some degree depending on the social and political context.

Repressive legislation is argued to exist when the legal system is intended, first and foremost, to ensure the power, authority and interests of the political elite:

> "Governing power is repressive when it gives short shrift to the interests of the governed, that is, when it is disposed to disregard those interests or deny their legitimacy." (2001:29)

The law is subordinate to political power, an instrument of coercion to achieve social control and to institutionalise the class order, 'disprivilege', and dependency (ibid.:44-45). In doing so, Nonet and Selznick argue that certain social groups are made more vulnerable 'depending on the distribution of power, patterns of consciousness, and much else that is historically contingent' (ibid.:30). Interestingly, repressive law is considered to be the more likely approach to social control when the political elite feel threatened or unable to deliver the expectations of the governed, which has a particular bearing in times of economic crises.

Although Nonet and Selznick contend that repressive law is efficient at imposing social order, they highlight that it does not produce stable or consensual societies. For long-term stability and rule by consent the law requires greater credibility in the eyes of the governed. To achieve this they argue that the law must appear independent, or autonomous, of the governing elite. Autonomous law, rather than being simply an instrument to exercise the power of government, is meant to act as a brake on its arbitrary pursuit of self-interest. The government creates the statute but the role of legal institutions, led by a judiciary, is to interpret, mediate and apply the law free from political interference. The outward stance of the law then becomes administrative: focussed on rules, procedure, regularity and fairness (ibid.:54); its autonomy from the power of government is the basis of its legitimacy.

The limitations of autonomous law stem from its strengths. The focus on procedure means, Nonet and Seznick argue, that the law takes a narrow view of the role of the law that is not substantive or outcome based, “thereby detaching legal thought from social reality” (ibid.:64). Furthermore, in applying the statutes of government, autonomous law accepts their underlying premises:

> “Thus, like repressive law, autonomous law remains closely identified with the state, a *Rechtsstaat* to be sure, but one nonetheless committed to order, control and subordination” (Nonet and Selznick 2001:.60).

However, because the autonomy of the law is meant to restrain the power of government, it necessitates and fosters some positive criticism, laying the seeds for an alternative approach to the law that is responsive to social change led by the interests and demands of the governed.

Responsive law does not see criticism as necessarily negative, but instead as an indication of what is needed to change, a source of knowledge and an opportunity for ‘self correction’ (ibid.:77). Rather than coerce citizens to follow a legal code ultimately created by elites distanced from their everyday lives, responsive law is ‘more receptive to cultural diversity, less prone to brutalise the deviant and eccentric’ (ibid.:91). At its heart is a participative, pluralistic and negotiated social order predicated on joint problem-solving. Fundamentally the focus is not on individuals seeking reparation on a case-by-case basis where justice is perceived as a close following of legal rules and established precedent. Instead the emphasis is on making institutions supportive of social goals that are valued by citizens so that injustice is rectified, or better still avoided, before it leads to individual cases.

Responsive legislation is not easily attained. Nonet and Selznick note that responsive law and repressive law have one similarity in that both are attuned to the political context rather than held separate as in autonomous law. The difference lies in whose interests the political and legal systems serve. Repressive law exists to protect the interests and power of the political elite at the expense of the rest of civil society. In responsive law legal institutions, political elites and civil society work together and, in so doing, share power. As Nonet and Selznick point out, responsive law is a ‘high risk’ strategy (ibid.:78); for governments it requires openness and a weaker grip on power and control in the face of a plurality of demands, whilst legal institutions forego the legitimacy of autonomy and the predictability of precedent. There are also some risks for vulnerable groups in civil society if their voices are drowned out by the louder demands of the majority or simply the more vocal.

Nonet and Selznick’s work was controversial at the time it was written. In the early 1980s mainstream academia began its rejection of ‘grand theory’ in favour of post-modernism, whilst politics and economics were speeding headlong into neo-liberalism and the cult of the individual. To be effective responsive law requires political support and, if it seemed 'high risk' to Nonet and Selznick, it would have been anathema to Reaganites and Thatcherites. Although Nonet and Selznick provide some examples of the stirrings of responsive law in the US, it was a concept that was ahead of its time (cf. Ayres and Braithwaite 1992).

3 Formal, Substantive and Reflexive Legal Systems

The ideas of Nonet and Selznick were taken up by German post-modern social theorist Gunther Teubner (1983). Drawing on social theorists Habermas and Luhmann and critiquing Nonet and Selznick, Teubner drew up a three stage typology of legal systems which he called formal, susbstantive and reflexive. In this typology, Teubner makes a distinction between responsive and reflexive law by arguing that legal systems, although influenced by broader social events, retain their own internal logic. For Teubner legal systems are 'self-referent' in that they view social events through legal lens, which 'selectively filter' (Teubner 1983:249) events to form their own construct of society. In a detailed critical analysis of Nonet and Selznick's formulation of responsive law, Teubner argues that it contains two forms of legal rationality – substantive and reflexive. Substantive rationality relates to the results oriented approach identified by Nonet and Selznick, whilst reflexive rationality relates to the structuring of institutions to achieve this (Nonet and Selznick 2001:251). Writing from a European perspective, Teubner correlates substantive law with the development of the welfare state and greater focus on collective regulation, concepts that may have had less bearing on Nonet and Selznick's US orientation to political influence on legal structures. Interestingly, Teubner contends that reflexive rationality was prompted by the crisis of the welfare state, which in 1983 was in the context of emerging neo-liberalism in Europe.

The key characteristic of reflexive rationality is that it does not impose greater regulation, but it seeks to guide institutions, through 'regulated autonomy' to reflect on their practices so they might bring about the redistribution of resources:

> "The role of reflexive law is to structure and re-structure semi-autonomous social systems…by shaping both their procedures of internal discourse and their methods of coordination with other social systems." (Teubner 1983:255)

In order to explain how legal systems move from one form of legal rationality to another in co-variance with social change, Teubner draws on the work of Habermas in relation to institutional and organisational learning based largely on historical materialism. He argues that adding this set of theories to Nonet and Seznick's provides a more three-dimensional model of change. To this Teubner adds the theories of Luhmann which apply evolutionary learning directly to legal institutions. Although, Teubner provides a detailed comparison and the addition of another stage of 'high cultural law' (ibid.:265), Luhmann's theories of archaic/high cultural law, positive and learning law still look remarkably like Nonet and Selznick's typology of repressive, autonomous and responsive law as does Habermas's conceptualisation of the law as a force for the democratisation of organisations.

Teubner's reading of Habermas and Luhmann does provide an interesting dimension to the work of Nonet and Selznick in its consideration of the conditions necessary for responsive legal systems to develop. The 'high risk' inherent in responsive approaches to the law, i.e. the redistribution of power to accommodate the participation of previously marginalised social groups, would not be easily accommodated by incumbent power holders. The reflexive function of responsive law is important here in that "reflexion structures within social subsystems become the main integration mechanisms in functionally differentiated societies" (ibid.:273). Teubner summarises this as "*law realises its own reflexive orientation insofar as it provides the structural premises for reflexive processes in other social subsystems*" (*ibid.* italics in original).

A further development in Teubner's (1983) work is to begin to identify what may confound the operation of responsive/reflexive law. In examining examples of where responsive/reflexive law might operate, Teubner notes that where the power and information differential between social groups is high, responsive law is unlikely to succeed unless the law develops reflexive structures to compensate for imbalances of power by defining "objective purposes and duties" (ibid.:277). However Teubner moves away from the position of participative democracy that is central in the theories of Nonet and Selznick and Habermas, to one in which the fostering of organizational conscience is enough to fulfil the requirements of reflexion and is somewhat illustrative of his focus on governance and procedure rather than on the governed and participation.[4]

4 Teubner (1987, 1993), in a similar fashion to Durkheim, later developed his theories by drawing on biological systems theories of *autopoeisis* as a metaphor of how social systems maintain and reproduce themselves

4 Responsive/Reflexive Legislation and Equality in the UK

In his concluding comments Teubner (1983) notes the need for more research on the applications of responsive/reflexive legislation. The following sections consider the application of theory to legislation in the UK. The clearest significance is in relation to UK equality legislation designed to influence better equality practice in public authorities. The early development of the legislation in the UK is analysed by O'Cinneide (2004) and later developments by Hepple (2010). O'Cinneide (2004) notes that early proactive equality legislation was preceded by gender mainstreaming initiatives in public authorities, which attempted to influence better organisational practice in relation to equality but, because of their voluntary nature, had been taken up very unevenly and with limited results.

The theories of Nonet and Selznick (1978/2001) and Teubner (1983) considered above highlight that transitions in legal approaches are often triggered by seemingly intractable social crises. In the UK this occurred in relation to two unrelated and quite different crises. The first were the on-going 'troubles' in Northern Ireland based on religious conflict. The second was the racist murder of Stephen Lawrence in 1993 and the deep-seated institutional discrimination it revealed. In both cases it was clear that neither the existing legislation nor voluntary approaches could offer a credible solution. In both cases, responsive legislation relevant to a specific social and political context was developed. Section 75 of the Northern Ireland Act 1998 is considered to be the forerunner of responsive legislation in the UK. The Act was a product of the 'Good Friday Agreement', a groundbreaking political agreement in the complex political context of Northern Ireland to share power between rival political and religious groups. Section 75 (1) imposes a positive duty on scheduled public authorities to have "due regard to the need to promote equality of opportunity… (a) between persons of different religious belief, political opinion, racial group, age, marital status or sexual orientation; (b) between men and women generally; (c) between persons with a disability and persons without; and (d) between persons with dependants and persons without.". Section 75(2) requires the same public authorities to promote "good relations between persons of different religious belief, political opinion or racial group." Section 76 of the Act reverts to restrictive legislation that prevents discrimination by public authorities on the grounds of political belief or religion, highlighting the point made by Nonet and Selznick (1978/2001) that both responsive and restrictive law is likely to coexist.

Section 75 is considered to be a particularly successful aspect of the Northern Ireland Act (O'Cinneide 2004; McCrudden 2007) and has been the model for responsive law, in the form of public sector equality duties that

Cover the rest of the UK. O'Cinneide documents similar early provisions devolved to Wales, Scotland and London, but notes that, because they were lacking in enforcement mechanisms, success depended largely on active political support. The first public sector equality duty covering the whole of England, Scotland and Wales was the race equality duty contained in the Race Relations (Amendment) Act 2000 and which came into force in 2001. The race equality duty was the culmination of a changed political environment following the general election of 1997, the Macpherson Report in 1999, which found endemic public sector institutional race discrimination had hampered the investigation of the murder of Stephen Lawrence and the Hepple et al. report in 2000 arguing for reform of the equality legislation (Hepple 2010). After a gap of six years a public sector equality duty covering disability was introduced as part of the Disability Discrimination Act 2005 and the gender equality duty followed in 2007 contained in the Equality Act 2006. The latter pieces of legislation were won following extensive lobbying and campaigning by disability and women's civil society groups (see Conley and Page 2015). The three duties supplemented the existing restrictive legislation on race relations, sex discrimination and disability discrimination. They were subsequently incorporated into s. 149 of the Equality Act 2010 to include further equality strands covering age, religious belief, sexual orientation, gender reassignment, pregnancy and maternity to meet the requirements of article 13 of the 1997 Treaty of Amsterdam and the resulting European Directives.

In addition to the public sector equality duty, other sections of the Equality Act 2010 contain provisions that have responsive/reflexive elements, which are considered in greater detail below. Before considering the impact of the current legislation in more detail, the following section examines the public sector equality duties in relation to the theoretical models of responsive and reflexive law.

5 Why are Equality Duties Different?

Public sector equality duties cover both public service employment and service provision. They are innovative because, unlike the established anti-discrimination legislation, they do not provide individual rights to seek reparation reactively after discrimination has occurred. As such, they do not place the responsibility on individuals to take legal action. Instead they require public authorities to act proactively to consider the impact of their policies and decisions on equality outcomes for protected groups. This aspect of the legislation is reflexive rather than responsive as it requires only internal consideration. The logic here is to avert discrimination in the workplace and in the provision of public services *before it occurs*. The three earlier duties covering race, disability and gender also contained a responsive element in that they required, to a different degree, public authorities to seek input from each of the respective protected groups. In the race equality duty there was an 'expectation' that groups affected by the policies and decisions of public authorities would be consulted. There was a specific duty in the disability equality duty to involve people with disabilities. However, the focus was on direct participation rather than collective representation. In the gender equality duty, there was a specific duty that required public authorities to consult stakeholders and their collectives, including trade unions, and to take into account their views in formulating gender equality objectives. The incremental progress in relation to strengthening the responsive element of the successive duties perhaps illustrates Teubner's view that responsive legislation has potential for organisational learning. The responsive element in the public sector equality duties made them a powerful tool for social movements, not only for getting their voices heard, but also for shaping the policy and decisions that affect public service employment and delivery by holding public authorities to account (Conley and Page 2010). In addition to these innovations, a core principle of the equality duties was to give minority groups, whose voices are usually drowned out in representative democracy, a statutory collective right to be consulted in relation to public service employment and provision, which addresses directly the concerns of Nonet and Selznick that vulnerable groups may not benefit from responsive law. However, Fredman (2011) makes the argument that focussing on equality only for protected minority groups risks the exclusion of those who suffer poverty and disadvantage but do not belong to legally defined categories.

The enforcement of the public sector equality duties is also innovative. Although there are no individual rights for reparation as in the anti-discrimination legislation, there are powers for the Equality and Human Rights Commission (EHRC) to serve compliance orders on public authorities that do not carry out their duties. There are also powers for individuals and groups to seek judicial review of any policies or decisions that they feel have an adverse impact on protected groups and have not been adequately considered under the duty. Although innovative, the enforcement mechanisms are considered to be problematic. The EHRC have made little use of their powers and there has been some concern that the use of judicial review to enforce the equality duties may have been used prematurely in some cases (Fredman 2011) or too late in others (Conley 2012). Ultimately, judicial enforcement is at odds with the concepts of reflexive and responsive legislation because it reverts to a negative (preventing unwanted behaviour) rather than positive (encouraging desired behaviour) role for the law. Despite these concerns there have been some glimpses of how powerful the enforcement of responsive/reflexive legislation can be, but also what 'high risk' might mean for states who adopt it. The following section analyses one of the leading cases that tested the gender equality duty prior to its incorporation into s. 149 of the Equality Act 2010.

6 The Power of the Duty: the Fawcett challenge

The Fawcett Society is a feminist organisation whose origins date back to the early suffrage movement in the UK. Suffragist rather than suffragette in its orientation, the original purpose of the Fawcett Society was to achieve women's emancipation by peaceful and legal means. In its contemporary form the Fawcett Society is a vocal lobby for women's rights and is outspoken in its opposition to the gendered effects of austerity measures taken by UK governments since 2010. In July 2010 the Fawcett Society launched a legal challenge on the emergency budget of the coalition government. The coalition between the Conservative and Liberal Democrat parties was formed following the general election in May 2010 that did not produce a majority government. Ninety days into their administration the coalition announced an emergency budget containing a range of austerity measures involving cuts to welfare benefits, public services and restraint on pay rises for public sector workers. The Fawcett Society used the powers contained in the Gender Equality Duty to apply for judicial review of the emergency budget. They argued that the austerity measures contained in the budget would have a disproportionate negative impact on women (Fawcett 2010) and claimed that the Treasury had not complied with the Gender Equality Duty in having 'due regard' as to its impact on women when deciding on how austerity measures would be implemented.

The case reached the High Court in December 2010 and, although the judge agreed that the UK government was covered by the Gender Equality Duty and that the Treasury had failed to fully comply with the law in drawing up the budget, the Fawcett Society was not granted permission to continue to judicial review (see Conley (2012) for a detailed analysis). The decision saved the coalition government from a constitutional crisis within months of its formation, making the case a good illustration of some of the theoretical points raised by Nonet and Selznick (1978/2001) in relation to responsive law. Firstly, it clearly demonstrates the interaction and power relations between the state, the law and civil society that are the focus of their theory. Secondly, it highlights how different aspects of law (repressive, autonomous and responsive) coexist. Thirdly, it demonstrates how responsive law could work to provide civil society groups with a powerful tool that extends beyond the ballot box to hold political elites to account for their decisions. Lastly, and conversely, the case illustrates the high risk responsive legislation poses for governments, particularly when faced with difficult economic and social conditions. The following section analyses the integration of the three separate public sector equality duties into the Equality Act 2010 and the political response following the Fawcett Challenge.

7 The Equality Act 2010: a lost opportunity?

The Equality Act 2010 (EqA 2010) was the final piece of legislation passed by the Labour government in power between 1997 and 2010, the fulfilment of the pledge on the last page of their 2005 Manifesto to 'simplify' and 'modernise' 40 years of complex equality legislation. The legislation underwent a protracted consultation and a difficult passage through Parliament, being heavily contested by the Conservative party in opposition (see Conley and Page (2015) for a detailed analysis). For a while it appeared that it would not be passed before the 2010 general election with the risk of being abandoned if the Conservatives took office. The Equality Act finally made it on to the Statute books on the 8th April 2010 – a month before the general election that resulted in the election of a Conservative-Liberal Democrat coalition government.

The Act, in addition to tidying up the existing equality legislation, introduced some innovations. The first provision was a new public sector socio-economic duty (s. 1), which required public authorities "…to consider how their decisions might help to reduce the inequalities associated with socio-economic disadvantage", which would address the concerns of Fredman (2011) that equality duties linked only to legally protected groups would miss large pockets of social deprivation. Other innovations included an extension to permitted positive action in the recruitment and selection of employees, allowing employers for the first time to make voluntary recruitment decisions based on protected characteristics where this would improve the representation of disadvantaged groups in the workplace (s. 159). In relation to equal pay the Act contained provisions for mandatory equal pay audits in workplaces with 250 or more employees (s. 78).[5] All of these innovations contain elements of responsive and reflexive legislation discussed above.

5 The Act also contained provisions that would allow discrimination claims which combine two protected characteristics, rather than making separate claims (s.14).

The three public sector equality duties were replaced by a single duty (s. 149), which was expanded to cover the additional protected characteristics of age, religion or belief, sexual orientation, gender re-assignment, pregnancy and maternity. As in the three separate duties the new duty contains two parts: a general duty which requires public authority to have 'due regard' to equality for those with protected characteristics in the exercise of its functions and a set of specific duties which provide procedural instructions on what authorities must do to demonstrate due regard. In the three original duties the requirement for public authorities to consult interested parties were contained in the specific duties.

On the face of it the EqA 2010 held some promise for transformative innovation, particularly in its use of responsive and reflexive legislation. However, the passage of the Act was not the end of the struggle for positive reform of the legislation because much of its content, certainly on any of the innovative aspects, was subject to secondary legislation. The reliance on secondary legislation meant that parts of the Equality Act could easily be shelved and, shortly after taking office, the Coalition government announced that it would not introduce the secondary legislation required to take forward the provisions for a socio-economic duty, or a combined discrimination provision. The requirement of mandatory equal pay audits was delayed until 2015 when, after an extensive public campaign, a last minute amendment to The Small Business, Enterprise and Employment Bill was successful in getting through Parliament shortly before the 2015 General Election.

Another important casualty of secondary legislation was the specific duties for the single public sector equality duty. The Act included only the provisions for the general duties. The provision for specific duties, the element of the legislation that provides the concrete procedural requirements, depended on secondary legislation giving Ministers of the Crown powers to impose specific duties on public authorities at a later date. The powers were devolved to the Scottish Parliament and the Welsh Assembly. After a long delay in their formulation, the specific duties for the equality duty in England are more limited than those for its predecessor duties, having no direct provisions for equal pay or requirements to consult trade unions as contained in the gender equality duty. The new specific duties covering England are far less prescriptive than those contained in the previous separate equality duties. Crucially, the requirement to consult stakeholders is absent meaning that the responsive element of the legislation has been lost (see Hepple (2011) and Fredman (2011) for a detailed analysis). The specific duties in Scotland are more extensive than the provisions in England, particularly in relation to collecting and reporting equality data including gender pay gaps. However, similarly, there is no provision that requires the engagement or consultation of public service users or employees. The specific duties for Wales are again far more detailed than both the English and Scottish provisions including specific duties in relation to addressing pay gaps on public authorities and requiring that employees are given training to understand the duty. Most importantly, from the perspective of responsive legislation, Regulation 5 contains the 'Engagement Provisions', which require public authorities to involve people with protected characteristics, their representatives and other parties with an interest in how decisions are made in the authority.

The precarious existence of the public sector equality duty did not end with its weakened transposition into the EqA2010. Its continued existence was threatened when Home Secretary and Equalities Minister, Teresa May announced on the 17th May 2012, when the Specific Duties were barely a year old, that a review of the PSED would be conducted as part of the 'Red Tape Challenge', a government initiative to strip away bureaucratic burdens to business. The review of the duty so soon after it had become fully operational was justified with concerns by government Ministers, including the Prime Minister, that it had become a bureaucratic 'tick box' exercise (Stephenson 2014). The review process was unorthodox in that it was not initially open to all stakeholders and was largely the remit of a government selected steering group, which did not contain any representatives of civil society groups who use public services.

The response of stakeholder groups to the threat that loomed over the public sector equality duty was vocal and concerted. The problematic nature of the review process came under widespread public scrutiny and criticism when Doreen Lawrence[6], the mother of Stephen Lawrence, wrote an open letter to the Prime Minister, Deputy Prime Minister and other political leaders questioning the composition of the steering committee and highlighting its bias towards public service senior managers rather than public service users. The letter asked that the review should "recognise that those who are to be held to account by legislation may have radically different views when compared to those who wish to use the legislation to hold public bodies to acount."

In the event a number of civil society groups 'gate-crashed' the review, submitting evidence without a direct invitation and Stephenson (2014:77) identifies that the majority of the eventual submissions to the review were 'broadly supportive' of the duty providing a wide range of instances where the public sector equality duty had succeeded in improving equality outcome in public authorities. In the face of such public support for the duty the government backed away from any changes to the legislation, ironically echoing

6 Doreen Lawrence was made a life peer in 2013, and is now Baroness Lawrence of Clarendon. She received an OBE in 2003 for services to community relations.

the initial advice from civil society groups that it was too soon to judge its effectiveness and postponed the review until 2016, but which did not take place. Even so, the report of the steering committee was largely negative and did not accurately reflect the weight of the evidence that it had received (Stephenson 2014). Although the Chair of the steering group could not get the support of the other members of the group, he personally recommended that the duty should be repealed (ibid.).

Since the review of the public sector equality duty the government has taken steps to limit the number of judicial reviews, many of which relate to the use of the duty, by reducing the amount of time to lodge a case and giving judges more powers to decide which cases can go forward to judicial review and what level of financial support will be allowed.[7] This move substantially reduces the remaining opportunities for civil society groups to use the legislation and therefore further limits its responsive elements.

8 Conclusions

There is little doubt that responsive and reflexive law underpins the most innovative legislative developments in the UK, particularly in relation to equality. The Equal Opportunities Commission recognised this when they declared the gender equality duty to be the most important development in women's equality since the Sex Discrimination Act 1975 (EOC, 2006). The main innovation of responsive legislation, as theorised by Nonet and Selznick (1978/2001), is a re-conceptualisation of the law as an agent for a participative, pluralistic and negotiated social order predicated on joint problem-solving. The emphasis is on making institutions supportive of social goals that are valued by citizens by requiring inclusive decision-making – a form of statutory participative democracy. The potential power of responsive legislation as a tool for civil society groups to hold the state to account for equality, in this case gender equality, is clearly demonstrated in the example of the Fawcett Society challenge to the 2010 emergency budget.

Although the Fawcett challenge demonstrated the potential power for enforcement of the duty, responsive legislation, in its most effective form, should not require judicial intervention. Teubner's (1983) theory of reflexive legislation, with its focus on the ability of legislative structures to reflect, learn and change helps the analysis at this point. The incremental development of the public sector equality duties between 2000 and 2008 provided

7 Criminal Justice and Courts Act 2015 and Civil and Legal Aid (Remuneration) (Amendment) Regulations 2015

greater powers for civil society groups to be involved in decision making processes – evidence that reflexive law can lead to legislative learning. The 2013 review demonstrated that the duty can also result in organisational learning as the majority of the public authorities who submitted evidence claimed that they had positively changed their practices and policy-making in response to the legislation (Stephenson 2014; Clayton-Hathway 2013).

Both responsive and reflexive law play their parts but there has been some theoretical drift in recent academic debate since Nonet and Selznick (1978/2001) and Teubner (1983) advanced their theories, with much of the focus leaning towards the concept of reflexive rather than responsive legislation. It is important to recognise that the two concepts cover substantively different elements. Briefly put, the participation of civil society is central to Nonet and Selznick's theories of responsive legislation, whilst Teubner's theories of reflexive law focus on processes that change behaviour within legal and organisational structures. The prioritisation of process over participation is echoed in changes to the public sector equality duty with the successive loss of opportunities for civil society groups to use the law to hold public authorities to account. The weakening of the responsive element of the duty is likely to have led to an emphasis on process rather than outcome, resulting in the criticism that the duty has become a 'tick box exercise'. It will be interesting to see how far the greater emphasis on engagement in Wales averts this.

Both Nonet and Selznick as well as Teubner emphasise the importance of state support for responsive and reflexive legislation and that crisis is likely to be a key trigger for the state to be more receptive. Teubner extends this to argue that the crisis in the welfare state has been a particular catalyst for change. In the UK this is only partly true and there is evidence that a distinction should be made between social and economic crises. The social crisis that resulted after the Macpherson Report identified endemic institutional race discrimination in key public services was such a catalyst for the race equality duty which, following extensive civil society campaigns, led to two further and progressively stronger duties. In stark comparison economic crisis followed by the political response of austerity has resulted in a substantial scaling down of the UK welfare state and a concerted political attack on the public sector equality duty, which provides a tool for civil society groups to challenge austerity.

Nonet and Selznick (1978/2001) warn us that responsive legislation is not easy to achieve because it is a 'high risk' strategy that requires the state to cede some of its power by making governments answerable to citizens beyond the ballot box. There is some evidence that other European nations may be willing to experiment with reflexive equality law. Legislation similar to the public sector equality duty was enacted in the Republic of Ireland in 2014 (s. 42 Irish Human Rights and Equality Act 2014). However the form it has taken resembles the weaker incarnation adopted in England rather than the stronger versions in Wales and Scotland. The precarious existence of the public sector equality duty since the enactment Equality Act 2010 is a clear example of the nervousness of UK government towards responsive legislation. Ideally we should be researching ways to strengthen and improve the public sector equality duty as the fifth generation of equality law (Hepple 2010) rather than defensively supporting what is left of it.

Discussion Questions

1. What is the difference between responsive and reflexive legislation?
2. How has it been applied to gender equality in the UK context?
3. Has responsive or reflexive legislation worked in the UK? If so, how? If not, why not?
4. How might responsive and reflexive legislation be utilised in a broader European context?

References

Alter, Karen J./Vargas, Jeanette (2000):Explaining Variation in the Use of European Litigation Strategies: European Commission Law and British gender Equality Policies. In: Comparative Political Studies, 33, 4 pp. 452-482.
Ayres, Ian/Braithwaite, John (1992): Responsive Regulation: Transcending the Deregulation Debate. New York: Oxford University Press.
Clayton-Hathway, Kate (2013): The public sector equality duty. Empirical evidence base. Oxford: Brookes Centre for Diversity Policy Research and Practice.
Conley, Hazel (2012):Using Equality to Challenge Austerity: New Actors, Old Problems. In: Work, Employment and Society, 26, 2, pp. 353-363.
Conley, Hazel/Page, Margaret (2010): The Gender Equality Duty in Local Government: The Prospects for Integration. In: Industrial Law Journal. 39, 3, pp. 321-325
Conley, Hazel/Page, Margaret (2015): Gender Equality in Public Services: Chasing the Dream. London: Routledge.
Dickens, Linda (2007): The Road is Long. Thirty Years of Equality Legislation in Britain. In: British Journal of Industrial Relations, 45, 3, pp. 463-494.
EOC (2006): Gender Equality Duty Code of Practice England and Wales. Manchester: Equal Opportunities Commission.
Fredman, Sandra (2011): The Public Sector Equality Duty. In: Industrial Law Journal, 40, 4, pp. 405-427.
Fawcett (2010): http://www.fawcettsociety.org.uk/index.asp?PageID=1165

Hepple, Bob/Coussey, Mary/Choudhury, Tufyal (2000): Equality: A New Framework. Report of the Independent Review of the Enforcement of UK Anti-Discrimination Legislation. Oxford: Hart.

Hepple, Bob (2010): The New Single Equality Act in Britain. In: The Equal Rights Review, 5, pp. 11-24.

Hepple, Bob (2011): Enforcing Equality Law: Two Steps Forward and Two Steps Backwards for Reflexive Legislation. In: Industrial Law Journal, 40, 4, pp. 315-335.

Macpherson, William (1999): The Stephen Lawrence Inquiry: Report of Inquiry by Sir William Macpherson of Cluny Presented to Parliament by the secretary of State for the Home Department by Command of her Majesty. CM4262-I.

McCrudden, Christopher (2007): Equality Legislation and Reflexive Regulation: A response to the Discrimination Law Review's Consultative Paper. In: Industrial Law Journal, 36, 3, pp. 255-266.

Nonet, Philippe/Selznick, Philip (1978, 2001): Law and Society in Transition. Towards Responsive Law. New York: Harper.

O'Cinneide, Colm (2004): Taking equal opportunities seriously: the extension of positive duties to promote equality. London: Equality and Diversity Forum.

Stephenson, Mary-Ann (2014): Misrepresentation and Omission. An Analysis of the Review of the Public Sector Equality Duty In: The Political Quarterly, 85, 1, pp. 75-80.

Teubner, Gunther (1983): Substantive and Reflexive Elements in Modern Law. In: Law and Society Review, 17, 2, pp. 239-285.

Veitch, Janet (2005): Looking at gender mainstreaming in the UK government. In: International Feminist Journal of Politics, 7, 4, pp. 600-606.

Hülya Şimga and *Zeynep Oya Usal*

A Case of Collateral Damage: widows of religious weddings in Turkey

1 Introduction

The family is the basic unit of society. It is a social and legal construct and, in various countries, a religious construct. In many states, the rights and responsibilities of married partners are governed by the principles of civil or common law, religious or customary laws and practices, or some combination of such laws and practices that do not comply with human rights of women and their social realities. Inequality in the family is a prevalent form of discrimination against women and is often justified in the name of ideology, tradition and culture.

The fundamental issue that instigates this article is the indirect discrimination women in Turkey in *de facto* partnerships – notably the religious marriages – suffer from especially in terms of the economic rights to be granted to spouses during or after the dissolution of their marriage. Taking the example of the Grand Chamber judgment of the European Court of Human Rights in *Serife Yigit v. Turkey*, this article examines the indirect discrimination suffered by women in Turkey who are bound with religious wedding and how this situation is, in fact, a clear example of the hermeneutical injustice experienced by those women. In its judgment *Şerife Yiğit v. Turkey*[1] – a striking example of this factual situation – the European Court of Human Rights (ECHR) examined the case of a woman, Şerife Yiğit, who was not recognized as the heir of a man to whom she had been married on a purely religious basis for 26 years as the only wife and mother of their six children. Living in a rural area of Turkey, Şerife Yiğit had been unable to claim retirement benefits – i.e. widow's pension – and health insurance on account of their marriage not being legally valid as they were not officially registered as married.

Having this judgment in mind, this article primarily aims to explore whether Turkey, as part of its obligations arising from the international human rights law, particularly under the European Convention on Human

1 Grand Chamber [GC] of the ECHR; application no. 3976/05; 2.11.2010.

Rights (Convention) and the Convention on the Elimination of All Forms of Discrimination Against Women (CEDAW), has positive obligations to prevent women in de facto partnerships who are exposed to indirect discrimination resulting from the nature of their relationship. Both instruments strictly prohibit discrimination on the grounds of sex and protect both men and women from treatment based on arbitrary, unfair and/or unjustifiable distinctions. CEDAW further goes beyond and focuses on discrimination against women, emphasizing that women have suffered and continue to suffer from various forms of discrimination because they are women. It therefore places an obligation on states to respect, protect, promote and fulfil this right to non-discrimination for women and to ensure the development and advancement of women in order to improve their position to one of de jure as well as de facto equality with men. By establishing the international legal framework for the situation of women in de facto partnerships, we discuss the applicable legal and administrative measures. Based on this, we argue that there is a pressing need to re-consider the de facto partnerships from the gender equality perspective in Turkey. Accordingly, we analyze if a new legal policy can help at all to scrutinize the indirect discrimination of women caused by the ambiguous attitude (having the secular laws in place but not enforcing them rigidly) the legal system exhibits vis-à-vis cultural practices in Turkey. In the course of our analysis, we base our arguments on the concept of epistemic, particularly hermeneutical injustice, as introduced by Miranda Fricker (2007). The hermeneutical injustice, as defined by Fricker, is structural and occurs when a society/person lacks the interpretative resources to make sense of the injustice they are suffering, due to their prejudicial epistemic marginalization. As in Şerife Yiğit v. Turkey, the women in de facto partnerships encounter this kind of injustice because they are wronged specifically in their capacity as a knower due to the lack of shared social resources – e.g. lack of education, access to justice – as to make sense of their experience. Therefore, hermeneutical injustice reveals a largely silent dimension of discrimination and thus we use it to lay the foundation of the reasons of indirect discrimination that women in de facto partnerships in Turkey are exposed to. Lastly, we find the comparison made by both the Turkish courts and the ECHR on the basis of religious v. civil marriage problematic on the account that their formalism failed to address the social reality in Turkey. No matter how women experience their de facto partnerships – in religious weddings or not – the factual situation does not change. Just like what Şerife Yiğit had experienced, as long as these women are not bound by civil marriage, they are not acknowledged as the rightful beneficiaries as to the consequences of their partnerships. Underlining this distinction to be the fundamental issue in our article, we argue that the better comparators to assess the situation of these women are, in fact, de facto partnerships v. civil marriage or in other words, long-standing and stable family relationship outside marriage on the one hand and marriage, as understood by the domestic legal system, on the other. We deem that such comparison is particularly felicitous in view of the new social realities, manifested in the growing number of stable relationships outside marriage, which are replacing the traditional institution of marriage without necessarily undermining the fabric of family life.

2 The ECHR and Other International Institutions Supporting Equal Opportunities

The non-discrimination principle is a well-established norm under international human rights law. Article 14 of the Convention stipulates a general ban against discrimination. It provides that the rights and freedoms set forth in the Convention shall be secured without discrimination on any ground such as sex, race, colour, language, religion, political or other opinion, national or social origin, association with a national minority, property, birth or other status. On one hand, Article 14 of the Convention has the limited scope of being an accessory right applicable only in relation to the enjoyment of the rights and freedoms otherwise protected by the Convention. On the other hand, it has a very wide range as it entails an open-model non-discrimination clause, which is not limited to an exhaustive list of discrimination grounds. This open structure of Article 14 has significant consequences as to its interpretation and application and provides for what may sometimes on the surface seem unstructured and perhaps conflicting case law (Armadóttir 2007:14).

The ECHR has established an analytical framework in its case law under Article 14. The test set out in the first Article 14 judgment, the *Belgian Linguistics*[2] case, is still instrumental. To begin with, the concept of discrimination and the analytical approach of the ECHR hold that a difference in treatment must exist. Sometimes, the ECHR adds to its express delimitation of the analytical framework that it is different treatment of persons in analogous or relevantly similar situations that must exist. In other cases, no express reference is made to this issue as part of the analytical approach, but it is generally implied and present in the reasoning of the Court. If the required difference in treatment and its basis are established the Court proceeds to the objective justification test. Under the objective justification test a violation occurs if the

2 Belgium Linguistics Case – 'In the case "relating to certain aspects of the laws on the use of languages in education in Belgium" v Belgium' (Application no 1474/62; 1677/62; 1691/62; 1769/63; 1994/63; 2126/64), 23.7.1968.

difference in treatment has no objective and reasonable justification. Such justification exists if the difference in treatment pursues a legitimate aim and if there is a reasonable relationship of proportionality between the means employed and the aim sought to be realised. While this reflects one of the possible manifestations of the prohibition against discrimination, the ECHR formulated a new test under Article 14 and placed the State under a positive obligation to accommodate different situations for the first time in the *Thlimmenos*[3] judgment in which it stated: "The right not to be discriminated against in the enjoyment of the rights guaranteed under the Convention is also violated when States without an objective and reasonable justification fail to treat differently persons whose situations are significantly different." The ECHR, thus, spelled out the *Thlimmenos* test in terms of a failure to meet positive State obligation to accommodate for differences when the same treatment results in discriminatory effects. The ECHR has also established yet another analytical test in relation to discriminatory effects analysis under Article 14. In *Hugh Jordan v. The United Kingdom*[4] it stated: "Where a general policy or measure has disproportionately prejudicial effects on a particular group, it is not excluded that this may be considered as discriminatory, notwithstanding that it is not specifically aimed or directed at that group."

These tests developed by the ECHR allow the examination of direct and/or indirect discrimination claims as far as they fall within the ambit of the Convention. The discrimination on the basis of sex has been discussed in numerous judgments and among others, in the *Konstantin Markin v. Russia* judgment, the ECHR concluded that "…[T]he advancement of gender equality is today a major goal in the member States of the Council of Europe and very weighty reasons would have to be put forward before such a difference of treatment could be regarded as compatible with the Convention ... In particular, references to traditions, general assumptions or prevailing social attitudes in a particular country are insufficient justification for a difference in treatment on grounds of sex."[5]

On the other hand, CEDAW also provides numerous legal guarantees as the first global and comprehensive legally binding international treaty aimed at the elimination of all forms of sex- and gender-based discrimination against women. CEDAW's aim is the elimination of all forms of discrimination against women both de jure and de facto, resulting from the activities or omissions on the part of States parties, their agents or committed by any persons or organizations in all fields of life, including the areas of politics, economy, society, culture, civil and family life. Its goal is the recognition and

3 Thlimmenos v. Greece [GC], no. 34369/97, 06.04.2000.
4 Hugh Jordan v. The United Kingdom, no. 24746/94, 4.5.2001.
5 Konstantin Markin v. Russia, [GC], no. 30078/06, 22.3.2012, § 127.

achievement of the de jure and de facto equality of women and men, which is to be achieved by a policy of elimination of all forms of discrimination against women incorporating all appropriate legislative and programmatic measures. A primary requirement for States parties is to "embody the principle of equality of men and women in their national constitutions or other appropriate legislation" and "to ensure… the practical realization of this principle" (Article 2 (a)). This requirement of practical realization of equality makes clear that CEDAW envisages substantive equality between women and men in the enjoyment of all human rights. It also provides a broad definition of discrimination against women as "[...] any distinction, exclusion or restriction made on the basis of sex which has the effect or purpose of impairing or nullifying the recognition, enjoyment or exercise by women, irrespective of their marital status, on a basis of equality of men and women, of human rights and fundamental freedoms in the political, economic, social, cultural, civil or any other field" (Article 1). This definition includes both direct and indirect discrimination against women, be it intentional or unintentional, in respect of law or practice, in all aspects of public and private life. Direct discrimination is intended to discriminate against women and constitutes apparent exclusion, distinction or restriction of rights of women as compared to men. Indirect discrimination occurs when apparently neutral legal standards or policies which do not seek to discriminate lead to consequences that, without justification, affect the enjoyment of rights by women disproportionally, simply because they are women. The fact that CEDAW addresses both direct and indirect forms of discrimination against women makes it a unique instrument in international law for the achievement of genuine (both formal and substantive) equality between men and women.

CEDAW further aims at enlarging our understanding of the concept of human rights, as it gives formal recognition to the influence of culture and tradition on restricting women's enjoyment of their fundamental rights. These forces take shape in stereotypes, customs and norms which give rise to the multitude of legal, political and economic constraints on the advancement of women. Noting this interrelationship, the preamble of the CEDAW stresses "that a change in the traditional role of men as well as the role of women in society and in the family is needed to achieve full equality of men and women."[6] States parties are therefore obliged to work towards the modification of social and cultural patterns of individual conduct in order to eliminate "prejudices and customary and all other practices which are based on the idea of the inferiority or the superiority of either of the sexes or on stereotyped roles for men and women" (Article 5). Similarly, the CEDAW Committee has

6 See Preamble of the UN Convention on the Elimination of All Forms of Discrimination against Women

consistently concluded that the elimination of discrimination against women requires States parties to provide for substantive as well as formal equality. Formal equality may be achieved by adopting gender-neutral laws and policies, which on their face treat women and men equally. Substantive equality, however, can be achieved only when the States parties examine the application and effects of laws and policies and ensure that they provide for equality in fact, accounting for women's disadvantage or exclusion.[7] Recently, the CEDAW Committee further concluded that, in respect of the economic dimensions of family relations, a substantive equality approach must address matters such as discrimination, the impact of gender stereotypes and gender roles on women's economic capacity[8].

3 Şerife Yiğit v. Turkey: a prominent example of indirect discrimination against women in de facto partnerships

3.1 Factual background and reasoning of the ECHR

The *Şerife Yiğit* case was initially discussed by the ECHR in a Chamber judgment of 20 January 2009[9] in which the ECHR held by four votes to three that there had been no violation of the right to respect private life under Article 8 of the European Convention on Human Rights (Convention). As mentioned earlier, the case was lodged by Ms. Şerife Yiğit after the Turkish courts had refused to entitle her the social security and pension rights of her deceased husband, the father of her six children, with whom she had been married in a religious ceremony. In examining whether the Turkish courts' decision had violated Şerife Yiğit's family life, the ECHR firstly noted that there was a current social trend, supported by the legislature, in certain member States of the Council of Europe towards the acceptance and even the recognition of stable forms of union such as cohabitation or civil partnership alongside the traditional marital bond. However, outside civil marriage, Turkish law did not provide for a union based on law creating a civil partnership that would allow two people of the same or opposite sexes to have rights identical or similar to those of a married couple. In this regard, the ECHR

7 See the General Recommendation no. 25 of the CEDAW Committee, 2004.

8 See the General Recommendation no. 29 of the CEDAW Committee (26 February 2013, CEDAW/C/GC/29).

9 Şerife Yiğit v. Turkey, Chamber judgment of 20 January 2009. Available at http://hudoc.echr.coe.int/sites/eng/pages/search.aspx#{%22itemid%22:[%22001-90786%22]} (last accessed 22.4. 2015).

stated that marriage remained an institution widely recognised as conferring a particular status to those who entered into it and Article 8 therefore could not be interpreted as requiring the establishment of a special regime for a specific category of unmarried couples. According to the ECHR, entry into a marriage signals acceptance of a distinct package of rights and responsibilities – as against one another *and* the State – that do not apply to cohabitees. A decision not to formalise the relationship thus is a decision not to 'opt in' to the associated rights and responsibilities.[10] In other words, through marriage a couple regulates their relationship with each other and with the State through their public contract. The couple puts the State 'on notice' of their relationship. A cohabiting couple make no such public contract. Thus, the ECHR concluded that the difference in treatment between married and unmarried couples with regard to survivors' benefits pursued a legitimate aim and was based on objective and reasonable grounds, namely the protection of the traditional family based on the bonds of marriage and therefore, it found no violation.[11]

After the Chamber judgment, Şerife Yiğit appealed against the decision and the ECHR relinquished the case to the Grand Chamber of the ECHR. This time, by virtue of the *jura novit curia* principle, the ECHR assessed the case on account of prohibition of non-discrimination in conjunction with the right to property and analysed whether the civil or religious nature of a marriage could be a source of discrimination. While the non-civil nature of her marriage to her partner was found as a source of discrimination, the ECHR nevertheless concluded that the difference in treatment in question had primarily pursued the legitimate aims of protecting women, particularly through efforts to combat polygamy and the reassurance of the principle of secularism in Turkey.[12] Having concluded that there had been a reasonable relationship of proportionality between the impugned difference in treatment and the legitimate aim pursued, the ECHR held that there had therefore been an objective and reasonable justification for the difference in question and thus there

---

10 See also Van der Heijden v The Netherlands, (no. 42857/05), Grand Chamber judgment of 3 April 2012.

11 ibid, para. 29-30. In the joint dissenting opinion of Judge Tulkens, Zagrebelsky and Sajō, the judgment has been criticised for failing to examine the case from the positive obligations on States to ensure the effective exercise of the right in question. Further, they underlined that the sole victims in such situations are women and not men. In this regard, the judges pointed out that this raises the issue of possible indirect discrimination (for instance, Hoogendijk v. the Netherlands (dec.), no. 58641/00, 6 January 2005) which the ECHR failed to take into consideration.

12 Şerife Yiğit v. Turkey, Grand Chamber judgment of 2 November 2010. Available at http://hudoc.echr.coe.int/sites/eng/pages/search.aspx#{%22appno%22:[%223976/05%22], %22itemid%22:[%22001-101579%22]} (last accessed 22.4.2015), see para. 75-82.

was no violation of the prohibition of non-discrimination in conjunction with the right to property.

In its reasoning, the ECHR considered it decisive that, in view of the relevant Turkish legal rules which are clear and accessible, Şerife Yiğit could not have had any legitimate expectation of obtaining benefits on the basis of her partner's entitlement. According to the ECHR, the Civil Code was clear as to the pre-eminence of civil marriage and being aware of her situation, Şerife Yiğit had known that she needed to regularize her relationship pursuant to the Civil Code in order to be recognized as her partner's heir. The ECHR further reminded that the Civil Code clearly states that the couple's religious marriage can only take place when the couple already holds the wedding certificate given at the time of the civil marriage and that people will be subjected to penal sanction, including the imams performing the religious ceremony, if they bond with religious marriage without first being bonded with civil marriage. Finally, the ECHR, emphasizing not only that an obligation to recognize religious marriages cannot be imposed upon the State but also that the State is not required to make special arrangements for unmarried couples, stated that there was no interference in private life on the part of the State since the State did not prevent Şerife Yiğit and her husband to have a family life.

3.2 Critical Reading of the Judgment in the Context of the Turkish Legal Setting

From a formalistic point of view, the Şerife Yiğit judgment may appear to be one that is reasonable, well justified and appropriate. However, when we take a glance at the social reality behind the judgment, one may ask the following question: is the situation after the judgment one where the legitimate aim of the protection of women is in fact ensured and the principle of secularism warranted or whether Şerife Yiğit is sacrificed as 'collateral damage' for the sake of these aims? Making a critical reading of the judgment, we argue that the situation of Şerife Yiğit is an example of indirect discrimination.

As stated before, indirect discrimination is the adverse effect of a neutral treatment to an individual or group with a protected characteristic, such as sex, race and sexual orientation. In the case of indirect discrimination, contrary to direct discrimination, the disputed treatment is neutral. It is not the form of the treatment but its effects are linked to the protected characteristic. In addition, indirect discrimination contests the consistency in treatment by putting a neutral treatment under scrutiny. The reason behind this contest is that "neutrality reinforces dominant values or existing distribution of power" and by doing so, a neutral treatment can in fact be a source of further inequality (Fredman 2001:154). Hence we contend that Şerife Yiğit suffers from indirect discrimination even though the Turkish law requiring civil marriage prior to religious marriage is gender neutral, the failure on the part of State authorities to enforce it – 'treatment' – puts her at a particular disadvantage as a woman compared to a man despite the law being applied on equal terms. We aim to investigate this case of indirect discrimination from two perspectives namely, in relation to the judgments given by the Turkish courts and in relation to the judgment of the European Court of Human Rights (ECHR).

As far as the legal setting and the related decisions given in Turkey are concerned, we contend that the indirect discrimination in question is primarily[13] caused by the State institutions' failure to take appropriate measures to make sure that the laws regulating religious marriage (commonly referred to as 'imam wedding') are properly carried out by the State organs. Pursuant to the Article 143 of the Turkish Civil Code,[14] the imam wedding cannot be concluded without submitting the civil marriage certificate. Furthermore, the Turkish Criminal Code[15] lays down a criminal sanction on the matter. According to the paragraph 5 of the Article 230 of the latter, individuals living together solely through religious weddings without a civil marriage are sentenced to two to six month in prison. Paragraph six of the same article further stipulates that the individual who carried out a religious wedding ceremony without seeing the relevant civil marriage document should also be imprisoned for two to six months.[16] Despite these legal obligations, we observe that

13 Indeed, beyond this factual matter of 'negligence', there is the more structural issue of the State's approach towards various forms of de facto partnerships which, as will be discussed, should have been the determining angle in the judgment of the ECHR.

14 Law no. 4721 adopted on 22.11.2001

15 Law no. 5237 adopted on 26.9.2004

16 These two paragraphs of Article 230 of the Turkish Criminal Code, however, had been annulled by the Turkish Constitutional Court (CC) with a very recent decision on 27.5.2015 (Anayasa Mahkemesi Kararı, Esas Sayısı: 2014/36; Karar Sayısı: 2015/51) The CC based its decision in a comparison it made between people living as a couple without religious marriage and those with religious marriage. It argued that „while individuals practically living together and having children without a religious ceremony or wedding are not being punished, punishing people who made choices in terms of their private lives and had religious marriages displays the [regulation's] intemperance on the issue. It thus concluded that the legislation in question is disproportionate and must be repealed." With this judgment, there is no longer any criminal prosecution of the imams conducting religious marriage without the submission of civil wedding certificate. However, we analyse the legal setting at the material time in the Şerife Yiğit case. Nonetheless, it must be stated that the recent Turkish Constitutional Court ruling spurred uproar among the legal and human rights' circles who argue that the move would threaten the rights of women and children in the country. Given that the judgment only came out at the time this article was just submitted for publication, we had to leave out the analysis of this judgment and its possible effect on the matter and we strictly bound ourselves with the applicable rules in the Şerife Yiğit case.

Şerife Yiğit and her partner were able to get religiously married without any prior civil marriage and neither they nor the imams, who are State officers under Turkish law, were subject to criminal proceedings.

The legal framework regarding the religious marriage has the appropriate objectives of protecting women from the ills of polygamy and the reassurance of the principle of secularism. The law regulating the terms of the religious marriage is part of the first Civil Code (in 1926) of the Turkish Republic. This and similar secular laws are acknowledged as paradigmatic indicators of the modernization and Westernization of the newly founded Turkish Republic which thereby became the only country with a predominantly Muslim population to entirely adopt secularism in its constitutional, legal and institutional structure.[17]

This historical background was also indicated in the Şerife Yiğit judgment by holding that monogamous civil marriage is a prerequisite for any religious marriage in Turkey aiming to put an end to a marriage tradition which places women at a clear disadvantage, not to say in a situation of dependence and inferiority, compared to men[18]. The judgment further recalls that Turkey also introduced the principle of gender equality for the same reason in the enjoyment of civic rights, particularly in relation to divorce and inheritance and prohibited polygamy. Marriage in accordance with the Civil Code is specifically aimed at protecting women, for instance by laying down a minimum age for marriage and establishing a set of rights and obligations for women, in particular in the event of the dissolution of the marriage or the death of the husband.

Against this background, we believe that a major reason for indirect discrimination against women bonded in religious marriages in Turkey is the ambiguous attitude the State institutions exhibit vis-à-vis cultural practices and tradition, especially those concerning the traditional place and role of women in the society. It is a marked characteristic of patriarchal societies that women are considered to primarily belong in the private sphere, notably the family, as mothers and wives.[19] There is no doubt that the secular State of

---

However, we deem that the CC ruling deserves a very thorough analysis as at the outset, the analogy it made appears to fail taking all crucial elements of the problem into consideration, particularly the situation of women.

17 Within a decade after the foundation of the Turkish Republic in 1923, secular education became mandatory for both girls and boys (1924) and women were granted equal political rights with men (1934). For an elaborate account and analysis of secularism in modern Turkey see for instance, Ahmad (2014), Zurcher (2007a), (2007b), and Mardin (2003; 2006).

18 Şerife Yiğit, para. 82.

19 As a prominent example of this perception at the State level, we can recall the replacement of the Ministry of Women and Family Affairs with the Ministry of Family and Social Poli-

Turkish Republic considers monogamy as the legitimate form of relationship for married couples. Considering that religious marriage is a very widely practiced custom in Turkey, the question remains as to why the State does not show a sincere will to eradicate the ills associated with the religious marriage by severely enforcing the laws.

4 The Concept of Family as a Determinant of the Problem

We believe that the most critical reason for the indirect discrimination in the Şerife Yiğit case seems to be associated with the very conception of 'the family'. As stated in the United Nations Declaration of Human Rights, the family is the fundamental unit of the society. The family which is a social, civil and economical structure also carries religious characteristics in many countries. The normative assessment regarding the structure and constitution of the family is specified not only by the legal constitutions of particular States but depends also on the social context of particular communities as well as the interpretive practices in tune with the religion(s), morals and traditions peculiar to those countries.[20] Accordingly, as the legal system, religion, morals and traditions differ from one country to another, an agreement on a 'universal' definition of the concept 'family' seems very unlikely. Although several international forums recognize family diversity, that is to say, its different manifestations in different cultural, political and social systems, many of the non-traditional forms of family are not recognized by all States. The family is often defined by legal systems as a unit founded on marriage between a man and a woman, affecting rights relating to, for example, inheritance, property, child custody, pensions, tax relief and social service provision. Given that State recognition is often a condition for families to receive services and benefits, such as accommodation and protection provided by the State and/or non-State actors, lack of recognition leads to the marginalization of these families just like in the Şerife Yiğit case.[21]

It appears that the applicable law in the Şerife Yiğit case aims, without reservations, at separating the domains of the traditional and the modern/secular/Western by clearly stating that the couple's religious marriage

cy in 2011. The renaming, seemingly small, is rather telling: the word 'women' has been taken out and the emphasis has been placed on 'family'.

20 For a background information on the effect of culture and religion in the definition of gender from human rights law perspective, see Raday (2003).

21 For the sociological and conceptual aspects of family in the context of discrimination against women and girls in cultural and family life, see Report of the Working Group on the issue of discrimination against women in law and in practice, United Nations (2015). See also, Aziz and Moussa (2014).

can only take place when the couple already holds the wedding certificate given at the time of the civil marriage and that people will be subjected to penal sanction, including the imams who perform the religious ceremony, if they bond with religious marriage without first being bonded with civil marriage. Together with the requirement of the civil marriage, the State also implies that as far as the laws and regulations are concerned, the only legitimate form of relationship for the couples forming a family is monogamy. Taking these into consideration, we believe that the rapport between the legally legitimate form of marriage and the valid structure of family needs further scrutiny to better assess the possible reasons of the 'negligent' attitude of the State institutions. The congruence of the State policies with the widely accepted approach to 'marriage' and 'family' seems to be positively affirmed as the law regarding the religious marriage considered together with the 'margin of appreciation'[22] of the Turkish State alluded to by the ECHR. This also implies that the State indeed has sincere will to do away with this custom's pernicious consequences. Here a question arises as to requisite conditions for the substantiation of the will to eradicate those pernicious consequences. Evidently, the existence of laws, such as the one requiring that couples first be bonded in civil marriage before the religious one, is a necessary but not sufficient condition to combat those consequences. We argue that what appears to be mere 'negligence' on the part of the State to enforce certain laws, should not be overlooked with such ease since an ever recurring negligence is a contradiction in terms, suspecting the 'sincerity' of the will in question. Indeed, customs, especially those that are grounded on religion, present highly complex issues in terms of secularism and have critical implications for law and politics.[23] The complexity of the issue becomes more evident and the 'sincerity' of the will appears more suspicious when the application of laws is thoroughly investigated. Despite the available legal sanctions, imams had

22 The case-law of the ECHR makes clear that each state is entitled to apply its own 'margin of appreciation' to determine which family form and related rights should be protected and ensured by the law. The ECHR also underlines that the widely accepted view is to seek the existence of 'legal marriage' bond and holds that marriage remains an institution conferring a particular status and rights on those who enter it and thus, regards the protection of traditional family structure provided by marriage to be an objective and reasonable justification for the different treatment between married and unmarried couples especially when the rights such as social security are in question. As known, a margin of appreciation refers to some "latitude of deference or error which the ECHR allows to national legislative, executive, administrative and judicial bodies", Yourow (1996:13).

23 In his most valuable recent book worth mentioning here, *The Secular State Under Siege: Religion and State in Europe and America*, Christian Joppke takes a historical approach to the connection (or the lack thereof) between religion and politics to critically discuss the current state of Western secularism where religion is no longer conceived as to be 'outside' politics and 'secular' law.

hardly ever been prosecuted for not performing their legal duties – i.e. asking proof of the civil marriage before conducting the religious ceremony. The situation of women in Turkey who are bonded by religious marriage only is thus a paradigmatic case at the intersection of customs, politics and law. The most recent decision of the Constitutional Court[24] that annulled the criminal sanctions applicable to imams though it appears to be grounded on a more liberal understanding of the relationships between the sexes at the outset, will rather please the religious voters of AKP and will potentially give rise to the worsening of the situation of these women unless it is supplemented with regulations to provide them with the same economic rights that women bonded in civil marriage benefit from.[25]

To reiterate, we claim that it is especially in terms of the traditions directly related to women that we encounter the 'negligence' of the State to rigidly enforce the laws indicative of its contraposition vis-à-vis tradition. As a characteristic of patriarchal societies, in Turkey too, women's traditional 'place' is the home. A woman is expected to get married, have children and take care of her family. Therefore, besides the fact that being married only by religious marriage – either as the only wife, or the second, third etc. to the wife also holding the marriage certificate – is a very widely practiced custom requiring a multi-dimensional struggle going beyond the enforcement of the related laws, the ambiguous attitude of the State vis-à-vis this practice is due to the understanding that although an unlawful one, the religious marriage sustains the traditional place and role of the woman in the family as the mother and the wife. According to the common morals of the society, there is discrimination between forms of heterosexual de facto partnerships. While a woman who 'lives together' (denoting that she is not religiously married) with a man or a mistress is considered 'indecent', a woman who is religiously married only is completely or better tolerated by the society. The State, by not rigidly enforcing the laws, in a sense becomes an accomplice and can even be said to behave as the 'guardian' of the customs resulting in the indirect discrimination of women.[26]

---

24 See footnote 8.

25 However, these regulations seem hard to come by any time soon, especially considering the patriarchal and paternalistic nature of Turkish culture where women, rather than being perceived as autonomous subjects having the same entitlement to economic, social and legal rights as men, are primarily defined in terms of their traditional roles in the family. Moreover, polygamy being a quite common practice in Turkey, governments would be reluctant to even propose laws granting the same property rights to women bonded only with religious marriage as well as in de facto partnerships due to the worry of their possible negative effect on the votes.

26 Ayşe Parla, in her award-winning article, "The 'Honor' of the State: Virginity Examinations in Turkey" (2000), explains how the modern Turkish State employs the traditional virtues such as chastity and modesty to fashion the modern women citizens of the Republic.

In its judgment, one of the reasons the ECHR advances for rejecting the case is that Şerife Yiğit already knew what was awaiting her upon the death of her husband hence almost rendering her the sole responsible party for the consequence she suffers namely, being denied social security. As much as the belief systems are a part of the cultural paradigm, this argument implies that she 'preferred' a traditional way of marriage when the 'modern' and secular alternative was already in place, thanks to the laws of the modern and secular Republic of Turkey. The same approach is shared by the State who denied Şerife Yiğit's appeal resulting in her applying to the ECHR as a last resort. The reason why the ambiguous attitude of the State is overlooked is because both the State of Turkey and the ECHR seem to take it for granted that the existing secular laws are sufficient to fight against the ills of traditions. More often than not, this facile reasoning which ignores the facts of social reality renders invisible the intentional as well as unintentional complicity and negligence of the institutions resulting in the violation of the rights of women.[27]

Here, another facet of the ambiguous relationship of tradition and modernity is revealed: the body of the woman becomes the site of the negotiations between traditional and modern values. She further explains that it is in terms of the interrelation of the legal and the cultural that the gendered social norms are put into effect by the State as manifested in the case of the state-enforced virginity examinations. While Parla's aim in this article is to argue that this practice, rather than being the „embarrassing remnant of tradition" (p. 66) is part of the surveillance mechanism of the modern nation-state of Turkey, we believe that it gives valuable insights regarding the discrimination that women may suffer due to influence of tradition upon legal systems.

27 Dicle Koğacıoğlu's article 'The Tradition Effect: Framing Honor Crimes in Turkey,' (2004) where she examines the case of 'honor crimes' or 'crimes of tradition', – a 'tradition' that in some instances happens to have very severe consequences for women (such as their being battered or killed) – offers a clear and useful analysis regarding the problematic attitude of the institutions vis-à-vis tradition: "Once…tradition is properly blamed, there remains no necessity to inquire into the ways in which a particular institution may be implicated in the making of honor crimes…Such framing enables actors in social institutions to eschew responsibility for their own complicity … These traditions are also presumed to be resistant to change … Consequently, not much effort goes into examining the ways in which an institution's own acts may be participating in the perpetuation of this allegedly timeless 'tradition' … This is what I call 'the tradition effect.'" (p. 121) We believe that a similar critical account is applicable to *Şerife Yiğit*'s case where, in its 'negligence' to enforce the law requiring the couple to be married in civil ceremony before the religious one, the State fails to fulfill its responsibility to protect Şerife Yiğit from the possible pernicious effects of the widely practiced tradition of being bonded with imam wedding only. In our words, the State fails to comply with its positive obligations – i.e. to take appropriate measures to remedy the situation. The most problematic consequence of this practice is that, although, culturally, these women are recognized as 'wives', having no legal right to claim their marriage rights, the sort of lives they would lead as widows is at the mercy of their families. The cost of the 'negligence' of the State is more often than not lesser lives for such women. With no pension and social security benefits to sustain themselves on their own, these women are bound to depend on their children or in-laws who may or may not actually care about their well-being. We believe that the ECHR should be vigilant and in-

The perspective of the ECHR is clear in terms of the common points that it shares with the perspective of Turkey; we can now turn our attention to some particularities in the judgment of the Court. With reference to the analysis under Article 8 in which it finds no interference with the respect for private life, the ECHR recalled that family life[28] is a factual matter and needs to be defined in accordance with the "real existence in practice of close personal ties."[29] It further states that Article 8 applies to the 'family life' of the 'illegitimate' family as it does to that of the 'legitimate' family. Accordingly, the notion of the 'family' is not confined solely to marriage-based relationships and may encompass other de facto 'family' ties where the parties are living together outside of marriage. In this respect, the ECHR does not consider the formal marriage relationship, deemed valid in accordance with the national law, blood link or adoption, to be necessary as conditions for family life. Despite this definition of the ECHR, in the legislation of many countries, there is no legal security for individuals in de facto relations[30] as to the implications/consequences regarding family life. An uncontroversial instance of this problematic state of affairs is the situation of Şerife Yiğit whose predicament is partly caused by the unclarity of the meaning and scope of the concept of 'family' giving rise to a double standard in terms of the legal implications/ consequences of family life.

There is no doubt that as far as they were concerned, Şerife Yiğit and her partner were married' and together with their children, had a family life no different than the family lives of men and women bonded in civil marriage. However, as far as the State is concerned, although Şerife Yiğit and her partner were not prevented from having a family life (in the sense of 'close personal ties'), their 'marriage' was not deemed to be a legally valid one, neither was their family recognized as 'legitimate'.[31] We argue that the ambiguity concerning the meaning of 'family' – that is to say, whether 'the existence of close personal ties' is sufficient to be a 'family' or whether these ties require

terpret the failure of monitoring the imams on the part of the State as a breach of the Article 5 (a) of CEDAW, a convention that is fully binding for Turkey since 1999.

28 For different aspects of what family life constitutes as discussed by the ECHR- see- *inter alia*- K. and T. v. Finland [GC], no.25702/94, § 150, ECHR 2001-VII. Johnston 9 and Others v. Ireland, 18 December 1986, § 55, Series A no. 112. Keegan v. Ireland, 26 May 1994, § 44, Series A no. 290, and Al-Nashif v. Bulgaria, no.50963/99, § 112, 20 June 2002.

29 See K. and T. v. Finland [GC], no.25702/94, § 150.

30 For the rights of de facto couples under international human rights law and in European countries, see Walsh and Ryan (2006).

31 To recall, alluding to the 'margin of appreciation', the ECHR unproblematically asserted that the State is under no obligation to recognize all forms of private life as legitimate forms of 'family'.

to be validated as such in civil marriage[32] – to be a major cause for the indirect discrimination against women whose case is exemplified in the person of Şerife Yiğit. Therefore, we think that, as the emphasis is on 'family' and 'family life', rather than substantiating the judgments given by Turkish domestic courts resulting in an unintentional distraction in terms of the central point of the case, it would have been more appropriate for the ECHR to carry on the comparison between *de facto* partnerships v. civil marriages instead of religious v. civil marriages. But before dwelling upon this suggestion, we will address another particularity in the judgment of the ECHR, where the reasoning appears to be questionable from the perspective of 'epistemic justice'.

5 Indirect Discrimination as an Effect of Epistemic Injustice

To recall, in its reasoning, the ECHR also argued that the relevant Turkish legal provisions governing the social benefits for widows – i.e., the pre-eminence of civil marriage – being clear and accessible, Şerife Yiğit should have known that she needed to regularize her relationship pursuant to the Civil Code in order to be recognized as her partner's heir. Hence, the Court has decided that Şerife Yiğit is partly responsible for her predicament. We believe that, being inattentive to the social reality behind the case, the Court also failed to notice the 'epistemic injustice' issues women such as Şerife Yiğit face. Moreover, as we have previously noted, the ECHR implied that it is Şerife Yiğit herself who had 'chosen/preferred' the traditional way of marriage to the 'modern' and secular alternative that was already in place for her. Hence, the Court decided that she has no grounds to object to the consequences naturally flowing from her 'preference'.

However, we believe that this formalistic argument overlooks the fact that what appears to be a 'preference' is deformed in various ways by oppression and deprivation where it is not really a preference but helplessness, oppression or discrimination that is the major determinant of the situation some women find themselves in.[33] Considering the actual circumstances of women

---

32 Naturally, with no aim to contest the birth rights of children, we find it important to point out that the pernicious effect of this ambiguity regarding the meaning and scope of 'family' is especially pronounced in the case of women. Although in the case of women, the 'strength' of family ties are judged by the existence (or the lack of) civil marriage and hence women are recognized as heir if and only if they are the lawful wives of their 'husbands', children are always recognized as heirs regardless of whether or not their parents are bonded in civil marriage.

33 In her article 'Oppression', referring to the experience of oppressed people, Marilyn Frye writes: " … the living of one's life is confined and shaped by forces and barriers which are

who are bonded with religious marriage only, it would be counterfactual to advance the accessibility of relevant information as a premise for the argument leading to the rejection of Şerife Yiğit's case. It is important to note that most of these women do not have any viable alternative but to endure the conditions that are imposed on them and more often than not, suffer various forms of hardship after the death of their partners or the dissolution of their 'marriage'.

In her ground-breaking book *Epistemic Injustice: Power and the Ethics of Knowing*,[34] Miranda Fricker elaborates two forms of epistemic injustice: the testimonial and the hermeneutical. Both, the testimonial and the hermeneutical injustice, have great relevance for our topic. According to Fricker, testimonial injustice occurs when a hearer discounts the credibility of a person's testimony due to prejudice against her social identity (Fricker 2007: 28). Hermeneutical injustice, on the other hand, takes place when "a collective hermeneutical gap prevents members of a group from making sense of an experience that is in their interest to render intelligible" (ibid.:7). Additionally, hermeneutical epistemic injustice implies testimonial epistemic injustice. Finding the idea of epistemic injustice to be highly illuminating for the problems related to the case in question, we believe that the somewhat hasty judgment of the ECHR may not only be due to the lack of requisite vigilance to social reality but also to the epistemic injustice issues relevant to Şerife Yiğit's case.

The ECHR in arguing that Şerife Yiğit should have regularized her relationship pursuant to the Civil Code seems to assume that although she had the 'capacity' or power to effect a change in her own situation – either refusing to be bonded in religious marriage unless she is first legally married or having the legal marriage as soon as possible after the religious ceremony – she chose not to exercise this power. However, considering the realities of the social world in which she dwelled, it would be extremely exceptional for a

not accidental or occasional hence avoidable, but are systematically related to each in such a way as to catch one between and among them and restrict or penalize motion in any direction" (Frye 2005:85).

34 Also see the special issue 'Epistemic Injustice' of *Social Epistemology* for the critical reception of Fricker's idea of epistemic injustice. One of the articles, Elizabeth Anderson's „Epistemic Justice as a Virtue of Social Institutions" is especially relevant for our topic. Anderson distinguishes between transactional injustice – wrongs committed locally at the site of individual transactions – and structural injustice – injustice manifested at the social or institutional level. Anderson, finding Fricker's emphasis on virtue at the level of the individuals insufficient as a remedy for epistemic injustice, argues that some epistemic harms must be corrected at the collective, policy level – i.e., structurally (Anderson 2012:163-164).

woman's 'social power' to accomplish that much.[35] As Fricker explains, the social power of an agent, her/his capacity "to influence how things go in the social world" (ibid.:9), is interrelated with "identity power" which depends "upon shared imaginative conceptions of social identity" (ibid.:14). Referring to gender as one such arena of identity power, Fricker says, "an exercise of gender identity power is active when, for instance, a man makes (possible unintended) use of his identity as a man to influence a woman's actions...He might, for instance, patronize her and get away with it in virtue of the fact that he is a man and she is a woman" (ibid.:14). Moreover, the stereotypes thus engendered inevitably affect the hearer's assessment of the interlocutor's credibility in a testimonial exchange (ibid.:16f.). Taking into view Turkish culture's patriarchal and paternalistic nature, it is not unusual for women to suffer from prejudices due to their gender identity giving rise to what Fricker calls "testimonial injustice" the central case of which is an "identity-prejudicial credibility deficit" (ibid.:28). We believe that, the judges of both the Turkish courts and the ECHR, are partly responsible from the testimonial injustice that Şerife Yiğit suffered from. To explain, the structural prejudices regarding women in general but especially women such as Şerife Yiğit, who do not have a profession, who are mostly uneducated (hence are also assumed to have poor intellectual capacities) and living in rural areas, possibly in poverty, engender a belief that they are content to be under the protection of a man regardless of the consequences. Accordingly, in terms of the case under investigation, we argue that there is ground to suspect the effect of these prejudices on the reasoning of the judges who, by alluding to Şerife Yiğit's 'failure' to regularize her relationship pursuant to the Civil Code, not only questioned the credibility of her testimony, but also took this 'failure' to be more central for the case than the obvious culpability of the State authorities who were inefficient and/or unwilling to enforce the laws.

In addition to testimonial injustice, we think that Şerife Yiğit also suffers from hermeneutical injustice. To express her situation in Fricker's terms, her highly patriarchal social world is one where women are systemically hindered from equal participation in the "practices through which social meanings are generated" (ibid.:6). Women thus being silenced, not only are their social experiences "inadequately conceptualized and so ill-understood" but also, as these experiences are not part of the "collective hermeneutical resources" making communication possible, they have difficulties to adequate-

35 It is important to recall that even though Şerife Yiğit was her partner's only 'wife', most of the time, women who are bonded with religious marriage only are the second or the third in relation to the legally married wife. Hence there is material impossibility for them to be lawful wives of their partners. We believe that it would be most appropriate for the ECHR to take these facts into consideration and place Şerife Yiğit's case in this broader picture before implying that she is at last partly responsible for her own predicament.

ly express themselves. Thus, not only are their utterances often not properly understood but, additionally, their voices unheard (ibid.:6f.). The example that Fricker uses as a central case of hermeneutical injustice is highly relevant for our discussion since it gives us valuable insights into the intimate relation between social power and the capacity to make one's own experience intelligible to oneself and others. Based upon a real event, it is the case of a woman who suffered sexual harassment but could not interpret her experience as such since this critical concept was not yet coined and hence, there was still a 'gap' in the collective hermeneutical resources not permitting her experience to become intelligible either for herself or for the others. As clearly expressed by Fricker, this woman's hermeneutical disadvantage not only "renders her unable to make sense of her ongoing mistreatment" but also prevents her from "protesting it", not to mention, "taking effective measures to stop it" (ibid.:151). Hence, it seems that the hermeneutically disadvantaged is also disadvantaged in terms of her/his capacity to effectuate a change in a given social situation. In other words, the hermeneutically disadvantaged has little or no social power.

In the light of these discussions, we argue that expecting Şerife Yiğit to have the social power to regularize her relationship with her partner pursuant to the Civil Code is unrealistic as well as unfair. Agreeing with Fricker, we argue "the powerful", in this case, men as social agents but also as state actors, have an unfair advantage in "structuring social understanding" (ibid.: 147). As is mostly the case in patriarchal cultures, these social understandings are not generated to include the perspectives of women. Hence, the social meanings specifically of concern to women are mostly missing. In Fricker's terms, these missing social meanings as 'gaps' make it very hard for women to adequately interpret their position as disadvantaged. Therefore, even though Şerife Yiğit might have known that being bonded with religious marriage only would put her in a disadvantaged position in the event of her husband's death, lacking a proper understanding of 'rights' or 'discrimination', it would have been almost impossible for her to interpret her disadvantage from these points of view. This factual situation was further worsened by the legal setting in Turkey. Despite the fact that the law requiring civil marriage prior to religious marriage is gender neutral, the persistent 'negligence' on the part of the 'powerful' to apply this law led to the inevitable outcome, namely, the denial of justice for Şerife Yiğit.

6 De Facto Partnership v. Civil Marriage as Better Comparators

In the light of these considerations, we argue that the ECHR does not exhibit a sincere will to protect the rights of women in these situations in that it interprets the margin of appreciation of the State and the specific conditions regarding polygamy and secularism too widely. According to the ECHR, marriage continues to be characterised by a corpus of rights and obligations which differentiate it markedly from the situation of a man and woman who cohabit it. Furthermore, it regards the decision whether to give a statutory right to pension provision to cohabitees following the death of a partner solely as a general measure of economic or social strategy of the State where a wide margin is usually allowed. Obviously, the fact that the case concerns an Islamic marriage also plays an important symbolic role. The ECHR attached a lot of importance to the place of the woman in Islamic marriage which it describes as follows: "Turkey aimed to put an end to a marriage tradition which places women at a clear disadvantage, not to say in a situation of dependence and inferiority to men".[36] Despite having stated that, however, the ECHR seems to turn a blind eye to the fact that the State systematically fails to monitor the conditions under which the religious marriages are carried out. Hence, it tolerates the unlawful acts of the imams who ironically happen to be state officials themselves. This narrow and formalistic interpretation of the ECHR can be said to be more pronounced in that it investigates the claim of discrimination only in terms of couples who are bonded in civil marriage versus those who are bonded in religious marriage. We claim that it would have been a more appropriate and progressive interpretation for the ECHR to draw on the comparison between *de facto* partnerships vs. civil marriages instead of religious vs. civil marriages. This could have been more in line with the generally accepted principle of the Convention as a 'living instrument'. In other words, the ECHR failed to interpret the case taking into account social realities.

To judge by the information supplied by the two parties, it is regrettable that the respondent State did not allow the applicant to claim an ordinary pension. Viewed objectively, this lack of any social welfare provision for widows who contracted a religious marriage is an infringement of the freedom of choice as to the form of 'family life'. The Court has stressed on numerous occasions that the notion of the 'family' is not confined solely to marriage-based relationships and may encompass other *de facto* 'family' ties where the parties are living together outside of marriage. This distinction is

36 Şerife Yiğit, §81.

particularly important given the other international human rights norms. For instance, the CEDAW Committee explicitly recommends that no discrimination should be made between women in unregistered marriages and de facto partnerships regarding the economic consequences of the termination of marriage or of family relations. Furthermore, the States are asked to protect the economic rights of women in all circumstances.[37]

Against this background, we contend that the ECHR should have started reconsidering its stance as to the justifiable distinction that it accepts, in certain matters such as children's birth rights, between civil marriage on the one hand and other forms of family life on the other, even when it comes to social security and related benefits. Recalling the Convention as a living instrument, such comparison is indeed a pressing need in view of the new social realities which are gradually emerging in today's Europe, manifested in a gradual increase in the number of stable relationships outside marriage, which are replacing the traditional institution of marriage without necessarily undermining the fabric of family life. By taking a more anthropological approach in the positions it adopts, the ECHR should aim to act by *not just exploring difference, but exploring it differently.* Otherwise, the Court is in danger of becoming entrenched in formalistic attitudes.

7 Conclusion

The purpose of this article is not to question the 'necessity' of the margin of appreciation of the States or to claim that religious marriage is as legitimate a form of marriage as the civil marriage. To wit, this article aims at underlining the problematic aspects of the most common form of *de facto* partnership in Turkey to determine the unfavourable and pernicious consequences for women of the present laws and the present social reality. We believe that these very laws that are said to be implemented to protect women, when not enforced, are primarily responsible for the indirect discrimination women in those partnerships suffer from. To be more precise, when the State does not seriously fulfil its positive obligations towards women who are bonded only with religious marriage and lack the sincere will to systematically enforce the laws, women in these conditions suffer indirect discrimination and are deprived of their economic rights regarding social security. The problem in the case of Şerife Yiğit seems to have its roots in such a lack of will. There would not have been such a case if the State monitored the imams and took

37 See the General Recommendation no. 29 of the CEDAW Committee (26 February 2013, CEDAW/C/GC/29).

the necessary precautions as well as penalized imams who break the law by not refusing to perform the ceremony if the couple is not already bonded in civil marriage.

We find it disappointing that in its examination of the case of Şerife Yiğit, the ECHR disregards this fact together with the pernicious consequences of the insinuated 'negligence' on the part of women, especially in a situation as Yiğit's. Exculpating the State from any serious fault, the Court seems to agree that by failing to regularize her relationship pursuant the Civil Code, it was Şerife Yiğit who single-handedly brought about her predicament onto herself. However, we find this hasty reasoning inadequate and claim that, had the Court examined the social reality determining the lives of these women, it would have seen the epistemic injustice problems that they are faced with, problems that make it very hard, if not impossible for them to possess the social power to effect a favourable change regarding the crucial aspects of their conditions. As explained, the injustices are mostly caused by the patriarchal understandings firmly established in the Turkish culture where it is very likely for women to suffer both from the testimonial and hermeneutical injustice. Therefore, drawing attention to the cultural influences on the conduct of the State vis-à-vis religious marriages, as also required by Article 5 of CEDAW, we conclude that it would have been more congruent with the ECHR's objectives and therefore more appropriate for the Court to reason from the distinction of de facto vs. civil marriage rather than the distinction of the religious vs. civil one, a point the elaboration of which exceeds the purpose of this paper.

Discussion Questions

1. What are the fundamental instruments that aim to ensure non-discrimination on the grounds of sex under international human rights law?
2. How would you define indirect discrimination? What features are distinctively different than direct discrimination? Can you think of any laws or policy measures that can be considered as an example of this form of discrimination?
3. In terms of the argument that the judgments of both the Turkish State and the ECHR result in the indirect discrimination of Şerife Yiğit, are there common prejudgments/premises/prejudices in these judgments that can be interpreted as discriminatory from a gender perspective?
4. Keeping in mind that religious marriage is a very widely practiced custom in Turkey and taking into consideration the 'negligence' of the Turkish State to enforce the law regarding religious marriages, discuss the

ECHR's argument from 'the margin of appreciation' in terms of its cogency.

5. How would have accounting for *Şerife Yiğit v. Turkey* case with an eye on the hermeneutical injustice problems that women in patriarchal societies suffer from contributed to a better assessment of the case by the ECHR?

References

Arnardóttir, Oddny M. (2007): Non-discrimination Under Article 14 ECHR: the Burden of Proof. In: The Scandinavian Studies in Law 51, pp. 13-40.

Aziz, Zarizana Abdul./Moussa, Janine.: (2015): The Due Diligence Principle and the Role of the State: Discrimination against Women in Family and Cultural Life, Report submitted to the United Nations Working Group on discrimination against women in law and in practice. Available from http://www.ohchr.org/Documents/Issues/Women/WG/Family/Written_Submissions/DDP_Submission_UNWG_Discr%20ag%20Women%20Family%20Cultural%20Life15.pdf (Accessed 10.1.2017)

Ahmad, Feroz (2014): From empire to republic. 2 vols. Istanbul: Bilgi University Press.

Anderson, Elizabeth (2012): Epistemic justice as a virtue of social institutions. In: Social epistemology: A journal of knowledge, culture and policy 26, 2, pp. 163-173.

Fredman, Sandra (2001): Equality: A new generation, In: Industrial Law Journal 30, 2, pp. 145-168.

Fricker, Miranda (2007): Epistemic Injustice: Power and the Ethics of Knowing. Oxford: Oxford University Press.

Frye, Marilyn. (2005): Oppression. In: Cudd, Ann/Andreas, Robin (eds.): Feminist Theory: a Philosophical Anthology. Malden: Blackwell Publishing, pp. 84-90.

General Recommendation no. 29 of the CEDAW Committee (26.2.2013, CEDAW/C/GC/29)

Joppke, Christian (2015): The Secular State under Siege: Religion and State in Europe and America. Cambridge: Polity.

Koğacıoğlu, Dicle (2004): The Tradition effect: Framing Honor Crimes in Turkey. In: differences: A Journal of Feminist Cultural Studies 15, 2, pp. 119-151.

Mardin, Şerif (2003): Laicism in Turkey. Istanbul: Konrad Adenauer Foundation Press.

Mardin, Şerif (2006): Religion, Society, and Modernity in Turkey. Syracuse: Syracuse University Press.

Parla, Ayşe (2001): The 'honor' of the State: Virginity Examinations in Turkey. In: Feminist Studies 27, 1, pp. 65-88.

Raday, Frances (2003). Culture, Religion and Gender. In: International Journal of Constitutional Law 1, 4, pp. 663-715.

Report of the Working Group on the issue of discrimination against women in law and in practice, United Nations General Assembly, Human Rights Council, A/HRC/29/40, 2 April 2015. Available from http://www.ohchr.org/Documents/Issues/Women/WG/Family/A.HRC.29.40_E.pdf (Accessed 10.1.2017)

Walsh, Judy/Ryan, Fergus. (2006): The Rights of *De Facto* Couples. The Irish Human Rights Commission (IHRC). Available from http://www.ucd.ie/esc/research/defacto.pdf (Accessed 10.1.2017)

Yourow, Howard C. (1996): The Margin of Appreciation Doctrine in the Dynamics of European Human Rights Jurisprudence. Dordrecht: Martinus Nijhoff.

Zürcher, Erik-Jan (2007a): Turkish Secularism in a European Context. In Nimrod, Goren/ Amikam, Nachmani (eds.): The Importance of Being European: Turkey, the EU, and the Middle East. Jerusalem: Hebrew University, pp. 131-140.

Zürcher, Erik-Jan (2007b): The Ottoman Legacy of the Kemalist Republic. In Touraj, Atabaki (ed.): The State and the Subaltern: Modernization, Society and the State in Turkey and Iran. London: I.B. Taurus, pp. 95-110.

Zürcher, Erik-Jan (2010): The Importance of Being Secular: Islam in the Service of the National and Pre-national State. In Kerslake, Celia/Oktem, Kerem/Robins, Philip (eds.) Turkey's Engagement with Modernity: Conflict and Change in the Twentieth Century. Basingstoke: Palgrave Macmillan, pp. 55-68.

Case law

Al-Nashif v. Bulgaria, no.50963/99, 20.6. 2002.

Belgium Linguistics Case – 'In the case "relating to certain aspects of the laws on the use of languages in education in Belgium" v Belgium' (Application no 1474/62; 1677/62; 1691/62; 1769/63; 1994/63; 2126/64), 23.7.1968.

Hoogendijk v. the Netherlands (dec.), no. 58641/00, 6.1.2005.

Hugh Jordan v. The United Kingdom, no. 24746/94, 4.5.2001.

K. and T. v. Finland [GC], no.25702/94. 12.7.2001.

Keegan v. Ireland, no 16969/90, 26.5.1994,

Johnston and Others v. Ireland, no. 9697/82, 18.12.1986.

Şerife Yiğit v. Turkey , [GC], no. 3976/05; 2.11.2010.

Thlimmenos v. Greece [GC], no. 34369/97, 06.04.2000

Van der Heijden v The Netherlands, , [GC], (no. 42857/05), 3.4. 2012.

Turkish Constitutional Court (CC), 27.5.2015 (Anayasa Mahkemesi Kararı, Esas Sayısı: 2014/36; Karar Sayısı: 2015/51)

Amel Grami

The Parity Law: Tunisian women's next battle

1 Introduction

Although Tunisian women participated massively in the Revolution of 14 January 2011 and affirmed themselves as political agents of change, they found themselves later victims of marginalization. The process of transition was in fact characterized by many attempts to exclude women from the public sphere, media, political participation and decision-making roles. Convinced that they should change this reality and claim their full rights and liberties as citizens, Tunisian women found themselves confronting a challenging patriarchal structure that still denies them their right to full equality and citizenship.

The mobilization of women's rights activists (at the level of both grassroots and institutional political participation) and feminist organizations highlights the active involvement in the improvement of women's rights and participation in socio-political transformations during the post-revolutionary transition. This article provides an assessment of the progress that has been made in Tunisia to promote equal rights and women's political participation since the revolution. It analyzes women's attempts to be included in the formation of the new regime against a background characterized by a debate on their actual situation, the perspectives of legislation on equality as well as the persisting gaps to be filled.

2 The Status of Tunisian Women: a historical overview

Tunisia has served as a model for women's rights in the Middle East and North Africa thanks to the promulgation of the Personal Status Code in 1956. The Code was established even before the adoption of the first post-independence constitution. The provisions of the PSC gave women a number of basic rights: Polygamy was abolished; the full consent of both parties is a pre-requisite to marriage and divorce may only take place in courts. The PSC also provided for a number of other issues that had burdened women, including the legalization of abortion. Tunisia was also one of the first countries in the Arab region to give women their right to vote in 1957 and shortly afterwards, the right to stand as a political candidate. Indeed, this legislation marked the beginning of the female egalitarianism process in Tunisia and created a new Tunisian identity centered on modern values and relative gender equality.

Habib Bourguiba, the first Tunisian president (1956-1987), made of women's equality in the public sphere a national policy. From 1956 to the mid-1970s, Tunisian girls and women increasingly took advantage of the newly acquired rights and freedoms. They pursued their education and they entered the workforce in record numbers; birth rates declined and a growing middle class emerged. A rise in the levels of urbanization, industrialization, and education led to an increase in women's awareness and mobilization. Moreover, economic and social conditions were conducive to the prominent roles offered to women by the new state. Indeed, the role of education in expanding the pool of feminist pioneers was important Tchaïcha, Jane D./ Arfaoui, Khedija (2012). Women felt qualified, motivated to stand for office and to participate in debates and reforms. Since that moment they become more visible.

Significant gains in women's rights and status are the result of decades of engagement by feminists. Feminist activism is still influential today using the established structures and new tools. Activists strategically used old and new communication technologies to achieve greater participation in the production and dissemination of knowledge and the establishment of alliances at inter/national levels to broaden their solidarity bases. This allowed women to overcome the censoring mechanisms of the state and the violence of conservative and fundamentalist groups.

Despite the implementation of a set of laws and women activists' efforts to push the Tunisian government under Bourguiba and later Ben Ali to adopt parity in electoral law, a gender gap is still visible at social and political levels and women's political participation has become a hot issue within the transition context since 2015.

Adoption of the Parity Law 2011 by the High Authority for the Achievement of the Objectives of the Revolution, Political Reform and Democratic Transition (HAAORPRDT)

It is important to note that both Bourguiba and Ben Ali used the strategy of instrumentalization of women's rights. The 'Woman question' has often been a symbolic terrain of political struggle. Tunisian women became both an alibi for and an emblem of cultural authenticity. They were transformed into symbols of the tensions between tradition and modernity, or between East and West.

Although many narratives celebrate the state's efforts to modernize the country and to empower women, society remained conservative. Moreover, old patriarchal structures still exist because reforms and gender policies were from above and the state failed to put provisions into practices and to change mentalities. According to Mounira Charrad, "The CPS was not a victory of feminism. It was the victory of a government strong enough to place a claim on Islam and enforce a reformist interpretation of the Islamic tradition" (Charrad 2011:108). We should acknowledge that many Tunisians consider that family laws constituted a radical shift in the interpretation of the Islamic laws.

If we look at the process of reform in Tunisia, we can say that it was highly symbolic because it signaled that both regimes were on the side of women's rights and only through the current rulers could further changes and reforms be achieved. It is no surprise that political parties, regardless of their different orientation and ideologies, denied women full and equitable access to positions of power within their leadership structure.

Under *Ben Ali* (1997-2011),[1] women held more than 20% of the seats in the Tunisian parliament (27.6% in the election of 2009). However, the political will to increase the number of women in the parliament did not enact a real democratic change in the country. The use of a quota system[2] by an unpopular dictator carried the danger of linking women's rights with an autocratic system of rule. Moreover, the effort of the state to increase women's quota served in reality to underscore the prevailing and popular image of a modern Tunisia. The problem is that gender quotas come at the expense of deeper reforms of the way in which candidates are selected and nominated. Yet Gender quotas may bring more women into the political arena but the dynamics of the process remain unchanged. In this respect, gender quotas reinforce the status quo, at least theoretically. The general perception was that women deputies were selected on the basis of their loyalty to the single party. They figured on the party's lists purely to boast the success of its gender policies and not on the basis of women's qualifications, their agendas or merit.

1 Zine el-Abidine Ben Ali was the second President of Tunisia. He assumed the presidency on 7 November 1987 in a bloodless coup d'état that ousted President Habib Bourguiba, who was declared incompetent. He ruled until the 14 January 2011 when after a month of protests, he was forced to flee the country to Saudi Arabia.

2 The insertion of political quotas is used to prove the commitment of the state to gender equality in the political system, but the legitimacy of gender quotas sparks debate. The use of quotas is far from creating a consensus among people, neither among its potential beneficiaries, nor among the others.

After the revolution (2011)[3], one of Tunisian women's dreams was to increase the number of women participants in political activities. All classes of women found 'political opportunities' to push for change even if they did not necessarily share the same ideology. Feminists aspired to implement the egalitarian model in other countries, particularly the Scandinavian model. They argued that the success story of Nordic gender equality was based on important women's inclusion into some formerly male dominated areas, basically the political sphere. The enthusiasm of women activists for the adoption of electoral gender quotas[4] was important. Sharing the belief that they are agents of change, women thought that it was the perfect time to adopt new strategies in order to change gender power relations and to make real change through politics.

It was evident to many women activists that improving the representation of women's interests in politics depends on: first increasing the presence of women in the parliament regardless of their ideologies and second through a form of 'constitutional parity'. As Brown et al. (2002), Camacho, Lara and Serrano (1997) and Reyes (2002) argue the demands for political rights emerge during periods of democratic transition or the creation of new democratic institutions as a means for guaranteeing the representation of traditionally underprivileged groups or establishing the national and international legitimacy of the new regime. Certainly, this was the case in Tunisia.

It is important to mention that Tunisian feminists benefited since 1980 from different networks: solidarity groups, Maghreb alliances such as *The Maghreb Collective of Autonomous Feminist Activists*, sharing experiences and learning new strategies. They turned to supranational institutions to put pressure on the state and to address the issues they felt were important. Al-Ali argues that one of the factors "which have helped the rise of independent women's organizations in some countries is the increased influence of international constituencies" (Al-Ali 2015:5) giving the examples of the United Nations and the World Bank. Also, the new political and social environment allows women activists to openly demand the implementation of parity law. The ability of women to produce alternative discourses and images about womanhood, citizenship, and political participation in their society was clear. Feminists were creating alternative discursive spaces where it was possible to

3 The Arab Spring started in Tunisia, it is often maintained, when a young Tunisian man Mohammed Bouazizi from the small town of Sidi Bouzid set himself on fire 17 December 2010, after having had problems with the local authorities when selling his fruits from a road-side stand. This event became a catalyst for the following uprisings in several Arab countries.

4 Feminist organizations claimed for a radical quota system. The so-called 'zipper-system' implies that 50% of the candidates shall be women, 50% men, and further men and women shall alternate throughout the candidate lists. If a candidate list does not comply with the rules, it will not be allowed to participate in the elections.

redefine patriarchal gender roles while questioning the socio cultural, economic, political, and legal institutions constraining them.

Rather than continuing the women's quotas system of the previous regime (20%), Tunisia's transitional government chose to implement a vertical zipper requirement for electoral lists. The reason behind this decision is that Tunisian quota policies may not have the aspired effect on the public. Problems of gender equality, perceived as something that is dealt with within the sphere of state intervention, are not often framed as a matter of broader public concern.

3 State Feminism

The state reforms represented the vision of a charismatic leader: Bourguiba the founder of the Republic. The new Republican Tunisian woman represented the modern, secular, westernized state. She was expected to talk, to behave and dress according to the modes decided and implemented by the State. No one can deny that state feminism under Bourguiba was grounded in a type of paternalism. He was called 'the father and the leader of the nation'. We should acknowledge that quotas as expression of state feminism 'from above' failed to temper the public gender-equality discourse and to change mindsets. The issue was promoted inviting action in both political and civil society organizations work. This benefited from a political opportunity structure, a growing consciousness of women themselves and a significant mobilization by women's organizations enlisting the support of international organizations such as the Association of Tunisian Democratic Women (ATFD), the Association of Tunisian Women for Research and Development (AFTURD) and other newly emerging associations such as 'Egalité et Parité' and 'Ligue des Electrices Tunisiennes'. The ideological commitment of a few politicians to gender equality and visible political have also contributed to sustaining the momentum.

Thanks to the support of many intellectuals, activists in the Tunisian Labor Union (UGTT), in the ATFD, in the Tunisian League for the Defense of Human Rights (LTDH) and in AFTURD as well as inside the High Authority for the Achievement of the Revolution Objectives, Political Reform, and Democratic Transition (HAARO) that supported gender parity from the beginning going along with a range of relevant protocols and structures (for example, CEDAW...), the campaign for parity was further embedded within a global dimension of women's rights and political empowerment.[5]

5 For more information see: Gender in the new Tunisian Constitution – UNDP Fact Sheet (28-1-2014) http://iknowpolitics.org/en/2014/01/gender-new-tunisian-constitution-undp-fact-sheet, accessed 19-08-2015.

In May 2011, the High Authority for the Achievement of the Revolution Objectives, Political Reform, and Democratic Transition (HAARO) adopted the Gender Parity Law. The law clearly obliges political parties to submit candidate lists that present men and women in an alternate manner, with the male-female ratio to be as close to 50% as possible. Article 16 of the Electoral Law stated that:

> *"Applications to candidacy are made on the basis of the principle of equality between women and men by ranking the candidates in lists alternating between them. Lists that do not respect this principle will be rejected, except in the case of an odd number of reserved seats in certain constituencies."*[6]

4 Women's Political Participation in the 2011 Election

While the so called 'Democratic block' (secular, liberal and leftists parties) were initially reluctant in their support to gender parity law and tried to exclude women from political leadership, *Ennahda* Islamist party decided to empower a group of women for pragmatic purposes. If we look at the reasons behind this attitude we find that those parties did not feel that they had a base level of female membership from which to draw 50% of their candidates. According to some political leaders,[7] women were reluctant to participate and were resistant to political activity particularly in a context of polarization between seculars and Islamists. No political party questioned its own failure to attract or convince women to run for elections. One exception was the Democratic Modernist Pole (*Pole Démocratique Moderniste*), which was the only party to apply the principle of parity in choosing the heads of their electoral lists.16 women were at the head of its 33 lists. We should keep in mind that many left wing, progressive, liberal and activist women joined the Democratic Modernist Pole after the revolution.

Women were in fact at the head of electoral lists on only 7% of political party lists, on 3% of independent lists, and on 35% of coalition lists. Of these 153 elected heads of lists, only 14 were women. This gave women 49 seats out of the 217 seats of the NCA (National Constituent Assembly),[8] that is 27% of the seats. Misogynic attitudes reflect, on the one hand, how women

6 For the full text of the 2011 electoral law, see: http://www.legislation-securite.tn/fr/node/30432

7 More than 60 political parties which stood for election did comply with the quota rules, alternating women and men throughout their candidate lists.

8 The National Constituent Assembly (*Assemblée Nationale Constituante*) was elected on 2011 and was charged with the task of writing a new constitution, but has also issued some new regulations.

are seen and utilized in the political sphere. At the same time, this shows how parties defending themselves as progressive and modernist manipulate women's rights. In addition, this attitude sends a message that sexism is still impacting women's political participation and can be an obstacle for all women seeking elective office and willing to achieve full gender parity. This can shed light on the outcomes of gender relations in the transition process.

Despite this hostile environment, women's participation in elections and campaigns was very successful with women being increasingly visible and partaking in political action on the ground. About 5000 women candidates participated in the 2011 election. Women also held several positions of power within the NCA. Yet the majority faced many challenges: exclusion because of dominant behavior, verbal violence and even marginalization from central party structures and decision taking processes. Women members of the NCA did not constitute a homogenous group. With diverse educational levels, professional backgrounds and age difference ranging from 23 years at the time of the election (the youngest NCA member) to 70 years old, women deputies were above all characterized by their diverse political experiences and ideological leanings. Some of them were vocal while others kept silent and remained invisible. Nonetheless, many succeeded in becoming a voice calling for change and defending issues beyond the scope of women's rights.

Although Tunisia has been known for the visible role of secular and liberal women in society (most of whom are well known in the history of women's movements), the majority of these activists were underrepresented in the constitutional body elected in 2011, particularly in comparison with Islamist women. Many of the leading figures of the women's movements and organizations were criticized and often publicly denounced for having kept silent about the injustices against Islamists. As Gana noted, "Although the regime's heavy involvement angered and alienated feminist activists, shared opposition to the perceived threat of Islamists' misogyny united them in partial alliance with Ben Ali and strained partnership developed between the two sides" (Marks 2013:232 in The Making of the Tunisian Revolution: Contexts, Architects, Prospects, ed. Nouri Gana. Edinburgh University Press (2013)).

Conservative forces played an important role in blocking opportunities for women to run for the 2011 election. For the majority of people, the empowerment of women had already gone too far while men were being victimized and disempowered. The belief that men have lost power and status was often enmeshed with a 'blaming' discourse that it was women who had brought about men's disempowerment and loss of his traditional social status. Even recent social problems such as unemployment have often been blamed on women's empowerment.

Despite the longstanding reverence for the Code of Personal Status,[9] there is a growing anti-Bourguiba sentiment that has emerged in the last decade among certain conservative segments of the population who believe that Bourguiba's social advances in education and work, many of which have benefited women, came about at the expense of Islamic religious identity and values. Tunisian society seems to resist state enacted legal rules. Ancestral habits, somewhat redefined, still persist.

Being aware of the impact of the emergence of Salafist movements and the power of religious groups using violence against women, secular and liberal women who succeeded to win seats positioned themselves as the voice of progressive women. They defended a social and legal order characterized by women's historical gains and social status. On the other side, the majority of women of the Islamist party *Ennahdha* tried to distinguish themselves from this movement and did not identify themselves as activists defending women and women's rights. They rather sought to be identified as engaged in political action within a broader Islamist movement.

Because of its success in winning several seats in each constituency, *Ennahda* party had the highest number of women in the NCA. 42 out of the 49 women elected to the NCA were from this Islamist party. Most of them did not have strong human rights backgrounds or a history of active participation in women's organization and rights. Some women think that their role in the NCA consisted in familiarizing themselves with the rules and guidelines of the political role they had to play, formulating strategies based on this knowledge.

From the ideological perspective, we can say that *Ennahda* NCA women members remained loyal to male political leaders in the party who encouraged them to run for the election. One deputy from *Ennahda* said she did not feel like she was ready to be a viable candidate prior to the October 23-elections, and had to discuss her political prospects with her father, fiancé and friends to dispel her concerns (Joline 2012). Obviously the influence of men on women, from outside the political and inside the political sphere, persisted and decided on their performance as NCA members. There was no common drive or objective bringing women at the NCA together on the basis of a common objective or a program benefiting and enhancing their socio-political situation. Regardless of their ideological background, women in the NCA can be divided into two groups: those who had a feminist conscientiousness or awareness and those who did not. Also, women's levels of gen-

9 This has been considered to be one of the most revolutionary family law codes in the Arab world and governs several critical areas including marriage, divorce, inheritance and child custody. The Code, preceding the 1959 Tunisian Constitution by three years and improved in 1992 and 1997, has guaranteed that Tunisian women are full citizens with full rights.

der consciousness varied according to socio-demographic characteristics and political ideology, with some women feeling no sense of group identification with other women at all.

The majority of women deputies from *Ennahda* accepted to be members in the Constituent Assembly by virtue of their familial relationships or close ties with officials and power holders at the central level. This situation was possible because under the proportional representation system used in the elections, people did not choose individual candidates, but parties. As a result, some of these candidates did not pass through a selection process and most likely were not interested in women's rights and not equipped to articulate the needs of their constituents.

5 The Debate on the Parity Law in the NCA – 2014

The Tunisian transition was characterized by a heated debate between the 'seculars' and the religious forces inside and outside the NCA. The process of drafting a new constitution reflected anxiety surrounding the place of religion in the new political system, how Tunisia's Arab Muslim identity should be expressed, the gender relationship and the role of law among other major political hot issues. The controversies have not been limited to the NCA; they have also taken place within society and in the media (websites, Facebook, Twitter, TV, Radio...). For this reason the ideological divide between deputies about gender parity law inside the NCA was very important.

Despite the fact that the number of secular and liberal women in the NCA was low, they played an important role in defending their rights. Feminists proposed that language be restructured in the Constitution to eschew sexism in recognition that the era of 'male-only' representation in texts is past, and in the 21st century, women have made enough impact in political and social life to deserve better representation on the pages of national documents. Also, activists believe that guaranteeing either gender specific or universal rights offers better protection to women than not having any constitutional commitment to the right at all. Although they benefited from the parity law, some women deputies from *Ennahda* were against it. Notably for the first time *Ennahda* representatives were split in their vote, they had failed to maintain party mass vote and consensus as instructed by the committee's recommendations. When the vote was over and the national anthem was sung, yelling broke out in the NCA, with the more extreme Islamists denouncing the result. This group of women refused to obey men's orders in their attempt to promote *Ennahda* as a moderate Islamic party. On the contrary, they preferred to defend Islamic values and traditional gender roles. The argument presented by this group of women was that positive discrimination violated the constitutional guarantee of equality but the reality shows that they were against full equality. Most of *Ennahda* NCA female members were conservative and did not conflict with society's traditions and male domination. To some of them, the fight against the old regime was a universal one, and there was no need to make it a gender-specific battle.

It is important to note that women deputies from *Ennahda* supported in 2012 their party's proposal for Art. 28 involving replacing the provisions of full equality in the Constitution by 'complementarity'. The project recognized women as a distinct group within the family and the moral foundation of society rather than referring to universal principles of human rights. Engaged in discussion, those women justified their passive positions by the desire to strictly observe religion and local cultural peculiarity to avoid the consequences of such universal rights. Such attitude highlights the intersection of gender and ideology and its implications for understanding women's political activism. It shows how Islamists (in Tunisia, Egypt, Jordan, Morocco and other countries) interpret and practice gender relations within the framework of Islam. But while *Islamist* women generally upheld a religious ideal of complementary gender roles, their actual practice often contradicted with and contested this ideal. Some women liberated themselves by means of education and by acquiring skills. They were against polygamy and the exclusion of women from important memberships. This shows the impact of feminism, education and urbanization which produced tremendous changes in religious practices, perceptions and visions.

Evidently, the women's movement in Tunisia has played an important role in influencing parliamentary positions on women's issues, especially on the family protection bill. But female parliamentarians are not necessarily sympathetic toward the women's movement. Even though we find many narratives celebrating the Tunisian model, the position of some Islamist deputies reflects the divide between Tunisian women. The divided attitude and votes of the women on key constitutional provisions reveal an important disparity regarding the status of women, in general and the impossibility of reaching a unified voice or vision for the future of women in Tunisia. There is a multiplicity of views but no clear perspective or common ground. Many women activists, even with their good will, have not been able to identify a background or a referent on which to build a common vision for women's rights in Tunisia. Many women's organizations failed initially to coordinate their movements and bring their voices to the political sphere. The ideological divide in the NCA was also visible at the level of the public spheres and other spaces including universities and the media. Indeed, studying conservative women's advocacy shows where feminism has made an impact and what lessons can be learned for the future.

In January 2014, despite resistance, political participation for men and women became constitutionally guaranteed and the principle of equality was enshrined in the new electoral law. This was achieved partially because the symbolic battle over the terms to be used in the provisions were challenged in the streets as women staged important protests denouncing the strange and ambiguous concepts Islamists tried to push through, making the Constitution a document with ambiguous terms. The term 'complementarity', contested widely as having no legal or human rights implication was dropped. This paved the way for other provisions to include clearly and explicitly the principle of equality. It is clear that the patriarchal positions of conservative parliamentarians, men and women, did not affect the voting pattern. Article 24 guarantees women's representation in all elected bodies (116-40 with 32 abstentions).This article requires 50/50 representation of male and female candidates on all lists. Further, Article 25 requires that every electoral list in a constituency with four seats or more must have at least one candidate under the age of 35 among the four top candidates on the list.

6 Disparities between Law and Practice in the Campaign for the 2014 Elections

The election of more women to the parliament and the support of female candidates running for the presidency had been a goal of women's movements for over two decades. In 2014, only 4 women dared practice their constitutional right in running for presidency but only one, *Kalthoum Kanou* who was a judge, was able to garner more than 15,000 signatures from across the country. She was the first Tunisian woman presidential candidate seeking a post higher than that of a parliamentarian. In fact, Kanou was an initiator in making something new happen. She was leading her campaign in all districts trying to explain her program. Also, *Kanou* was on the media discussing politics and negotiating her views with others candidates. There is no doubt that *Kanou* contributed to breaking the 'psychological barrier' that kept women from running for the highest office. The decision of *Kanou* was in fact a symbolic move. She was sending a letter of hope for the coming generations saying that it was possible for Tunisian women to consider and seek this post.

It is important to note that many political parties tried to gain women's support by placing women's issues on the political and electoral agenda. For this reason, women appeared to have just made up the majority of voters. According to some international reports, 50.5% of registered voters were women.[10] Despite the establishment of electoral 'gender parity', women aspiring to be deputy in the new parliament were often sidelined in the run-up to the parliamentary and presidential elections in 2014 for political and socio-economic reasons:

- Lacking trust and tradition, many women did not have any interest or motivation to run for the parliament or for other positions.
- A gender gap in political knowledge, activity and skills as well as lack of access to well-developed education and training systems for women's leadership in general, and for orienting young women towards political life.
- Lack of belief that politics can lead to positive change. Also, some rural women believe that politics is exclusively a male domain and they underestimate the importance of their political voice.
- Lack of solidarity and support among women. The creation of an informal women caucus was proposed within the NCA. However, internal disagreements and above all the reluctance of parties to see some of their women members acting outside their control quickly brought this initiative to an end. Feminists have been reluctant to work within a religious framework for a better outreach; they limited their work only within a human rights framework and avoided any religion-based arguments.
- Women activists didn't succeed to bring young women to the struggle for women's rights. Young women have been in the leadership of activism for democracy, but they didn't give priority to the objectives of gender equality, they had other priorities.
- Lack of party support. Most political parties, both Islam-oriented and secular, continued their patriarchal practices and insisted on maintaining outdated political positions despite the societal changes that occurred over the past decades. The male dominance of internal party structures is a real obstacle for women's higher political participation. There are no traditions or newly established provisions at the level of party structure and by-laws that obligated the nomination of women in political decision-making positions.
- The nature of the electoral system, which may or may not be advantageous for women candidates. The structure of voting amplified the systematic male preference. Using a proportional list-based voting system places great emphasis on the order of the candidates on the list. The proportion of votes received per party determines in fact how many candi-

10 (http://www.gnrd.net/GNRD%20%26%20IIPJHR%20JOINT%20MISSION%20TO%20TUNISIAN%20PARLIAMENTARY%20ELECTIONS%202014%20REPOR.pdf), accessed 22-7-2015.

dates, starting from the top of the list, will become deputies. Due to the paucity of female-headed lists, the proportion of men elected far outpaced that of women.

- The existence of a set of stereotypes such as the belief that women did not have the temperament or capability to participate in politics, or that women belong to the private sphere or that women are incapable of providing political leadership. Stereotypes were codified in political thought. The parties, through their management, continue to devalue women and perpetuate stereotypes. Fundamentally, there is no real conviction of the need to involve women and the role that they could provide.
- Political parties remain 'private clubs for men'. A 'politics of men's solidarity' places restrictions on policymaking within the gender-equality field. The resistance of the majority of deputies and political leaders against setting 'women' up against 'men' was important and visible.
- The prevalence of the 'masculine model' of political life and of elected government bodies. For *Nidaa Tounes* (liberal party), that presents itself as the defender of women's rights and the most feminist party, the low level of women as heads of party lists is a result of the country's political realities: choosing heads of lists "is not a matter of taking a specific position to make history, but instead involves caring about efficiency… we have only been concerned with competence and efficiency in order to win elections" (Dami 2014).
- In some cases, the perceptions of female politicians were dominated by images and judgments associated with their party more than their gender. In the 2014 election, many women candidates from the Congress for the Republic (CPR) or the Democratic Forum for Labor and Liberties *(Attakatol),* for example, failed to attract support because of policies taken by leaders of those parties against liberties and in favor of the islamization of the country.
- Lack of female political role models who may have an 'empowering' effect on marginalized groups, leading them to be more aware of and responsive to their representative's policy record. It is important to emphasize that the lack of women appointed to top government posts in the transitional government had an important impact on women's choices.
- Cultural attitudes toward the role of women in politics. According to many political leaders and voters, it is more difficult for women to achieve credibility and attract supporters because conservative norms remain important in society.
- Cultural and religious barriers. Women who do make the choice to go into politics have to deal with societal judgments or their own feeling of

guilt because of choosing politics over their families. Family care responsibilities often limit the work and contributions of women. More women than men have problems handling the pressure of management positions.

- Islamist Channels played an important role in emphasizing the place of women in society. Conservative radical preachers made of TV a powerful pulpit from which they could reach Muslims all over the world and sensitize them to a more conservative interpretation of Islam (Lynch 2012; Tchaïcha and Arfaoui 2012).
- Women dispose of less resources to participate in politics. Time to participate in politics is a critical resource.
- Lack of media coverage of women candidates. Many qualified women were invisible during their campaign.
- Lack of sustained contact and cooperation of some candidates with other public organizations such as the trade unions and women's groups.
- The impact of economic crises on women's condition. The resurgence of 'traditional' values is in some ways complemented by the economic changes taking place. Indeed, economic development may also have indirect effects. As Richard Matland notes: "Development leads to weakening of traditional values, decreased fertility rates, increased urbanization, greater educational and labor force participation for women, and attitudinal changes in perceptions of the appropriate roles for women" (Matland 1998:114).

All these factors show where and why gender equality was in a dead lock. We should keep in mind that the process of writing the new constitution was influenced by many events such as strong polarization and political violence. In that specific context, it was not easy to learn how to discuss and reach some compromise. Moreover, historical, social and structural factors influenced the legislative activities of both female and male legislators. We should take into account that the historical marginalization of women and the construction of gender norms have long-lasting effects on the levels and patterns of activity.

The adoption of parity law reveals the interplay between gender and the specific country context. As Tønnessen notes, "there is an array of gender ideologies at play, some fiercely calling for equality between the sexes, others advocating equity and complementarity between men and women and some take it even further and demand gender segregation" (Tønnessen 2013: 4). Also, it reflects the impact of the process of democratization on gender relations. At first glance, it would appear that parity law and positive action policies emphasize women's inclusion dynamic but there has been resistance to opening up the power structures. Recently, resistance of men in politics to put the parity principle into action is even more visible. Although many scholars avoid using the concept of 'crisis of masculinity', it is my contention that the impact of 'crisis of masculine identity' on everyday lives of women is part of the factors impacting the post-revolution politics of gender. Recently we witness the birth of new style of militarized masculinity and a subservient femininity that embrace violence denouncing equality and universal rights in the name of a more radical, 'good' and 'pure' Islam.

7 Conclusion

According to the gender parity requirement in the Constituent Assembly elections 2011, which specifies that every other name on a list must be a woman theoretically, men and women should have equal representation in the new Constituent Assembly. However in 2011, only 49 women have received seats in the NCA, out of a total 217 seats, (42 from *Ennahda*) making their representation in the Assembly approximately 24% of the body.

Regarding the substantial disparity between the number of female candidates and the resulting number of female deputies we can say that the issue remains the divide between laws and cultures at all levels of practice, whether it is political structures, social structures or even institutions. Many male political leaders understood parity law as a tool to win votes. For this reason they encourage some female members in their parties to run for the election but they refuse at the same time to put them on the top of the list. This way of interpreting Article16 and Article 23 which uses language nearly identical to the 2011 electoral law: "Nominations to candidacy are made based on the principle of parity between women and men and the rule of alternation between them on the [electoral] list. Any list not respecting this principle will be rejected, except in the case of an odd number of reserved seats in some districts"[11] is related to religious norms and patriarchal ways of interpreting religious texts such as a hadith (sayings) attributed to the Prophet *Muhammed*: "A nation which entrusts its affairs to a woman shall never prosper" or else "A woman may not lead a man in Prayer, nor may a Bedouin lead a believer of the Muhajirun or a corrupt person lead a committed Muslim in Prayer" or else "The best rows for men are the first rows, as opposed to the last ones, and the best rows for women are the last ones as opposed to the first ones".

---

11 For the full text of the electoral law passed, see: http://majles.marsad.tn/fr/lois/loi_electorale/chapitre/1.

As a result of this narrow understanding of the concept of parity, political parties restricted women's political participation. Similarly, the heads of *Ennahda* lists were male-dominated. However, the relative popularity of this party in comparison to individual secular parties ensured that more than just the candidates at the head of the lists were elected. This resulted in the election of a higher number of female deputies in comparison to secular ones, despite similarly narrow definitions of parity.

Evidently women's political participation in post revolution Tunisia (2011-2014) highlights how gender equality is understood. For some political leaders and activists, this participation is in terms of a harmonious, linear process of gradual development, whereas, for other politicians gender equality is typically understood in terms of a gender-power system, conflicting interests and political deficiencies. The analysis of some political discourses shows differences in the way gender equality is understood and addressed in public. It helps us also understand how national elite groups provide different meanings, strategies and arguments in order to respond to some crucial questions such as the reason why all the interim governments reduced the numbers of women in decision making or why top positions in office, nationally and locally, are still dominated by men even after the adoption of the new constitution and promises given by the newly elected *Nida* leaders to support women's participation according to parity principles.

Indeed, considerable progress has been made in the protection of gender-specific constitutional rights in Tunisia. The new constitution is an important channel for entrenching women's equal right to vote and access positions of leadership in government. However, the continued underrepresentation of women in elective office remains puzzling. Women who were meaningfully involved in the constitution-making process, argue that their rights must be fully protected and defendable and must not be subordinate to men's will, customary or religious laws. According to them, the success of Tunisia's democracy will depend on its newly elected leaders to defend the Constitution and protect the rights of all Tunisian citizens. For the first time the concept of 'parity democracy' was discussed. No one can deny that the process of democratization illuminates how variations in the nature of the ruling parties enabled the mobilization of different aspects of women's identity.

Since 2014, women's groups and other members of civil society started to be more vocal about the incompatibility of some government choices (nomination of ministers and governors) with Tunisia's constitutional guarantee of gender equality. Article 46 provides that the State has a responsibility to protect the established rights of women and strengthen and develop these rights. It also obliges the State to ensure that men and women enjoy equal opportunities and have access to all levels of responsibility in all domains. Moving from the status of protected groups by the state, women themselves became protectors of the process of democratization defending accountability and respect of laws.

Women activists are aware of the necessity of future activism. Obviously, the new struggle of Tunisian women is to change the mentality, gender and power relations. For them 'blind loyalty' in descriptive representatives may diminish accountability for substantive representation. Additionally, women are strongly determinate to reform gender parity law and to push the new government to adopt a good strategy for a better representation of women in the government and political parties. Despite their ideological differences many activists (Secular, liberal and Islamists) are against the continual utilization of women's rights as a mechanism of state power or political Islam and consolidation, under the guise of modernism, upholding the image of a progressive Tunisia. Today, some Islamist women are defending the parity law and willing to be active members in their parties. All of them are seeking to define their own means of activism and wish to be autonomous from any oversight, both political and organizational. Will they succeed to liberate themselves from political male domination? There is perhaps more room for optimism in Tunisia. Evidence of this can be seen in the mobilization of many activists as well as women's organizations. Indeed, Tunisian women have a lot to do in order to affirm their full citizenship. The journey began a long time ago and will certainly continue with fervent enthusiasm.

Discussion Questions

1. In what way have Tunisian women's and feminist organizations changed their agendas in relation to the improvement of women's rights and participation in socio-political transformations during the post-revolutionary transition?
2. What are the socio-political conditions that make the reforms possible or encourage policy makers to make them?
3. Is there one single meaning to the concept 'parity'?

References

Al-Ali, Nadje S. (2015): Women's Movements in the Middle East: Case Studies of Egypt and Turkey. Geneva: United Nations Research Institute for Social Development. Retrieved from: core.ac.uk/download/pdf/2788043.pdf (Accessed: 5 August 2015).

Brown, Alice/Barnett Donaghy, Tahnya/Mackay, Fiona/Meehan, Elizabeth (2002): Women and Constitutional Change in Scotland and Northern Ireland. In: Parliamentary Affairs 55, pp. 71-84.

Camacho, Rosalia/Lara, Silvia/Serrano, Madrigal E. (1997): Las cuotas mínimas de participación de las mujeres: Un mecanismo de acción afirmativa: aportes para la discusión. San José, Costa Rica: Centro Nacional para el Desarrollo de la Mujer y la Familia, Promoción de la Ciudadanía Activa de las Mujeres.

Charrad, Mounira (2011): Tunisia at the forefront of the Arab world: two waves of gender legislation. In: Sadiqi, Fatima/Ennaji, Moha (eds.): Women in the Middle East and North Africa: Agents of Change. London: Routledge, pp. 105-114.

Dami, Samira (2014): Tunisie: Femmes et listes électorales – Les 'têtes' sont ailleurs...In: All Africa. September 4. Retrieved from: http://fr.allafrica.com/stories/201409040998.html (Accessed: 12 February 2015).

Joline, Courtney (2012): Women in Post Revolutionary Tunisia: Political Inclusion and Prospects for the Future. Independent Study Project (ISP) Collection, 1272. Retrieved from: http://digitalcollections.sit.edu/isp_collection/1272 (Accessed: 1 January 2014).

Lynch, Marc (2012): The Arab Uprising: The Unfinished Revolutions of the New Middle East. New York: Public Affairs.

Marks, Monica (2013): Women's Rights before and after the Revolution. In: Gana, Nouri (ed.): The Making of the Tunisian Revolution: Contexts, Architects, Prospects. Edinburgh: Edinburgh: University Press, pp. 224-251.

Matland, Richard E. (1998): Women's Representation in National Legislatures: Developed and Developing Countries. In: Legislative Studies Quarterly, 23 (1), pp. 109-125.

Reyes, Socorro L. (2002): Quotas for Women for Legislative Seats at the Local Level in Pakistan. In: International IDEA, Perempuan di Parlemen: Bukan Sekedar Jumlah. Stockholm: International IDEA.

Tchaïcha, Jane D./Arfaoui, Khedija (2012): Tunisian women in the twenty-first century. Past achievements and present uncertainties in the wake of the Jasmine Revolution. In: The Journal of North African Studies 17 (2), pp. 215–238.

Tonnessen, Liv (2013): Marriage is politics: Prospects for Women's Equality after the Arab Spring. In: CMI Insight 1. Retrieved from: https://www.cmi.no/publications/file/4761-marriage-is-politics.pdf (Accessed: 22 July 2015).

Gender and Diversity Studies: concepts and methods

Anna Temkina and *Elena Zdravomyslova*

From Discovery to Politicization: the trajectory of Russian gender studies

1 Introduction

In this paper we focus on the trajectory of gender studies in Russia within the last two decades. Currently Gender Studies is threatened by the hegemonic conservative ideology in Russia. The political arena largely influences the academic field and public sociology. The intersection of the political and academic field in the current Russian context has made academia submit to the State promoted ideology by restricting the autonomy of social sciences. The authoritarian turn in the Russian political regime in combination with the hegemonic conservative ideology has led to the implementation of several laws and launching of ideological campaigns in the 2010s. Media is dominated by the ideology and propaganda of the State, legitimized by issues related to national security controlled through financial aids. In this chapter, we address the impact of the intersection of authoritarianism and conservatism on the field gender studies.

In this piece we discuss the uneasy development of gender studies in Russia.[1] We focus on the Russian context of 'doing gender studies', highlighting the dilemmas we faced. For empirical evidence we concentrate mainly on our own experiences in the Gender Studies Program at the European University in St. Petersburg, but we also refer to the other cases of Gender

1 This piece is a slightly edited version of the article by Temkina and Zdravomyslova (2014).

Studies Centers in Russia. We observe how the political and academic context of the 1990s created opportunities for academic innovations that ideologically challenged Soviet patriarchy and invoked gendered criticisms of post-Soviet changes. We discuss the effects of the rapid but partial institutionalization of gender studies in the Russian academic context and how gender became the umbrella term for both feminist and anti-feminist standpoints in 1990s. We claim that since international support for the gender studies diminished in the 2000s, the trend and economic benefit of doing gender studies has declined, with only a small group of researchers maintaining their commitment to the feminist approach to gender. We focus on the politicization of gender studies in the last decade of Putin's Russia and the role of feminist researchers in the analysis of the new cultural conservatism, as expressed in gender ideology.

2 The 'Discovery' of the Gender Approach within the Sociological Profession

We became involved in gender studies in the early 1990s. Our interest resulted from the overlapping of our professional careers and the political and institutional environment. We entered sociology during the Soviet period, when the discipline was under control of the State apparatus (Firsov 2012).

Gorbachev's reforms of glasnost and democratization (called the period of Perestroika: 1985-1991) opened doors of opportunities for the Russian academia. Sociology began to play an indispensable and meaningful role in supporting democratic reforms and criticizing the existing regime. It became clear to us that sociology and democratic reforms would advance hand-in-hand. The possibilities of institutionalizing sociology were dependent on the new political regime. Without the consolidation of democracy and civil society, empirical sociology as a professional enterprise would be distorted being under the party-State censorship.

During Perestoika we conducted a research on social movements and the emerging civil society. During this time western researchers took the opportunity to study Russia in transition, while Russian scholars were able to further their academic knowledge through international networks made through exchange programs and joint research projects. Our participation in IREX, an exchange program organized by the United States of America in the early 1990's, helped us advance our knowledge in the field of sociology. Most western researchers we met were interested in knowing about Russian gender practices; on the one hand, issues related to gender equality, women's emancipation and women's role in the domestic sphere and paid labour, and on the other hand, the existence of sexism, patriarchy and the absence of men's participation in reproductive work. An 'outside perspective' legitimized the problem areas within the existing gender relations in society and highlighted the inconsistency between discourses and practices. The international academy introduced us to the institutional nature of feminist research, academic centers for women and gender studies and the study of gender inequalities from a philosophical standpoint.

Our effort to understand the political transformations in Russia led us to examine the absence of feminist mobilization in the process of democratization in Eastern Europe and post-Soviet space. The very term 'feminism' was considered abusive and irrelevant in spite of recognition of gender glass ceiling in waged labour and low representation of women in politics. Such issues as sexual harassment and domestic violence hardly interested Russian researchers. But why? Did it mean that such phenomena did not exist? No, this was not true. The answers to these questions did not emerge clearly or immediately. These circumstances brought us a new awareness of our roles as feminists who are committed to academic research in the field of gender studies. Our professional goal was the 'happy marriage' of sociologically informed gender studies and qualitative research methodology

We considered gender studies not only an academic field, but also a platform for feminist conscious-raising efforts and public debate. Through our research we aimed at spreading awareness about feminist and gender related issues relevant to the Russian society, which were repressed by the Soviet State policies (see also Zdravomyslova 2013).

To summarize, the overlapping of our socio-political background, our academic interest in collective mobilization, our active participation in social movements, our increased awareness with our experiences in the western world urged us to apply the new knowledge we had gained in the field of gender studies to the Russian context.

3 Dilemmas of the 'Gender-flavoured' 1990s[2]

Perestroika had given rise to feminist initiatives in the sphere of academia and civic activis Crisis centers for women, shelters providing refuge from domestic violence and institutions for gender studies came to be established as an after-effect of Perestroika. Between 1991 and 1992, two conventions

2 Irina Zherebkina's book 'Gender-flavoured 1990s' (2003) focuses on the post-Soviet transformations of gender representations in the 1990s. We use this metaphor to signify this period and the comparatively favourable political and ideological conditions for the development of gender studies in Russia.

for women's NGO'S, namely the All Russia Forums of Women's NGO'S, were organized by Russian activists with the support of international feminist organizations which took interest in issues related to gender and development in Eastern Europe and post-Soviet countries. Gender studies, undoubtedly played a crucial role at these events.

3.1 The Rise of Gender Studies

As international assistance increased, the membership of research institutes and NGOs began to overlap, reflecting a habitus shared by academic feminists and their partners in civil society. We were oriented towards developing our professional careers; participated in the democratic civic activism during the Perestroika period; were involved in international academic feminist networks; recognized the existence of gender inequalities in Russian society; shared democratic liberal values; and believed in the importance of public intellectuals in the process of democratization of the Russian society.

Academic feminists in the CIS (Commonwealth of Independent States) became more active in the 1990s. Some of them initiated new educational programs and seminars; others launched new gender studies' centers in Universities and registered them as NGOs. To name those which were important for us: the Moscow Center for Gender Studies in the Institute of Demography of the Russian Academy of Sciences (N. Rimashevskaya, A. Posadskaya, O. Voronina, E. Kochkina), Centers for Gender Studies at Tver University' (V. Uspenskaya, N. Kozlova), Samara University (L. Popkova, I. Tartakovskaya), Saratov Technical University (P. Romanov, E. Yarskaya-Smirnova), Kharkov University (Ukraine: Irina and Sergei Zherebkins) and European Humanitarian University in Minsk (Belarus: E. Gapova, A. Usmanova). We have been collaborating with these institutions until date.

The Russian academic authorities looked favorably at these institutional innovations. But, why? There were two sets of reasons – politics and economy.

During the Presidency of Boris Yeltsin, the newly established Russian state was seeking integration into international politics. As the Russian Federation earlier ratified the UN Convention on the Elimination of All Forms of Discrimination against Women (in 1981), it was in this context that the state authorities supported education and research as well as corresponding organizations with a similar agenda. The second set of reasons for the favorable disposition toward gender studies was the sorry state of the budget in the Russian academy, which had lost a substantial share of its funding from the government. This encouraged the administration of academic institutions and universities to support new projects that promised to bring international grants. The creation of centers for gender studies, based on international institutional and financial support was at the same time welcomed by academic managers, who hoped to improve the economic situation, if not to salvage academic institutions by innovative projects. Thus, the new gender centers helped the academy to survive economically and renovate substantially. The political and economic situation thus encouraged academic entrepreneurship, and feminist researchers, although very few at the time, used this chance of institutionalization gender studies centers.

However, the key objectives that we set for ourselves were inspired by the principles of public sociology (Burawoy 2008) – our aims were not purely academic but also political – the knowledge was seen as the instrument to facilitate gender equality and to fight against sexism. A significant part of our agenda was gender education, both for academics and for the wider public.

The gender perspective, theoretically, was quite novel for the Russian academia; it was an unplowed field with no division of labor. During the 1990s, we did a little of everything, including translations, interpretations of theoretical writings that were new to us, elaboration of the conceptual apparatus and research directives, public education and linking empirical research with activism. Research in this new field required a lot of skill and knowledge and, of course, required active collaboration with the international research community.

This is the story of how one of us was drawn into the feminist tide. In 1993, four sociology students from St. Petersburg University asked one of us to teach an extra-curricular course on feminist theory. They were eager to obtain this new knowledge, having heard about it somehow somewhere, but the department's curricula included not much related to this topic. We took up the challenge and every two or three weeks met with the student in the private setting. It was a feminist self-education in the form of a kitchen seminar, outside any institutional arrangement.

Discussions among St. Petersburg's feminists also contributed to the development of gender studies. Olga Lipovskaya and a group of colleagues opened St. Petersburg's Center for Gender Issues. Feminist education was an essential part of its activity: seminars, consciousness-raising groups and research projects (on topics such as unemployed women and sexual harassment at work). We, as academicians were needed as lecturers, researchers, commentators and participants in the events outside of the academy, open to the interested public.

At this time, there emerged a movement of summer schools in gender studies, sponsored by international foundations. In the 1990s these schools took place in Russia and other post-Soviet countries such as Ukraine, Kazakhstan, Belarus, Hungary, the Czech Republic and Lithuania and became the platform for gender education and the consolidation of an interdisciplinary gender community consisting of a small number of academic feminists. In this connection, new universities, specifically the Central European University, and later the European Humanities University in Minsk played a major role. In old Universities new initiatives also emerged – one of the most important endeavor in the post-Soviet space was the Center for gender studies in Kharkov Karazin University (Ukraine).

It was out of this broth, that our feminist commitment was born and our gender research developed. At that time, we wrote a lot about the specifics of the emerging field of gender studies in Russia as compared with the West and about the role of the women's movement in the development of feminist theory and sociology. First and foremost, we were interested in the sociological branch of gender studies. Analyzing the Russian context, we appropriated the categories of 'gender order,' 'gender regime,' and later the idea of 'intersectionality' in gender studies.

3.2 International Collaborations

Meanwhile, the Russian academia was undergoing institutional changes. The 1990s created a demand for new knowledge resulting in the establishment of new state-independent research and educational institutions. In St. Petersburg, examples for these institutional innovations are the Center for Independent Social Research (established in 1992) and later the European University at St. Petersburg (established in 1996). These new institutions have developed transnational strategies making the effort to integrate Russian social scholars in the international discussions. To meet academic market demands, these institutions had to be innovative, flexible and open for new themes and methodologies. We regularly participated in international projects. Due to the geographic proximity between St. Petersburg and Finland, we enjoyed an especially close collaboration with Finnish sociologists. Initially, these research projects were aimed at studying civil society issues. The world was interested in the post-Soviet transformations, and for the foreign scholars joint projects with Russian colleagues became a reliable way of discovering what was really happening. The opportunities for field research became available. Dr. Anna Rotkirch, a sociologist and feminist, became the key figure in this collaboration. Together, we conducted a number of research projects related to gender relations in Russia. In collaboration with Dr. Rotkirch and her senior colleagues Prof. Elina Haavio-Mannila and Prof. J. P. Roos, we undertook studies of sexual biographies and the 'new everyday life', both framed from a gender perspective. These joint projects with Finnish sociologists were very successful, thanks to our convergent worldviews, our friendly relations and the collegiality that emerged, as we carried out the projects. Another example is collaboration with Dr. Martina Ritter in the joint project on Russian middleclass families based on feminist methodology. It was important from the very beginning that, we – the two authors of this piece – worked together. Our 'academic duo' was and still is expressed in co-authorship of publications, as well as in collaboration on projects, teaching and educational outreach. This mutual support helped in promoting the new field, which despite many obstacles, found its place in the Russian academy.

It was important that we were not alone in our academic endeavor. The networks of cooperation linked the gender centers in Tver', Samara, Ivanovo, Moscow, Minsk and Kharkov, as well as researchers from the city we live in – St. Petersburg. We regularly organized conferences and meetings, participated in summer schools and conducted joint projects. If we were to respond to the needs and requests of the community of academic feminists and civic activists, it was imperative that we shared our methodology, pursued common interests and goals and continually supported each other.

One of the most significant academic innovations was the opening of the European University in St. Petersburg in 1996. We belong to the first cohort of the faculty in the Department of Political Science and Sociology. Gender studies found a supportive home in this fast developing institution of postgraduate education in social sciences, that was committed to the advancement of modern academic knowledge in Russia. For several years, we taught courses on feminist theory and the Russian gender relations. Although these courses were optional, they always appealed to the interests of students – and not just women. During this time, interest in the subject grew among young researchers-, firstly, because of its innovative nature and, secondly, because this subject resonated with the many existential problems young people faced.

During the 1990s, international foundations were very active in Russia, providing grants to explore new academic areas including gender studies. In the beginning, grants from international foundations were the only source of funding for the European University and its Gender studies program inside this institution. Since we had a record of academic initiatives that stretched over several years, we qualified for institutional grants from the MacArthur and Ford Foundations to develop the program for gender studies in the department of political science and sociology. This funding in different forms (individual and institutional) continued until 2009. International foundations also supported the gender studies networks. In addition, we received individual research grants from the Open Society Foundation and the Heinrich Böll Foundation.

Thus, the resources of feminist camaraderie, solidarity within the western and Russian colleagues, institutional support from the European University and financial support from international foundations made it possible for us to introduce gender studies into the European University in St. Petersburg.

3.3 Gender Studies in the Context of Patriarchy

During the 1990s, a fragile academic feminism became a civic initiative and public sociology domain. Gender researchers worked with NGOs, created networks and promoted institutional and ideological innovations in academia and beyond. In truth, gender research was public sociology in the 1990s, or more precisely, public interdisciplinary transnational studies. Gender studies did, indeed, cross borders, and later they would be attacked for being divorced from their original context, being alien to Russia and having a western orientation. Although they would later be accused of being separated from activism, academic feminists interacted with publics, recruiting young people, activists and representatives of various disciplines and professions (for example, during summer schools) as well as appearing in the mass media.

Gender researchers became able to project gender categories and feminist themes into public discourse. Having been previously treated as a 'foreign' in origin and cultural essence, now, slowly but surely, gender and with it, the feminist agenda – reached the public. In a fragmentary way, it also appeared in the Russian media. All this took place due to pressure from the local academic feminists, civic activists supported by international community.

Here is a list of issues that our colleagues and we studied: the balance between work and family, discrimination in the workplace, sexual harassment, under-representation of women in politics, the gender profile of employment, the prevalence of abortion, the lack of sexual education, problems of sexual minorities, the 'care deficit' and the dilemmas of care-giving and care-receiving. We tried to analyze all these issues by paying attention to the specific gender dynamics within Russia, the consequences of Soviet gender policies and the impact of post-Soviet transformations on the gender arrangements. We introduced terms such as 'State patriarchy,' 'state-approved gender order' and the contract of the 'working mother.' The trend of 'patriarchal renaissance' was discussed by Anastasia Posadskaya, Natalia Rimashevskaya and others (see Posadovskaya 1993; Zakharova et al. 1989). However, the broad public was not very interested in these issues. The reaction to the Soviet legacy of gender mobilization under the banners of sexual equality turned patriarchal models of gender divide with its naturalization of gender roles, into an appealing alternative. Ideologies of gender equality and emancipation seemed ever more out of place, as the rhetoric of getting back to Russian cultural traditions backed by the Orthodox Church infiltrated public discourse and set the terms of choice.

It is a challenge to cultivate gender studies in an atmosphere of intensification of patriarchal discourse, which rightly considered gender studies a threat to gender hierarchies. Gender sensitivity in the society remained rather limited. In this context we consider education and research the main instruments for the gender conscious raising. Indeed, our two main public roles were as educators and experts, although there was not a great deal of public interest in our approach to gender. Still, we used every opportunity to deliver lectures and seminars; we never refused an interview with the media; and, most important, we continued to work with our students.

3.4 Dilemmas of Gender Studies in the 1990s

During the 1990s, the gender studies' community actively discussed two intertwined issues dealing with institutionalization of the innovative academic field in the Russian context: first, the criteria for the authentic gender studies and second, strategies for the integration of gender studies in the Russian academy. With regard to the first, the 1990s saw all sorts of people and organizations gather under the gender banner. As soon as gender issues received state support international interest and funding, they attracted a flow of attention, both of the feminists and traditionalists who, under the name of gender studies glorified traditional gender regimes. In the latter case under the brand name of 'gender,' the critical drive of feminism was transformed into a toothless reproduction of role theory at best.

We took the following positions in these discussions (Temkina and Zdravomyslova 2014; Barchunova 2000; Brandt 2003; Doing Gender na russkom pole 2005; Gurko 1998; Kletsin 1998; Kletsina 2002; Ushakin 2000; Voronina 2001; Zvereva 2003). Firstly, we agree with those who claimed that gender studies in Russia had developed into an umbrella category that contained both critical and opportunistic positions. Secondly, we tried to pursue our own path in gender research rather than sinking our energies into internal quarrels and purges. We sought to strengthen contacts with friendly researchers in Russia and abroad and to support the feminist wing of gender studies. Thirdly, we believed that the crowding of gender studies was the result of fashion and innovation and that over time the ballast would disappear. In our view this is indeed what has happened, and we will discuss this in the following text. Fourthly, we positioned ourselves as experts, emphasizing the need for a scholarly approach towards gender issues and tried our best to demonstrate this in our research.

In the course of the discussion over the second issue, we tried to follow a dual strategy for institutionalizing gender studies in Russia (Zdravomyslova and Temkina 2001). We realized that gender studies was marginal within the Russian academy for reasons that went beyond the backwardness of Russian social science, the lack of institutionalization and the effects of the political and economic conjuncture. The marginality of gender studies was supported by the entire cultural context of patriarchy that regarded feminism in any form (liberal or radical) as opposing essentialist traditions of Russian culture. One more reason for lack of recognition of gender studies was its open political standpoint which contradicted the conventional idea of politically neutral social science. The balance of forces was heavily weighted against feminism. In order to prevent gender studies from sliding into an academic ghetto, it was necessary to bring gender sensitivity into mainstream social science and humanities. In this way, we hoped that academic audiences would hear the feminist voice and join discussions on the subject, something they had avoided so far. This would mean recognizing scholars who were not known to mainstream scholarship. We named this as the 'institutional strategy of academic integration' (it can well be called mainstreaming of gender approach).

The second institutional strategy of 'autonomization' on the other hand, implied building an interdisciplinary, transnational gender community where researchers share common methodological positions and are involved in scholarly communication across the borders of countries and institutions. This was an ambitious program that could not be realized in the short run.

4 Conservative Attack and the Demand for Gender Expertise in the 2000s

Thus, by early 2000s, gender researchers had formed a community, although fragmented and weak in nature. Gender issues along with the demand for education and expertise in gender received a limited public resonance. Media interest was ridiculously driven by the two calendar dates – 8th of March – the International Women's Day and – 23rd of February – the Day of the Russian Armed Forces, commonly known as a 'man's holiday'. Our effort to communicate with various audiences did not have much effect. Gender studies while being torn apart by the dilemmas of its own contradictions remained on the periphery of the Russian academia and public discourse. Strategies to incorporate gender perspectives into established institutions contributed to the withering away of the critical stance, leading to strained relations between activists and academic feminists. Furthermore, the gender 'window-dressing' –

an imitation of gender studies – and limited gender awareness in the public sphere contributed to gender studies not entering mainstream academia.

The political and economic environment saw changes in the early 2000's. Many international foundations changed their priorities and left Russia that experienced economic growth at that time and established new rules of control over international foundations. Several centers for gender studies closed down due to lack of funding. Those who saw gender studies as a source of grants resigned from the field. Academic feminists, although in shrinking numbers and with limited support, gained more experience and confidence in comparison with 1990s. However, soon the picture began to change – Russian politics started talking gender. We would like to share some examples regarding the politicization of gender issues during contemporary times in the following paragraphs.

Gender Issues in Putin's Russia

In the last decade, attack from the conservatives led to politicization of gender issues and this ideological and political shift has had a huge influence on gender studies. Initially, in Vladimir Putin's Russia, gender issues were raised in connection with demographic policies. In 2006 the president came forward with a proposal to overcome Russia's demographic crisis by stimulating the birth rate. Reproductive decisions would be shaped by a 'maternal capital' – a single but financially substantial payment to the families with two or more children that should be used for three administratively defined purposes: improvement of the family housing conditions, education of children and mother's pension. Feminist researchers and demographers criticized this program, stressing it's gender insensitivity, it's inefficiency as a tool for demographic growth and the consequences of drawing women out of the labor market.[3]

By the end of the 2000s, gender issues started to be intensively pursued in the legal sphere. Conservatives (law-makers and civic organizations) blocked the Law on gender equality, pushed through bills that would limit women's reproductive rights and submitted bills against the rights of sexual

3 To estimate the effects of this monetary pronatalist policies, we interviewed mothers with two or more children, who were beneficiaries of the State assistance. We voiced their concerns about the underdeveloped and limited measures for supporting families and their distrust of the government and bureaucrats. The results were presented not just in academic publications but also in public forums (both real and virtual). The regional authorities in St. Petersburg supported our study of the gender dimensions of social policy. Our conclusions were included in the recommendations of the city committee for gender equality (Borozdina et al., 2012).

minorities. As a result, gender issues entered public debate and became politicized. In the course of those debates, various ideological positions emerged, inaugurating the fight between different gender ideologies. In these confrontations, the conservative discourse was particularly powerful, demanding a return to traditional Christian orthodox values – to the 'normal' family, with corresponding conventional gender roles. We witnessed our opponents having learnt the lesson rather well. Now, they understand the meaning of gender studies and gender ideology.

Therefore, paradoxically, the conservative political atmosphere created a demand for expert knowledge which directed against the conservative turn in gender ideology and in support of the ideology of gender equality and sexual and reproductive freedom. Now, let's have a look at how gender issues have been expressed in the political and public arenas in more detail.

Firstly, the very term 'gender' triggered protest from the conservatives. Interestingly, they had the correct interpretation of the term, matching its definition as a social construction of femininity, masculinity and sexuality. The conservatives made their position very clear during the 2012 Duma debates on the Law on Gender Equality.[4] In its press release, the organization Family, Love and Fatherland (2012) declared, 'After examining this Bill, representatives of Families and Parents' Orthodox Patriotic organizations came to conclusion that the Bill poses a threat to the demographic security of Russia and endangers family institutions and fundamental cultural and moral values'. This quotation reveals intersection of nationalistic and gender conservative rhetoric.

Secondly, at the end of 2011 Russian 'pro-lifers' submitted the Duma amendments to the Health Protection Law, which would have substantially reduced women's reproductive rights by limiting access to abortions. This led to protests by some feminist organizations over the Internet and even on the streets. While most of these amendments were ultimately rejected both sides promoted their views in the public media. They used different forms of mobi-

4 As stated in Article 1, this Bill is intended to regulate 'relations regarding the protection of citizens' rights and freedoms with respect to discrimination by gender and/or by reasons associated with the presence of children.' The key categories used in the document are 'gender equality,' 'gender discrimination,' 'gender balance' and 'positive discrimination.' In particular, gender equality is defined as 'the equal judicial status of men and women, including the provision of equal access to resources, and eliminating gender discrimination.' The bill prohibits gender discrimination against pregnant women or against men and women more generally 'for reasons associated with the presence of children.' The draft law defines the objectives of state policy as providing for gender equality in political and professional spheres of society. In addition, the law requires 'the support of families and people with family responsibilities and the formation of responsible motherhood and fatherhood.' As a mechanism to guarantee gender equality, the Bill proposes the creation of a Commission for Issues of Gender Equality within the Government of the Russian Federation and the introduction of a Commissioner for Issues of Gender Equality.

lization to present their perspectives: pickets, demonstrations, participation in talk shows and the distribution of petitions. Activist feminist groups organized a public campaign under the slogan 'Fight against abortions, not against women!' This took place in 2011, and at the same time anti-abortion organizations (such as 'Warriors for Life' or 'Resistance to Killing Children') continued to participate in public debates and in Russia-wide protests to ban abortion. Each side drew on their own experts.

Thirdly, the Federal 'Gay Propaganda Law' was passed in the Duma on 25 January 2013. This Bill is an amendment to the RF Child Protection Law making propaganda of non-traditional sexual relationships among minors a criminal offence. This Law suffers from inconsistencies and terminological ambiguity: as the term 'propaganda' is not defined, the law could be easily used to restrict freedom of speech and criminalize the gay/lesbian community. It has powerful repressive potential, symbolic significance and practical implications as a tool to suppress political opposition. Moreover, it makes it more difficult to deal with the real, complex problems of pedophilia, violence and the vulnerability of children. Although mild, nevertheless it is reminiscent of the laws of the Stalinist period.

Fourthly, the Law on Juvenile Justice was blocked. Similar to the previous cases, it was opposed by conservative mobilization that included the so-called 'community of parents' and organizations that act as the transmission belts of the Russian Orthodox Church. All these legislative moves are part of a broad conservative mobilization against gender equality, reproductive rights and sexual education.

Fifth, in February 2012, against the backdrop of protests organized under the banner of 'Free Elections,' the punk group Pussy Riot with its unsanctioned performance provoked exciting public debate about many issues including gender. The punk group called itself feminist. They held a protest performance in the major Cathedral of Moscow, calling it a punk prayer with the refrain 'Our Lady, Take Putin Away!' The court sentenced two of the participants to two years in prison for hooliganism. The third one was given a two-year suspended sentence. The trial caused a major stir not only in Russia but also abroad. There were actions in defense of Pussy Riot and collective appeals to the President calling for the release of the participants. However, the Orthodox community and Russian Orthodox Church remained unmoved. They demanded heavy punishment for offending the feelings of their believers. Pussy Riot's protest defined Putin's regime as patriarchal and broadened the agenda for Russian feminism to include the fight for political democracy and against authoritarianism.

Later the Head of the Russian Orthodox Church, Patriarch Kirill gave the following assessment of the feminist values:

> "I consider feminism very dangerous phenomenon. This is because feminist organizations proclaim pseudo-freedom of women which should be realized basically outside family and marriage. In the core of feminist ideology is not the family, not the children but another function of women which as often juxtaposed to family values. This is probably the reason why most of the feminist leaders are unmarried women (...). Feminist ideologists reduce all the nuances of human relationships – love, care, fairness, responsibility – to the social, political monetary and to distribution of power and influence".[5]

All these events are symptoms of the strengthening of conservative ideology in Russia, which goes beyond official authorities to include segments of civil society that exist through the support of the Russian Orthodox Church, itself allied to the ruling powers. The conservatives are fighting for ideological hegemony, decrying gender and feminism as their adversaries and as threats to the moral foundations and security of Russian society. Democratic and liberal resistance to this 'new morality' discourse is fragmented, but it exists, nonetheless, and opposes the conservatives.

5 Political Context and the Growth of Traditionalism

The public discussion of gender issues has taken place in a particular political context. Conservative hegemony exercise influence on public discourse and academic gender studies. Researchers who study political processes in Russia have concluded that the 2000s in Russia were marked by 'recentralization of State governance and institutionalization of the authoritarian regime in the country' (Gelman and Ryzhenkov 2010:132). Although *de jure* Russia has a multi-party political system, *de facto*, political competition does not exist (Golosov 2012:54). At the same time, the ruling authorities and the leaders of the Russian Orthodox Church have supported the conservative mobilization. In the context of the authoritarian political tendencies of the 2000s, there has been a move in public discussion toward de-secularization, including growing attention to issues of religion in the mass media and an increase in the activity of religious organizations and their leaders (Verkhovsky 2009).

The conservative turn of official ideology, with its demands for a return to traditional values and its criticism of any signs of westernization, was especially apparent in the debates concerning gender values and gender ideologies. Society is severely split on these issues, with the result that the conservative party has been consolidated while liberals are still weak and scattered. Both parties have influential representatives in the structures of power. Both seek expertise from their own segments of the Russian academy.

---

5 Taken from the official webpage of the Russian Orthodox Patriarchy, translation by the authors. Retrieved July 3, 2017 (http://www.patriarchia.ru/db/text/2899463.html).

The Growing Demand for Gender Expertise

In such political contexts, there is a need for gender expertise. The demand comes from the democratic gender-sensitive community; NGOs whose status is threatened by charges of being foreign agents; sexual minorities that are in danger of repression; feminist human rights activists who are advocates of equal opportunities and reproductive rights for women; and officials from the Regional Committee for Social Policy, who support gender equality. Gender researchers provide verbal advice, write expert reviews of bills, participate in Internet forums, sign petitions against conservative laws and conduct empirical research.

Our educational activities are also aimed at students, NGOs and the general public. In addition, we help to develop gender-sensitive networks and civil society by contributing expertise, research and direct participation. Our studies carry a civic significance. Together with our students, we investigate the mechanisms of conservative mobilization and identify their alliances, resources and support strategies; we also study family and sexual policies and their gendered effects. There are emerging friendly media that are not afraid of feminist agenda and realize that democrats must form a common block against authoritarianism and support the gender agenda.

6 Conclusion

When gender studies were launched, public interest was very limited. This was the case although, during the 1990s, gender studies had both an academic and a political mission to promote democracy (with respect to gender equality) and civil society (supporting initiatives against sexism and violence). Public interest in gender was so modest because of prevailing essentialist visions regarding gender differences and generalized beliefs that feminist goals are irrelevant in the Russian context and alien to Russian society. Gradually, under the influence of academic and activist feminism and with the support of an international community, gender approach infiltrated the public sphere. This process was accompanied by frequent misunderstandings and reformulations of gender research, and often reducing it to the study of the conventional gender roles in society. Gender studies became the umbrella term that included both feminist and traditionalist understanding of masculinity and femininity; men's and women's position in society. The gender studies community remained small and fragmented.

The public role of gender researchers was to educate and to offer expertise on social inequalities structured by intersection of gender/sexuality/class/

and ethnicity. NGOs, university students, students of summer schools and researchers and social science lecturers who wanted to advance their knowledge and skills were our audiences. We relied on interdisciplinary and transnational networks of gender studies.

During the first decade of the twenty-first century, the favorable phase of gender studies ended. Gender studies became narrower and more critical, since today it does not bring money or compliments, but, on the contrary, it can bring disgrace and ideological pressure. At the same time, gender issues have become the focus of intense political debates. The authorities developed powerful new technologies of public manipulation as they pursued the gendering of politics. In these conditions, researchers face an open dismissal of their gender and feminist approaches. This is due to the competition for ideological hegemony, in which the conservatives are the most active, forming a united front with a section of the political elite, the Russian Orthodox Church and part of civil society. Gender conservative attack is taking place in the context of authoritarian trends in Russian politics, the growth of nationalism and anti-western attitudes that promote traditional values and traditional gender roles, protest sexual education and repress sexual minorities.

At the same time, there has also been an opposing trend – the development of a feminist community. Ideas of gender equality and gender freedom are common among educated young people. Our expertise and our educational efforts, on any given local agenda are addressed to them.

We consider gender studies to be one of the most promising and important directions for public sociology. The anti-patriarchal potential of gender studies in the context of authoritarian tendencies can help the democratic opposition to authoritarianism. We find supportive sectors within the academia that include scholars of disability, youth sub-cultures, and the sociology of health, social movements and ethnicity.

Discussion Questions

1. Which factors explain the emergence of Gender Studies in Russia in the beginning of 1990s?
2. Who has been targets of conservative attack and who supports this? To which interest groups do these belong ?
3. Why does an authoritarian rule coexist with conservative gender ideologies?

References

Barchunova, Tatijana (2000): Erkskljuzija i inkljuzija soobshchestva gendernykh issledovatelei [Exclusion and inclusion in the community of gender researchers]. In: Preodoleniye. Novosibirsk, Russia:SibNovCenter, pp. 216-226.

Borozdina Ekaterina, Zdravomyslova, Elena and Temkina, Anna (2012): Materinskij kapital: sotsial'naja politika I strategii semej [Maternal capital: Social policy and family strategy]. In: Demoskope Weekly, 23 January–5March, pp. 495-496. (demoscope.ru/weekly/2012/0495/analit03.php).

Brandt, Galina (2003): Gendernye issledovanija v Rossii: osobennosti i problemy [Gender studies in Russia: Specifics and problems]. In: Popkova L./Tartakovskaya I. (eds.): Gendernye otnoshenija v sovremennoi Rossii, Issledovanija 1990-kh godov [Gender Relations in Contemporary Russia, 1990s Research]. Samara: Samara University Press, pp. 23-30.

Burawoy, Michael (2008) Za publichnuju sotsiologiju [For public sociology]. In: Yarskaya-Smironova E./Romanov P. (eds.): Sotsialnaja Politika v Sovremennoj Rossii: Reformy i Povsednevnost [Social Policy in Contemporary Russia: Reforms and Everyday Life]. Moscow: CSPGI, Variant, pp. 121-163.

Doing Gender na russkom pole: kruglyi stol [Doing gender in the Russian field: Round table] (2005). In: Gendernyje issledovanija [Gender Studies] 13, pp. 190-217.

Family, Love and Fatherland (2012): The real truth about gender. Retrieved June 11, 2013. (ruskline.ru/analitika/2012/02/23/nastoyawaya_pravda_o_gendere/)

Firsov, Boris (2012): Istorija sovetskoj sotsiologii 1950-1980-kh gg. Ocherki [History of Soviet Sociology. Essays]. St. Petersburg: EUSP Publishing House.

Gelman Vladimir, Ryzhenkov, Sergei (2010): Lokal'nye rezhimy, gorodskoe upravlenie i 'vertikal vlasti' v sovremennoj Rossii. Politicheskaja ekspertiza [Local regimes, municipal governance and 'vertical power' in contemporary Russia. Political expertise]. In: Politeks 6, 4, pp. 130-151.

Golosov, Grogorii (2012): Demokratija v Rossii: Instruktsija po Sborke [Democracy in Russia: Instruction for Set Up]. St. Petersburg: BKhV-Petersburg.

Gurko, Tatiana (1998): Sotsiologija pola i gendernykh otnoshenij [Sociology of sex and gender relations]. In: Yadov V. (ed.): Sotsiologija v Rossii [Sociology in Russia]. Moscow: Institute of Sociology, RAN, pp. 173-195.

Kletsin, Alexander (1998): Dilemmy gendernoj sotsiologii [Dilemmas of gender sociology]. In: Zherebkina, I. (ed.): Gendernye Issledovanija: Feministskaja Metodologija v Sotsial'nykh Naukakh [Gender Studies: Feminist Methodology in Social Sciences]. Kharkov: KhHCGI, pp. 187-193.

Kletsina, Irina (2002): Razvitije gendernykh issledovanij v psikhologii [Development of gender studies in psychology]. In: Obshchesrvennye nauki i sovremennost 3, pp. 181-192.

Popkova, Ljudmila/Tartakovskaya Irina (2010): Akademicheskij optimism mezhdu tajushchej podderzhkoj fondov i udushajushchimi ob'jatijami gosudarstva: razvitie gendernykh issledovanii v Kazakhstane i Kirgistane. Unpublished manuscript.

Posadskaya, Anastasia (1993): Zhenskoe izmerenije sotsial'noj transformatsii: ot Foruma k Forumu [Women's dimension of social transformation: From forum to forum]. In: Materialy Vtorogo Nezavisimogo Zhenskogo Foruma [Proceedings of the Second Women's Independent Forum]. Dubna, Moscow: CGI IESPN RAN, pp. 13-19.

Pravmir.com (2013): Patriarch Kirill believes feminism is a very dangerous phenomenon. Retrieved February 10, 2013 (www.pravmir.ru/tag/feminizm/)

Temkina, Anna/Zdravomyslova, Elena (2002): Feministische Übersetzung in Russland, Anmerkungen von Co-Autoren. In: Cheaure E./Heyder C. (eds): Osteuropaforschung 43: Russische Kultur und Gender Studies. Berlin: Verlag, pp. 15-34.

Temkina, Anna/Zdravomyslova, Elena (2014): Gender's crooked path: Feminism confronts Russian patriarchy. In: Current Sociology 62, pp. 253-270.

Ushakin, Sergei (2000): 'Gender' (naprokat): poleznaja kategorija dlja nauchnoj kar'ery ['Gender' for rent: A useful category for academic career?] In: Muravjeva, M. (ed.): Gendernaja Istorija Pro et Contra [Gender History Pro and Contra]. St. Petersburg: Rossiskij gosudarstvennyj pedagogicheskij universitet im. A.I. Gertsena, pp.34-39.

Verkhovsky, Alexander (2009): Religioznye organizatsii i vozmozhnosti ideologicheskogo proektirovanija v putinskoi Rossii [Religious organizations and opportunities for ideological projects in Putin's Russia]. In: Dvadtsat' let religioznoi svobody v Rossii. M. Moscow: ROSSPEN, pp. 160-188.

Voronina, Olga (2001): Formirovanije gendernogo podkhoda v sotsial'nykh naukakh [Formation of a gender approach in social sciences]. In: Malysheva, M. (ed.): Gendernyi kaleidoskop [Gender Kaleidoscope]. Moscow, Russia: Academia, pp. 8-32.

Zakharova, Natalia/Rymashevskaya, Natalia/Posadskaya, Anastasia (1989): Kak my reshaem zhenskij vopros [How we deal with the woman's question]. In: Communist 4, pp. 56-65.

Zdravomyslova, Olga (2013): Gendernye issledovanija kak opyt publichnoj sotsiologii [Gender studies as public sociology experience]. Retrieved April 15, 2017 (genderpage.ru/content/zdr.htm)

Zdravomyslova, Elena/Temkina, Anna (2001): Institualizatsija gendernykh issledovanij v Rossii [Institutionalization of gender studies in Russia]. In: Malysheva, M. (ed.): Gendernyi kaleidoskop [Gender Kaleidoscope]. Moscow, Russia: Academia, pp. 33-51.

Zherebkina, Irina (2003): Gendernye devjanostye ili Fallasa ne sushchestvujet [The Gendered 1990s, or The Phallus Does Not Exist]. St. Petersburg: Alateija.

Zvereva, Galina (2003): 'Chuzhoje, svoje, drugoje...': feministskie i gendernye kotsepty v intellektual'noi kul'ture postsovetskoi Rosii ['Alien, own, other...': Feminist and gender concepts in the intellectual culture of post-Soviet Russia]. In: Repina, L. (ed.): Adam i Eva. Al'manakh Gendernoj Istorii [Adam and Eve. Gender History Review.] Moscow: IVI RAN; St. Petersburg: Alateija, pp. 389-427

Martina Tißberger

At the Intersection of Gender and Racism: critical whiteness as a method of hegemonic self-reflection

1 Introduction

At the advent of 'diversity' in the field of the social sciences in the 1990s, many feminist scholars and activists expressed concerns about the disempowerment of gender as a category of critical inquiry and political struggle if it was subsumed under a range of various differences between people. Many saw 'sex difference', that is, 'sexual difference' as the master category of discrimination, which apparently concerned 'all women*' – worldwide. Likewise, 'gender' had threatened feminism earlier in the 1990s – a feminism that was understood as the field of study and activism regarding discrimination against 'women*'. The worry was, that by the deconstruction of the category 'woman*', all the political power of feminism would disappear. By the time of the introduction of the concept of 'intersectionality' later on, the field had already gone through a certain transformation. Most of those acting in it had understood that subjects are always identified with more than one category within our society's matrix of powerful signifiers, and were therefore positioned interdependently; in some relations or constellations more, in others less, powerful. More importantly, they finally realized that there were powerful differences between women* and that white* women* were not only victims of patriarchy but also perpetrators of racism. The "chorus of victims in feminism had finally fallen silent" to use a phrase by Christina Thürmer-Rohr (1984). It was racistically marked women* who had conducted all of these interventions in feminism and they addressed the notorious whiteness as a signifier of dominance in feminism and gender studies. Critical whiteness studies were introduced as a field of inquiry which followed the request of Audre Lorde, bell hooks, Toni Morrison and others to research the signifying rather than the signified of race*, not the 'victims' of racism but its perpetrators, and thereby focusing not only on the violent forms of racism but the "racism, which does not leave corpses" (Howitt/Owusu-Bempah 1994:35). Racism, like sexism, is a constitutive element of (Western) societies and not just a phenomenon at their margins, such as right wing extremism and white supremacy groups.

This chapter will give an insight into the critical studies of whiteness and its relations with gender (studies). It will focus on the mechanisms of ontologization, which are at the core of both power relations – gender and racism – as body politics. Furthermore, the chapter will discuss critical whiteness as a method and didactics of hegemonic self-reflection in the nexus of gender and racism, a nexus where positionings of power switch (for white* women*). The focus of the chapter is on the subject of sexism and racism. While both power relations operate through discourse and on the structural, institutional and symbolic level of society, it is the subject – the individual – through which these racist and sexist discourses performatively get 'real'. People are subjectivated within society and its power relations and only if they understand how they operate in these structures, can they interrupt and change them. Given, that "race does not exist but it does kill people" (Guillaumin 1995:107), its signifier – whiteness – operates mainly in the realm of the unconscious, at least with white* people. A methodology of hegemonic self-reflection must therefore delve into the realm of the unconscious of racism and gender.

2 The Production of Difference: gender and race*

The perception that women* are fundamentally different to men* is a constitutive element of Western societies. The binary construction of men* and women* as rational versus emotional, intelligible versus palpable, active versus passive and their association with mind versus body, professional and public life versus domestic life and motherhood puts men* and women* not only in a complementary relation but a hierarchical one, too. Men* are the carriers of all appreciated qualities of the Western value system whereas women's* qualities are disregarded. It is no coincidence that non-white* people are ascribed the same devalued attributes as white* women* in this value system, leaving non-white* women* at the lowest point of the scale. I mark essentializing gendering as well as racializing terms with an asterisk in this text in order to direct readers' attention to the fact that women* and (non-) white* people are effects of signifying practices and not 'natural' entities. For the same reason I use the phrasing 'racistically marked' or 'unmarked', pointing to the fact that it is the act of marking which produces race* – that racism is the act of marking, and race* the effect of racism, not vice versa. Therefore, it would be backward to use the term 'racial' and speak of 'racial marking' since 'raciality' is the effect of the act of marking. I do not use the term 'people of colour', which is currently considered the politically correct term in the eyes of many, because of its semantic proximity to 'coloured people'.

Howitt and Owusu-Bempah argued this in 1994 (p.13). In contrast to race* gender is a post-essentialist term, which deconstructs 'sex'. 'Whiteness', however, points to a symbolic (power) structure and is therefore not marked, as 'femininity' or 'non-whiteness' are not, for example, since such terms point to ideas rather than ontological entities.

The alleged intrinsic differences between the sexes* and races* have never been neutral and purely descriptive in Western cultures. Their meanings always carried an evaluation in worth and value, subordinating 'the darker races' and all women* to white* men*. Along with this process of discrimination came the unequal distribution of power and labour: (white*) women's* unpaid care work and the exploitation of non-whites* in the course of imperialism and colonialism which found its peak in slavery. The powerful effect of this production of differences is the white* man's* position of hegemony. This hegemony has survived all legal measures for human rights whereby the latter at first excluded women*, non-whites* and many economic, social, religious and political groups anyway. Current human rights laws encompass a large part of (formerly) discriminated-against groups but white* men* are still situated more powerful than any other group – globally.

Hegemony means more than power or dominance as in authoritarian regimes. The hegemony of white* men* as the effect of the intersectional power relations of sexism and racism operates in Antonio Gramsci's (1991ff.) sense as a *cultural hegemony*. It goes beyond political power and encompasses the symbolic, institutional and structural levels of society, but also the unconscious of society and the individual. Equal opportunity and anti-discrimination laws and politics such as gender mainstreaming and diversity have been developed and implemented in order to address these power imbalances and discriminations, which take place despite the human rights laws. Because of antidiscrimination laws, beginning with the Civil Rights Act in 1964, through to the Equal Treatment Directives which have now been implemented in the European Union – including the 'Antidiskriminierungsgesetz' (*Allgemeines Gleichstellungsgesetz* – AGG), people who experience discrimination in the job market, for example, can enforce their rights judicially. These laws are cornerstones in the struggle against discrimination. However, discrimination and power imbalances operate on levels beyond the formal order of society. The hegemony of whiteness and masculinity is anchored in epistemology – our theory of knowledge. That means that our ways of gaining knowledge about a subject or a culture are already coined through that hegemonic order.

Interestingly, the production of differences along the constructions of gender and race took place at the same time as Europe went through a period of emancipation with the development of Enlightenment thought and its ideals of freedom and equality. Nobel Prize winning Afro-American literary critic Toni Morrison remarked, in reference to sociologist Orlando Patterson, that we should not be surprised about this apparent contradiction in Enlightenment thought because:

> Nothing highlighted freedom – if it did not in fact create it – like slavery … For in that construction of blackness *and* enslavement could be found not only the not-free but also, with the dramatic polarity created by skin color, the projection of the not-me. (Morrison 1993:38)

While European men* struggled to overcome institutional authority, as in the church and monarchy and their belief systems, by defining reason, freedom, analysis and individualism for themselves, they used this very tool – science – to deprive the majority of the world's population of freedom and individualism. All women* and non-white* men* became the field of projection for those qualities which were split off in the process of creating the ideal subject of Enlightenment. Thereby arose interdependence. Femininity and non-whiteness became a before-in-the-service-of-an-after[1] – white* masculinity. The subject of the Enlightenment was generated as white* and male* *through* the construction of a 'primitive' past, which was coded as non-white* and female* and as a foundation from which development emerges. The scientific study of women* and non-whites* became instrumental for the subordination of these groups under the 'class' of white* males*. Biology was the ground on which the Enlightenment philosophers' *ideas* about the differences in sex* and race* *manifested.*

Biologically based classificatory sciences sought to define 'natural' differences through empirical studies of bodies – in particular of skulls. Both white* women* and women* and men* of colour were said to possess smaller brains than white* men*, a factor taken to signify their lesser powers of reasoning (Weedon 1999:9). The term 'primitivity' was introduced and coded with female* as well as non-white* codes, which became key elements in the epistemic violence (Spivak, 1994 [1988]:76) of many Western sciences, as we shall see later on in this text.

The scientific disciplines involved in the study of sex* and race* differences were biology, medicine and what was to become psychology. In the 18th and 19th centuries, when these theories of race* and sex* differences were developed, psychological research was untertaken within the disciplines of philosophy, biology and the life sciences, as well. A popular protagonist of this research was psychologist Gustave Le Bon "who is regarded as the founder of social psychology and who was part of Paul Broca's French

1 I owe this phrase to Judith Butler in her foreword to Patricia Purtschert's „Grenzfiguren" (2006:8).

school of craniometry" (Weedon 1999:9). Le Bon writes: "All psychologists who have studied the intelligence of women, as well as poets and novelists, recognize today that they represent the most inferior forms of human evolution and that they are closer to children and savages than to an adult civilized man" (Le Bon 1897, cited in Weedon 1999:8). The few 'exceptional' distinguished women* of his time were, to Le Bon, monstrous like "a gorilla with two heads" (ibid.).

Proofs for the claimed parallels between (white*) women*, all non-white* people, children and animals were produced through the measurement of body, brain size or facial angles in the then scientific fields of phrenology, craniology and sociobiology. The inferiority of women* and non-whites* legitimated their deprivation from (higher) education, suffrage and civil rights. Drawing on the pseudo scientific race* theories of Carl von Linné, Johann Friedrich Blumenbach, Immanuel Kant, Peter Camper, Georges Cuvier, Jean Baptiste Bory de Saint-Vincent, Arthur de Gobineau, Francis Galton, Houston Stewart Chamberlain, Jean-Baptiste de Lamarck or Ernst Haeckel, it was argued that African people were biologically suited to slavery and the brutality against non-whites* in the course of colonialism, slavery and segregation was declared a necessary measure (Brickman 2003; Gould 2007; Hentges 1999; Jahoda 1999). Most of these race* theorists produced evolutionist scales of human development as a continuum from 'primitivity' to civilization, aligned phenotypes with skin color and situated black* people as the missing link between human and animal. Medical scientist Peter Camper (1722-1789), for example, measured facial angles and aligned black* people with apes.

While those brute forms of racist science no longer exist, many of its principles live on in contemporary scientific work. For example, the principle of setting a norm according to the Enlightenment ideal of the human subject and describing everything which differs from that as deviation or lack – *not quite/not white**, to use Homi Bhabha's (1994) term. Likewise, the principle of identifying differences between people and cultures and grounding them in biology is a practice which is still widespread in the social and life sciences. Many of the principles which were developed in the racial* sciences of the 18th and 19th centuries have become part of – and are hidden in – an epistemology which is still very much alive.The founder of psychoanalysis Sigmund Freud, for example, adopted Ernst Haeckel's recapitulation theory for his theory of psychosexual development, which, again, has been incorporated in many other psychological theories that do not relate to psychoanalysis and are still widely applied. Psychoanalytic theory, even though never established in formal academia, is the psychological theory which has spread most widely – in the social sciences as well as in everyday thought. Many of its theoretical aspects have become common sense. Following Jean-Baptiste de Lamarck (ontogenesis recapitulates phylogenesis) and Charles Darwin (origin of species), the concept of recapitulationism claims that a human being recapitulates in its individual development (ontogenesis) the evolution of the human species (phylogenesis) – from primitivity to civilization. 19th century cultural anthropology translated Darwin's theory of the evolution of physical marks onto mental and cultural phenomena (Brickman 2003:58). According to Darwin, all species originate in one primordial form and due to natural selection the fittest survive. In its translation into social theory the term *species* in Darwin's evolution theory was sometimes replaced with the term race*. Generations of morphology and embryology were organized by this theory.

Psychoanalysis situates sexual difference in the body too, even though Freud was innovative for his time, arguing that gender and desire were acquired in the process of psychosexual development. The baby was 'polymorphously perverse' according to Freud, by which he meant its entire body surface was identified as an erotic zone. During the oedipal phase of development, however, children discover that there are some who have a penis and others who *lack* it, and Freud claimed that this induces boys* to fear castration and girls* to feel castrated, thereby suffering from penis envy ever after. The male* becomes the norm, and the female* stands for deviation, lack and inferiority. Freud called the clitoris a 'primitive organ', the inferior little penis of women* (Freud 1927:388). Female* sexuality was termed a *dark continent* (1926:303), thus allegorized as Africa. Antisemitic discourse in Freud's *fin de siècle* Vienna called the clitoris 'Jew' and female* masturbation 'playing with the Jew', but that is another story. The psychoanalysis of the patient 'Little Hans', which brought Freud to develop the concept of the Oedipus Complex – the theory of castration – contains a footnote in which Freud explains that little Jewish Hans learns in Kindergarten that Jews are castrated (circumcised) (Boyarin 1998:224, in reference to Gilman and Freud).

I chose the example of psychoanalysis because nowhere have the intersections of race*, gender and sexuality become as virulent, and nowhere can it be better observed how discourses of a particular period in time enchroach on scientific theory (see Tißberger 2013). Current research on gender, racism and postcolonialism within psychoanalysis exists because of the virulence of these registers and their intersectionality in psychoanalytic theory. While the sexism of Freudian as well as Lacanian psychoanalysis theory has been criticized elaborately, not least by Judith Butler (1990; 1993), its inherent racism and coloniality still mostly goes unconsidered (e.g. Truscott and Hook 2014; George 2016).

The idea of the primitive as the beginning of everything – both of the individual and of humanity – is a repeat of European medieval philosophy's presumption that 'savages' lived in the childhood of human development and that 'civilized' children recapitulate the human wilderness (Brickman 2003: 58). According to Brickman, Darwin believed that defeat in the 'survival of the fittest' lead to infertility, and that military and economic strength were a proof of biological strength, and he thereby produced a theory which allowed for the naturalization of the subjection and extermination of the colonized. Those who were on the wrong side of the imperial battlefield simply "lost the biological struggle for survival" (ibid.:48) and were naturally determined to die out. Their extinction simply placed them "back into the dead prehistoric world where they belonged" (Stocking, cited in Brickman, ibid.). Civilization and colonization were soon to be understood as the biologically constituted capacities of a distinct race*, which was due to natural superiority destined to win the survival of the fittest competition and to conquer other races*.

Contemporay body politics of racism and sexism are gounded in this evolutionism. The evolutionist axis with the poles of primitivity and civilization has a racist and sexist inscription, which parallels darkness and femininity with primitivity and lightness and masculinity with civilization. It positions dark skinned and female* phenotypes close to the beginning of human development and in kinship with apes, and light skinned and male* phenotypes close to civilization, progress, development and success. The darker a person appears, the more primitively he or she was represented, the lighter, the more civilized. Steretypes of non-white* people and in particular black* people – both negative and celebratory – as being more physical, more sexual, more intuitive, more spiritual, as having a lesser sense of justice and being more criminal, less rational and less sophisticated than whites* (Weedon 1999:153) are the effect of the transfer of biology. It is the mapping of physical markers onto cognition and psychology – mind and psyche. Even though these theories are obsolete, they are still practiced widely in everyday racism. This process of ontologization is what often goes unrecognized in contemporary racism and sexism.Take the sexual violence and theft on New Year's Eve 2015, in Cologne, Germany, for example. Immediately the media, as well as politicians and other commentators, focused on the perpetrators' majoritarian male* Muslim migrant and refugee background and contrasted it with the victims' femaleness*, German nationality and whiteness, thereby linking the incident with the so called refugee crisis (Dietze 2016a; 2016b; 2017; Hark and Villa 2017). None of the frequent gang rapes at the Oktoberfest or football matches with white* autochthonous rapists ever had that kind of media attention. This ethnosexism reinforced Samuel Huntington's (1996) notorious thesis of the 'Clash of Civilizations', and with it the belief that 'those backward Orientals with their patriarchal and sexist cultures will never fit in our emancipated Western societies'.

3 Dark Continents: ontologization and the unconscious

Sigmund Freud's allegorization of white* women's* sexuality as a *dark continent* at a time when the colonial plundering and exploitation of Africa's natural and human resources was at its peak, is remarkable. It discloses the confluence of gender, race* and sexuality not only in colonial fantasy but also in its various manifestations in contemporary post/neo/colonial politics. Freud distinguished two kinds of the unconscious, the topological and the dynamic. The dynamic unconscious carries the revolutionary potential of psychoanalysis. It explains the mechanisms of transference, defence and other aspects of the psyche, which are not only helpful but also indispensable in understanding power relations, for example. The concept of the topological unconscious – and the *dark continent* refers to this – was developed out of evolutionist thought as described above. Herein lies the reactionary potential of psychoanalysis.

In *Totem and Tabu* (1912) Freud explains that in the beginning of culture and civilization was the primal horde – an adapted fantasy of his contemporary, anthropologist James George Frazer (1854-1941). The primal horde was headed by the primal father who 'owned' all women* and thereby, so goes the story, deprived all the other men* of the horde (the 'brothers') of sexuality. The brothers united one day and killed the father. But that posed another problem because all of them wanted to replace the father and 'own' the women* now. Thus the taboo of incest and killing was established, and Freud sees that as the beginning of civilization – the capacity to renounce one's 'drives'; that is, the love and death drive. According to Freud, this phylogenetic 'incident' (in fact a fantasy) is sedimented in every individual psyche and recapitulated in the Oedipus complex when the little boy* – desiring his mother – understands that the mother is 'owned' by the father. Consequently, he has to renounce his desires, to love and sexually own his mother and kill his father, and wait until another woman* is 'given' to him. French psychoanalyst Jacques Lacan developed this theory further. The manifest – penis – gets replaced by the symbolic – phallus – in the process of Oedipal desire, castration threat and renunciation. With the 'cut of the signifier' – the phallus – determination (satisfaction) is replaced by an undetermined desire. The phallus stands for lack, and woman* for phallus. Lacan's famous phrase *La femme n'existe pas* (the woman* does not exist) means that she *is* lack, in the symbolic.

The subject, as becomes obvious here, is male* in psychoanalysis. Freud fails to fathom what happens to the girl* child and develops ideas such as *dark continent* and penis envy. We can already observe how femininity and non-whiteness, both associated with primitivity (the qualities of the savage primal horde), come to serve as 'constitutive outside' – the other – in the creation of a subject ideal which is white* and male*; the phallus not just refers to the masculine* penis (Butler 1993:84) but also to whiteness: the phallus is white* (Tißberger 2013:70ff.). The 'other', coded by femininity* and non-'whiteness' serves as a *before-or-outside* of the subject; in Judith Butler's theory, this is referred to as the 'other' as object becoming 'abject'. For Butler,

> '... the "abject" designates that which has been expelled from the body, discharged as excrement, literally rendered "Other." This appears as an expulsion of alien elements, but the alien is effectively established through this expulsion. The construction of the "not-me" as the abject establishes the boundaries of the body which are also the first contours of the subject' (1990:169).

Psychoanalysis is only one, but a good example for the inscription of the social and political structure of patriarchy into the 'nature' of the individual psyche. Much feminist and gender research has made that point, not least by Judith Butler (1990; 1993). Less problematized in scholarly writing is how psychoanalysis is an example for the inscription of racism, evolutionism and the normativity of whiteness into the theories of the social sciences. Psychoanalysis is interesting as a science for the examination of sexism and racism on three levels. First, it has written both sexism and racism into its meta theory. Second, its descriptions for the acquisition of gender and civilization (a code for whiteness) in ontogenesis read against the grain, exposes this apparently natural process as a process of subjectivation under the power structures of society. In her critique of psychoanalysis, Gayle Rubin (1975) has called it a feminist theory *manqué* because it was Freud who showed that gender was not innate but acquired through infant experieces in the family as representative of society – but then naturalized this process. Daniel Boyarin (1998) indicates in his examination of the meaning of the phallus in the work of black* psychoanalyst Frantz Fanon and Jewish Sigmund Freud, that psychoanalysis is a theory about racism manqué. Third, with the description of the dynamic unconscious, it shows the psyche's possibilities to deal with power structures ranging from subjection to resistance.

I suggest the reading of what Freud called the topological unconscious as the field of sedimented power structures – sexism, racism and other relations of discrimination – in the psyche. However, the structuralism with reference to archaic events must be rejected. What Freud claimed to be archaic truths should be understood as an archive of racist and sexist knowledge which has been circulating for centuries. It goes back to real historic events – in the case of racism the epochal event of 1492's 'discovery' of 'America' by Columbus and 'knowledge' about Europe's 'others' produced since then, as well as the spread of race theories in the 18th and 19th centuries with the systematicity of racism they introduced. Sexism, the subordination of 'women' under 'men', is usually represented as a universal, ancient condition. However, gender relations took different forms in history, changed over time and are anything but homogenous in different cultures. Not everywhere and always have men* ruled over women*. Even the understanding of sex*, gender, woman* or man* varies from culture to culture; scholars such as Ifi Amadiume (1987, 2000), Oyewùmí Oyèrónké (1997) or Ilse Lenz and Ute Luig (1995) have made that clear. Even though with the hegemony of European culture its gender norms have spread globally, gender and sex* differences are by no means universal and homogenous.

Gender theory has shown that gender is produced through habitual and performative means and that heterosexuality is *constructed* and *produced* as a dominant norm and is not 'natural'. These poststructuralist theories have overcome the essentialism which had characterized some earlier feminist theories. The same holds for constructions of 'cultural' and race* differences. Critical race* theory, postcolonial critique and cultural studies have shown that essentialisms might be useful strategically, at the most (Spivak 1994). Poststructuralist thought has replaced identity politics and cultural essentialism, the idea that there is an essence of femininity* in women*, of masculinity* in men*, of blackness* in Africans or European-Africans etc. The growing interdisciplinary field of intersectionality (e.g. Hill Collins and Bilge, 2016) documents this development. In the more conservative scientific fields as well as in everyday practice, however, ideas of 'female* morals', 'black* culture' or heterosexuality as a norm, for example, are still very much alive. It is therefore necessary to understand the mechanisms of *ontologization* on the discoursive level as well as on the level of the individual and its unconscious.

Ontology is part of metaphysics and claims to produce knowledge about becoming, being and the reality of certain entities. The talk of 'identity' as a popular discourse as well as a social science discourse since the 1950s might be seen as a modern version of the attempt to tell the story of being and origins[2]. Applied to the human being, ontology and identity fall precicely into the field of gender and diversity studies, critical race* theory and critical whiteness studies, which all struggle with the effects of the application of sexism, racism, ableism and other '-isms' onto people – their bodies and psyche. Ontology however, is not concerned with power relations or discourse. Steming from Greek philosophy, it follows a different thread of thought than contemporary poststructuralist theories of the subject. The social sciences, the humanities and psychology in particular always had a great interest in the

2 For an elaborate critique of the discourse of identity in the social sciences see Jungwirth (2007).

faculty of offering knowledge about subjects and their behaviour. Industry offers applied sciences a lot of money for producing this kind of knowledge about the customers of their products. At the moment, the sciences and associated scholarships are under a lot of financial pressure due to the increasing privatization of universities. Basic research is hardly funded anymore and in order to get funding, scholars have to offer research topics which suit the interests of industry. Uncritical sectors of diversity studies attend to these interests and offer knowledge about alleged different cultures' needs, for example. The outcome of such diversity studies might be profit for Ford by selling more of its Transit model cars, through to Turkish-speaking promoters in front of the central vegetable market in Berlin. Essentialist gender studies might be serviceable for the industry as well by offering knowledge about alledged female* skills to be 'used' in the course of production, as well as knowledge about alledged female* needs which could be served by industrial products – cosmetics, health products, or cars.

Critical scholarship on gender, diversity, racism or culture – critical subject theory and cultural studies in general – do the opposite of such 'utilization science'. The object of research is rather to understand how people come to be *represented* and hence treated as woman*, 'migrant' and 'the other', the processes of subjectivation in societies that are structured through gender, race* and other regimes. Understanding the *ontologization* of constructions like gender and race* is therefore key to unterstanding how these power relations work.

Ontologization is the process in which ideas get inscribed into the subject. It usually takes the path from the social through the body into the psyche. Ontologization nowadays takes place usually in order to hide the power relations of society in the biology of the subject – a register of the subject, which despite the scholarship of Donna Haraway or Judith Butler is still thought of as undeceiveable truth. For example, the idea that women* are more emotional because their brain shows more activity in the limbic system than men's*, visible through the magnetic imaging resonance apparatus, when exposed to emotionally stirring scenes. Such processes of naturalization are supposed to immunize categories against their deconstruction. Brain research is an intersting field on which these politics of ontologization can be observed. At the same time that neuroscience and brain research 'find out' that women's* brains show more emotionality and men's* more sexual drive e.g. they teach us that the most important finding in the field is the fact of the brain's plasticity, and that it develops in dependence on the experiences which a subject has from the moment it is born – and even before. They therefore deliver perfect proof for the *materialization* of the social, cultural and political in what is considered the 'biological' – the neurons etc. Behaviour then *follows* the context and structures in which a subject grows up, including sexist and racist power relations. That is what I mean by refering to Rubin's remark that psychoanalysis is almost a feminist theory. Reading the Oedipal complex against its grain, we can understand it as the process when the child internalizes the gender power structures of its context, and we can add the racist power structures as well. The child learns to desire everything which is associated with whiteness and masculinity* and to reject everything that is culturally coded as abject – the feminine* and non-whiteness.

One dimension in the process of ontologization is science and the scientific discourse as described above. The other part is on the level of the individual – as part of society but also in individual psychological terms. Scientific discourse would mean nothing if people did not believe in it. Key to ontologization is the individual, which believes that women* are the better care takers and that black* people are less intelligent than white* people. Another key to ontologization is in the fact that those who are subjectivated as women* believe that they are better care takers than their male* partners and that those who are subjectivated as black* believe that they are less intelligent than their white* classmates and therefore aspire only to manual work. Much of this individual process – identification, desire etc. – is unconscious and this is where the work of a counterhegemonic subjectivation begins.

4 Critical Whiteness

Black* scholars and activists, as has been mentioned above, initiated critical studies of whiteness. Sojourner Truth (1798-1883), an African-American woman* who was active in both the abolitionist and the women's* rights movement – a former slave herself – might be mentioned as one of the first who named whiteness as a blank spot at the intersection of gender and racism in her famous speech of 1851: 'Ain't I a Woman?'[3]. She pointed to the racism in feminism and to the fact that non-white* women's* situation was not considered in the movement. Remarkably, the first women's* movement in the U.S. arose in connection with abolitionism and thereby at the intersection of racism and feminism. Until this day the connection between feminism and anti-racism is important, and critical studies of whiteness as an academic field started through debates about racism in feminism/gender studies. However, African-American sociologist W.E.B. DuBois must be named here, too, as somebody who published his scholarly work on racism as early as 1896 and analysed carefully the workings of whiteness. DuBois coined the phrase

3 See also bell hooks (1986).

Wages of Whiteness (1965), pointing to the surplus resources that racism creates for whites* and therefore the intersection of racism and class/economy[4]. David Roediger (1994; 2002) developed his critical work on whiteness in alignment with this point in DuBois. Charles Mills' (1999) *The Racial Contract* is another important work in this field. Mills shows how white* *supremacy* has survived slavery, Apartheid and segregation and until this day continues to guarantee what in contemporary critical whiteness studies.[5] is called 'white* privilege' – actually a euphemism.

Besides the afore mentioned scholars and activists, Audre Lorde (1984), bell hooks (1984; 1989; 1994a; 1996), Toni Morrison (1993) and also Patricia Hill Collins (1991) refused their inclusion in a 'universal sisterhood' of white* feminism. The volume by editors Cherríe Moraga and Gloria Anzaldúa (1981) *This Bridge Called My Back*, as well as the volume *Making Face, Making Soul – Haciendo Caras,* edited by Anzaldúa in 1990, were influential works for the development of critical whiteness studies. In the German speaking context a volume by Katharina Oguntoye, May Opitz (later Ayim) and Dagmar Schulz titled *Confessing Colour* ("Farbe bekennen") from 1986 was an early work on racism in Germany. The Afro-German authors not only wrote about their lives as affected by racism in Germany, but were some of the few and first who reminded Germany of its colonial history, a theme which was concealed in public discourse until 2004 when the uprising of the Herero in colonial 'Deutsch-Südwest', now Namibia, had its hundredth anniversary. Another early work in the debate on whiteness and gender in the German context was Martha Mamozai's 1982 published book *Black Woman, White Mistress* ("Schwarze Frau, weiße Herrin"), on white* women* in the German colonies. The issue of white* women* in colonialism was only picked up and researched much later in the German speaking context (Zantop 1999; Kundrus 2003a, 2003b; Schneider 2003; Dietrich 2004, 2007; Walgenbach 2007; Wildenthal 2001).

In the English speaking academic realm critical whiteness studies were established in the 1990s, beginning with Ruth Frankenberg's *White Women, Race Matters* published in 1993, and of course Toni Morrison's *Playing in the Dark: Whiteness and the Literary Imagination* from 1993. Richard Dyer's monograph *White* from 1997 was the next influential work. Edited volumes followed, such as *Female Subjects in Black and White* in 1997, the proceedings of a conference in which non-white* and white* feminist scholars discussed race*, psychoanalysis and feminism, edited by Elisabeth Abel, Barbara Christian and Helen Moglen. Ruth Frankenberg also edited a volume: *Displacing Whiteness* in 1997. *The Making and Unmaking of Whiteness* edited

4 See also Gilroy (2002).
5 See also Leonardo (2005).

by Birgit Brander Rasmussen et al. in 2001, David Roedigers' *The Wages of Whiteness* (2002) and *Towards the Abolition of Whiteness* (1994), also edited by Roediger, need to be named here too. The first text on whiteness in the German speaking world was Ursula Wachendorfer's *Soziale Konstruktionen von Weiß-Sein. Zum Selbstverständnis Weißer TherapeutInnen und BeraterInnen* published in 1998. Substantial scholarship into critical studies of whiteness were also taken up at the beginning of the 21st century, first with scattered articles, for instance Tißberger (2001); then edited volumes (Eggers et al. 2005; L'Homme 2005; Tißberger et al. 2006), monographs (Wollrad 2005; Amesberger/Halbmayr 2008; Röggla 2012; Husmann 2010; Tißberger 2013, 2017) and further articles (Tißberger 2006a, 2006b, 2007; Kerner 2013; Tißberger 2014a, 2014b) followed. I name here just a few works on whiteness. There are now too many publications in English and also in German to be listed here.

Critical studies of whiteness mark a paradigm shift in the research on racism. Inspired by those who were the 'objects' of racism and its gaze, the gaze was returned (Bannerji 1993) and directed towards the subjects of racism, namely white* people – and not just right wing extremists or neo-nazis but the unsuspicious well meaning liberal in the center of society who is perpetuating racism, often despite better knowledge and against their will. In the German speaking context this was particularly unsettling for the majority of the people but also for many researchers on racism. Until that point one could see racism to be a problem at the margins of society, perpetrated by some politically misrouted extremists or as often portrayed in psychological research on racism, people with psycho-social problems (i.e. König 1998; Erdheim 1992). The taboo on the term *Rasse** (race*) and *Rassismus* (racism) following the shame about the Nazi-history of Germany, with the intention that the taboo would erase racism, failed. Racism in Germany remained omnipresent, but the language to address it adequately was prohibited. Terms like *Fremdenfeindlichkeit* (fear of strangers) or *Ausländerfeindlichkeit* (hostility against foreigners) replaced 'racism' and 'culture', or 'ethnicity' replaced race*. These terms did not explain, however, what happened in Germany, Austria or Switzerland. Targets of violent attacks or everyday racism were not white* Swedes or white* Canadians but Afro-Germans, Albanian-Austrians or Turkish-Swiss. The reason for the hostility against them and their social exclusion is not their ostensible strangeness but the imagination of a dangerous difference grounded in biology and therefore immutable. Some work on racism had already used discourse analysis following Foucault (Magiros 1995; Terkessidis 1998) or Bourdieus theory on habitus (Weiss 2001), and had thereby shown that racism is not an exception or a deviation but widely spread in Western societies, such as in Germany. The center of society and the 'normal white*' subject, however, remained unsuspicious of racism. That might be due to the fact that even the last-mentioned works concentrated on the level of discourse, institutions and the political, and argued that the subjects are always racist because of a discourse or instituional structures. Actionability – the capacity not to be racist – therefore is enabled only by the change of discourses, institutions or politics. But who changes these discourses, institutions and politics and how?

The starting point of change, respectively the overcoming of racism, must be the subject itself – and I am not following an individualistic idea with this thought. As long as those who profit from racism do not become fully conscious of their involvement – the fact that they are the perpetrators of racism – racism will always be the problem of 'others'. Violent racism is terrible but much more widespread than this form is that of subtle everyday racism. Colette Guillaumin's aforementioned ascertainment that "race does not exist but it docs kill people" (1998:107) points to the social construction of the term and violent forms of racism, but it also refers to the fact that racism leads to the social death of racistically marked people through the regime of whiteness. It is easy for white* people to say "I am not a racist" and support such a statement by examples: "I am a member of Amnesty International", "I have a lot of black* friends" and "I recently campaigned for the hiring of migrant colleagues in our team". It is less easy to say: "I am not white*". Being white* in a society, which is characterized by a racist power structure – what Birgit Rommelspacher (1998) called a 'dominance culture' – in which whites* are automatically superior and privileged, makes everybody in this society who profits from racism a racist. In other words, "the racist is the normal individual in a racist society" (Dolan et al. 1991:71).

Critical whiteness studies approach racism as constitutive of Western societies with whiteness as the signifier of race*, which works primarily on a symbolic and epistemological level and disseminates from there into every pore of society and its individuals. I have shown in the first chapter how evolutionist thought and race* theories in the 18th and 19th centuries built a structure in which the white* male* subject stands for the ideal and everybody else is some sort of deviation – lack, less, inferior. While race* theories and social evolutionism are no longer accepted, whiteness has remained as the dethematized, unconscious and disavowed but all the more powerful signifier of white* supremacy. Charles Mill's (1999) argument that white* supremacy has survived the abolition of slavery, segregation and Apartheid but also human rights and anti-discrimination laws, as well as many pedagogical and political attempts to overcome racism, is founded in the fact that whiteness as a cultural symbolic has become the invisible centre from which all the apparently obsolete racisms continue to work.

The examination of the effects of one's own whiteness therefore requires more than punctual anti-racist activities. It requires a constant dealing with (one's) whiteness as a powerful signifier in the cultural symbolic of white* dominance societies. It requires the awareness to notice not only obvious racism but also the subtle exclusions and inclusions, the subtle otherings, privilegings and the nuances in racist speech – of oneself and others. There is no 'comfort zone' anymore for whites*, just like for racistically marked people, who cannot choose whether or not to deal with racism. They have to. But racistically marked people are not responsible for racism, whites* are – and therefore they need to do the work to overcome it.

George Yancy (2004) writes that whiteness "will never be innocent" as long as it constitutes "an ensemble of power relations", in which whites* are invested with power and advantages vis-á-vis non-whites* (p.6). These very power relations are mostly ignored by those who profit from them. Only when those who are de-marked in racism acknowledge their whiteness as a marker, will they be able to develop consciousness about whiteness and that is the precondition for the capacity to act – provided that they want to. We must not forget that there are still many people who believe in white* supremacy and openly admit to it. That is why the 'critical' is important in studies of whiteness. Racism, of course, is not limited to the personal level, but works on the epistemic and institutional level as well. The subject, that is, the personal, is not prior to the epistemic and institutional. Poststructuralist subject theories, following Foucault and Butler, have shown how subjectivation is an entangled process between the individual, the symbolic, the institutional, the epistemic and other dimensions (see, for example, Meißner 2010). It requires awareness for these subjectivation processes, for racist knowledge and the racist institutional structures in order to interfere – performatively, habitually and discursively – and shift relations of racism, destabilize them and ultimately, at least theoretically, overcome them.

5 Critical Whiteness as Practice of Hegemonic Self-Reflection

So, what is meant by critical whiteness? How can we envision a hegemonic self-reflection in the context of critical whiteness? In the preceding sections I tried to address some of the most important points for this project in preparation for the answer of these questions. In the following I will sketch some ideas about how these points could be translated into critical whiteness as a practice of hegemonic self-reflection. Such practice might be used as a method and be applied didactically according to the context. I am focusing on the aspects that concern the individual – white* – person's hegemonic self-reflection. Obviously, the decolonization and the erasing of racism on the discursive level – the media, schoolbooks, politician's articulations – as well as institutional changes etc. are just as necessary.

First, we need to be aware of the productions of differences and their hierarchization. Whenever an identity is appealed, difference is a necessary 'side-product' (Hall 2004). That happens as soon as we say: "I am a student of gender studies" or "I am German". It also happens when we ask somebody: "where do you come from?" If the person is racistically marked and/or has a name that is uncommon in the culture where the conversation takes place, or speaks with an accent, the question is not a neutral one. Identification had taken place before the conversation started. Were it not for the physiognomic or other markers of the one asked and the empowered gaze of the one asking, the conversation would not have taken place at all. Such a question is based on the presumption that the person asked is not a member of the society where the conversation takes place; that her or his 'origins' are somewhere else. The hierarchy is there without saying and it goes unnoticed by the one with power to ask, and therefore questions the belongingness of the one asked. Difference is also produced when a staff department hesitates to employ a young woman*, assuming that she might get pregnant and thereby giving the job to a slightly less qualified male* applicant. The first applicant is *produced* as a woman* in that moment, and her procreative capacity becomes an issue only through the assumptions of the staff department members. She might be not interested in having children. She might have a partner who will take over the primary parent role etc. but none of that counts anymore. She is fixed as a 'woman* who might get pregnant' and will therefore be less of a human resource for the company. Anti-discrimination laws have made it possible to dispute such incidents, but it takes courage to claim one's rights. It would be much better if people were aware of these subtle and obvious discrimination practices and instead of asking "where do you come from" question their own *curiosity* and reflect upon their motivation for asking. Why is it important to them to know? Which desires are they trying to saturate with the answer? Which uncertainty needs to be overcome?

I took examples from everyday personal life. We might as well look at the media, schoolbooks or social networks to observe productions of difference and deconstruct them. With the latter example – one that we have access to – we can shift the meanings of difference by our own performative participation.

Once we are sensitive to the production of differences and our involvement in it, we might focus a bit more on what the production of difference – the act of othering – does to *ourselves*. As mentioned before, difference and identity are inseparable. Going back to the previous example, what happens to me when I ask another person because s*he seems 'different' to me, "where do you come from?" What does it mean, that I apparently have the right and the power to ask such a question? Where does this power come from? What happens to my 'identity' in the process of such a conversation? What interdependence arises in the process and becomes activated? How is my 'belonging' to an imagined community (Anderson 2006) entangled with the construction of a 'stranger', 'foreigner', 'other' etc.?

The more we observe, think and gain consciousness of the processes of othering – of producing hierarchical difference – we might see how simple words such as 'foreigner*', 'woman*', 'worker' or 'Asian-German' *act* in us and in the context of the uttering. Once we know that, we might change our behaviour and thereby make a given society a safer place for racistically marked and gendered people and therefore a better place for all of us. In the long run the marking and unmarking along the lines of race* and gender might stop and that is where we want to get to.

The constructions of difference work not only along the binary of 'identity' and a constitutive outside. We also have the axis of before-in-service-of-an-after as interdependence. The Enlightenment's ideas of freedom and autonomy did not develop in a vacuum, as Toni Morrison (1993) reminds us. We can observe the heritage of this constellation in contemporary contexts, for example a counselling situation between a counsellor who belongs to the white* dominance society and a racistically marked migrant. How is the apparent *lack* of education, emancipation, independence and resources of the client linked with the legitimacy and professionalism of the counsellor and her*his representation of the opposite qualities? Such questions are everything but easy to answer in the particular situation. It is difficult to disentangle these complex relationships immediately. One needs to be patient – to get comfortable with being uncomfortable (hooks 1994b; Tißberger 2005) – because many certainties are questioned in the necessary process of hegemonic self-reflection. However, if one stays in the course of examination and works through the consequential intellectual and emotional turbulences, the learning process can be fundamental.

Whiteness is not talkative. It works in the quiet and is therefore all the more effective. It works through grammar: 'not yet', 'already', 'still' in descriptions of people and thereby positioning them – and us – on an evolutionist developmental track where 'they' will always be behind 'us' in 'their' development, not realizing that 'I' arrest 'their' development through my powerful attitude. It works through other dimensions of language and speech without the appearance of words that refer directly to race*, for example 'foreigner', 'illiterate' or 'headscarf'. It works in our unconscious when we do *not* notice that there are only white* people at our birthday party even though the city that we live in is 'diverse'.

If we sensitize ourselves to these processes of othering and realize when ontologization takes place, when an evolutionist ideology rules our ideas about the development of our clients, students and neighbours, when difference gets represented as deviance, ab-norm-ality and lack and how social and cultural difference gets inscribed into the body of a person, we can stop that and find more constructive ways to interact with each other. What might sound like the attempt to burden individuals with problems that are grounded in the structures, the institutions and the politics of society – racism, sexism and other relations of discrimination – is only the attempt to change these more sustainably. It is the people who run the institutions, practice politics and build the structures of a society. Since whiteness is a power structure that is probably more than five hundred years old, inscribed in every part of culture and society and sedimented in our unconscious, it requires more than some weekend training to change that power structure. First, our minds have to be decolonized before we do the work in society, be it teaching, counselling, hairdressing, work in the media or governing a country. You, the readers, will be engaged in one or the other field. You will carry the responsibility for maintaining racism and other discriminations and be consciously or unconsciously part of the problem, or part of the solution and work for a society with more justice and less discrimination.

Discussion Questions

1. What is meant by an 'archive of racist and sexist knowledge'?
2. Describe the term 'ontologization' and its relation to gender and racism.
3. What can be achieved with critical whiteness studies in comparison to other forms of anti-racism?
4. Name a few methodological aspects of hegemonic self-reflection in the context of racism and sexism.

References

Abel, Elisabeth/Christian, Barbara/Moglen, Helen (eds.) (1997): Female Subjects in Black and White: Race, Psychoanalysis, Feminism. Berkeley: University of California Press.

Amadiume, Ifi (1987): Male Daughters, FemaleHusbands. London: Zed Books.

Amadiume, Ifi (2000): Daughters of the Goddess, Daughters of Imperialism: African Women struggle for Culture, Power and Democracy. London: Zed Books.

Amesberger, Helga/Halbmayr, Brigitte (2008): Das Privileg der Unsichtbarkeit. Rassismus unter dem Blickwinkel von Weißsein und Dominanzkultur (Bd. 22). Wien: Braumüller.

Anderson, Benedict (2006): Imagined Communities: Reflections on the Origin and Spread of Nationalism. London: Verso. Orig. 1983.

Anzaldúa, Gloria (ed.) (1990): Making Face, Making Soul – HaciendoCaras. Creative and Critical Perspectives by Feminists of Color. San Francisco: Aunt Lute Books.

Bannerji, Himani (ed.) (1993): Returning the Gaze: Essays on Racism, Feminism and Politics. Toronto: Sisterversion Press.

Bhabha, Homi K. (1994): The Location of Culture. London, New York: Routledge.

Boyarin, Daniel (1998): What Does a Jew Want?; or, the Political Meaning of the Phallus. In: Lane, C. (ed.): The Psychoanalysis of Race. New York: Columbia University Press, pp. 211-240.

Brander Rasmussen, Birgit/Klinenberg, Eric/Nexica, Irene J./Wray, Matt (eds.) (2001): The Making and Unmaking of Whiteness. Durham & London: Duke University Press.

Brickman, Celia (2003): Aboriginal Populations in the Mind: Race and Primitivity in Psychoanalysis. New York: Columbia UP.

Butler, Judith (1990/1999): Gender Trouble. New York: Routledge.

Butler, Judith (1993): Bodies That Matter: On the discursive limits of "Sex". New York: Routledge.

Butler, Judith. Foreword in Purtschert, Patricia (2006): Grenzfiguren. Kultur, Geschlecht und Subjekt bei Hegel und Nietzsche. Frankfurt a/M.: Campus.

Dietrich, Anette (2004): Die unmarkierte Weiße Frau. Feministische Debatten über den Deutschen Kolonialismus. iz33w(275), pp. 30-33.

Dietrich, Anette (2007): »Weiße Weiblichkeiten«: Konstruktionen von »Rasse« und Geschlecht im deutschen Kolonialismus. Bielefeld: Transcript.

Dietze, Gabriele (2016): Ethnosexismus. Sex-Mob-Narrative um die Kölner Sylvesternacht. movements 1(2): 1016.

Dietze, Gabriele (2016): Das ‚Ereignis Köln'. Femina Politica 1: 93-102.

Dietze, Gabriele (2017): Sexualpolitik. Verflechtungen von Race und Gender. Frankfurt a.M., Campus.

Du Bois, W. E. B. (1965): Black Reconstruction in America: An Essay toward a History of the Part Which Black Folk Played in the Attempt to Reconstruct Democracy in America, 1860–1880. New York: The Free Press.

Dyer, Richard (1997): White. London: Routledge.

Eggers, Maureeen Maisha/Kilomba, Grada/Piesche, Peggy/Arndt, Susan (Hg.) (2005): Mythen, Masken und Subjekte. Kritische Weißseinsforschung in Deutschland. Münster: Unrast.

Erdheim, Mario (1992): Das Eigene und das Fremde. In: Psyche. Zeitschrift für Psychoanalyse und ihre Anwendungen 8, 46, pp. 730-744.

Frankenberg, Ruth (ed.) (1997): Displacing Whiteness: Essays in Social and Cultural Criticism. Durham: Duke University Press.

Frankenberg, Ruth (1993): White Women, Race Matters: The social Construction of Whiteness. Minneapolis: University of Minnesota Press.

Freud, Sigmund (1912): Totem und Tabu. Studienausgabe (Bd. IX). Frankfurt a.M.: Fischer.

Freud, Sigmund (1926): Die Frage der Laienanalyse. Studienausgabe (Ergänzungsband). Frankfurt a.M.: Fischer.

Freud, Sigmund (1927): Fetischismus. Studienausgabe (Bd. III). Frankfurt a.M.: Fischer.
George, Sheldon (2016):Trauma and Race: A Lacanian Study of African American Racial Identity. Waco, Texas, Baylor University Press.
Gilroy, Paul (2002): The Black Atlantic: Modernity and Double Consciousness. London: Verso.
Gould, Stephen Jay (2007): Der falsch vermessene Mensch. Frankfurt a/M.: Suhrkamp.
Gramsci, Antonio. (1991-2002). Gefängnishefte. Hamburg: Argument.
Guillaumin, Colette (1995): Racism, Sexism, Power and Ideology. London & New York: Routledge.
Hall, Stuart (2004): Wer braucht ‚Identität'?. In: Koivisto, J./Merkens, A. (eds.): Ideologie, Identität, Repräsentation. Ausgewählte Schriften 4. Hamburg: Argument, pp. 167-187.
Hark, Sabine/Villa, Paula-Irene (2017):Unterschieden und Herrschen. Ein Essay zu den ambivalenten Verflechtungen von Rassismus, Sexismus und Feminismus in der Gegenwart. Bielefeld, Transcript.
Hentges, Gudrun (1999): Schattenseiten der Aufklärung. Die Darstellung von Juden und "Wilden" in philosophischen Schriften des 18. und 19. Jahrhunderts. Schwalbach/Ts.: Wochenschau.
Hill Collins, Patricia (1991): Black Feminist Thought. Knowledge, Consciousness, and the Politics of Empowerment (Vol. 2). New York: Routledge.
Hill Collins, Patricia/Bilge, Sirma (2016): Intersectionality. Cambridge, Polity.
hooks, bell (1984): Feminist Theory: From Margin to Center. Boston: South End Press.
hooks, bell (1986): Ain't I a Woman: Black Women and Feminism. London: Pluto Press.
hooks, bell (1989): Talking Back: Thinking Feminist, Thinking Black. Boston: South End Press.
hooks, bell (1994): Black Looks: Popkultur – Medien – Rassismus (K. Meißenburg, Übers.). Berlin: Orlanda.
hooks, bell (1994): Teaching to Transgress: Education as the Practice of Freedom. New York: Routledge.
hooks, bell (1996): Sehnsucht und Widerstand. Kultur, Ethnie, Geschlecht (H. Pfertsch& M. S. Charnitzky, Übers.). Berlin: Orlanda.
Howitt, Dennis/Owusu-Bempah, J. (1994): The Racism of Psychology. Time for Change. New York: Harvester Wheatsheaf.
Husmann, Jana (2010): Schwarz-Weiß-Symbolik. Dualistische Denktraditionen und die Imagination von "Rasse". Religion – Wissenschaft – Anthroposophie. Bielefeld: Transcript.
Jahoda, Gustav (1999): Images of Savages: Ancient roots of modern prejudice in Western culture. London: Routledge.
Jungwirth, Ingrid (2007): Zum Identitätsdiskurs in den Sozialwissenschaften. Eine postkolonial und queer informierte Kritik an George H. Mead, Erik H. Erikson und Erving Goffman. Bielefeld: Transcript.
Kerner, Ina (2013): Critical Whiteness Studies: Potentiale und Grenzen eines wissenspolitischen Projekts. In: Feministische Studien, 2013, 2, pp. 278-293.
König, Hans-Dieter (1998): Sozialpsychologie des Rechtsextremismus. Frankfurt a/M.: Suhrkamp.
Kundrus, Birthe (Hg.) (2003): Phantasiereiche. Zur Kulturgeschichte des deutschen Kolonialismus. Frankfurt a/M.: Campus.
Kundrus, Birthe (2003): Moderne Imperialisten. Das Kaiserreich im Spiegel seiner Kolonien. Köln, Weimar, Wien: Böhlau Verlag.

L'Homme. Europäische Zeitschrift für Feministische Geschichtswissenschaft 16(2) (2005) Whiteness. Wien: Böhlau.

Lenz, Ilse/Luig, Ute (Hg.) (1995): Frauenmacht ohne Herrschaft. Geschlechterverhältnisse in nichtpatriarchalischen Gesellschaften. Frankfurt a/M.: Fischer.

Leonardo, Zeus (2005): The Color of Supremacy: Beyond the Discourse of 'White Privilege'. In: Leonardo, Zeus (ed.): Critical Pedagogy and Race. Malden MA: Blackwell, pp. 37-52.

Lorde, Audre (1984): Sister Outsider: Essays and Speeches. Trumansburg, New York: The Crossing Press.

Magiros, Angelika (1995): Foucaults Beitrag zur Rassismustheorie. Hamburg: Argument.

Mamozai, Martha (1982): Schwarze Frau, weiße Herrin. Reinbek bei Hamburg: Rowohlt.

Meißner, Hanna (2010): Jenseits des autonomen Subjekts. Zur gesellschaftlichen Konstitution von Handlungsfähigkeit im Anschluss an Butler, Foucault und Marx. Bielefeld: Transcript.

Mills, Charles Wade (1999): The Racial Contract. Ithaka: Cornell UP.

Moraga, Cherríe/Anzaldúa, Gloria (eds.) (1981): This Bridge Called My Back: Writings by Radical Women of Color. Watertown: Persephone Press.

Morrison, Toni (1993): Playing in the Dark: Whiteness and the Literary Imagination. New York: Vintage.

Oguntoye, Katharina/Opitz, May/Schultz, Dagmar (Hg.) (1986): Farbe bekennen. Afrodeutsche Frauen auf den Spuren ihrer Geschichte. Frankfurt am Main: Fischer.

Oyewùmí, Oyèrónkẹ́ (1997): The Invention of Women: making an African Sense of Western Gender Discourses. Minneapolis, MN: University of Minnesota Press.

Roediger, David (ed.) (1994): Towards the Abolition of Whiteness: Essays on Race, Politics and Working Class History. London: Verso.

Roediger, David R. (2002): The Wages of Whiteness: Race and the Making of the American Working Class. London: Verso.

Röggla, Katharina (2012): Critical Whiteness Studies und ihre politischen Handlungsmöglichkeiten für Weiße AntirassistInnen. Wien: Mandelbaum.

Rommelspacher, Brigit (1998): Dominanzkultur. Texte zu Fremdheit und Macht. Berlin: Orlanda.

Rubin, Gayle (1975): The Traffic in Women: Notes on the "Political Economy" of Sex. In: Reiter, R. R. (ed.): Toward an Anthropology of Women. New York: Monthly Review Press, pp. 157-210.

Schneider, Rosa B. (2003): Um Scholle und Leben. Zur Konstruktion von "Rasse" und Geschlecht in der deutschen kolonialen Afrikaliteratur um 1900. Frankfurt a/M.: Brandes&Apsel.

Spivak, Gayatri Chakravorty (1994/1988): Can the Subaltern Speak. In: Patrick Williams, L. C. (ed.): Colonial Discourse and Post-Colonial Theory. A Reader. New York: Columbia University Press, pp. 66-111.

Terkessidis, Mark (1998): Psychologie des Rassismus. Opladen/Wiesbaden: Westdeutscher Verlag.

Thürmer-Rohr, Christina (1984): Der Chor der Opfer ist verstummt. beiträge zur feministischen theorie und praxis: Frauenforschung oder feministische Forschung, 7(11).

Tißberger, Martina (2001): Über Frauen und andere Ent- fremd-ete. Psychologie und Gesellschaftskritik. Eigenes, Fremdes., II/III (98/99), pp. 95-124.

Tißberger, Martina.(2005): Uncertainty and Method: Whiteness, Gender and Psychoanalysis in Germany. European Journal of Women's Studies. Special Issue: Transformative Methodologies in Feminist Studies 12, 3, pp. 315-328.

Tißberger, Martina/Dietze, Gabriele/Hrzán, Daniela/Husmann-Kastein, Jana (eds.) (2006): Weiß – Weißsein – Whiteness. Kritische Studien zu Gender und Rassismus. Critical Studies on Gender andRacism. Frankfurt a/M: Peter Lang.

Tißberger, Martina (2006): Die Psyche der Macht, der Rassismus der Psychologie und die Psychologie des Rassismus. In: Tißberger, Martina/Dietze, Gabriele/Hrzán, Dana/Husmann-Kastein, Jana (eds.): Weiß-Weißsein-Whiteness. Kritische Studien zu Gender und Rassismus. Frankfurt a/M: Peter Lang, pp. 13-29.

Tißberger, Martina (2006): 'Wir wollten die Welt entdecken'. Projekt(ion)e(n) der Zivilisation und feministisches Sendungsbewusstsein. In: Bechhaus-Gerst, Marianne/Gieseke, Susanne (eds.): Koloniale und postkoloniale Konstruktionen von Afrika und Menschen afrikanischer Herkunft in der deutschen Alltagskultur. (Bd. 1). Frankfurt a/M.: Peter Lang, pp. 79-92.

Tißberger, Martina (2007): The project(ions) of 'civilisation' and the counter-transferences of whiteness: Freud, psychoanalysis, 'gender', and 'race' (in Germany). In: Deventer, V. v./Blanche, M. T. /Fourie, E./Segalo, P. (eds.): Citizen City. Between Constructing Agent and Constructed Agency. Cape Town, South Africa: Captus University Publications, pp. 406-425.

Tißberger, Martina (2013): Dark Continents und das UnBehagen in der weißen Kultur. Rassismus, Gender und Psychoanalyse aus einer Critical-Whiteness-Perspektive. Münster: Unrast.

Tißberger, Martina (2014): »[...] ist doch auch das Geschlechtsleben des erwachsenen Weibes ein dark continent für die Psychologie«. In: Hostettler, K./Vögele, S. (eds.): Diesseits der imperialen Geschlechterordnung. (Post-)koloniale Reflexionen über den Westen. Bielefeld: Transcript, pp. 121-157.

Tißberger, Martina (2014): Critical Whiteness – eine Figur hegemonialer Selbstreflexion. Philosophie indebate. http://philosophie-indebate.de/1901/schwerpunktbeitrag-critical-whiteness-eine-figur-hegemonialer-selbstreflexion-1/#more-1901

Tißberger, Martina (2017): Critical Whiteness. Zur Psychologie hegemonialer Selbstreflexion an der Intersektion von Rassismus und Gender. Wiesbaden: Springer VS

Truscott, Rossand/Hook, Derek (2014): Lessons from the postcolonial: Frantz Fanon, psychoanalysis, and the psychology of political critique. Palgrave Handbook of Global Political Psychology. C. Kinnvall, T. Capelosand P. Nesbitt-Larking. London & New York, Palgrave.

Wachendorfer, Ursula (1998): Soziale Konstruktionen von Weiß-Sein. Zum Selbstverständnis Weißer TherapeutInnen und BeraterInnen. In: Castro Varela, María del Mar/Vogelmann, Silvia /Weiß, Anja (eds.): Suchbewegungen. Interkulturelle Beratung und Therapie. Tübingen: Deutsche Gesellschaft für Verhaltenstherapie, pp. 49-60.

Walgenbach, Katharina (2007): »Die weiße Frau als Trägerin deutscher Kultur«. Koloniale Diskurse über Geschlecht, „Rasse" und Klasse im Kaiserreich. Frankfurt a/M.: Campus.

Weedon, Chris (1999): Feminism, Theory and the Politics of Difference. Oxford: Blackwell.

Weiss, Anja (2001): Rassismus wider Willen: ein anderer Blick auf eine Struktur sozialer Ungleichheit. Wiesbaden: Westdeutscher Verlag.

Wildenthal, Lora (2001): German Women for Empire, 1884-1945. Durham and London: Duke University Press.

Wollrad, Eske (2005): Weißsein im Widerspruch: feministische Perspektiven auf Rassismus, Kultur und Religion. Königstein/Taunus: Helmer.

Yancy, George (ed.) (2004): What White Looks Like: African-American Philosophers on the Whiteness Question. New York: Routledge.

Zantop, Susanne M. (1999): Kolonialphantasien im vorkolonialen Deutschland (1770-1870). Berlin: Erich Schmidt Verlag.

Heike Weinbach

Social Justice Training: a dialogic approach to diversity education

1 Introduction

This article introduces the concept of social justice dialogic training under the general rubric of the Mahloquet approach. The development and spread of gender and diversity training is closely linked to the implementation of anti-discrimination directives and to the European Charter of Human Rights. These are aligned with the UN Charter of Human Rights. Social group affiliations incorporating human rights and legal drafting form the basis of all antidiscrimination policies: "Any discrimination based on any ground such as sex, race, colour, ethnic or social origin, genetic features, language, religion or belief, political or any other opinion, membership of a national minority, property, birth, disability, age or sexual orientation shall be prohibited" (Charta 2000). In this chapter I will set out the context and the structure of social justice dialogic training, the 'Mahloquet' method, theory and practice, and some differences to other kinds of training.The text intends to explain what it means to use a strong cognitive and dialogical approach in social justice and diversity education training.

2 The Development of Diversity Training in the EU Context

Diversity training in Germany incorporates the legitimization of international and European identity-orientated human rights policy and adopts its categories. When the European Union established the concept of Gender Mainstreaming around 1995, this coincided more or less with the establishment of antidiscrimination and diversity policies. In 2011 the European Union published a programme entitled 'Managing Diversity at Work,' which brought together the diversity charters of different member states, Germany included.

Both gender mainstreaming and European antidiscrimination directives led to obligatory transposition into legislation in the member countries. In

Germany, the concept of gender mainstreaming was implemented in 2000 by the Federal Government, with the General Equal Treatment Act (*Allgemeines Gleichbehandlungsgesetz*/AGG) being implemented 2006. From the beginning, diversity considerations were incorporated into gender mainstreaming and gender equality, although at first the term *diversity* was not used but instead the term *multiple discrimination*. The law on general equal treatment on the basis of sex and sexual orientation is very comprehensive, in order that the social disadvantages of lesbian, gay or transgender identities can be taken as a theme; the concept of gender mainstreaming in Germany has until now remained relatively unchanged. That means gender mainstreaming, despite social changes, still focuses on the categories of *Ms* and *Mr*. This corresponds with EU policy, as the 2015 report on equality between women and men illustrates; the icon on the title page shows a female sign and a male sign interrupted by a jagged line encompassing both sexes, which could be an indicator of the presence of both sexes. The strategic EU programme for the period 2016 to 2019 demonstrates a significant change from earlier programmes. The aspect of multiple discrimination and the necessity for training are no longer evaluated. In this case, it is a question of serious shelving of EU policy compared to earlier gender equality programmes. In Germany, the training programme for gender and diversity is only at its early stages, and this EU programme could perhaps contribute to the reduction in training work in the field of gender and diversity.[1]

The question of how gender mainstreaming and antidiscrimination policy can be implemented in the training context has occupied the EU at the beginning of the discussions about multiple discrimination.The focus on antidiscrimination policy has repeatedly resulted in studies and pamphlets which make practical recommendations and provide training exercises. The studies and practice recommendations concentrate first and foremost on individual cases of discrimination; an awareness of intersectionality is nevertheless present (Bell 2012).

In Germany this policy is implemented at the state level by the Federal Anti-Discrimination Agency and by the German Institute for Human Rights. In the field of gender mainstreaming, the task of implementing training programs was undertaken by trainers in ministries, schools, universities and other administrations.

In consequence, a further range of independent associations, institutes, training bodies and firms have been established who propose training offers. They pursue the goal of implementing EU policies with their own special emphasis. For example the training programme ‘A World of Difference’, set

1 See the article by Ahrens and van der Vleuten in this book.

up by the Anti-Defamation League and the Bertelsmann Foundation, and Anti-Bias-Training[2] or social justice training developed by university based trainers – are established programmes in Germany.

There are also numerous Diversity Management training programmes in the economic context (Genkova/Ringeisen 2016) as well as special training (gender training, antiracist training, training for the awareness of religious discrimination and others). Despite the multitude of diversity training courses that have been in use for quite a long period of time, there has been relatively little research in this field (Bendl, Hanappi-Egger and Hofmann 2012). The training courses differ in their origin, their methods, and their understanding of plurality and diversity. There are also differences in the thematisation or non-thematisation of forms of discrimination. The effects of these programmes are hardly investigated (ibid.).

One must assume that there could be differences in reflection on the impact of social categorisation in the training process. Whether the programmes are open-source based or licensed training programmes also makes a difference. Open-source training is accessible to everybody who speaks the language in which the training is available. The training can also be carried out in an autonomous context and it can be subject to change by many people. Licenced training programmes are accessible to people who can afford it and who are prepared to adhere to the training programme. Regarding all of these aspects, no comparable studies have been available until recently. Regarding the inclusion of intersectional perspectives, the analysis of gender training likewise confirms the need for action:

> "Training policy makers and civil servants about gender+, gender inequalities and diversity has become an important key for establishing, enhancing and improving gender equality policies in the European Union. While there is a huge market for such training, one can also examine the lack of quality measures and standards for trainers, commissioners and participants of gender+/gender/diversity trainings. An analysis of contemporary training manuals for gender and diversity trainings within the EU and the UN shows that intersectionality is a concept which is rarely explicitly used in the training field." (Baer, Keim and Nowottnick:22).

An online survey conducted by Fernuni Hagen (Rohmann, Maziotta and Piper 2013) concludes that diversity training in Germany has some common aspects, for example the determination of perspective-taking as an important building block; discussion as a central method; the target group of multipliers as well as the number of recruiting trainers with a university degree. The survey identifies the need for an intellectual exchange of ideas about the training and any shortcoming in the assessment of training offers. Diversity training

2 See the article by Schwärzer-Dutta in this book.

courses are integrated into their respective political and philosophical contexts. These are determined by the structure of the political system in the country, its power relations, history and debates in the social movements themselves, which are addressed at the level of international and European human rights. In the following section, I would like to introduce the social justice training Programme, inspired byAmerican and Jewish methods; which has been adapted, reworked and reinvented in the German context. In this way the training programme has resulted from the interactions between participants and trainers in a continuous and never-ending process of development.

3 Social Justice and Diversity Training

The training programmes were created by Leah Carola Czollek, Gudrun Perko and Heike Weinbach around 2000 in Berlin. They came from different theoretical and personal backgrounds and realized that they were thinking about similar questions, which were:

- Why is it such a challenge for people to understand and acknowledge difference and different perspectives, even if these perspectives are not threatening them in any way at all?
- Why do people blame other people or politicians for injustice in society?
- What does it mean to look at society from a structural perspective? Is that something you can learn?
- What does it really mean to make a significant contribution to change society? As an individual, as a group, as a community?

The trainers and authors of the social justice training were introduced to the idea of a Social Justice and Diversity training by studying the programme given by the University of Massachusetts (Adams, Bell and Griffin 2007). They soon realized that a transformation and adaption of such a programme cannot work because the American and German societal contexts are too different in terms of educational traditions, history and theory, and hence they transformed the whole programme and created a different form of training based on a different method – the dialogic concept of *Mahloquet*. However, they kept the strong approach of their American colleagues by focusing on structural contexts, and ensured that individuals were seen as of the structures of society (Czollek, Perko and Weinbach 2012).

3.1 Structure and Background of the Trainings

The underlying method is the Jewish dialogic approach *Mahloquet* which represents the modus of a dialogic conversation and an ethical-dialogic mindset. Participants learn and practise this approach in a short-term (a weekend) or a long term training programme (six month or one year). Language and acts of recognition are important, as well as responsibility between the participants: taking care of each other during training.

Trainers give short inputs on the history theory and structural aspects of different forms of discrimination and the intersectionality of the subjects. Participants do exercises on this content on their own during training: for example, biography work, but also structural analysis. At the end of the training programme there is a strong focus on actions for change, which might be individual actions or collective actions, such as organising an exhibition, founding a group, writing a paper, reading a book, or even talking to people in the streets. During long term training a significant period of time will also be given to train-the-trainer questions and/or meta-cognitive reflections.

There are many modules with different topics, and in each module the trainers follow a similar methodological structure. Over a period of fifteen years the modules were augmented, resulting in the following modules being taught: ableism; ageism; adultism; antisemitism; anticiganism; classism; lookism; east/west = GDR/FRG power structures and discrimination; racism/migration; gender and queer: sexism/heterosexism; religion and belief discrimination; Mahloquet (dialogue training).

The theoretical background, fully explained in the 2012 book by Czollek, Perko and Weinbach, is in theories of social justice: economic equality, participation, recognition, visibility (Young 1990, 1996; Fraser 2001,, 2003; Weinbach 2006; Honneth 2003); diversity theory: political and critical diversity, intersectionality theory (hooks 2014; Collins 2009; Czollek,Perko and Weinbach 2009a, 2009b; Czollek and Perko 2012); the philosophy of deconstruction (Derrida 1972, 2007); theories of plurality (Arendt 2005, 2006; Castoriadis 1990) and theories of dialogue (Buber 1973, 1995; Levinas 1995; Bohm 1996).

3.2 The Dialogic Approach 'Mahloquet'

Mahloquet (Hebrew/French) means 'disputation'. The word Mahloquet is an old Jewish concept, and was relayed and probably rediscovered by the French Rabbi Ouaknin (Czollek 2003). That is the reason why we pronounce Mahloquet with a French intonation. Originally it means discussion and disputation between two teachers, and later between teacher and student, and amongst students. It is a discussion based on the old Jewish texts, like the Thora or Talmud or other books. This discussion is a specific way to dialogue, which Mendelsohn describes:

> "The students had the freedom to interrupt myself, creating new arguments, focus on the discussion between themselves and I often stopped my lecture and discourse to let them enjoy their dialogue." (Czollek 2003:127)[3]

The Rabbi or the teacher is not the main authority in a Mahloquet dialogue; every student is allowed to question everything at all times, and inspire the discussion with new and contradicting ideas. With interruption and lively discussion the students are nevertheless expected to listen to each other, and use the ideas of the other students as an opportunity to think further. Mahloquet is a method and an attitude, a mindset, and a concept of human beings as well. A conversation in the modus of Mahloquet needs the other person, since in the dialogue people share their different views and perspectives on the same text, as well as make references to others who have had different interpretations of the texts. There is no correct interpretation, as every perspective will be accepted and there is no need for compromise or looking for consent during a lively debating process. It is not the individual who is the focus of the dialogue, as each voice will be heard and listened to, so that the plurality of perspectives is attended to. There is no finality of debe or perspective, because each one can be questioned at any time. There is no concept of 'truth'. The plurality of perspectives facilitates a challenge to ossified beliefs and structures of thinking. The dialogue might alter the outlook of the students. In this setting, no perspective can become a dogma or an ideology because the space is open for ambiguity and plural meaning. Every person in a group is enabled and encouraged to speak out, and everyone in the group needs to take care that the speaker will be listened to. The idea behind this is that every person has a very special view of the world, politics and life in general; every person has knowledge and experience. And people can only change their own views while listening to others and being exposed to new ideas. Rabbi Ouaknin follows the Talmud, which means a logic of *sense* instead a logic of *truth*. Sense is a category which includes the personal and social dimension; that is, something does make sense for someone in a specific context at the moment, although it might be different tomorrow (Czollek 2003). What makes sense for me during the dialogue may change while discussing and debating a subject. Mahloquet, in an educational context, therefore means opening yourself consciously to other perspectives, letting them touch you, and enjoying questioning your own obvious and commonplace ideas.

3 Translation from the German original version by the author.

3.3 *Method and Ethics of Mahloquet in Social Justice Training*

There is a special way to practice Mahloquet or to learn to act in a dialogic setting. It means: there is no leader (every person leads the dialogue), no moderation and no list of speakers, and we do not need to ask someone for permission to speak. Everybody takes care of everybody during the dialogue, and everybody is responsible for the balance of the dialogue.Every speech and every contribution within the dialogue is treated as equal. There is no hierarchy and every view will be respected.The focus is on the subject of the dialogue. Similar to Ruth Cohn's *themenzentrierte Interaktion* (theme-centered interaction) (Cohn 1993), it is the issue which makes it possible to connect, to share, to talk to each other instead of talking only to yourself and about yourself. You do not label other people in a dialogue, you ask them questions about their ideas, experiences, and different views. And youcommunicate the background of your question. Questions are a difficult thing. A question can easily make people feel embarrassed or culpable, or just left wondering, while explaining the reason for the question brings transparency and understanding into the dialogue.Participants will be encouraged to reflect before speaking. It isnot necessary to speak out about everything, and no one expects you to be honest in one sense: I simply tell you what is in my mind.. A dialogical setting should support participants to think before they speak, and reflect on the consequences of speech and the way and structure of their own speech. Historical, theoretical and empirical perspectives (from literature, science, views from your grandparents and other people) can be used as reference and further perspectives within the dialogue. Trainers introduce participants to some attitudes which might be helpful, and encourage them to try out these attitudes, but participants are also allowed to question and discuss these, as the whole concept is open to be developed and changed and rethought at all times.

Attidudes of speech in a dialogue are, for example:

- Humbleness, which means keeping in your mind that your view of the world is not the right view, it is only one view among a lot of others; leave the idea of omnipotence behind.
- Enjoying differences and allowing yourself to feel touched by difference and strangeness.
- Think of the person next to you as a friend. This is based on the Greek concept of friendship (Derrida 2007): everybody in a dialogue is a guest of the other person and should be treated like a guest in the sense of hospitality.
- Taking responsibility for each other in a dialogue, for the needs and interests of the other participants.

- No reward is intended. People should focus on their interest in other people's views due only to their interest in widening the perspectives of everybody.
- Ongoing and never-ending questioning and examining of meanings, values, ideas.
- Speaking and acting without an intention; there is no intention to convince other people, due to the concept that nobody knows the truth

Attitudes of *de*-hierarchy are, for example:

- Every subject is treated as an equal.
- Equal relations between the group and the individual, which means the individual is as important as the group and vice versa.
- No victims; no individual will be sacrificed to the group or to an idea.
- No one will be forced into structure, for example fixed group identities.
- Individuals speak for themselves only, not in the name of a group, and cultural identity is only in the background of the unique and special individual.
- There is no solution and no synthesis of contradictions or different outlooks; diverse attitudes remain different point of views.
- Solutions can be win-win Encouraging the thought of possibilities beyond a compromise; that there might be a third, fourth or many more solutions (Czollek/Perko 2006).
- There is no one in the group who tells you what is wrong or right. You need to make up your own mind.

Usually people ask if these ideas could really work in practise. As thexperience shows they *can* work, but there is one condition *sine qua non*. That is: the absence of violence. Where violence kicks in the Mahloquet dialogue has to stop at once, and can only go on after the situation has been changed. Of course,hat people regard as a violent act can be different. But at the moment when someone describes the atmosphere in a group as 'violent' we need to stop the dialogue, reflect upon the situation, and change something. That can happen in a short or longer break, or in the group discussion itself – or if necessary, though moderation (mediation, conflict resolution etc.) (Czollek/Perko/Weinbach 2012).

3.4 *Theory, Evaluation and Implications of Mahloquet in Educational Settings*

Here I will make some relevant theoretical and philosophical points and link them to the experiences and evaluations of the social justice training programme.

> "Every culture institutes itself through the unilateral imposition of some politics of language. Mastery begins, as we know, through the power of naming, of imposing, and legitimating impositions." (Derrida 1998:39)

This not only happens in society in general, in the structures of the society, but also in every classroom, and even in private conversations. People try to convince others, ignore the reality of others, and others do accept the power structures thus created. Some people focus on themselves and their own views of the world, and they believe that the world would be a better place if every person shared their ideas. The challenge in an educational setting is to create a space where people regard the presence and the voice of every other person to be as important as their own. If this happens no view or perspective can become dominant, and no culture can be imposed on another.

Two evaluations of training sessions with young people from different cultural and religious backgrounds took place, and one of a training session with children in a primary school. There were similiar responses from the young people. For them the most effective and most interesting experience was: *we could tell our viewpoints, we were not blamed, everbody told their ideas and opinions, we listened to each other, we all were concentrated.* And from the teacher: *I was astonished how different they are and what the pupils think.*

Hannah Arendt (1996), again and again, emphasizes the idea of understanding: 'I want to understand'. Understanding means listening to what people think. Understanding means realising differences in thinking, feeling, articulating, living a life. Understanding needs the attitude of not categorizing, and not forcing what I hear and see into the categories which are in my mind. Understanding as it is practiced in the Mahloquet concept means allowing the meaning, sense and explanations of other people to have an affect on myself. In social justice training this seems to be the most difficult thing, as people tend to question the experiences of others , and tend to go back to their own views shortly after having listened to extraordinary stories from members of the group, just as if it never took place. Doing simple exercises can enable participants learn how to be inspired by and focus on what other people have to tell us. Following Hannah Arendt's concepts of plurality we get an idea of diversity as a natural condition and process:

> "Human action, like all strictly political phenomena, is bound up with human plurality, which is one of the fundamental conditions of human life insofar it rests on the fact of natality, through which the human world is constantly invaded by strangers, newcomers whose actions and reactions cannot be foreseen by those who are already there and are going to leave in a short while." (Arendt 2006:174)

When people come together there always is plurality. But without making plurality visible, the imagination can eliminate the awareness of plurality, and people may impose their own fears and anxities, and create pictures of others whom they have never spoken to before.

In a dialogic process the imaginings, fantasies and constructions of the participants will be questioned and challenged, and as far as they get into such a process, new imaginings and new ideas can be created. During social justice training such a process happens all the time for everyone in the group. Everyone realises how deeply structurally involved they are in their own constructions and fantasies of what other people are like, and how little they really know about themselves or someone else. Over and over there are moments of humbleness, when participants realise what Martin Buber pointed out: what you know about another person is only what that person tells you (Buber 1995). Knowledge about and from other people comes out of dialogues and encounters, though it is always a fragment, a moment, a suprise and a present in the present.

4 Differences between Social Justice Training and other Training Programmes

Social justice training focuses on an understanding of diversity as taking into account discrimination and being critical of the discriminating aspects of diversity (Czollek/Perko 2012). From the beginning, intersectionality was part of social justice training. Intersectionality here is understood to be a model of multiperspectivity and the overlapping structural analysis of discrimination. Diversity categories must not be reduced and one discrimination category should not be subsumed under another (for example antisemitism under racism). The aim is to make all forms of discrimination visible (Perko 2017).

From the online questionnaire of the Fernuniversität Hagen (Rohmann, Maziotta and Piper 2013), similarities and differences between social justice training and other diversity training could be observed. Social Justice Training, like other forms of training, involves perspective-taking. Here it is important in a sense of broadening perspectives and learning to appreciate cognitive recognition, the plurality of perspectives and the differences in perspectives. Deepening the ability to empathise is, in social justice training, better described as ‘intellectual empathy’ (Linker 2014). In the arena of Jewish dialogue, Hannah Arendt describes this as an attitude of longing for deep understanding (Arendt 1996). This understanding also includes a metacognitive reflection on the training session and the method itself. Roleplay, which was used by 88% of the participants of the questionnaire, is not part of social justice training programmes because the dialogue in a real encounter is the most important part of the method. Changing perspectives here happens through a deep cognitive understanding and not through a simulation. Similar to other training programmes the analysis of stereotypes and structural discrimination is a central part of the training method, and this includes intersectional approaches. Identity categories and social group categories are regarded as being based on political and societal structures. In the dialogues these categories have to be challenged again and again. A social justice training programme strives to see ‘identity’ as being a fluid construct which should be questioned from a metacognitive perspective.

5 Conclusion

Like other types of training, social justice training is an educational approach to promote awareness about discrimination and diversity in society. It depends on how much change people are prepared to make in their daily life practices. Trainers have the obligation to reflect on the effects and longterm outcomes of their methods by being aware of the ambiguous and and unpredictable structure of those learning processes.

Discussion Questions

1. Carry out research on the term and concept of *Mahloquet*; find out more about the history and the method. Discuss the results with other students.
2. With a group of six to ten people choose a text and discuss it using the rules of the Mahloquet method. Afterwards reflect on your discussion in the same way.
3. Create one exercise to make participants aware of intersectionality. Practise the exercise with other students. Reflect on the exercise and write a short essay about the challenges of incorporating intersectionality into diversity training.

References

Adams, Mauriann/Bell, Lee Ann/Griffin, Pat (1997, 2007): Teaching for diversity and social justice. A sourcebook. New York, London: Routledge.
Arendt, Hannah (1993): Between Past and Future: eight exercises in political thought. New York: Viking Press.
Arendt, Hannah (1996): Ich will verstehen. Selbstauskünfte zu Leben und Werk. München: Piper.
Arendt, Hannah (2006): Denken ohne Geländer. Texte und Briefe. Edited by Heide Bohne and Klaus Stadler. München: Piper.
Baer, Susanne/Keim, Janet/Nowottnick, Lucy (undated): Intersectionality in Gender + Training. Retrieved June 6, 2017 (http://www.quing.eu/files/WHY/baer_keim_nowottnick.pdf)
Bell, Marc (2012): Anti-Discrimination Law and the European Union. Oxford: Oxford University Press.
Bendl, Regine/Hanappi-Egger, Edeltraud/Hofmann, Roswitha (eds.) (2012): Diversität und Diversitätsmanagement. München: UTB
Buber, Martin (1995): Ich und Du. Stuttgart: Reclam.
Buber, Martin (1973): Das dialogische Prinzip. Heidelberg: Lambert Schneider.
Bohm, David (1996): On Dialogue. London und New York: Routledge
Castoriadis, Cornelius (1984): Gesellschaft als imaginäre Institution. Entwurf einer politischen Philosophie. Frankfurt: Suhrkamp.
Charter of Fundamental Rights of the European Union. Retrieved from: http://www.europarl.europa.eu/charter/pdf/text_en.pdf (17.6.2017)
Cohn, Ruth/Klein, Irene (1993): Großgruppen gestalten mit Themenzentrierter Interaktion. Ein Weg zur lebendigen Balance zwischen Einzelnen, Aufgaben und Gruppe. Mainz: Matthias Grünewald Verlag.
Collins, Patricia Hill (2009): Black Feminist Thought: knowledge, consciousness, and the politics of empowerment. New York: Routledge.
Derrida, Jacques (2007): Von der Gastfreundschaft. Frankfurt/M.: Suhrkamp.
Derrida, Jacques (1972): Die Schrift und die Differenz. Frankfurt/M.: Suhrkamp.
Derrida, Jacques (1998): Monolingualism of the Other; or, the Prosthesis of Origin. Stanford: Stanford University Press.
Czollek, Leah Carola (2003): Am Anfang war das Wort. Aspekte jüdischen Dialoges und die Vielstimmigkeit von Multikulturalismus. In: Czollek, Leah Carola/Perko, Gudrun (eds.): Verständigung in finsteren Zeiten. Interkulturelle Dialoge statt 'Clash of Civilizations'. Köln: Papyrossa, pp. 44-64.
Czollek, Leah Carola/Perko, Gudrun (2006): Mahloquet als integrative Methode des Dialoges: ein Mediationsverfahren in sieben Stationen. In: Perspektive Mediation. Beiträge zur KonfliktKultur 4. Wien.
Czollek, Leah Carola/Perko, Gudrun/Weinbach, Heike (2009a): Lehrbuch Gender und Queer. Grundlagen, Methoden und Praxisfelder.Weinheim: Juventa Beltz
Czollek, Leah Carola /Perko, Gudrun/Weinbach, Heike (2009b): Radical Diversity im Zeichen von Social Justice: Philosophische Grundlagen und praktische Umsetzung von Diversity in Institutionen. In: Castro Varela, Maria do Mar (ed.): Soziale (Un)Gerechtigkeit. Kritische Perspektiven auf Diversity, Intersektionalität und Antidiskriminierung. Weinheim: Juventa Beltz, pp. 260-276.

Czollek, Leah Carola/Perko, Gudrun/Weinbach, Heike (2012): Praxishandbuch Social Justice und Diversity. Theorien, Training, Methoden, Übungen. München/Weinheim: Juventa Beltz.

European Commission Justice (2012): Managing Diversity at Work. Brussels. Retrieved June 16, 2017. (http://ec.europa.eu/justice/discrimination/files/managing_diversity_atwork_en.pdf)

European Union Report on equality between women and men (2015). Brussels. Retrieved June 16, 2017. (http://ec.europa.eu/justice/gender-equality/files/annual_reports/2016_annual_report_2015_web_en.pdf)

European Union (2016): Strategic Engagement for Gender Equality 2016-2019. Brussels. Retrieved June 16, 2017. (http://ec.europa.eu/anti-trafficking/eu-policy/strategic-engagement-gender-equality-2016-2019).

Fraser, Nancy (2001): Die halbierte Gerechtigkeit. Schlüsselbegriffe des postindustriellen Sozialstaates („Justice interruptus“). Frankfurt/M.: Suhrkamp.

Fraser, Nancy/Honneth, Axel (2003): Umverteilung oder Anerkennung? Eine politisch-philosophische Kontroverse. Frankfurt/M.: Suhrkamp.

Genkova, Petra/Ringeisen, Tobias (eds.) (2016.): Handbuch Diversity Kompetenz, Bd. 1, Perspektiven und Anwendungsfelder. Berlin, Heidelberg: Springer.

Honneth, Axel (1992): Kampf um Anerkennung. Frankfurt/M.: Suhrkamp.

Honneth, Axel (2000): Das Andere der Gerechtigkeit. Aufsätze zur praktischen Philosophie.Frankfurt/M.: Suhrkamp.

hooks, bell (2014): Feminist Theory: from margin to center. New York: Routledge.

Levinas, Emmanuel (1995): Zwischen uns. Versuche über das Denken an den Anderen. München, Wien: Carl Hanser Verlag.

Linker, Maureen (2014): Intellectual Empathy: Critical thinking for social justice. University of Michigan Press: Ann Arbor.

Perko, Gudrun/Czollek, Leah Carola (2012): Social Justice und Diversity Training: Intersektionalität als Diversitymodell und Strukturanalyse von Diskriminierung und Exklusion. Retrieved May 10, 2017 (http://portal-intersektionalitaet.de/startseite/).

Perko, Gudrun (2017): Social Justice im Zeichen von Diversity, Pluralität und Perspektivenvielfalt: Philosophische Grundlagen für eine diskriminierungskritische Soziale Arbeit. In: Perko, Gudrun (ed.): Philosophie in der Sozialen Arbeit. Weinheim, Basel: Juventa Beltz, pp. 48-69.

Rohmann, Anette/Maziotta, Agostino/Piper, Verena (2013): Diversitytrainings im deutschsprachigen Raum. Hagen. Retrieved June 16, 2017. (https://www.fernuni-hagen.de/psychologie/psychologisches_institut/wp-content/uploads/2016/06/Diversity-Trainings_im_deutschsprachigen_Raum.pdf).

Weinbach, Heike (2006): Social Justice statt Kultur der Kälte. Alternativen zur Diskriminierungspolitik in der Bundesrepublik Deutschland. Berlin: Dietz Verlag.

Young, Iris Marion (1990): Justice and the Politics of Difference. Princeton: Princeton University Press.

Young, Iris Marion (1996): Fünf Formen der Unterdrückung. In: Nagl-Docekal, Herta/ Pauer-Studer, Herlinde (eds.): Politische Theorie, Differenz und Lebensqualität. Frankfurt/M: Suhrkamp, pp. 99-139.

Dagmar Vinz

Transdisciplinarity with 'Science & Fiction'

1 Introduction

Transdisciplinary Research[1] (TR) is highly important for intersectional Gender and Diversity Studies. Many Gender and Diversity Studies Programmes and Institutes in Germany and worldwide pursue the goal to analyse culture and society, power and politics or bodies and identities from a transdisciplinary perspective. It is to merge and 'transcend' the diverse disciplinary approaches towards an enhanced understanding of gender and diversity in the form of 'Super-Interdisciplinarity'.

Apart from the institutionalization of TR as an important feature of Gender and Diversity Studies Programmes at universities, a second form of TR has gained importance: TR, understood as participatory and applied science, has become an important element of research at independent research institutes. The solution of 'real-world-problems' and the implementation of strategies for sustainable transformations with the involvement of all relevant stakeholder lie at the heart of TR as an applied science. As I will show gender has become an important category for the analysis of actors and for the implementation of strategies in the context of the transdisciplinary German 'SÖF Programme' (Sozial-Ökologische Forschung), which I will present later in more detail.

Thirdly, I will portray my innovation of TR as a hybrid form, which I call 'Science & Fiction'. TR in this form serves the communication of knowledge, experiences or research results by merging scientific and literary creative writing projects. My approach of 'Science & Fiction' uses the mark '&' instead of 'and', in order to stress the intersection between science and fiction which is supposed to be more intense than a pure addition (plus) of both approaches. The idea for this approach stems from my experience of teaching in the context of an applied master's programme of Gender and Diversity Studies. I found that there was a lack of literature related to practice and devoted to the qualification of change agents in organizations. I also

---

1 I will abbreviate Transdisciplinary Research as TR.

found that there is a lack of literature about gender and diversity, which bridges the gap between academic feminism and popular culture. There is a need for literature, which opens ways from the 'bubbles of alternative subcultures' to the mainstream.

In this article I refer to different pieces of literature, particularly in the German speaking world, as relevant for my approach of 'Science & Fiction'. Furthermore, I give reasons for researchers and students to contribute to this field. The creative writing about change agents and their social and political experiences can help to reach a broader audience. It can also help to improve the knowledge and strategies of change agents on how to engender transformations in organizations. Furthermore, it can prevent to repeat the same mistakes by improving the dialogue between the generations, e.g. between first wave feminists and today's gender equality officers. TR that follows the understanding of my approach 'Science & Fiction' does not only target the public opinion but also implies practical and strategic advice for change agents in the field of Gender and Diversity Politics. It is also a counter hegemonic project against the dominance of quantitative research and the undue preference of peer reviewed 'A-journals' in social sciences. It provides knowledge for a broader audience and aims to improve the quality of the public discourse e.g. on the introduction of new technologies or on strategies for sustainable transformations. It also has the potential to sensitize for gender bias or to overcome other stereotypes. Whereas traditional research is often characterized by an intense division of labour and directed to a small number of experts, TR attempts to be integrating and to provide 'generalists' with expertise.

The first part of my article is devoted to present definitions of transdisciplinarity and to discuss the three levels of TR with respect to their relevance for intersectional Gender and Diversity Studies. Secondly, I will give examples of literature, which can be seen as a contribution to my approach of 'Science & Fiction'. Last but not least, I will give examples of possible formats to the field of 'Science & Fiction' in order to both inform and to encourage students and scholars of Gender and Diversity Studies to develop research designs or creative writing projects in this field.

2 Trans-X

Before I discuss the different definitions and mottoes of TR I want to shed the light on the prefix 'trans'. In hundreds of words the prefix 'trans' is used with the meanings 'across, through, over, beyond or outside of'. In everyday life words like 'transport', 'transaction' or 'transatlantic' are widely used. In the academic world every student or scholar of Gender and Diversity Studies is confronted sooner or later with 'trans' as a prefix in very diverse empirical phenomena or research perspectives. Thus I want to suggest all readers of this article to remember and reflect their knowledge about and their experience with the prefix 'trans' (see Question 1).

From my personal experience the prefix 'trans' is often associated with a superior or more developed concept for very diverse matters like research strategies, identity formations or policy strategies. The prefix 'trans' in these constellations is thought to overcome binary oppositions and to destabilize hierarchies between dualisms like reason-emotion, male-female, up-down etc. Thus it is meant to cross borders and to create new entities. Some regard trans-perspectives therefore as postmodern.

My personal historiography of 'trans' as an important prefix for research starts with Judith Butler and the notion of performance for the representation of 'transgender', 'transwomen' or 'transsexual'. I then came across Karl Polanyi (1978/1997) and his important work on 'The Great Transformation', which shaped capitalist structures in England. The change of economy, culture and politics is described as a revolutionary process, which brings about entirely new forms of social relations. Transformation according to David Harvey (2011) from a dialectical perspective means that everything is in process, everything is in motion. Ludger Pries (2008) has raised recognition with his work on 'Transnationalization' as a phenomenon going beyond and across the nation state. He discusses transnational life worlds (family, ageing), transnational organizations like EURO work councils and the change of social institutions like labour markets or inequality. Last but not least, the term 'translational' has gained my attention as a term, which comes from medicine. It refers to research that 'translates' findings into diagnostic tools, policies or health education. Translational research is thus, closely tied with the understanding of TR as an applied science.

Definitions of TR

To begin with, I have collected two definitions of TR which imply different understandings of TR:

- TR is "research conducted across existing fields of study with results applicable to all involved"[2].

2 Quora.com gives an overview over different schemata of TR: https://www.quora.com/Does-the-following-model-correctly-explain-the-differences-between-multidisciplinarity-interdisciplinarity-and-transdisciplinarity (14/08/2017).

- TR is a "new form of learning and problem solving involving cooperation among different parts of society and academia in order to meet complex challenges of society" (Thompson Klein et al. 2001:7).

Firstly, TR integrates different disciplinary perspectives ('across existing fields'). Secondly, it has to be mentioned that TR is participatory and lives from the involvement of various groups in the research process ('involving cooperation among different parts of society and academia'). Thirdly, TR is an innovative way of learning and problem solving ('results applicable to all involved'). In this form several research stages for TR have been developed: It starts with the analysis of real world problems and ends with the suggestion of solutions under collaboration of all relevant stakeholder.

Stages of TR

TR organizes team-based research along different stages. The differentiation between specific phases in the process of gaining knowledge shall help researchers to work together effectively and to be sensitive to other (disciplinary) perspectives. It shall also foster researchers' awareness of 'real world problems' and of the need to produce knowledge for the 'solution' of social or ecological problems.

The literature on TR presents various models for the organization of the research process in phases or stages. Two of them are presented in the table below. At this point it merely has to be mentioned that the models for different phases of TR do not draw a strict division line between the stages in a temporal order. Researchers rather have to be aware that a shifting between the different levels of research is often necessary for gaining good results. The phase models thus can be seen as a blueprint for the mind in order to reflect the research process and its ups and downs more consciously.

Table 1 (Stages of TR)

	Model 1 (Three Stages)	**Model 2 (Four Stages)**
Source	e.g. www.transdisciplinarity.ch	Hall (et al.) 2012
Stage 1	Problem Identification	Development
Stage 2	Analysis of Real World Problems	Conceptualization
Stage 3	Bringing Results to Fruition	Implementation
Stage 4		Translation

Mottoes of TR

More than other fields of research, TR is a science that has to sell itself. Therefore, various 'mottoes' have been created to promote TR, which I have collected in the following lines:

- "Stimulating Synergies, Integrating Knowledge" (UNESCO. Social Science Sector 1998:2).
- TR "is, essentially, team science".[3]
- TR "may not be located on the prevailing disciplinary map" (Gibbons et al 1994:5).
- TR "is dynamic. It is problem solving capability on the move" (ibid.).

Key words to characterize TR are 'team', 'integrating' and 'problem solving capability'. I am sure that more slogans for the positive characterization of TR could be found. TR presents itself as an innovation of applied science and it stresses its potential for solving problems of the modern world. TR is however research that sells itself. In particular independent and applied research institutes refer to TR for money laundering and for the legitimation of research that does not follow the dominant path of quantitative research.

Perspectives on TR – Pros and Cons

To give an impression of contradicting perspectives on TR, I have listed some arguments for and against TR , which I have been confronted with on several occasions when diskussing TR.

Pros

- TR is a "process of minimizing the bias of each perspective" (Häberli et al. 2001:7);
- TR as "prerequisite for progress in single disciplines" (ibid).

Contra

- TR as 'incompetent involvement in other disciplines';
- TR as 'ill-disciplined';
- TR as 'too ambitious' and too 'cost-intensive';
- TR as 'overburdening researchers'.

---

3 TREC Center: http://www.obesity-cancer.wustl.edu/en/About/What-Is-Transdisciplinary-Research (14/08/2017).

Both perspectives can come true in the process of research. Therefore, costs and requirements have to be critically examined before starting research. The awareness of one's own disciplinary belonging also has to be reflected upon in order to take an enhanced transdisciplinary perspective. Altogether sensitivity of all actors in the research involved is necessary – awareness of chances and risks, of advantages and disadvantages, and of benefits and losses.

3 TR and Gender Studies in Germany

Transdisciplinarity has gained importance in German Gender Studies by the foundation of inner-university transdisciplinary institutes and by the institutionalization of Gender Studies degrees with combinations of disciplinary and transdisciplinary approaches.[4]

The success of the notion of transdisciplinarity for the institutionalization of Gender and Diversity Studies in Germany can be explained by the fact that it is a very promising concept. It claims to provide new insights for theoretical, methodological and empirical research on gender relations. It enhances the dialogue between researchers and students with different disciplinary backgrounds and helps to critically reflect theoretical and methodological foundation of one's own discipline. Thus it helps to generate knowledge that exceeds the constraints of one's own discipline. The combination of these elements and perspectives contributes to the quality and potential of Gender Studies in Germany.[5]

Research and teaching in the field of Gender and Diversity Studies at German *universities* mainly refer to transdisciplinarity as a way to productively overcome boundaries between already established academic disciplines. Theoretical foundations, methodological approaches and empirical observations in one discipline are questioned by researchers of another discipline; ways to find a common language are entered and mutual support helps to be in uncharted waters. Research at independent German research *institutes*, however, has developed another understanding of TR: to overcome not the gap between the disciplines, but the cleavage between academic disciplinary

4 Vinz (2016) gives an overview on Gender and Diversity Studies in Germany, Austria, and Switzerland. Furthermore there is the Collection of the 'Netzwerks Frauen- und Geschlechterforschung NRW': http://www.gender-curricula.com/gender-studies/gender-studiengaenge/(14/08/2017).

5 Exemplary for the German debate about the relevance of TR for Gender Studies, I want to list the following references, which refer both to transdisciplinary research and to the integration of transdisciplinary skills in B.A. and M.A. programmes of Gender Studies: Kahlert/Thiessen/Weller (2005), Baer/Hornscheidt (2011, in English), and Schier/Schwinger (2014).

research and 'real-world problems', between 'theory' and 'practice', between researchers and policy actors, between academic experts and 'real-world-experts'. In Germany, this understanding of TR has been particularly developed in the programme Social-ecological Research (Sozial-Ökologische Forschung, SÖF), which was set up by the Federal Ministry of Education and Research (BMBF) in 1999.[6] In an agenda process SÖF was theoretically, methodologically and empirically further developed with participation of all relevant stakeholder.

From a gender perspective, it is of high importance that the research projects, which were funded under the umbrella of the transdisciplinary SÖF programme from 2000 to 2005, were *obliged* to integrate gender perspectives in their research design. Thus knowledge produced by SÖF should combine TR with the simultaneous consideration of gender relations. After 2005 gender perspectives should only be implemented voluntarily in the context of SÖF. Most recently, Schultz/Schramm/Hummel (2015) give a concise overview over SÖF as TR. They argue that SÖF should be systematically evaluated from a gender perspective: How was gender implemented as an important social dimension theoretically, conceptually and practically in TR? In what ways did the solutions brought forward by TR contribute to both solving ecological problems and enhancing gender equality? The authors argue that an analysis of the results of TR in the context of the SÖF programmes from a gender perspective would be a treasure for further research and policies and should thus be funded. In this context the authors understand gender as an integration dimension ('Integrationsdimension'), which becomes relevant to research and policies and to all relevant forms of 'transdisciplinary knowledge' ('Target Knowledge', 'Systems Knowledge', and 'Transformation Knowledge') (ibid.: p. 223).

4 Approaches /Levels of TR

To summarize what has been said by now, I want to give an overview over the three different main levels of TR:

6 Further information on SÖF can be found in: http://www.fona.de/de/19711 and as an English summary in: http://www.fona.de/en/index.php (14/08/2017).

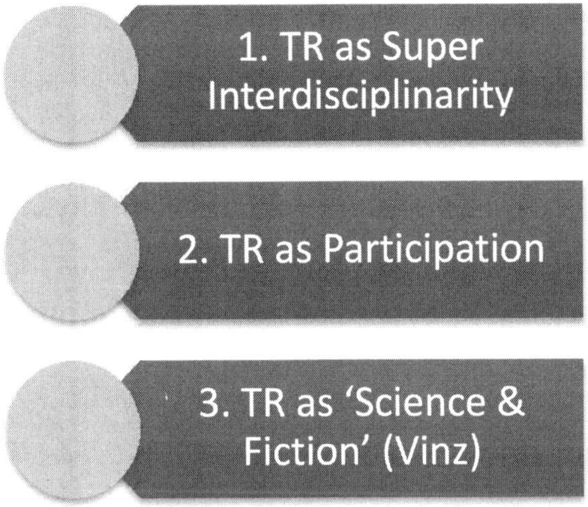

Level 1: The characterization of TR as Super Interdisciplinarity is most common in Gender Studies. It goes beyond inter- or multidisciplinarity:

> "In mainstream research interdisciplinarity is often just an exchange of findings (…). In gender studies, interdisciplinarity usually means that researchers from two or more disciplines define a similar research interest, discuss and combine methodological approaches and enhance findings" (Baer and Hornscheidt 2011:169).

Surpassing inter- or multidisciplinarity TR is understood as 'reflexive research':

> "Transdisciplinarity, in our understanding, is thus not a farewell to disciplines but rather a strong commitment to quality in disciplines. It is in no way their dissolution; in reflecting the presuppositions of a discipline, its strengths can often be formulated more clearly, beyond avoidance of bias. At the same time, transdisciplinary collaboration helps to understand when and how it can be productive to work together with other disciplines, how disciplines are themselves constructions based on complex decisions, inclusions and exclusions, with strengths and limitations" (ibid.:171).

Following this understanding of TR is very challenging. How to conduct transdisciplinary research as a student or PhD scholar thus remains an open question. An understanding of one's own disciplinary belonging with respect to theories, methodologies and empirical analysis is required. Furthermore, it is necessary to consciously overcome disciplinary boundaries when integrating transdisciplinary elements in students' research. Hopefully transdisciplinary institutes for Gender Studies, which are already institutionalized at some universities, can enhance knowledge about the implementation of TR in master and PhD theses. Whereas research institutes or think tanks perform TR mainly as teamwork by the institutionalization of a dialogue between researchers from various disciplines, students and PhD scholars often work on their own and thus cannot profit from the direct dialogue with researchers from other disciplines. Therefore, universities and Gender Studies Programmes have to train their students to shed the light on relevant research and policy fields from various disciplinary perspectives. Baer and Hornscheidt (2011) use research on discrimination as an example and discuss it from the perspective of linguistics and legal studies (ibid.:169). A conference on 'The Family'[7] brought forward analyses from different disciplinary perspectives (Psychology, Legal Studies, History, Medicine, Sociology, Economics). This kind of conference conception could serve as a model for university classes or textbooks: One phenomenon analysed from different disciplinary perspectives – a model for students and researchers to become aware of potentials and boundaries of one's own discipline. A second step would be to enable students and scholars to take on transdisciplinary perspectives, which go beyond the traditional generation of knowledge. To understand transdisciplinarity as 'Super-Interdisciplinary' (Level 1) is a challenge for scholars and even more for students of Gender and Diversity Studies. Therefore, more literature is needed that introduces students and early stage scientists to the integration of TR as 'Super-Interdisciplinarity' in their work. Since I do not want to elaborate this point now and here, I rather want to suggest an understanding of TR in other ways (Level 2 and 3), which are more easy to integrate in students' works than the production of knowledge which serves the demanding approach of TR as 'Super-Interdisciplinary'.

Level 2: The definition of TR as participatory refers to the involvement of all relevant actors in the field. These can be powerful actors, who are decision makers like politicians, leaders of non-governmental organizations or managers. But actors, relevant to research, can also be all persons who experience positive or negative effects of decisions e.g. on their bodies or their life worlds. Even though in a relatively powerless position, these persons become experts on the transformation of their neighbourhoods and their other environments. The participatory approach is designed both to integrate this knowledge 'from below' in the research process and to empower participants for reforms in their life worlds and for improvements of their life quality. Participation as an important element of applied research has a strong tradition in 'action research', which has been introduced by Kurt Lewin in the 1940s and has been further developed since then. Even though the term 'em-

7 German Association of University Professors and Lecturers (Deutscher Hochschulverband, in short DHV): DHV-Symposium 'Vater, Mutter, Kind? – Familie im Spiegel der Wissenschaft', 28.10.2015, Bonn.

powerment' had not been so widespread as today, the strengthening of democracy and participatory procedures was on the agenda of action research. It became an important point of reference for the 1968 movement. Interestingly most authors who express an understanding of TR as participatory do not refer to action research. Therefore, it is hard to draw a clear distinction between action research and the participatory approach of TR. Further work is needed to reflect similarities and distinctions between action research and TR as participatory research. A good starting point for this work could be the discussion of TR as double-boundary-transgression by Mückenberger/Timpf (2006):

- TR as super-disciplinarity firstly transforms the border between disciplines;
- TR as participatory secondly overcomes the dualism between experts and target groups.

The result is an understanding of TR as double-boundary-transgression. As an exemption to the rule Mückenberger and Timpf discuss the relevance of aims and methodologies of action research for TR and merge both approaches in order to create TR in the form of 'real world experiments' in post-fordist city districts. To sum it up, the integration of knowledge from different actors in the process of research can be combined with the empowerment of disadvantaged groups. Research methods for the implementation of TR as participatory approach can reach from quantitative approaches for the empirical investigation of the related 'life world' by surveys to qualitative research in various forms (e.g. narrative interviews, future workshops, 'real world experiments' or town hall meetings). Mückenberger and Timpf (2006) argue that not only qualitative but also quantitative research can profit from the participation of target groups: e.g. the quality of questions for opinion polls is enhanced when reflected by both researchers and target groups (ibid.:231).

Level 3: The third level of TR is called 'Science & Fiction' and is an approach, which – as has been said before – I have developed and which will be discussed in the following. Fitting at least partly under the umbrella of 'Science & Fiction', I will present a corpus of already existing literature on the lives of change agents in organizations, on career patterns of disadvantaged groups or on the future development of social relations from a Gender and Diversity perspective. This literature can be regarded as belonging to the approach of 'Science & Fiction' since it already has a hybrid form: For example, data about existing inequalities between men and women is used as a basis for the formulation of different scenarios about the lives of future women.

Future work of students, PhD candidates or researchers though has to strengthen the merging of 'Science' and 'Fiction':

- *'Fiction' needs to be informed by 'Science'*: Quantitative and qualitative data are to be the basis of an informed story telling; theories from social and natural sciences are to be used for the complex writing about human relations or social relations to nature.
- *'Science' vice versa needs to integrate 'Fiction'*: the communication of scientific findings can be improved by their presentation in a literary form; academic theories and debates can reach a broader audience if students and PhD scholars were allowed or even encouraged to present part of their work in the form of fiction.

Thus my hope is that future work will connect and unite 'Science & Fiction' more closely and make work in this field more accepted as a valued contribution to both academia and the desired transformation of human relations towards sustainability and social justice. As we remember Marx's famous thesis: 'The philosophers have only interpreted the world, in various ways; the point is to change it' (MECW 1888/1969:6-8). 'Science & Fiction' can contribute to this goal by providing knowledge for change and by referring to authors like Donna Haraway (1991) who already works with the mixture of 'Science' and 'Fiction', e.g. in her 'Manifesto for a cyborg'.

5 'Science & Fiction' in the Existing Literature

By now I have sketched an outline of my approach for 'Science & Fiction'. In the following section I will refer to six examples of literature, which deal with the work of change agents, with the description of organizational change or other creative forms of writing, which I regard as relevant for Gender and Diversity Studies. I will shortly present these publications. Then I will describe in which ways both Gender and Diversity Studies and my approach 'Science & Fiction' can profit from these cases.

'Science & Fiction' in the Field of Social and Political Thought

Before I discuss the selection of literature, which can be interpreted to a greater or lesser extent as a contribution to 'Science & Fiction' and to 'Gender & Diversity', I want to mention that there is a need and desire in the public sphere for contemplation and critical reflection. In the last decade, several books have become bestsellers in the German speaking world, which 'translate' philosophical, social and political thought for the general public: Wilhelm Weischedel published in 1975 'Die philosophische Hintertreppe. 34 große Philosophen in Alltag und Denken' (Philosophical Backstairs: 34 grand philosophers in everyday life and thinking). He was one of the first who presented Aristotle, Descartes, Kant or Hegel in an understandable way for a broader audience. Bestsellers in Germany and many other countries became Jostein Gaarder's 'Sofies Welt: A Novel about the History of Philosophy' (1991 in Norwegian, 1993 in German, 1995 in English) and Dietrich Schwanitz' 'Bildung. Alles, was man wissen muss' (1999) (Education: all one has to know; a Spanish translation from 2006 exists).

From an intersectional 'Science & Fiction' perspective, 'Sofies Welt' fits best due to its hybrid form: a narration builds the framework in which political thought of relevant philosophers is presented. The other examples mentioned above fall more in the category of a non-fiction book.

From an intersectional Gender & Diversity perspective it has to be mentioned that Weischedel (1975) sets a canon of Western male philosophers as a standard. Schwanitz (1999) integrates at least a chapter on the history of gender debates (Chapter 7) in his work and Gaarder chooses a girl as a leading character of his book. I suggest perceiving this work as a contribution to a greater permeability between the academic world and the broader public. As such it strengthens the reflection on moral values and virtues and contributes to the creation of a critical public sphere, which is, according to Habermas (1962/1996), the basis for a functioning and participatory democracy.

'Science & Fiction' in the Field of Feminism and Gender Equality

The three examples mentioned above became bestsellers by contributing to the transfer of social and political thought to the general public. They have to be complemented by three examples of bestsellers on gender equality: (1) In the form of an essay Virginia Woolf (1929/2000) describes 'A Room of One's Own' as a precondition for female writing, self-determination and emancipation. (2) In the form of a novel Gerd Brantenberg describes in 'Egalia's Daughters' (1977: original Norwegian version, 1980 German version, 1985 English version) a reverse 'matriarchal' world, in which men raise children, wear 'Penis Holder' (PHs), this ironically refers to the German abbreviation of bra as BH, and cannot become 'seawoman'. The author transforms the language consequently so that feminine forms are universal and masculine forms detect the inferiority of men as the 'weak gender'. (3) Choosing the form of a Science Fiction Marge Piercy describes in 'Women at the edge of time' (1976, German: Frauen am Abgrund der Zeit, 1986) a radical democratic and sustainable future in which gender as a dual category has been overcome technologically (referring to Shulamith Firestone). Feminist thought on gender equality and the emancipation of women is transported by these exemplary writings to the public sphere and the audience can be made politically aware of discrimination and prejudices against women. In political and feminist theory, the need for 'utopias' and 'dystopias' as a prerequisite for change is reflected, particularly by Holland-Cunz (1988) and also by Vinz (2005).

The six readings mentioned above are highly recommended for students and scholars in the field of gender and diversity. They encourage to let one's inspiration run and to question reigning social relations. Even though these readings have provoked public debate and helped to overcome the boundary between the academic ivory tower and the 'real world' they mainly fall either in the category 'fiction' or in the category 'non-fiction literature' ('Sachbuch'). This dualism shall not be seen negatively, but I will argue that the education of change agents in the field of Gender and Diversity politics could profit from an understanding of 'Science & Fiction' as an intersectional, close relation. With the following five examples I will introduce 'best practices' for addressing a broader audience and for combining 'Science & Fiction'.

Example 1
Edding, Cornelia (2000): Agentin des Wandels. Der Kampf um Veränderung im Unternehmen. München: Murmann Verl.

The title of this book can be translated into English as 'Change Agent. The battle for change in the company'. It was first published by Cornelia Edding in 2000. In the form of a novel it describes projects and strategies of an equal opportunity officer (called Ms. P.). A process of five years duration is depicted, in which the 'heroine' develops various projects and strategies – successful and unsuccessful ones. The heroine's experiences can help actors in the field of equal opportunity policies to improve their projects and strategies and to reflect on their position in the organization and on existing power relations.

Firstly, our heroine recommends to start the change process with small projects designed for little, but quick success. Why? In the beginning, the management board has to justify the expenditure for the position of an equal opportunity officer and our 'heroine', vice versa, has to strengthen her position in the organization. Secondly, the change agent becomes aware that she is confronted with many divergent expectations of her colleagues: Some come up with very individual problems, others demand the support of their interests and third ones want her to improve the company's image. We learn from our heroine that change agents have to become aware of their role in an organization in order to design appropriate targets and strategies and to cope decently with high expectations or well-meant advice of others. Important to note: Ms. P. compares her present task with her former work as conference organizer and realizes that she does not get so much recognition, support, and compliments as before. Thus, change agents need to be aware that they might become lone warriors and that they do not get much emotional support for their endeavour. Thirdly, Edding discusses why and how resistance emerges in the organization: on the surface, discrimination and prejudices against women are banned and perceived as inadequate with the self-image of working for a modern, innovative and open company. Below the surface and hard to see, however, prevails resistance against equal opportunity policies. Methods of resistance are the three Vs: '(nicht eingehaltene) **V**ersprechen, **V**erschleppen, **V**ermeiden' (neglected promises, delay the proceedings, avoidance). Edding presents various coping strategies with resistance. In the end however, her 'heroine' decides to leave the company – with mixed feelings and the wish for new and other challenges.

An Intersectional Gender & Diversity Perspective:
From a Gender & Diversity perspective, Edding's book can be read as a source for practical advice. In this form, it can help students as future change agents to design strategies and projects for the implementation of gender equality in organizations. Even though the terms are not used, Gender & Diversity perspectives intersect when Edding describes how the change agent fails to mobilize the support of women working in the production line: She does not succeed in reaching working-class women as a target group. Besides this, competition dominates between Ms. P. and the powerful female trade unionist who formerly applied for the position of the change agent. The way in which gender and class interact shows that an appropriate analysis of the constellation of actors – a method of the policy-analysis – can help to build coalitions or to understand how and why an empowerment of women fails to come into existence.

An Intersectional 'Science & Fiction' Perspective:
Edding merges 'Science & Fiction' by narrating in the form of a novel about practical experiences, thoughts and emotions of a change agent in the 'battle for change'. Students and scholars of Gender and Diversity Studies thus get insights into equal opportunity policies, which are neither part of scientific literature nor included in glossy brochures of organizations. Therefore, they should read Edding as part of the canon of Gender and Diversity Studies and unmerge 'Science & Fiction'. From a scientific perspective, students and scholars of Gender and Diversity Studies can use policy analysis or organizational research to explain both success and failure of projects and strategies described by Edding. Reading the scientific work of Erfurt Sandhu (2010) and Mergaert/Lombardo (2014) can help to understand resistance against the change agent and to discuss coping strategies. From the perspective of fiction, students can finally be encouraged to create literature on gender and diversity relations according to their own experiences or on the basis of qualitative interviews.

Example 2
Schwanitz, Dietrich (1995): Der Campus. Eichborn: Frankfurt am Main.

The novel 'Der Campus' by the university professor Dietrich Schwanitz became a bestseller after its publication in 1995. It was filmed as a movie by the well-known German director Sönke Wortmann in 1998. It deals with a (fictitious) professor at the University of Hamburg who is falsely accused of having raped a student and who is consequently dismissed. Critics like Möller (2003) regard the novel as clearly antifeminist due to the stereotypes, which are used to describe the university's women's representative. Thus he regards the novel as part of the antifeminist backlash in politics and culture in the decade after the German reunification. Reviewers of mainstream journals like the German weekly journal *Die ZEIT* stressed that all figures of the novel are portrayed in an ironical or even sarcastic way. The affair between the main character and a female student becomes public since a young, naïve and inexperienced journalist writes articles on the basis of speculation and half-truth. The president of the disciplinary committee accuses the main character of rape since he thus expects to improve his position for the election as Vice President. Deals, personal ambitions, intrigues and lies dominate life on Schwanitz's campus and they are presented in the form of a political satire. It is true that the women's representative and feminist student groups are presented in a stereotypical way, it is true in equal measure that both play a minor role in the novel – the press and the university administration are the driving force for the creation of a scandal.

An Intersectional Gender & Diversity Perspective:
Gender and diversity relations are quite traditional at Schwanitz' (1995) (fictitious) University of Hamburg: white German men hold most positions of power. Individual vanity, personal hunger for power and material interests are relevant for decision making, not the strive for truth and justice. Gender and Diversity policies, however, are normatively based upon the latter. Students and scholars of Gender and Diversity Studies can thus discuss how the university as a learning organization can be reformed in order to stimulate and support transparency, fairness, inclusiveness, and truth.

An Intersectional 'Science & Fiction' Perspective:
My approach 'Science & Fiction' can learn from 'Der Campus' that irony and exaggeration can be important tools for transdisciplinary 'story-telling' about competitive relations, hierarchies and power games in the academic world. It can also be a basis for the discussion about the adequate treatment of and communication about cases of sexual harassment and rape at university.

Example 3
Curruca, Sylvia (1996): Als Frau im Bauch der Wissenschaft. Was an den deutschen Universitäten gespielt wird. Freiburg/Basel/Wien: Herder Verlag GmbH

The novel of which the title can be translated as 'As a woman in the belly of the sciences' was published by Curruca (a pseudonym) in 1993. It ironically describes hierarchies and gender relations at a German university and depicts career patterns and the work of appointment committees with poignant sarcasm. It describes both professors who have elaborate strategies to avoid work and professors who are so career oriented that they regard students and colleagues alike either as competitors or as time-wasters. With chapters on 'Promotion' (Ph.D.), 'Lehre' (teaching), 'Habilitation'[8] and 'Personalpolitik' (Human Resource Management), the author covers a wide range of experiences within the university as an organization. In the end, she describes several unfruitful attempts to apply for appointments outside of academia.

An Intersectional Gender & Diversity Perspective:
The author describes authentically, what it means to be one of the first female scientists who holds a doctorate and a 'Habilitation' in the organization. Recognition of a scientist's work in research and teaching is rare. Even after her 'Habilitation', she has to do a lot of unqualified work like photocopying. Result is a lack of time for publishing. Authentically, the permanent visibility of our scientist as a woman (tokenism) is described. Furthermore, the incompatibility of the organization's working time with the family life is critically analysed. Sexual harassment also becomes an issue in the

8 'Habilitation' is a further thesis in the German education system, located in the post-doc period for the qualification as a professor at university. It is also referred to as a ‚second doctoral thesis'.

reflection of gender relations. Things have changed in Germany since 1993. The introduction of the Assistant Professorship ('Juniorprofessur') has improved the working and power position of junior scientists, and the 'Habilitation' has vanished in many disciplines. Being a woman and holding a Ph.D. is no longer an exemption: in 2013 the share of women holding a dissertation in legal studies, economy and cultural studies amounts to 36.1%, the share of women holding a second doctoral thesis amounts to 27.1%.[9] Both Gender Equality Offices and Family Offices are set up to install the university as a learning organization. How do gender and diversity intersect in the novel? Main diversity dimensions like race, religion or sexuality do not come into play. Class is only touched when the role of trade unions or the hierarchies in the organization are discussed. Most interesting for diversity as a concept is the creation of categories for the different types of professors and scientists and the roles they play in the organization.

An Intersectional 'Science & Fiction' Perspective:
What can we learn from this publication for our approach of 'Science & Fiction'? Students and scholars gain insight into the work of appointment committees and the power games, which can be part of the process. On this basis, coping strategies with success and failure could be developed and fairness in the academic world could be enhanced. Apart from this, things have changed in academia since the publishing of the novel in 1993. Even though we still face male dominance in many research organizations and a gendered division of labour according to the lines of feminized and masculinized disciplines, the access for women to research has improved, even if equal opportunity policies have to become more aware of the intersection of gender with other dimensions of discrimination. Power games in the work of committees and in the process of decision-making remain – scholars and students of Gender and Diversity Studies thus can still learn a lot from Curruca's (1996) report, hopefully without being frustrated and discouraged from the author's often sarcastic and negative perspectives.

Example 4
Meinecke, Thomas (1998): Tomboy. Frankfurt a. M.: Suhrkamp Verl. / Meinecke, Thomas (2011): Tomboy. Las Vegas: Amazon Crossing, English translation.
With 'Tomboy', a term becomes a book title, which describes girls, who are acting or dressing in a boyish way. Thomas Meinecke published the novel Tomboy in 1998. It appeared in 2011 as an English translation, which is criticized as sticking too much to German grammar and as such being difficult to understand. The novel portrays students of the University of Heidelberg who read and discuss deconstructivist authors in the field of Gender Studies. The author refers among others to Butler, Haraway and Fraser, to Foucault and Lacan, and to the misogynist Otto Weininger. Parallel reading of the novel 'Tomboy' and the quoted literature could fill a whole university seminar. Even though Meinecke's writing is in parts difficult to follow, the reflections and discussions of the characters in his novel give insight in gender theories and 'Gender

9 Source: CEWS-Statistikportals: http://www.gesis.org/cews/unser-angebot/informationsangebote/statistiken/ (14/08/2017).

Trouble' (Butler 1991). Being lesbian, bisexual or transsexual, the main characters in 'Tomboy' represent a world, in which identities and sexual orientations are floating and in which theories and writings of prominent authors like Judith Butler or Donna Haraway fuel the destabilization of hierarchical binary oppositions like male-female, reason-emotion, hard-soft, strong-weak etc.

An Intersectional Gender & Diversity Perspective:
Thomas Meinecke concentrates on authors, which are primarily characterized as belonging to the field of gender studies. Intersectional Gender & Diversity perspectives come in when the lives and self-reflections of bi-, inter- and transsexual characters are portrayed. The notion of 'queer' has not yet found its way into the academic students' scene, which ranges from the 'coerced heterosexual' Vivian Atkinson over the bisexual Korinna Kohn to the lesbian PhD student Frauke Stöver.

An Intersectional 'Science & Fiction' Perspective:
My approach 'Science & Fiction' could take the novel 'Tomboy' as an example for discussing complex theories of Gender and Diversity Studies in the context of everyday life, here the academic world of students' lives. Thus a broader public could access academic work more easily.

Example 5
McCorduck, Pamela/Ramsey, Nancy (1996): Die Zukunft der Frauen. Szenarien für das 21. Jahrhundert. Frankfurt a.M.: Fischer Verl.
Corduck, Pamela/Ramsey, Nancy (1999): The Futures of Women: Scenarios for the 21st Century. Reading/Massachussetts: Addison-Wesley.

On the basis of existing economic trends and an analysis of global gender relations in the midst of the 1990s, the authors develop four future scenarios for 2015. The four scenarios are:

1. 'A Golden Age of gender equality' in which women and men alike can develop their potentials in a peaceful and economically prosperous world. In both, North & South and East & West, poverty and inequality are reduced, and access to education is broadened.
2. 'A worldwide Backlash' fosters traditional allocation of roles and stereotypical thinking on gender relations. Women are excluded from attractive or powerful positions in politics, economy or society. Only few professions like nursing and elderly care or secretary and waitress are feminized. Unbelievingly, the veil becomes a fashionable couture in the West.
3. A 'Two Steps Forward, Two Steps Back scenario' presents several uneven developments in the context of a stagnating world economy, which limits the scope of international women's networks. Access to education is restricted due to the fact that even formerly prosperous welfare states have to spend most money for the provision of elderly care in the context of demographic change. Simultaneously, the advancement of careers cannot be combined with care obligations – another reason why women stay behind.
4. A 'Separate: Yes please'-scenario fosters the development of social cultures with women- and men-only communities.

An Intersectional Gender & Diversity Perspective:
From a critical perspective, it has to be mentioned that the German translation always uses the term 'die Frauen' ('the women'), which tends to be homogenizing and essentializing: Women en bloc are opposed to men en bloc, sometimes in terms of their capabilities, sometimes due to their social and emotional skills. This tendency to homogenize the group 'die Frauen' is compensated by the international perspectives of the authors, which can be very helpful for scholars and students of Gender and Diversity Studies. The policies of international institutions are discussed and a great variety of country specific portrays of gender relations are presented. Thereby images of women and men become more nuanced and intersections between race, class and gender are depicted. From an intersectional Gender & Diversity perspective, scholars and students can broaden their perspectives by embracing the international perspectives of the two authors and the interplay between the development of the world economy and gender equality. They can also profit from analyzing and evaluating how the authors integrate intersectional perspectives on race, class or sexuality in their writing on 'The futures of women'. Seminars for international students could provide the knowledge for developing scenarios for the futures of women in the students' home countries.

An Intersectional 'Science & Fiction' Perspective:
Science and Fiction are in many respects commendably merged in 'The futures of women'. Current figures and trends are presented and further developed in the form of future scenarios. It has to be mentioned that the authors understand each scenario as focussing on one trend and that future development will be a mixture of the scenarios presented. Scholars and students of Gender and Diversity Studies can profit from 'The futures of women' and shall be encouraged to gain expertise in the methodology 'Future Scenarios' as it has particularly been developed in Sustainability Studies (again Gender and Diversity Studies can profit from Sustainability Studies).

Example 6
'I Diversity, I Intersectionality': a dialogue in black and white with a bit of sarcasm

Another form of 'Science & Fiction' is the creative dialogue, which I have invented. As an example I present a dialogue in black and white between 'I Intersectionality' and 'I Diversity'. It uses irony as an important element of political discussion and exaggeration as a strategy for drawing a clear distinction between intersectionality and diversity and for contrasting intersectionality with diversity.

"I, Diversity, am so practical".

"I, Intersectionality, am theoretically superior and methodologically more manifold".

"I, Diversity, please men and women, gays and lesbians, the faithful and atheists, thick and thin people, whites and blacks, large and small...".

"I, Intersectionality, criticize the construction of binary oppositions and demand following approaches like critical whiteness or queer theory with their aim to foster the deconstruction of categories".

"I, Diversity, find it important to give recognition for difference – following Axel Honneth and Nancy Fraser. Therefore, I have no problem to approve that particular groups have specific skills or capabilities".

"I, Intersectionality, am critical towards uneven power relations and question hierarchies. I analyse how social inequality rises in the process of globalization along the categories race, class, and gender".

"I, Diversity, take care that the diversity of society is mirrored in transnational companies on all hierarchical levels. Thus I contribute to the reduction of discrimination and social inequality".

"I, Intersectionality, analyse multiple discrimination and the interdependency of different social categories".

"I, Diversity, do the same".

"As if!"

"I, Diversity, am underestimated and discredited as neoliberal management strategy. This is mean! I do have a theoretical foundation in the form of theories of difference. Apart from this, diversity is a positive term, which has a utopian dimension. This is often forgotten".

"I, Intersectionality, insist: You, Diversity, are the comrade of the bosses ('Genosse der Bosse'), whereas I, Intersectionality, personalize the critique of capitalism with a strong reference to the category class".

"I, Diversity, am upset about so much phrase mongering. I object to this snobbish perspective. Even in socialism or post growth societies there will be the necessity to reduce discrimination and to develop intercultural competence and to foster social justice in organizations. There I'm game".

"I, Intersectionality, question hierarchies as such and stand for more democracy, in particular in business organizations. Trade Unions are my allies, whereas you, diversity, alienate them due to your location near the board of management".

"I, Diversity, am critically eyed by trade unions. Likewise, I observe them critically as an organization and ascertain that trade unions are governed by 'dominant groups' (white, heterosexual, male, family head). A shot of diversity would not be too bad for trade unions. Apart from this, I am sure that the management of diversity will be of advantage for all employees, will contribute to the identification with the workplace and enhance the achievement on all levels of the hierarchy. An organization without hierarchies? Hard to imagine, even though there are first and still marginalized examples for democratically organized enterprises. An organization with meaningfully divided levels of hierarchies and the possibility to realize one's potential in the work process: the realization of the multicultural organization (Cox 2001) as utopia?"

"You, Diversity, are concerned with the winners of globalization, who are occupied in large transnational corporations and who are accordingly privileged. I, Intersectionality, deal with the situation of single mothers, chronically ill people, welfare recipients or early school leavers. I choose the perspective from below, whereas your perspective, Diversity, is from above. Therefore, you are and you remain, following Foucault (1976), a technology of dominance".

"You, Intersectionality, perceive yourself as superior. If you devaluate me you bar the way for a peaceful coexistence based on the division of labour. I, Diversity, invite you, Intersectionality, to a constructive dialogue in research and teaching, particularly in political and social sciences".

If and how this goes on, the future will show…

6 Change Agents and Organizational Transformation

'Science & Fiction' is an approach that has a scientific foundation. For the proper analysis of organizations and the performance of change agents I suggest to consider the three levels which can be seen in the chart below.

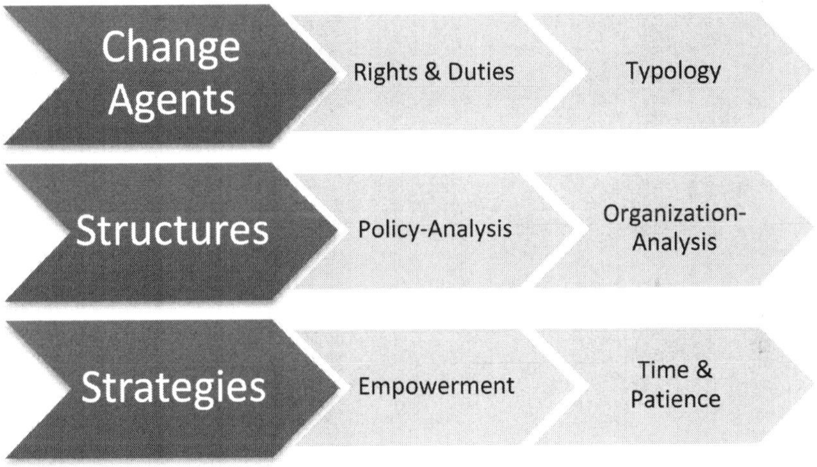

Firstly, I differentiate between (a) change agents, (b) structures and (c) strategies. Research on organizational change has to take these three levels into consideration:

To understand change agents (a), it is necessary to know which rights and duties they have, e.g. by analyzing legal guidelines, job descriptions or organization charts. Different types of change agents can be examined: at university, for example, the full time women's officer and the student women's officer;

Elements of policy analysis or organizational analysis can help to understand the structures (b), which both can enable and prevent organizational change;

Last but not least, strategies (c) have to be developed as part of the solution oriented perspective of TR and serve for the empowerment of the change agent and his/her target groups. Strategies have to take into consideration that change is a 'hard business', which requires time and patience.

'Science & Fiction' enables change agents to learn from the experience of other actors and strengthens the analytical capabilities for understanding success and failures of strategies for the implementation of equal opportunity policies and other social and environmental justice strategies.

Normative Foundations, Ethical Challenges and Methodology of TR on Change Agents

TR in the form of 'Science & Fiction' needs information from change agents in the real world. Therefore, a dialogue is necessary with ensured anonymity, with recognition and respect and last but not least, not only with scepticism but also with optimism:

Granted Anonymity – contracting!
Support through organizational partnerships;
'Affidamento' – the Milano Approach[10];
Respect of 'Otherness', of difference;
Scepticism – every perspective is relative. There is more than one truth.
Optimism – 'Another world is possible' (*Association for the Taxation of financial Transactions and Citizen's Action*, ATTAC: an activist organization critical of neoliberalism and promoting the control of financial markets and fair trade). And: 'Yes we can'.

---

10 Affidamento, also known as the Milano Approach (Libreria delle donne di Milano 1988), rests on the mutual respect between women and suggests women to relate to each other as 'symbolic mothers' and 'daughters'. In contrast to traditional gender equality policies, which enforce the adaption to a male norm, affidamento serves female empowerment. Envy and competition between women shall be overcome and be substituted by gratitude towards the symbolic mother. Knapp (1991) has profoundly criticized the approach due to its concentration on the symbolic sphere as the relevant realm of power and due to its tendency to homogenize women and to exclude intersectional perspectives on race or class. In spite of these – very fundamental deficiencies – the approach directs attention to the need for mutual respect and valuation between women and between change agents in whatever organization as an important prerequisite for success.

TR in the form of 'Science & Fiction' can potentially make use of the whole range of methods in the field of political and social sciences. From my perspective, qualitative interviews, expert interviews and future scenarios are of particular importance. Group discussions, policy analysis and critical discourse analysis can also be relevant, not to forget organizational analysis, manifestos and portraits (e.g. political biographies).

7 Conclusion

TR is a key competence and a challenge for scholars and students in the field of Gender and Diversity Studies. Understood as 'Super-Interdisciplinarity' (1) it is both necessary to comprehend an issue from different disciplinary angles and to integrate these perspectives on a novel level. Understood as participatory (2) TR demands from scholars and students to address and understand relevant actors in different areas, be it in an organization or in a specific policy field. TR thus includes the competence to involve and to empower actors in the research process and is to be combined with the challenge to solve 'real-world-problems'. Understood as 'Science & Fiction' (3) TR fosters the competence of scholars and students to write creatively and to translate and communicate knowledge, which is gained in scientific research, to a broader audience. Vice versa authors can integrate scientific findings in their story telling and thus contribute to reducing the gap between the academic world and the general public. In both directions, which are mentioned above, the flow of knowledge between science and members of the public is of utmost importance: not only as a prerequisite for individual, organizational or political learning, but also as a basis for deciding reverberatory on contested issues in the framework of a participatory democracy.

Of course, students and scholars in the field of Gender and Diversity Studies need a profound training in theories and methodologies of their home discipline. Similarly research perspectives in neighbouring disciplines and interdisciplinary approaches have to be part of the curriculum in B.A. and M.A. Gender and Diversity Studies Programmes. In addition to this clearly scientific focus, as I want to argue here, it is the task of Gender and Diversity Studies Programmes to train future change agents practically, particularly in the field of equal opportunity and anti-discrimination politics. Hands-on experience, know-how and internships should be part of the curriculum. Therefore the whole potential of the term 'transdisciplinarity' (1, 2, *and* 3) has to play an important role in Gender and Diversity Studies programmes. Both the integration of change agents in the research process and the enhanced communication of research results with the merging of 'Science' and 'Fiction' in creative writing projects should be honoured as valued contribution to knowledge in the field and should be accepted as evidence of academic achievement and alternative to classic examinations like essays or tests.

As you can see below, TR is also a political project – it is counter-hegemonic against the dominant forms of quantitative research. In this sense, TR is and could become a light tower in the scientific landscape:

- *Light Tower* against the undue hegemony of quantitative science in many fields;
- *Light Tower* against the isolation of research in subsystems of expert communities and against the isolated dissemination of research results in 'Refereed Journals only';
- *Light Tower* against English as 'Science language only';
- *Light Tower* against the 'tacit knowledge' of privileged groups in organizations, e.g. about career patterns or 'appropriatc' bchaviour;
- *Light Tower* for the empowerment of change agents, for participatory democracy and fairness and for 'learning from mistakes';
- *Light Tower* for 'a better world'.

Discussion Questions

1. Describe your experiences with the prefix 'trans' and discuss their meanings.
2. Present your own definition of the prefix 'trans' and the term TR.
3. What is your motto when you imagine doing TR?
4. Create a table with the stages of TR. Choose a topic on which you have already written an essay. Try to 'organize' your topic as TR and to fill in the table accordingly.
5. Visit the homepage of SÖF. Search for three research projects and discuss how they implement TR.
6. Read the information on future scenarios for women again. Collect relevant data for the future of women in your home country. Develop at least one possible future scenario.
7. Read the information on the analysis of change agents in organizations again. Choose one organization, which you have been a member of (e.g. school, university, company, hotel). Analyze and discuss how gender and diversity relations are organized in this organization. What could or should be changed?

References

Baer, Susanne/Hornscheidt, Antje (2011): Transdisciplinary Gender Studies. Conceptual and Institutional Challenges. In: Buikema, Rosemarie/Griffin, Gabrielle/Lykke, Nina (ed.): Theories and Methodologies in Postgraduate Feminist Research: Researching Differently. New York: Routledge, pp. 165-179.

Brantenberg, Gerd (1987): Die Töchter Egalias. Ein Roman über den Kampf der Geschlechter. München: Frauenoffensive. Engl.: (1985): Egalia's Daughters: A Satire of the Sexes. Emeryville, CA: Seal Press.

Butler, Judith (1991): Das Unbehagen der Geschlechter. Frankfurt a.M.: edition suhrkamp, Engl.: (1990): Gender Trouble. Feminism and the Subversion of Identity. New York: Routledge.

Cox, Taylor (2001): Creating the Multicultural Organization. San Francisco: Jossey-Bass.

Curruca, Sylvia (1996): Als Frau im Bauch der Wissenschaft. Was an den deutschen Universitäten gespielt wird. Freiburg/Basel/Wien: Herder Verlag.

Edding, Cornelia (2000): Agentin des Wandels. Der Kampf um Veränderung im Unternehmen. München: Murmann Verlag.

Erfurt Sandhu, Philine (2010): Nicht wichtig, keine Zeit, fehlende Beweise – Widerstände bei der Implementierung von Gender Mainstreaming und Diversity Management. In: diversitas – Zeitschrift für Managing Diversity und Diversity Studies, 02/2010, pp. 11-17. http://www.zf-diversitas.eu/resources/11+01+20+Diversitas+02+Art+EP.pdf (06/09/2017).

Foucault, Michel (1976): Der Wille zum Wissen. Sexualität und Wahrheit 1. Frankfurt a. M.: Suhrkamp Verl., Engl.: (1998): The Will to Knowledge: the history of sexuality v. 1. London: Penguin Books, reprinted.

Gaarder, Jostein (1993): Sofies Welt – Roman über die Geschichte der Philosophie. München/Wien: Carl Hanser Verl., Engl.: (1995): Sophie's World: the Greek philosophers. London: Phoenix.

Gibbons, Michael (et al.) (1994): The New Production of Knowledge. The Dynamics of Science and Research in Contemporary Societies. London et al.: Sage Pub.

Habermas, Jürgen (1962/1996): Strukturwandel der Öffentlichkeit. Frankfurt a.M.: Suhrkamp Verlag, Engl.: (2015): The Structural Transformation of the Public Sphere. New York: John Wiley & Sons, E-Book, First Edition.

Häberli, Rudolf et al. (2001): Synthesis. In: Thompson Klein, Julie et al. (ed.): Transdisciplinarity: Joint Problem Solving among Science, Technology and Society. An Effective Way for Managing Complexity. Basel: Birkhäuser, pp. 6-12.

Hall, Kara L. et al. (2012): A Four-phase Model of Transdisciplinary Team-based Research: Goals, Team Processes, and Strategies. In: Transl Behav Med., 2 (4), pp. 415-430. http://www.ncbi.nlm.nih.gov/pmc/articles/PMC3589144/ (06/09/2017).

Haraway, Donna (1991): A Cyborg Manifesto: Science, Technology, and Socialist-Feminism in the Late Twentieth Century. In: Haraway, Donna: Simians, Cyborgs, and Women: the Reinvention of Nature. New York: Routledge, pp. 149-182.

Harvey, David (2011): Marx' Kapital lesen: Ein Begleiter für Einsteiger und Fortgeschrittene. Hamburg: VSA Verl., Engl.: (2010): A Companion to Marx's Capital. London/ New York: Verso.

Holland-Cunz, Barbara (1988): Utopien der Neuen Frauenbewegung. Gesellschaftsentwürfe im Kontext feministischer Theorie und Praxis. Meitingen: Corian Verlag.

Kahlert, Heike/Thiessen, Barbara/Weller, Ines (ed.) (2005): Quer denken – Strukturen verändern. Gender Studies zwischen Disziplinen. Wiesbaden: Verlag für Sozialwissenschaften.

Knapp, Gudrun-Axeli (1991): Zur Theorie und politischen Utopie des ‚affidamento'. In: Feministische Studien, 1991, Heft 1, Jg. 9, pp. 117-128.

Libreria delle donne di Milano (1988): Wie weibliche Freiheit entsteht. Eine neue politische Praxis. Berlin: Orlanda Verlag.

Marx, Karl/Engels, Friedrich (1888/1969): Selected Work, Vol. 1, Theses on Feuerbach, pp. 13-15. Moscow, Soviet Union: Progress Publishers.

McCorduck, Pamela/Ramsey, Nancy (1996): Die Zukunft der Frauen. Szenarien für das 21. Jahrhundert. Frankfurt a.M.: Fischer Verl., Engl.: (1999) The Futures of Women: Scenarios for the 21st Century. Reading/Massachussetts: Addison-Wesley.

Meinecke, Thomas (1998): Tomboy. Frankfurt a.M.: Suhrkamp Verlag, Engl.: (2011): Tomboy. Las Vegas: Amazon Crossing.

Mergaert, Lut/Lombardo, Emanuela (2014): Resistance to Implementing Gender Mainstreaming in EU Research Policy. In: Weiner, Elaine/MacRae, Heather (ed.): European Integration Online Papers (EIoP), Special Issue 1, The Persistent Invisibility of Gender in EU Policy, Vol. 18, Article 5, pp. 1-21. http://eiop.or.at/eiop/pdf/2014-005.pdf (06/09/2017).

Mückenberger, Ulrich/Timpf, Siegfried (2006): Transdisziplinarität als doppelte Grenzüberschreitung: Realexperimentelle Raum-Zeitgestaltung in urbanen Quartieren. In: Sozialwissenschaften und Berufspraxis 29, 2006, 2, pp. 225-248. http://nbn-resolving.de/urn:nbn:de:0168-ssoar-38725 (06/09/2017).

Möller, Simon (2003): Operation gelungen. In: Der Freitag, 2003, March 21, https://www.freitag.de/autoren/der-freitag/operation-gelungen (06/09/2017).

Piercy, Marge (1985): Die Frau am Abgrund der Zeit. Hamburg: Argument Verlag, Engl.: (1976/1996): Woman on the Edge of Time. New York: Alfred A. Knopf,

Polanyi, Karl (1978/1997): The Great Transformation. Politische und ökonomische Ursprünge von Gesellschaften und Wirtschaftssystemen. Frankfurt a.M.: Suhrkamp Verlag, Engl.: (1957/1971): The Great Transformation: political and economic origins of our time. Boston: Beacon Press.

Pries, Ludger (2008): Die Transnationalisierung der sozialen Welt. Sozialräume jenseits von Nationalgesellschaften. Frankfurt a.M.: Suhrkamp Verlag.

Schier, Carmen/Schwinger, Elke (eds.) (2014): Interdisziplinarität und Transdisziplinarität als Herausforderung akademischer Bildung: Innovative Konzepte für die Lehre an Hochschulen und Universitäten. Bielefeld: Transcript Verlag.

Schultz, Irmgard/Schramm, Engelbert/Hummel, Diana (2015): Gender als Integrationsdimension in der transdisziplinären SÖF (Sozialökologischen Forschung). In: Katz, Nina et al. (eds.): Nachhaltigkeit anders denken. Veränderungspotenziale durch Geschlechterperspektiven. Wiesbaden: Springer Fachmedien, pp. 217-230.

Schwanitz, Dietrich (1995): Der Campus. Frankfurt a.M.: Eichborn Verlag.

Schwanitz, Dietrich (1999): Bildung. Alles, was man wissen muss. Frankfurt a.M.: Eichborn Verlag.

Thompson Klein, Julie et al. (2001): Transdisciplinarity: Joint Problem Solving among Science, Technology, and Society: An Effective Way for Managing Complexity. Basel/Boston/Berlin: Birkhauser Verlag.

UNESCO. Social Sciences Sector (1998): Charter of Transdisciplinarity, International Symposium of Transdisciplinarity, Val-d'Oise, France, 25-29 May, 1996. http://unesdoc.unesco.org/images/0011/001146/114694eo.pdf (06/09/2017).
Vinz, Dagmar (2005): Zeiten der Nachhaltigkeit. Perspektiven für eine ökologische und geschlechtergerechte Zeitpolitik. Münster: Westfälisches Dampfboot.
Vinz, Dagmar (2016): Gender- und Diversity-Studies in Deutschland, Österreich und der Schweiz. In: Genkova, Petia/Ringeisen, Tobias (ed.): Handbuch Diversity Kompetenz. Band 2: Gegenstandsbereiche. Wiesbaden: Springer, pp. 297-312.
Weischedel, Wilhelm (1975): Die philosophische Hintertreppe. 34 große Philosophen in Alltag und Denken. München: dtv Deutscher Taschenbuch Verlag.
Woolf, Virginia (2001): Ein eigenes Zimmer /Drei Guineen. Frankfurt a.M.: Fischer Taschenbuch Verlag, Engl.: (1929/2000): A Room of One's Own and Three Guineas. London: Penguin Random House.

Audio-Books /DVDs (Selection)

Audio-Book: 1998 Der Campus. Gelesen von Christian Baumann. Der Hörverlag: München.
Audio-Book: 1998 Tomboy (Intermedium Records).
Audio-Book: 2005 Weischedel, Wilhelm: Die philosophische Hintertreppe 1-3.
Audio-Book: 2009 Sofies Welt. Der Hörverlag (Audio Drama) and (Original Version).
DVD: Der Campus. 123 min. Deutschland 1998. Regie: Sönke Wortmann, Drehbuch: Dietrich Schwanitz, Produktion: Bernd Eichinger, Verleih: Constantin Film. Starlight Video 22588.

Constanze Schwärzer-Dutta

Unlearning Discrimination: experiences with the anti-bias approach in adult-education in Germany

1 Introduction

The anti-bias approach to education for diversity and against discrimination was developed in the USA in early childhood education and in South Africa in adult education. Both approaches were introduced in Germany at the end of the 1990s from the USA and South Africa. In this period marked by an ongoing divide between East and West Germany, a rise in racist violence and a widespread denial of racism, the anti-bias approach provided a new way to open dialogues about racism and other forms of oppression by taking peoples' personal experiences in their multiple and intersecting identities into account. Anti-bias is based on the assumptions that everyone holds biases and that everyone has the potential to be an agent and a target of discrimination at some point in life. The anti-bias approach used in adult education distinguishes itself by its strong focus on power relations and on the links between interpersonal and structural discrimination. This article explains the key concepts of the anti-bias approach and traces the history of anti-bias practice in Germany from the project "Learning from the South"[1] to current applications in professional development, specifically my own experience as a trainer and facilitator in adult education with my network ZSIMT Berlin.[2] I highlight the strengths of anti-bias in uncovering unintentional discrimination through the concept of internalized dominance, drawing on my experience in counseling and in counselor training. In the end possible risks and limits of anti-bias

1 See INKOTA-Netzwerk (2002). The Anti-bias approach discussed in this article goes back to this learning exchange between South African and German educators.

2 ZSIMT stands for Zentrum für soziale Inklusion, Migration und Teilhabe (Center for social inclusion, migration and participation) and is a network with hubs in the cities of Bonn and Berlin. It was founded in 2013 by Dr. Prasad Reddy as a successor of the network Global Skills for Change. I am indebted to my teacher Dr. Prasad Reddy for making the experience discussed in this article possible. I would like to thank Dr. Prasad Reddy, Georg Klauda and Anna-Lena Dohmann for their comments on this article. Its shortcomings are all mine. My own perspective is not unbiased: as a white german heterosexual temporarily able-bodied ex-christian adult cis-woman from an upper middle class family I am privileged in many ways. My personal experiences as a target of discrimination are mainly due to sexism.

workshop methods and experience-based antidiscrimination workshops in general will be discussed.

2 Origins and Historical Background of the Anti-Bias Approach

2.1 From Multicultural Education to an Anti-Bias approach to Early Childhood Education in the USA

The anti-bias approach was developed by Louise Derman-Sparks and Carol Brunson Phillips[3] together with a group of faculty and students at Pacific Oaks College. Their starting point was a criticism of existing approaches to diversity, inequality and specifically racism in pedagogical contexts. Derman-Sparks (1989:6f.) highlights two approaches this criticism is directed at, the "tourist" approach and the "color-blind" approach.

"Tourist curriculum" is what multicultural education often deteriorates to in practice: Paying a visit to 'other' cultures by tasting foods and learning about religious holidays, while the dominant culture is not presented as one culture among many but remains the norm. This reinforces stereotypes and inequalities by depicting people of non-European descent as 'others' and by often treating children of immigrant families as representatives of their parents' or grandparents' country of origin (Derman-Sparks 1989:7).

To avoid falling into these traps, and out of a preoccupation that talking about differences might draw childrens' attention towards them, many educators have taken on a "color-blind" approach. The reasoning behind this is that prejudice and discrimination can best be avoided by ignoring differences and treating all children the same. However, by the time they are three or four years old children notice that there are differences in gender, skin color and physical ability and that status differences are frequently attached to these (Derman-Sparks 1989:2ff.). When adults seem uncomfortable talking about these topics, they unwillingly send the message that difference is a problem. Not taking differences into account also makes it impossible to address historical inequalities.[4]

---

3 Today Carol Brunson Day

4 Derman-Sparks (2001) highlights how in the US educational system before the Civil Rights Movement, white dominance was enforced by the segregation of schools for Black and white children, the forced sending of Native American children to boarding schools, or the prohibition of the Spanish language.

A third point of criticism of traditional multicultural education is that it addresses only the children. The anti-bias approach emphasizes that teachers and institutions have to embark on their own anti-bias journey and provides them with tools for working on their own attitude, for working with parents and for creating an environment in which diversity is represented in an adequate and non-stereotypical way and which provides equal learning opportunities for each child.

2.2 The Anti-Bias Approach in the Context of Transition from Apartheid to Democracy in South Africa

In the beginning of the 1990s the transition from the Apartheid[5] regime towards a democratic South Africa was decided. The anti-bias approach was one answer from the educational sector to the enormous task of constructing an integrated, diverse and democratic society out of a racially segregated and oppressive one. Schools and other institutions had to be prepared for teaching *white* and Black children together, for dealing with language and cultural diversity, but also with persistent inequalities in income, housing, health care etc. (Hermanus 2011).

Various antiracist and other progressive organizations, such as the Anti-Racism Training Network (ART) Gauteng and the Early Learning Resource Unit (ELRU), were looking for concepts to counter racism and other forms of oppression in the educational and social sector. ELRU worked with US diversity and anti-bias trainers like Derman-Sparks, Valerie Batts and Julian Sonn to develop an anti-bias training course for adult multipliers (Hermanus 2011). This training concept is laid down in the manual *Shifting Paradigms* which is still the book of reference for anti-bias work with adults (ELRU 1997). While focusing primarily on racism and sexism, the South African anti-bias approach is flexible enough to integrate any form of discrimination participants might have experienced. Sexism, racism, classism, anti-semitism, religious oppression, adultism, ageism, heterosexism, ableism and linguicism are mentioned in the handbook (ELRU 1997:12).

5 Apartheid was the segregation of *white* and Black people and the supremacy of the *whites* which was installed legally in 1948 and was enforced with brutal violence. Black people were forced to live in rural 'Homelands' and urban 'Townships' and were allowed to enter *white* areas only with a permit to work. They did not have equal access to education and their right to vote applied only inside the 'Homelands'. Sexual relationships and marriages between Blacks and *whites* were forbidden for a long time. Everyday life was ruled by segregation. After decades of resistance from political organizations and large parts of the Black majority population, by the end of the 1980s it was clear that Apartheid would end.

3 The Anti-Bias Approach in Germany: historical context and today's practice

3.1 Germany in the 1990s: a country of immigration and racism in denial

The end of the 1980s saw a rise in racist and right-wing extremist violence which peaked after Germany's reunification.[6] This violence was usually attributed not to racism but to 'Ausländerfeindlichkeit' (hostility to foreigners) or 'Fremdenfeindlichkeit' (hostility to strangers) by politicians and media, although it mainly affected Black Germans and German residents of African, Asian or Turkish descent. To see German residents of Color and/or from immigrant families as 'foreigners' is in line with the everyday language of those times, due to a historically rooted ethnic understanding of the nation. Strict nationality and naturalization laws contributed to the disenfranchisement of a large number of people affected by racism. When in 1998 the government finally declared Germany to be a country of immigration, over 7 million non-German citizens were living in Germany. In the years after, steps were taken to modernize nationality and immigration law and integration policies were implemented. Some of these were directed not only at immigrants but also at 'persons with migration background', a new category in statistics and social research which includes immigrants' children and sometimes grandchildren. While the statistical category 'migration background' was determined with the aim to get a better understanding of the composition of the social structure and social inequality in Germany, it is misleading to use it synonymously with being affected by racism. To see people affected by racism as 'foreigners' or as 'people with migration background' enables to divert the attention from racism and blame the disadvantages people thus labeled suffer on presumed cultural differences.

Moreover, the term racism was associated with Nazi ideology and the Holocaust in public discourse, so that contemporary racist violence, let alone institutional or everyday racism, was trivialized.

At the same time, after the reunification in 1990, Germany continued to be divided in East and West economically and socially. There is a far higher per-capita incidence of racist violence in the East (Zeit Online 2015), which makes it easy for media and politicians to depict racism as a problem of its victims and violent extreme right-wing eastern young men as the stereotypical perpetrators – the 'others' and the 'other others' (Güler 2009:33) – and to

6 As I am writing this in 2016 there is a new peak in violence against refugees.

deny its systemic quality and its intertwinement with ethnic nationalism and migration regimes. Since the early 1990s government-sponsored programs were undertaken to combat right-wing-extremism and violence – at first only in Eastern Germany – and to support their actual and potential victims – i.e. 'people with migration background' – through counseling and labour market integration programs. Diversity education is also part of European Union funded programs for labour market integration of disadvantaged groups (XENOS), of programs supporting the implementation of the 2012 *Anerkennungsgesetz* (Federal Recognition Act regarding foreign professional qualifications) and since 2015 many projects with newly arrived refugees.[7] Although the funded projects are quite diverse, the target direction of the programs left a difficult legacy on antidiscrimination and diversity education in Germany, since they were initially designed to address participants either as potential right-wing-extremists, implying a strong accusation, or as potential victims of these.[8]

3.2 Learning from the South: how the anti-bias approach came to Germany

The South African anti-bias approach was introduced in Germany through the project '*Vom Süden lernen*' (Learning from the South) by the developmental NGO INKOTA (2002). This project was designed to reverse traditional strategies of development cooperation by bringing experts from the Global South to Germany so that German educators could learn from them. Especially the anti-bias trainings conducted by South African trainers fell on fertile ground. The transition from Apartheid to democracy in South Africa set a model for societies in transformation worldwide. For Germany as a society in transformation and an immigration society with a severe racism problem, the anti-bias approach opened up new possibilities by taking into account that agents and targets of every form of discrimination may be present at a workshop. The trainers from South Africa made it clear that German educators had to deal with racism and with the East-West divide (Giesche/ Reddy/Reddy 2002). Anti-bias provides methods to work with heterogeneous groups in a sensitive and productive way. In practice, they enable facilitators to overcome stereotypes like the racist unemployed Easterner, and to show

7 For detailed information about past government programs and their political and theoretical background see Reimer (2011:281-311).

8 The reasoning behind the labor market programs is also partly problematic. While seeking to mend some of the effects of structural discrimination, they also seem to follow the logic that racism would somehow diminish if racists and their victims had better jobs.

participants who fit into these categories that their own concerns about unemployment and discrimination are taken seriously, which makes it much easier to then talk about racism.

At about the same time a group of early childhood educators in Berlin began to look for up-to-date approaches to deal with diversity and discrimination in kindergartens. They started adapting the US anti-bias approach to German context and applying it in various institutions through the project *Kinderwelten* (childrens' worlds).[9]

3.3 Adaptions and Applications of the Anti-Bias Approach in Germany

In educational work the South African anti-bias approach has set new standards in Germany. Various groups and projects have dedicated themselves to adapt and apply it to different fields.[10] For a long time, the anti-bias approach was mostly realized in extracurricular and further education. In recent years, it has increasingly been integrated into university curriculums of pedagogy, social work, and social and political sciences. There are also various anti-bias projects in schools and kindergartens. Support programs for international students and first-generation university students also work with anti-bias.

Anti-bias still has an important place in development education. Government-sponsored volunteer programs such as *weltwärts* ('worldwards'), which send young people often without professional training from Germany to work in social projects in Africa, Asia, and Latin America, have come under criticism for their structural racism and colonial division of work. The government responded to this by introducing a 'reverse' component in the programs, and many organizations have included anti-bias components in their preparatory seminars. Education for sustainable development and global citizenship education can also be improved with an anti-bias lens. Too often stereotypes of the Global South as needy and polluted are reproduced and the presence of Southern knowledge, e.g. via immigrant families, in Germany is neglected.

Applications of anti-bias outside the educational sector and in other formats than workshops and seminars are being developed. Anti-bias is finding

---

9 For more information, see the project's website, https://situationsansatz.de/fachstelle-kinderwelten.html, or Wagner 2013.

10 Among these are the *Anti-Bias-Werkstatt*, the *Anti-Bias-Netz*, ZSIMT, glokal e.V., the project *Perspektivwechsel* of the ZWST (Central Welfare Office of Jews in Germany), *Fortbildungsinstitut für die pädagogische Praxis* Fipp e.V. Berlin, *Institut für konstruktive Konfliktaustragung und Mediation* IKM e.V. Hamburg and the *Bremer Institut für Soziale Arbeit und Entwicklung* e.V. BISA+E.

its way into continuous professional training for social workers and counselors and even public authorities.[11] Practitioners of anti-bias have long seen its potential for organizational development, but there is little corresponding practice outside of kindergartens. The new leading image of inclusion could open up new discussions about barriers and discrimination in institutions, which anti-bias can help uncover and dismantle.

3.4 Anti-Bias Compared to other Approaches to Diversity, Antiracism and Antidiscrimination Education

The prevailing method of antiracist pedagogy in Germany and the one favored by many state-funded programs was for a long time the imparting of knowledge about history, mainly about the Shoah. While being undoubtedly important, this is not enough to combat contemporary forms of racism. Firstly, it focuses on antisemitism, while other racist histories like German colonialism, the genocide of the Herero and Nama, and the Porajmos[12] remained almost forgotten for a long time. Secondly, historical pedagogy is not enough to understand contemporary racisms. Thirdly, it seems to be addressed mainly at non-Jewish *white* Germans whose grandparents and great-grandparents were among the perpetrators and it fails to take into account the family histories of a large part of the immigrant population.[13] Anti-bias methodology follows the principle 'start with self', which means that real life experiences are shared, compared and linked to societal structures and theoretical concepts.

Like 'diversity' approaches, anti-bias addresses participants in all their identities and works best in heterogeneous groups. However, anti-bias distinguishes itself from those business approaches to 'Diversity' which neglect power relations by placing a strong focus on relations of power and inequality which enable discrimination. Participants are required to position themselves as advantaged or disadvantaged along the lines of different categories of inequality. This makes both experiences emotionally accessible to participants. It also makes intersectionality understandable as a personal experience.

---

11 This is not to say that anti-bias in adult education is widely funded or applied by government institutions. Organizations delivering training courses for labor market institutions for example sometimes hire anti-bias trainers but then often expect them to deliver diversity or intercultural trainings.

12 Porajmos or Samudaripen are Romani terms for the Holocaust of the Roma and Sinti committed by the (non-Jewish, non-Roma) Germans during National Socialism. As with the Jews, the Nazis aimed at exterminating the Romani people as a whole.

13 While the need has been seen to modify historical pedagogy to honor the experiences of young people from immigrant families, including Palestinian refugees, their interpretations of history are often dismissed as false (Attia 2015:83).

Anti-bias shares with critical whiteness and empowerment approaches a focus on the ways structural oppression influences personal emotions, thoughts and interactions, summed up under 'internalized dominance' and 'internalized oppression'. While theoretical insights of critical whiteness studies combine well with anti-bias, the methods are fundamentally different because anti-bias works with agent and target groups of racism and other forms of oppression simultaneously. Precisely this makes anti-bias so powerful because it enables participants to gain emotional access to both experiences. Being seen in all their identities and having the respective 'other' as a mirror to reflect on their own words and deeds fosters a self-reflective, self-critical stance of privileged participants, which also makes it easier for respectively disadvantaged participants to demand changes. I will explore some of the challenges of working experience-based in heterogeneous groups in the last two chapters.[14]

4 Key Concepts of the Anti-Bias Approach

4.1 Topics and Goals of the Anti-Bias Approach for Children and Adults

Anti-bias workshops tend to not have fixed goals and schedules but rather follow participants' learning process in sharpening their emotional and cognitive understanding of how discrimination works and how to dismantle it. Nevertheless Derman-Sparks and Edwards (2010:4f.) name the following four main topics and goals of anti-bias education which Rubaica Jaliwala (2012:89) reformulates for older youths and adults:

1. Constructing identity: Children should feel good about their personal and their group identity, without feeling superior or inferior to other people and other groups (Derman-Sparks 2001). Making diversity visible in a non-stereotypical way is important to achieve this. For adults it is important to examine "the constructedness of identity" (Jaliwala 2012:89) and the need to actively construct an antiracist, antisexist etc. identity. Anti-bias closely links the discussion of identity to power relations (Jaliwala 2012:75). In practice this requests a careful balance between respect for individuals' identities and a critical stance on the social categories and power relations through which identities are often constituted. Con-

14 For the pros and cons of antiracism trainings in mixed versus segregated groups, also see Boger and Simon (2016).

temporary critical approaches like postcolonial or queer/feminist ones were not systematically integrated into the 'classic' anti-bias texts and methods. Criticism from a feminist perspective was directed at some anti-bias methods for failing to recognize the construction of gender or cultural identities (Frey 2002). However, since anti-bias does not work with an essentialist concept of identities it is possible to integrate these approaches and individual facilitators and researchers such as Jaliwala (2012) are doing this.[15]

2. Generating empathy: For children this means to be comfortable with human diversity and to develop "deep, caring human connections." (Derman-Sparks/Edwards 2010:4). In anti-bias work with adults empathy is generated mainly through the methodology which relies on an exchange of experiences. Listening to each other's experiences fosters a cognitive and emotional understanding of discrimination and its effects, without necessarily blurring the differences between different forms of oppression in their societal, historical and personal impact. However, facilitators should be conscious of the boundaries of empathy across the lines of structural oppression experiences (Jones 2004). In our trainings for counselors we explicitly work on these boundaries.
3. Becoming aware of biases: For children this means to "recognize unfairness, have language to describe unfairness, and understand that unfairness hurts." (Derman-Sparks/Edwards 2010:5) This can start by criticizing books or toys as unfair or wrong. Here, Derman-Sparks and Edwards treat stereotypes mainly as misinformation. With adults, this means a critical self-reflection to become "aware of our own biases and the ways in which we intentionally and unintentionally feed into the oppression of others and ourselves" (ELRU 1997:7).
4. Acting against discrimination: To be empowered and have "skills to act, with others or alone, against prejudice and/or discriminatory actions." (Derman-Sparks/Edwards 2010:5) For preschool children this means to learn to defend themselves and others by saying 'no' or getting help. The overall goal of anti-bias education for adults is to "challenge any form of prejudice, stereotyping, bias and discrimination which occurs at a personal, structural and/or cultural level in the institutions in which we work, and within the structures of society." (ELRU 1997:10)

15 The concept of 'identity' is rarely treated explicitly in German language anti-bias work. I suspect that this is mostly due to the difficulty to assume being German as an identity because of the historically exceptional crimes committed in the name of this.

4.2 *Bias, Stereotypes, and Prejudice*

Bias is usually taken to mean the same as prejudice, but it's more complicated. Derman-Sparks (1989:3) defines bias as "[a]ny attitude, belief, or feeling that results in, and helps to justify, unfair treatment of an individual because of his or her identity." So biases work like prejudices or stereotypes, but not only prejudices or stereotypes can work as biases. While the term prejudice emphasizes the psychological motives and the term stereotype emphasizes the cognitive mechanisms behind attitudes, the term bias emphasizes attitudes' consequences. This distinction is important because anti-bias encourages participants to question their biases as a starting point to interrupt mechanisms of discrimination, but aims at combating discrimination which is ultimately defined by discriminatory effects and not by the intentions of the discriminating agent.

Prejudice is defined in social sciences similar to the everyday use of the term. Gordon Allport defines "ethnic prejudice"[16] as "an antipathy based upon a faulty and inflexible generalization. It may be directed toward a group as a whole, or toward an individual because he is a member of that group" (Allport 1979:9). The classic studies in prejudice (Allport 1979, Adorno et al. 1950) focus on the psychological functions of prejudice for the individual, for example the projective ascription of own devalued personality traits or wishes on 'others', or the diversion of aggression and blame through scapegoating. They combine psychological and sociological insights. However, they focus on societal structures' impacts on the individual psyche, and not on these structures' contribution to creating the stereotyped categories, ascriptions and valuations.[17]

Stereotypes are ideas about collective traits of social groups, that is, groups of people who are taken to share an identity based on certain characteristics like race, gender, or class. They are widely shared and they come to our minds regardless of our personal opinion or more adequate information we may have. The research on stereotypes suggests that stereotypes play into cognitive processes in which our brain organizes our perceptions into categories, although the social categories and the contents of stereotypical ascriptions are learnt.[18] However, stereotype research cannot explain how the categories and the stereotypes' contents come about (Terkessidis 1998:37).

---

16 Most research on prejudices and stereotypes has been done on racist or 'ethnic' prejudice. Its applicability to other categories is often sustained but not proved. The same holds true for most models used in anti-bias work.

17 The contemporary research on GMF (Gruppenbezogene Menschenfeindlichkeit or group-related hostility to humans) follows the same logic. For a criticism of GMF see Attia 2013a and Terkessidis 2004:39-44.

18 For cognitive psychological research in stereotypes see Banaji/Greenwald 2013 for example.

Most practitioners of anti-bias would attribute biases neither to individual psychological needs nor to universal cognitive processes.[19] Rather they see biases as part of discourses or ideologies which are learnt by individuals (Reddy 2002:36, Schmidt 2009:102f., Jaliwala 2012:37).[20] They are learnt for example through schoolbooks and other media, but also by the observation of the world around us, trying to make sense of societal structures and our own lives' realities. The contents of stereotypical ascriptions reflect the existing power relations in society and the norms of the dominant group. This is in line with contemporary research and theories on racism that have turned towards the critical analysis of the interplay of power and knowledge in dominant discourse. Theories on racism that are informed by discourse[21] and ideology theory conceptualize racism not as individual prejudice plus power, but as a complex or apparatus (Terkessidis 1998:74) of knowledge and power which structures society but also produces racialized subjects. The way for these theories was paved by Robert Miles' definition of racism and Stuart Hall's application of ideology and discourse theory to the analysis of racism. In the German context I refer to the groundbreaking work of Mark Terkessidis (1998, 2004) and Grada Kilomba (2008) here.

Grada Kilomba's (2008:42) definition of racism draws on the classic formula 'prejudice + power' which is also widely used in anti-bias workshops, but specifies it to answer the questions who produces racist categorizations and ascriptions and who benefits from them. The first component of racism according to her, the "construction of difference" is connected to a "construction as 'different'" "from the white norm". This can also be achieved through discrimination. The second component of her definition is the application of hierarchical values to this difference and the third is the combination with power. She emphasizes that historically only *white* people had the power to install racism in this sense and thus the definition of racism should be restricted to prejudice + power of *white* people.

Terkessidis (1998:59f.) rejects the term prejudice and proposes the term 'racist knowledge' to refer to the production of specific categories and their

19 For a thorough criticism of prejudice and stereotype research and a critical discussion of the equally relevant social categorization and social identity theories, see Terkessidis 1998:17-37.

20 Reddy (2007:48) explicitly distinguishes a 'northern' and a 'southern' paradigm as different perspectives on stereotypes. The northern perspective sums up the psychological and cognitive explanations of prejudice and stereotypes, the southern perspective sees 'prejudice' as systematically created and applied in power structures and learnt by individuals. Jaliwala (2012) incorporates findings from prejudice and stereotype research but emphasizes that stereotypes tend to be created through processes of 'othering' and structural discrimination.

21 The term discourse here refers to the later Foucault's concept of discourse as a complex of knowledge, power and praxis.

content. Institutions play a key role in the production of this knowledge and power/practice complex. For example, the social group of the Germans is defined by nationality law, the category 'people with migration background' is defined by the federal statistical office, integration policies and media. Unlike 'stereotype' or 'prejudice', racist knowledge is not an error, or an attitude that some individuals have and others don't.[22] It is an explanation and at the same time a (pre)condition of the status quo. Its content reflects the values of the dominant group. For anti-bias work, the concept of racist knowledge is valuable because it provides a necessary understanding of the relations between biases and power structures. Terkessidis (2004:99) maintains that categorization is already part of racist knowledge, that there need not be a negative valuation attached or rather the valuation is inherent because the 'other' and its ascribed traits are made to represent the opposite of the dominant group and its values. The process of constructing an 'other' from a position of power can be well described with the concept of 'Othering', a term coined by postcolonial theorist Gayatri Chakravorty Spivak (1985:252). It is through constructing others as others that the dominant group constructs itself as the norm(al). This othering can be achieved by negative stereotyping thereby confirming the dominant groups' values and identity, but it can also be achieved by misrepresenting the 'other' in various ways, e.g. as 'exotic' or 'interesting'.[23]

4.3 Power and Privilege

Power is understood in anti-bias work as a prerequisite of discrimination and oppression in the sense of 'power over', but also as 'power to', that is an individual or collective ability to act. In this sense, anti-bias wants to empower everyone to stand up against discrimination and to develop alternatives to discriminatory practices. anti-bias literature distinguishes various levels on which power can be assigned and exercised. My classification is based on Schmidt (2009:124), Attia (2013b:150) and my reading of Terkessidis' (2004) findings on everyday racism. It is an important part of anti-bias workshops to asses individuals' power on various levels with the aim of finding ways to share it and/or use it in a non-discriminatory way. Definitional power in this context means to have the power to decide which identities of oneself

---

22 This is one point of criticism at classical research in prejudice and GMF. These conceptualize prejudice as a deviation, only to state its commonness according to surveys.

23 Othering in Spivak's use implies epistemic violence and is connected to legitimizing and exercising colonial power. Unlike prejudice or stereotype, it is a historically specific concept.

or of others are recognized or seen as salient in a certain context. An example of appropriating the definitional power over others in interpersonal contact would be the question 'Where are you (really) from?', because the person posing the question is implying that the person asked can't be from 'here'. Situational power is the power transferred to someone due to a certain situation, for example, by being a part of the majority group in that situation, or by spatial settings. Institutional power is the power of an institution or of a person due to laws or regulations. For example a teacher has the power to give grades, an immigration official can grant or deny visa. The most important level but also the one most difficult to understand in practice is the individual's position of power in society, what is commonly called privilege. For some workshop participants it is unusual to see themselves in terms of social categories like race, gender, class etc. Persons who enjoy many privileges tend to see themselves as unmarked, as 'normal' or as mere 'individuals'. For example, a *white* workshop participant maintained that she could not know if she discriminated against her students of Color because she didn't have any *white* students to compare. She construed herself as neutral and did not acknowledge the societal power she had as a *white* person. The described levels of power are interconnected. People who are privileged in various identities have more access to institutional power and are likely to find themselves in settings where they have situational power, for instance by sitting behind a desk or standing in front of a class. Jaliwala (2012:95) adds to these levels of power their respective current and historical dimensions, which is important when it comes to the internalization of dominance and oppression.

4.4 Discrimination and Oppression

Discrimination is defined in law and the social sciences as the differential and/or disadvantageous treatment of a person or a group based on the social group they are perceived to belong to. Social scientists usually reserve the term for those forms of discrimination which build on and correlate with systemic forms of social inequality like racism, sexism, classism and other inequalities (Scherr 2012).

In anti-bias work the term discrimination is used, referring not only to an individual level but including the analysis of power on multiple levels: personal, interpersonal, structural, discursive and internalized. In English language anti-bias work the term oppression is often used when in the German context we talk of discrimination (ELRU 1997:11).[24]

---

24 For a critique of an individualized concept of discrimination see Attia (2013b).

One of these two definitions are used as a working model of discrimination in many anti-bias workshops: prejudice + power > (read: can lead to) discrimination (1) or differentiation + power > discrimination (2) (Schmidt 2009:82, Anti-Bias-Netz 2016:15). Their strength is that they provide an easy to handle analytical tool for participants to assess their own everyday thoughts and actions as to whether they can lead to discrimination. The weakness of this model in my reading is that it does not provide an explanation of the link between biases and power structures. It may also be mistakenly read as a causal chain, in the sense that biases precede power and discrimination.

Fig.1: 'Old' anti-bias discrimination model

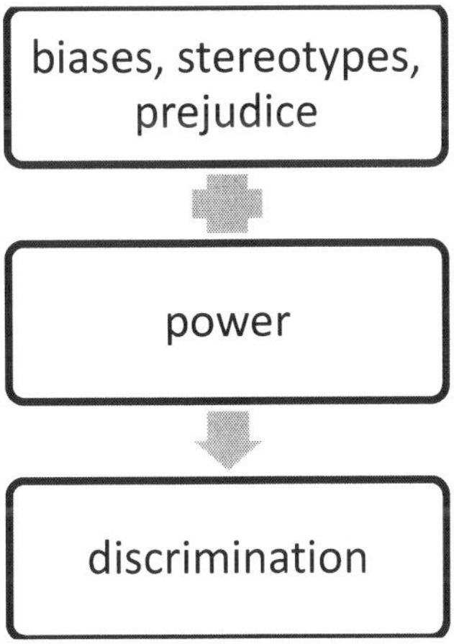

Source: Own presentation, inspired by Anti-Bias-Werkstatt/Europahaus Aurich 2007

I propose a revised discrimination model taking into account Gayatri Chakravorty Spivak's concept of othering and Mark Terkessidis' definition of racism. Terkessidis defines racism, inspired by Robert Miles, as consisting of the following three elements (Terkessidis 1998:74-77):

1. "Racialization": the process of categorization of groups as 'natural', referring to biological, cultural or sociological traits, and the definition of the 'nature' of this group with reference to the 'own' group.
2. "Exclusionary practice": This includes practices that have an unequal effect, what in anti-bias work would be called discrimination.
3. "Differentiating power", which alludes to the fact that, to install racism, a group must be able to enforce categorizations and exclusionary practices through different means, including violence (Terkessidis 1998:79).[25]

25 This definition is inspired by Robert Miles.

This model implies that the categorizations which discrimination builds on are made from a position of structural power and at the same time serve to consolidate that power. Positive or negative ascriptions ('prejudice') are often mere effects of power and categorization. To analyze individual motivation for discrimination we do not necessarily need the concept of prejudice. I argue that the preservation of a position of power is enough motivation to discriminate.[26]

Fig. 2: A new anti-bias discrimination model

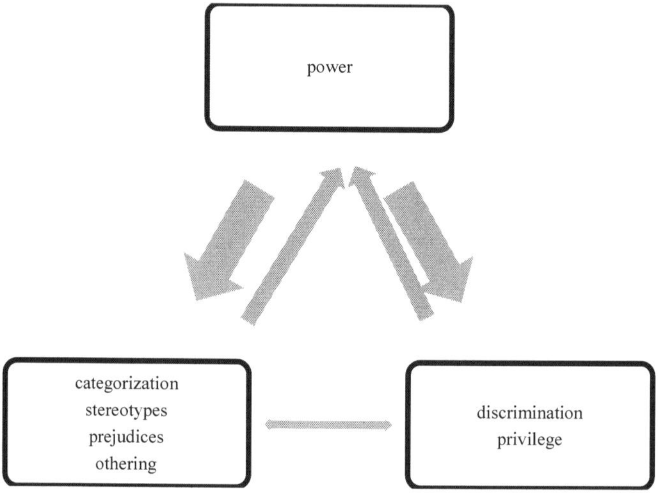

Source: Own presentation

Ultimately, discrimination is best defined by its effects and not by the intentions of the discriminating person or institution.[27] A challenge for anti-bias workshop facilitators is to respect individual experiences while maintaining a firm stance on historically and systemically embedded forms of discrimination that need to be addressed in order to construct a more just and equitable society. The relatively open definition of discrimination does not endorse ideas such as 'reverse racism'.

26 With this new model I also hope to better grasp contemporary manifestations of racism which operate without explicit racist categorization such as 'color blindness' (vgl. Terkessidis 1998:76).

27 Defining discrimination by its effects is in line with a human rights perspective on discrimination such as the one laid down in the United Nations' International Convention on the Elimination of All Forms of Racial Discrimination (ICERD).

In line with different levels of power, we distinguish different levels of discrimination. Personal level discrimination comprises discriminatory actions which can take place even if no target group member is present, like discriminatory speech acts. Discrimination on an interpersonal level comprises all forms of disadvantageous treatment by other persons, e.g. insults, harassment and violence. Institutional or structural level discrimination encompasses "laws, customs, traditions and practices" which systematically favor one social group and disfavor another (ELRU 1997:14). It can occur without conscious intention, through structures and rules that are seemingly neutral but perpetuate one-sided norms. Cultural or discursive level discrimination refers to values, norms and practices which promote or sustain biases, power relations and discrimination, making them seem normal or justified.

4.5 Internalized Dominance and Internalized Oppression

One important goal of anti-bias is the dismantling of internalized power relations which Jaliwala (2012:81) also terms "decolonizing the consciousness".[28] Some dynamics of internalized power relations are summed up in the model of 'modern racism' and 'internalized oppression' by Valerie Batts (2002).

'Modern racism' and 'modern sexism' are used in social psychology to describe forms of subtle or covert prejudice leading to or justifying discrimination. While 'old-fashioned' racism claims an inherent superiority and inferiority of racialized groups, modern racism may articulate itself through a strong preference for the group perceived as 'own' and its values, through the overemphasizing of cultural differences, or through resentment of antidiscrimination measures like affirmative action or women's quota. In ELRU (1997) and Batts (2002) modern racism is introduced as a way racist bias and treatment occurs and is defended in times of legal and seemingly widely accepted equality. In this sense the psychological concept of modern racism is similar to the concepts 'neo-racism' or 'cultural racism' used in social sciences. Another way to conceptualize "modern racism" is to see it as internalized dominance (ELRU 1997:18), that is, the ways in which a lifetime of experiences of being privileged and of being able to discriminate against others has formed our feelings and actions.[29] This concept provides a link between

28 Jaliwala takes this term from Claudia Lohrenscheit's (2004:258) study on Human Rights Education including anti-bias work in South Africa.

29 It is important to distinguish between dominance and power. Power is to be found on all sides, it generates resistance which is also a power. Dominance means consolidated power on various levels, including structural and cultural, so the term describes practices of privileged groups in society (Rommelspacher 1998:25).

the personal, interpersonal and structural levels of power and discrimination. Internalization is not understood in a psychological sense. The oppressed person does not have to believe in their own inferiority. Internalized oppression refers to the internalization of individual strategies to deal with the continued exposure to biases and discrimination. Many of these strategies are useful or even necessary in a short-term perspective, but become counterproductive in the long term because they do not challenge the power relations that make discrimination possible. Actions which can be read as manifestations of internalized dominance or oppression can also be employed consciously and strategically. Especially on the oppressed side actions such as 'playing the system' or 'avoidance of contact' can be smart or necessary, sometimes for survival. To avoid the labeling of tactics from the outside, I will not elaborate on the side of internalized oppression here (full model see Batts 2002, ELRU 1997:19-25; Mamutovič 2016:123).

The model used in anti-bias work (ELRU 1997:21) is built around some common manifestations of internalized dominance and internalized oppression. It is especially relevant for professional development in different helping professions, where professionals are often well-meaning and operate from a position of structural power. I will introduce this side of internalized dominance here by illustrating it with an example from my educational work.

In Germany currently there are many programs for integrating young refugees into the apprenticeship system. While some programs provide good opportunities, others provide training in low paying 'dead end' jobs. Moreover, being in an apprenticeship can protect deportation. I worked with a group of *white*, non-migrant instructors in such a program.[30] Instead of recognizing these draw-backs of from the program, some instructors would emphasize possible benefits, even if the program was obviously not well suited to the needs of several refugee participants. This could be seen as an example of internalized dominance which is called *dysfunctional rescueing.* This refers to help which is motivated more by the helping person's needs and assumptions than by the needs of the person being helped.

Other examples of internalized dominance can be seen in the expectation of subservience of the refugee participants, complaining about their 'lack of gratefulness', when they, for example, listened to family members or social workers rather than to the instructors. Instead of recognizing the complexity of the refugees' social situation, the instructors would rather *blame the victim* – for example, resorting to cultural stereotypes and criticizing the oppressed person's behavior and their survival strategies rather than acknowledging

30 Of course the group of instructors was not a homogeneous entity. It was diverse in terms of gender, age and organizational status, for example. I generalize here to illustrate my point and maintain anonymity.

their situation. This can be seen as another example of internalized dominance in the sense of *"denial of political, historical, economic, psychological and social significance of differences"* (ELRU 1997:21). Not knowing "how to handle these youngsters," lead some of the instructors to employ another tactic of internalized dominance, the *denial of differences* or *color blindness* which in practice lead, for example, to a disrespect for some students' religious food rules. Underlying all this was a category of internalized dominance called *avoidance of contact* and a lack of self-reflection. In order to not act out internalized dominance, instructors would have had to come to terms with their own positions in society, their own interests, their own scope of action and to explore their own biases. This is exactly what anti-bias is about.

5 Potentials and Limits of the Anti-Bias Approach in Professional Contexts: some examples from my experience

5.1 Potentials: power and diversity conscious counseling

To illustrate the potential the anti-bias approach has for professional training in counseling and social work, I want to draw on a training format I have developed together with my colleague Karun Dutta at ZSIMT Berlin. We started from our experience working in coaching and counseling, as a lawyer and as an activist and volunteer, and from our knowledge as anti-bias trainers to find a new approach to transcultural counseling.[31]

First of all, counseling would need to be power and diversity conscious which entails the examination and becoming aware of the counsellor's own social position with regard to the construction of race as well as the social position. This is essential because the dynamics of power, closeness and distance which have to be handled in every counseling process can be increased when counseling across the categories of social inequality. Dynamics of (internalized) dominance and oppression have to be controlled in order to build up trust and maintain a counseling process with an open result in which the counseled person remains agent of their own case at all times.

31 Transcultural counseling is used here as an umbrella term for counseling across cultural or social differences that might affect communication, trust and psychological dynamics of the counseling process. The main topic is counseling across differences in migration status and between people who belong to possible agent and target groups of racism. In Germany this is still mostly called intercultural counseling. I call it transcultural, alluding to the dynamic and constructed character of culture, for lack of a better term.

One danger, I encountered in my own experience of coaching is *dysfunctional rescueing.* For example, trying to console the person seeking support or making unrealistic promises, which serves to maintain a counselors' self-image as good and non-racist and to shield oneself off from dealing with feelings of hopelessness, despair or anger – the counseled persons' and their own.

With regard to research about intercultural competence,[32] racism and discrimination in counseling and social work (Erdem 2011, Melter 2006, Castro Varela et al. 1998), it seems that considering Batts' model of internalized dominance can give important further insights. For example, it would be interesting to examine to which extent the "denial of political, historical, economic, psychological and social significance of differences" (ELRU 1997: 21) takes place and how cultural differences are emphasized in the sense of culturalization or cultural racism or differences are denied in the sense of color blindness.[33]

From our experience with a training course for counselors on the basis of the anti-bias approach, we observe how the counselors can be enabled to self-reflect on their motivation for this work in the context of their biographical experiences and the history of their organizations and society. With anti-bias methods, emotional and cognitive understanding of discrimination and empathy with the persons affected by discrimination can be deepened, while the boundaries of empathy across different positions in society, e.g. between Black and *white* people, between non-migrants and refugees, also become clear.[34] Through anti-bias methods, case studies and communication exercises we explore the internalization of dominance, links between communication styles and power relations and the exacerbating of harmful psychological dynamics in counseling through the influence of societal power relations. Inspired by anti-bias methods we enable participants to constantly shift between the perspectives of counselor and counseled and of agent and target of discrimination.

---

32 This is because counseling and social work in the context of racism are still often framed as 'intercultural' in the German context.

33 As one participant in our courses rightly pointed out, the denial of differences and the over-emphasizing of differences can go hand in hand when intersectionality is not taken into account. Fatma Erdem (2013) provides the example of a German woman of Turkish descent who was assigned a social worker by the youth office on the basis of ethnic matching, who didn't meet her needs because of what she perceived as arrogant, probably classist behavior. The client emphasized that both cultures, Turkish and German, were part of herself and rejected the youth office representative's one-dimensional view of her identity.

34 With the example of police violence against Black people, Janine Jones (2004) analyzes how empathy can be generated and argues that it might be hardly possible to empathize with a person who lives an experience you structurally cannot make and to which there is no analogous situation in your experience.

Drawing on participants' feedback[35], they profited from being sensitized with regard to their own position of power for example as *white* non-migrant counselors as well as to the needs of their immigrant clients and clients of color. Participants reported falling less into the traps of dysfunctional rescuing or avoidance of contact. Many reported paying closer attention to letting persons in coaching and counseling decide and speak for themselves instead of the counselors making assumptions about their needs and speaking for them. Some stated being more open about the results in the counseling processes, others reported a measurable increase in their use of professional interpreters to assure mutual understanding. Participants, including participants of Color and immigrants, also reported to having benefited from reflecting class or ableism privileges and from the improvement of communication and empathy skills.

A question not yet fully answered is the benefit of this course for counselors who can become targets of oppression.[36] While all participants stated that they benefited from the course in their professional role, the personal benefit did not seem to be equally distributed among *white* participants and participants of Color. This leads me to the limits, risks and side-effects of Anti-bias methods in the following chapter.

5.2 Limits: unlearning discrimination without reproducing it?

The biggest challenges in anti-bias work are about dealing with biases, racism, triggers, and trauma in the workshops or seminars. Some might even argue that reproductions of discrimination are part of the process, since some anti-bias methods are designed to help participants discover and disclose their own biases. But these should come in small and manageable doses so that they can be sufficiently analyzed and contained in a way that limits their hurting and maximizes their learning potential. I will name some of the risks I see in anti-bias work here. These are not specific to anti-bias methods but apply to all experience based antidiscrimination and diversity workshops.

35 We evaluated both participants' satisfaction and learning at the end of the course and through an anonymous online survey a month later.

36 Implicitly our program may have been more adapted to *white* counselors, since the literature we used was mostly about *white* counselors, often in relation to clients of color or immigrant clients. While being careful not to reproduce the stereotype that all counselors are *white* in our method and materials, we lacked theoretical tools to explicitly address the role of counselors of Color. As I am writing this the role of counselors of Color still seems to be under-theorized. Some exceptions are Castro Varela 1998, Mecheril 1998, Dhillon-Stevens 2011, Alleyne 2011.

Firstly, anti-bias methods are designed so that participants learn from their own and each other's experiences, but sometimes participants pursue their learning process at the expense of others. Opening a space where bias and discrimination can be talked about without fear can easily be misunderstood as opening a space where people can expose their racism or ask everything they always wanted to know e.g. from people of Color, people with disabilities, or trans*people. It is therefore important for facilitators and participants to know and respect their own and each other's boundaries. Facilitators have to be careful that no participant becomes a 'resource person' for one of their social positions or self-identification or is even pushed in a co-trainer role, like being asked by other participants: 'What is your perspective as a Black woman?'

Secondly, participants could experience being reduced to or being made invisible in one of their identities in the seminar. Therefore, every topic should be looked at from different angles to avoid a re-centering of *white* or other dominant perspectives. Anti-bias methods provide for this but are not always put into practice fully. This is a danger especially in professional training like ours where participants are implicitly addressed more in their powerful roles. Facilitators should always keep in mind that agent and target-group members of every kind of discrimination can be present at the seminar.

Third, experiences of discrimination and oppression are often traumatic. In the best cases, the telling of the stories in an appreciative and self-critical environment can be healing, but people can also be triggered by remembering their own or listening to other participants' stories. Stories of discrimination can also set off dynamics of internalized dominance among the participants. Facilitators need to be very open and sensitive to participants' feelings especially after small group sessions.

Fourth, the experience-based methodology comes with its own limits. Listening to each other's experiences is a powerful way to embark on the journey of unlearning biases and interpersonal discrimination and develop more empathy. However, one should be conscious of the limits of one's own emotional experience which also limits the capacity to truly empathize with people who have real life experiences oneself can structurally never have.

Fifth, the experience based methods work best when the participant group is as heterogeneous as possible. The facilitator team should also represent different perspectives and experiences. If a social group which is minoritized in society represents a minority in the workshop, risks one and two pose a very real danger. If some perspectives are missing at all, there has to be more theoretical input.

Sixth, structural oppression cannot be understood solely from personal stories and experiences, because it cannot be put down to a series of single experiences of discrimination. Structural oppression even deprives people from making contacts or entering into spaces where these single events can occur or the events are not conceived as discrimination as long as the oppressive structure is soundly in place. That is one of the reasons why the personal accounts have to be grounded with some theoretical inputs.

Seventh, while remaining true to the principle 'start with self', participants need to keep in mind that unlearning interpersonal discrimination is not enough. Institutional racism and institutional discrimination has to be dealt with also beyond the training on a structural level, for example through political engagement. Anti-bias tools and models can make structural discrimination visible, but it has to be tackled outside the workshop. These are of course limits not of one specific approach but of educational work per se.

6 Conclusion

Keeping these dangers in mind and navigating around them, we draw a positive conclusion of our ongoing project. Anti-bias workshops provide a laboratory where living in a more diversity-conscious and less discriminating society can be practiced, with all the foreseeable and unforeseeable obstacles in the way. Of course this requires attentiveness and dedication of facilitators and participants. Dialogue across different power positions and different life realities does foster empathy and understanding, and experiencing the limits of this exchange is also an important learning experience.

Reflecting their own real life experiences together with others and being required to position themselves does have a deeper impact on participants than a merely cognitive input or merely learning about 'others'. For persons in a privileged position, the presence of the respective 'other' as a mirror and the decentering of privileged perspectives however contribute to the motivation to change. For persons in a disadvantaged position, it can be empowering to have feelings, experiences, knowledge and criticism taken seriously. Change can and has to be practiced in the workshop already. This requires privileged participants to move beyond guilt and shame which often lead to the reproduction of internalized dominance. Although empowerment elements can be integrated, anti-bias trainings do not aim at replacing empowerment spaces and approaches.

As forms and discourses of discrimination change, so will anti-bias methods and models. It is an ongoing task to analyze current manifestations of racisms, sexisms, etc. and include them in the workshops. Some of the behaviors named 'risks' here – like appropriating knowledge, forcing contact – will have to be among them. By presenting the anti-bias approach in a self-critical way I hope to contribute to this process.

Discussion Questions

1. Which challenges did and does antidiscrimination education face in the historical context of 1990s' Germany and today? How does anti-bias answer these challenges?
2. Compare the anti-bias approach to other approaches in diversity and antidiscrimination education you have experienced or read about. What do they have in common? What are their differences? Which potentials and limits do you see in each approach?
3. The theoretical foundations of the anti-bias approach exposed briefly here focus on racism. What would you have to consider or add to explain other forms of discrimination or oppression? Choose one you already have fairly good knowledge about.

References

Adorno, Theodor W./Frenkel-Brunswik, Else/Levinson, Daniel J./Sanford, R. Nevitt (1950): The Authoritarian Personality. New York: Harper & Brothers.

Alleyne, Aileen (2011): Overcoming racism, discrimination and oppression in psychotherapy. In: Lago, Colin (ed.): The Handbook of Transcultural Counseling & Psychotherapy. Maidenhead, New York: Open University Press, pp. 117-129.

Allport, Gordon W. (1979 [1954]): The Nature of Prejudice. 25th Anniversary Edition. Reading: Addison-Wesley Publishing Company.

anti-bias-netz (ed.) (2016): Vorurteilsbewusste Veränderungen mit dem Anti-Bias-Ansatz. Freiburg: Lambertus.

Anti-Bias-Werkstatt/Europahaus Aurich (Hg.): 2007: Methodenbox: Demokratie-Lernen und Anti-Bias-Arbeit. Aurich: Europahaus.

Attia, Iman (2013a): Das Konzept der „gruppenbezogenen Menschenfeindlichkeit“. Einige kritische Anmerkungen. In: Soziologische Revue, Heft 1/2013, S. 3-9.

Attia, Iman (2013b): Institutionelle Diskriminierung und struktureller Rassismus in modernen Gesellschaften. In: Opferperspektive e.V. (ed.) (2013): Rassistische Diskriminierung und rechte Gewalt. Münster: Westfälisches Dampfboot, pp. 139-15.

Attia, Iman (2015): Geteilte Erinnerungen. Global- und beziehungsgeschichtliche Perspektiven auf Erinnerungspolitik. In: Attia, Iman; Köbsell, Swantje; Prasad, Nivedita: Dominanzkultur reloaded. Neue Texte zu gesellschaftlichen Machtverhältnissen und ihren Nebenwirkungen. Bielefeld: transcript, pp. 75-88.

Banaji, Mahzarin R.(Greenwald, Anthony G. (2013): Blindspot. Hidden Biases of Good People. New York: Delacorte Press.

Batts, Valerie (2002): Is Reconciliation Possible? Lessons from Combating "Modern Racism". In: Douglas, Ian T. (ed.): Waging Reconciliation: God's Mission in a Time of Globalization and Crisis. New York: Church Publishing, http://visions-inc.org/wp-content/uploads/Is-Reconciliation-Possible.pdf (accessed 09.02.2017).

Boger, Mai-Anh/Simon, Nina (2016): zusammen – getrennt – gemeinsam. Rassismuskritische Seminare zwischen Nivellierung und Essentialisierung von Differenz. In: move-

ments. Journal für kritische Migrations- und Grenzregimeforschung, 2, 2, pp. 163-174.
Castro Varela, Maria del Mar (1998): Die Lage ist normal. Normalisierungsdiskurse in der Aus- und Weiterbildung. In: Castro Varela, María del Mar; Schulze, Sylvia; Vogelmann, Silvia; Weiß, Anja: Suchbewegungen. Interkulturelle Beratung und Therapie. Tübingen: Dvgt-Verlag, pp. 117-126.
Castro Varela, María del Mar/Schulze, Sylvia/Vogelmann, Silvia/Weiß, Anja (1998): Suchbewegungen. Interkulturelle Beratung und Therapie. Tübingen: Dgvt-Verlag.
Derman-Sparks, Louise (2001): Anti-Bias Arbeit mit jungen Kindern in den USA. Translated speech at a conference of the project Kinderwelten „Kleine Kinder – keine Vorurteile?", 15.3.2001, Berlin.
https://situationsansatz.de/files/texte ista/fachstelle kinderwelten/kiwe pdf/Derman-Sparks_Anti-Bias-Arbeit in den USA.pdf (accessed 09.02.2017).
Derman-Sparks, Louise and the A.B.C. Task Force (1989): Anti-Bias Curriculum. Tools for Empowering Young Children. Washington, DC: National Association for the Education of Young Children.
Derman-Sparks, Louise/Edwards, Julie Olsen (2010): Anti-Bias-Education for young children and ourselves. Washington, DC: National Association for the Education of Young Children.
Dhillon-Stevens, Harbrinder (2011): Issues for psychological therapists from black and minority ethnic groups. In: Lago, Colin (ed.): The Handbook of Transcultural Counseling & Psychotherapy. Maidenhead, New York: Open University Press, pp. 105-116
ELRU – Early Learning Resource Unit (1997): Shifting Paradigms. Using an anti-bias strategy to challenge oppression and assist transformation in the South African context. Lansdowne: Early Learning Resource Unit.
Erdem, Fatma (2011): Interkulturelle Kompetenz in der Sozialarbeit. Sozialpädagogische Familienhilfe (SPFH) am Beispiel türkischer Migrantenfamilien in Berlin. Uelvesbüll: Der Andere Verlag.
Erdem, Fatma (2013): Interkulturelle Kompetenz in der Sozialpädagogischen Familienhilfe (SPFH) am Beispiel türkischer Migrant_innenfamilien in Berlin. Journal für Psychologie, 21, 1,
https://www.journal-fuer-psychologie.de/index.php/jfp/article/download/261/303 (accessed 09.02.2017).
Frey, Regina (2002): Von Gender und anderen Ausgrenzungskategorien. Über das Verhältnis von Gender und Anti-Bias. In: INKOTA-Netzwerk (ed.) (2002): Vom Süden lernen. Erfahrungen mit einem Antidiskriminierungsprojekt und Anti-Bias-Arbeit. Berlin: INKOTA-Netzwerk e.V., pp. 76-81.
Giesche, Dorothea/Reddy, Anita/Reddy, Prasad (2002): Der Weg in den Süden führt über den Osten. Vom Süden lernen heißt Vorurteile abbauen. In: INKOTA-Netzwerk (ed.): Vom Süden lernen. Erfahrungen mit einem Antidiskriminierungsprojekt und Anti-Bias-Arbeit. Berlin: INKOTA-Netzwerk e.V., pp. 28-32.
Güler, Serdal, (2009): Die Konstruktion der Anderen. Rassistische Legitimations- und Herstellungspraktiken. Diplomarbeit. Berlin: FB Erziehungswissenschaft und Psychologie, Free University Berlin.
Hermanus, Beryl (2011): Speech at the Anti-Bias-Days Conference at Oldenburg University, 7th to 9th of September 2011.
http://www.anti-bias-tage.de/?q=en/beryl_hermanus_speech (accessed 09.02.2017).

ICERD International Convention on the Elimination of All Forms of Racial Discrimination, New York, 7 March 1966, United Nations, Treaty Series, vol. 660, p. 195.

INKOTA-Netzwerk (ed.) (2002): Vom Süden lernen. Erfahrungen mit einem Antidiskriminierungsprojekt und Anti-Bias-Arbeit. Berlin: INKOTA-Netzwerk e.V.

Jaliwala, Rubaica (2012): Political education in plural societies. Using the Anti-bias approach to challenge oppression in Bombay and Berlin. Doctoral Thesis. Kassel: Faculty of Social Sciences, University of Kassel.

Jones, Janine (2004): The impairment of empathy in goodwill whites for african americans. In George Yancy (ed.), What White Looks Like: African-American Philosophers on the Whiteness Question. New York and London: Routledge, pp. 65-86.

Kilomba, Grada (2008) Plantation Memories. Episodes of Everyday Racism. Münster: Unrast.

Lohrenscheit, Claudia (2004): Das Recht auf Menschenrechtsbildung. Grundlagen und Ansätze einer Pädagogik der Menschenrechte. Frankfurt am Main, London: IKO – Verlag für Interkulturelle Kommunikation.

Mamutovič, Žaklina (2016): Empowerment und Anti-Bias – Gemeinsamkeiten und Unterschiede. In: anti-bias-netz (ed.): Vorurteilsbewusste Veränderungen mit dem Anti-Bias-Ansatz. Freiburg: Lambertus.

Mecheril, Paul (1998): Angelpunkte einer psychosozialen Beratungsausbildung unter interkultureller Perspektive. In: Castro Varela, María del Mar; Schulze, Sylvia; Vogelmann, Silvia; Weiß, Anja: Suchbewegungen. Interkulturelle Beratung und Therapie. Tübingen: Dvgt-Verlag, pp. 287-311.

Melter, Claus (2006): Rassismuserfahrungen in der Jugendhilfe. Eine empirische Studie zu Kommunikationspraxen in der Sozialen Arbeit. Münster: Waxmann.

Reddy, Prasad (2002): Vorurteile verlernen. Antworten auf die Frage: Was ist Anti-Bias? In: INKOTA-Netzwerk (ed.): Vom Süden lernen. Erfahrungen mit einem Antidiskriminierungsprojekt und Anti-Bias-Arbeit. Berlin: INKOTA-Netzwerk e.V., pp. 33-38.

Reddy, Prasad (2007): From Victims to Change Agents: Learning from the South – Towards Effective Intercultural Development Education in the North. Frankfurt am Main: IKO Verlag für interkulturelle Kommunikation.

Reimer, Katrin (2011): Kritische politische Bildung gegen Rechtsextremismus und die Bedeutung unterschiedlicher Konzepte zu Rassismus und Diversity. Ein subjektwissenschaftlicher Orientierungs-versuch in Theorie- und Praxiswidersprüchen. Berlin: Fachbereich Erziehungswissenschaft und Psychologie, Free University Berlin.

Rommelspacher, Birgit (1998): Dominanzkultur. Texte zu Fremdheit und Macht. Berlin: Orlanda Frauenverlag.

Scherr, Albert (2012): Diskriminierung: Die Verwendung von Differenzen zur Herstellung und Verfestigung von Ungleichheiten. Vortrag 36. Kongress der Deutschen Gesellschaft für Soziologie. Plenum Diversity und Intersektionalität. portal-intersektionalitaet.de/theoriebildung/ueberblickstexte/scherr/(accessed 27.09.2016).

Schmidt, Bettina (2009): Den Anti-Bias-Ansatz zur Diskussion stellen, Oldenburg: BIS-Verlag.

Spivak, Gayatri Chakravorty (1985): The Rani of Sirmur: An Essay in Reading the Archives. In: History and Theory, 24, 3, pp. 247-272.

Terkessidis, Mark (1998): Psychologie des Rassismus. Opladen, Wiesbaden: Westdeutscher Verlag.

Terkessidis, Mark (2004): Die Banalität des Rassismus. Migranten zweiter Generation entwickeln eine neue Perspektive. Bielefeld: transcript.

Wagner, Petra (ed.) (2013): Handbuch Inklusion – Grundlagen einer vorurteilsbewussten Bildung und Erziehung. Freiburg: Herder.

Wagner, Petra (2014): Geschichte von Kinderwelten. http://www.situationsansatz.de/files/texteista/fachstellekinderwelten/kiwe pdf/Geschichte Kiwe.pdf (accessed 09.02.2017).

Zeit Online (2015): Jede zweite rassistisch motivierte Gewalttat im Osten verübt. 18.08.2015. http://www.zeit.de/gesellschaft/zeitgeschehen/2015-08/rassismus-gewalttaten-ostdeutschland-statistiken (accessed 09.02.2017).

Changing Social Inequalities

Peter Streckeisen

The Business Case for Diversity: Europe 2020, the economic approach and antidiscrimination policies

1 Introduction

This chapter is about EU labour market policy. Today the European Commission certainly is a key actor advocating equal opportunity politics. Labour market policy is one important arena where such concepts are promoted. EC directives and policy recommendations set norms and principles national governments must respond to. The performance of every member state is regularly assessed through indicators relating to equal opportunity principles. While these policies to some extent are consistent with the goals advocated by social movements contesting inequality and discrimination, they might produce new forms of social exclusion and social control at the same time. I argue that EU labour market policy embodies a rising form of power that rests on the individual responsibility of every person able to participate in the labour market. In fact the European Commission's policy choices and priorities are strongly influenced by economic imperialism, that is, the application of economic concepts, for example human capital theory, to all domains of human activity. Legal, ethical and social arguments against discrimination are not the only reasons why the European Commission advocates equal opportunity politics. These arguments go hand in hand with economic reasoning and the question is whether they are, more often than not, even outweighed by economic interests.

The first section of this chapter briefly explores the notion of the labour market. The second section discusses two concurrent processes: the transition from Fordism to post-Fordism and the ascendancy of economics. After that, three sections are dedicated to EU labour market policy. First, I describe the main components of the Europe 2020 policy framework, giving special attention to the rise of social investment as a leading rationale. Second, I analyze how a new conception of full employment is closely related with diversity management and antidiscrimination policy aiming at maximal labour market integration of population groups marginalized or excluded under Fordism (women, the elderly, people with disabilities and others). The following section addresses governance issues: I argue that institutional tools and arrangements like the Open Method of Coordination or the European Semester, are quite evocative of what Foucault calls the economic tribunal. My chapter ends with concluding remarks highlighting the ambivalence of diversity and antidiscrimination policies based on economic reasoning.

2 Labour Markets

Labour markets are key institutions of capitalism. But why do we call it labour market? Actually people do not sell and buy labour on these markets, neither labour as an activity (one cannot detach it from the active person in order to sell it), nor labour as a product, i.e. accomplished labour. Rather, employers buy the capacity to work and the readiness to work of those persons we often call the workforce. But labour markets are not like slave markets either, where human beings are sold and bought. In a way, talking about the workforce is misleading because this notion mistakes the working capacity of people for these people themselves. Instead of that, in capitalist labour markets workers remain owners of their own person even if they must involve much of their personality in the working activity and may strongly identify with their work.

Like all markets, labour markets are neither natural nor universal in human history. Polanyi (2001) in his pioneering book about 'The Great Transformation', that is, the historic transition from feudal society to capitalism reminds us that markets have existed in various human communities and historic societies but never before capitalism there existed an integrated market system regulated by price mechanisms. As long as markets remain relatively small and disconnected they show no natural tendency for expansion, neither penetrate all domains of human activity. But when an all-embracing market system is established economy becomes a realm of its own and markets show a tendency to subordinate society. For that reason, Polanyi argues that market economy leads to market society, that is, to the development of a society strongly penetrated by market mechanisms.

In this process labour markets are of crucial importance. Polanyi (2001: 71-80) calls labour, as much as land and money, a 'fictitious commodity'. Contrary to ordinary commodities, members of the workforce are not produced for sale on the market. Human beings exist in their own right, even those persons who sell their working capacity to other people. But labour markets treat workforce as if it existed only, at least primarily, for sale in these markets. Polanyi rightly insists that talking about labour means talking about human beings, just as talking about land means talking about nature. As far as capitalism relies on labour as a 'fictitious commodity', it inevitably penetrates all spheres of human activity and transforms the societal conditions and forms of people's everyday lives. Because their capacity to work and their readiness to work is not naturally given, it depends on socialization in the family, at school, during leisure time, on the job and so forth. In many spheres of human activity, capitalism shows a tendency to treat human beings as if they existed for sale or as very things to invest in. At the same time, capitalist economy really works only if most people behave as if labour was a commodity like all the other commodities being sold and bought on the market.

In his chapter about the buying and selling of labour-power in *Capital Volume One*, Marx (1990:146-147) stresses that nature,

> "… does not produce on the one side owners of money or commodities, and on the other men possessing nothing but their own labour-power. This relation has no natural basis, neither is its social basis one that is common to all historical periods. It is clearly the result of a past historical development, the product of many economic revolutions, of the extinction of a whole series of older forms of social production."

Labour market policy, a notion that did not yet exist in Marx's times, is very much about transforming human beings into workforce. Marx (1990:619-643) described how at the beginning of capitalism poor people were expropriated and brutally forced to work by the state (in so called work houses, amongst others), whereas later in history the working class got accustomed to the new economic regime and state intervention decreased. Nevertheless, the transformation of human beings into workforce is never achieved for good in the history of capitalism because workers' children are born as human beings, not as workers. Moreover, this transformation regards not only, maybe not even primarily, the separation between workers and means of production, but over and above the making of people's working capacity and readiness to work. Today more than ever, this process is perceived to continue during the whole life span of every individual. Hence, labour market policy is closely related to family policy, education, public health, old age policy and so forth.

3 Another Great Transformation

If neoliberal economists like Friedman (1975) like to say that 'there's no such thing as a free lunch', critical sociologists might respond: 'There's no such thing as a free market!' Inspired by the findings of Polanyi and others, economic sociology offers an impressive literature about markets being social institutions. Capitalism gives birth to an economy, which is a relatively autonomous realm of human activity (like politics, mass media, religion, art, literature, sport and so forth). Even if it is true that capitalist economies display disembedding tendencies, markets always remain imbedded in social relations and they are heavily influenced by politics. State intervention occurs in order to create markets and to make them work, as well as in order to protect human beings and nature against negative effects of market mechanisms. Labour market policy is not an exceptional case. It always confronts this kind of potentially conflicting goals.

During the last decades, much has been written about structural changes in labour markets. For Castel (2011:9) we are witnessing another great transformation, quite comparable to the one analysed by Polanyi. Many scholars discuss these changes in terms of deregulation and privatization, highlighting the picture of a retreating state, surrendering to or intentionally leaving the field over to market forces. Bearing in mind the key findings of economic sociology, it seems more promising to investigate how and why state intervention and political regulation are qualitatively changing and to ask how labour markets are socially and politically reengineered, rather than focusing on the somewhat misleading debate about more or less state intervention. In a recent book (Scherschel/Streckeisen/Krenn 2012) we have investigated the so called active labour market policies in five European countries (United Kingdom, Germany, Poland, Austria and Switzerland). The 'activation turn' since the 1990s is a good example for changes that cannot be adequately understood in terms of more or less state intervention. When governments try to shift the focus of their policies from 'passive' to 'active' measures (e.g. cutting unemployment benefits and spending more on training of the unemployed), a qualitative transformation of state intervention is at stake.

The debate about Fordism and post-Fordism can be helpful to understand current labour market transformations. Inspired by French regulation school (Boyer 1990) various scholars investigate the changing relations between 'regimes of accumulation' and 'modes of regulation', that is, between economy and politics in contemporary Western capitalism. Fordism relied on mass production, raising living standards and corporatist regulation of the economy by business, trade unions and the state. Unions accepted the capitalist order in the shop floor and restrained from industrial action in exchange for a 'fair' distribution of productivity gains and welfare state development. Fordism appeared to be a period of full employment, that is, of low unemployment. But large population groups were more or less excluded from the labour market. In line with the male breadwinner model, with the implementation of old age and disability insurance, elderly people, persons with a handicap and married women (mothers) obtained the right to a living without immediately earning their everyday income themselves. More generally, the 'price to pay' for that attainment were different forms of discrimination and exclusion in labour markets and throughout society. At the same time, numerous persons (mostly immigrant workers) saw their economic activity constrained to low income jobs without promising future prospects. As Fordism is fading away since the 1980s or 1990s, in the context of economic globalization and liberalization of financial markets, many scholars observe a tendency towards flexibilisation of labour markets and precarisation of living conditions, making vulnerable large parts of the working population in ancient core lands of Fordism. As we will see further on, a new conception of full employment gains momentum. This time, all population groups are supposed to be active economically or to be 'activated' in order to join the workforce, with a special attention turned to those having been largely excluded at the age of Fordism.

A missing link in regulation school analysis regards theory and scholarship influencing political debate and design of particular policies. It is not enough to investigate relations between economy and politics because the intellectual world of scholars, experts, think tanks, research departments and policy entrepreneurs is of crucial importance. My contribution rests upon the assumption that the transition from Fordism to post-Fordism goes hand in hand with a growing influence of economists in public debate and political consulting. "Economists are everywhere" observes Fourcade (2009:1) at the very beginning of her book about the history of the economic science in the United States, Great Britain and France. But what counts is not only the influence of economists per se, but the ascendancy of specific views and concepts within the field of economics. Milonakis & Fine (2009) describe the transformation of classical Political Economy into Economics, a 'pure science' of rational behavior under conditions of scarce means applicable to alternative uses (following the famous 1932 definition by Lionel Robbins) having gotten rid of societal and historical variables. Foucault (2008:215-260) in his lectures about "American neoliberalism" has pioneered the investigation of how this paradigm of economic theory allows economists to claim their truth over fields of research hitherto controlled by other disciplines. Today, an economist is no longer seen only as expert on problems of economy. He can also be in great demand when it comes to family, education, politics, criminology, migration, arts or any other sphere of human activity.

The invention of human capital theory by American scholars in the 1960s (Jacob Mincer, Gary S. Becker, Theodore W. Schultz and others) strongly contributed to the ascendancy of a new economic approach, connecting the investigation of macroeconomic aggregates (production, consumption, savings, investment and so forth) to the analysis of supposedly rational individual behavior. In this theoretical perspective, *homo economicus* is less a merchant than an investor, someone investing rationally in his own human capital. If every human being is regarded as his (or her) own entrepreneur, differences of class, sex, nationality or age appear to be less relevant. They are taken account of as mere market disturbances. In politics, human capital theory therefore offers a strong 'business case' for antidiscrimination measures in the name of economics. As Foucault holds, American neoliberalism somehow inverts the relations between economy, society and politics: society is now entirely perceived in terms of market relations. Over and above, politics is permanently subjected to a kind of "economic tribunal" (Foucault 2008: 247), measuring its inputs and outputs, markets telling the truth about its achievements and failures.

This conquest of new research and expertise fields by economists, at the expense of other social sciences, is called economic imperialism (Radnitzky/Bernholz 1987; Lazear 1999). It truly represents a great transformation in the world of ideas. Consider education, for example. Philosophers perceived it since the Enlightenment period as a means to self-emancipation and full deployment of one's personality. Later on, the nation state propagated a civic conception of education, its goal being the instruction of good citizens knowing and respecting the law, participating in public debate and political elections. As for the social-democratic idea of education, it insists mostly on social integration and access to good jobs and a decent living standard. The new economic approach is quite different. Education appears as a form of investment, either by individual actors investing in themselves or by collective actors: states investing in their population, firms investing in their workforce and so forth.

4 Europe 2020: acting to avoid Europe's decline

Europe 2020 is the current overall policy framework of the European Commission for the decade 2010 to 2020. It succeeds to the so called Lisbon Strategy (2000 to 2010), which aimed at making the European Union the most competitive and dynamic knowledge-based economy in the world. There is considerable continuity from the Lisbon Strategy to Europe 2020 with some changes and new priorities. Due to the economic crisis of 2008-09 the new policy framework conveys a strong feeling of urgency calling upon member states to act fast and with determination. In its communication of March 3rd 2010 the Commission admits that the recent crisis has exposed "Europe's structural weaknesses" in a context of fierce and intensifying global competition. Three weaknesses are mentioned (European Commission 2010a:7): First, the "productivity gap" is due to

> "differences in business structure combined with lower levels of investment in R&D and innovation, insufficient use of information and communication technologies, reluctance in some parts of our societies to embrace innovation, barriers to market access and a less dynamic business environment."

Second, insufficient employment rates are disadvantaging Europe in comparison with other leading economies of the world.

> "Only 63% of women are in work compared to 76% of men. Only 46% of older workers (55-64) are employed compared to over 62% in the US and Japan. Moreover, on average Europeans work 10% fewer hours than their US or Japanese counterparts."

Third, demographic ageing is a major challenge. "The combination of a smaller working population and a higher share of retired people will place additional strains on our welfare systems." The conclusion is clear: "Europe must act to avoid decline." (European Commission 2010a:8)

Europe 2020 deploys three priorities, five measurable targets and seven inspiring flagship initiatives. The first priority, very much in continuity with the Lisbon Strategy, is "smart growth" aiming at "developing an economy based on knowledge and information". For this goal, the target is investing at least 3% of Europe's GDP in research & development. The second priority is "sustainable growth" with energy policy targets (reducing greenhouse gas emissions, more energy from renewables and higher energy efficiency). The third priority of "inclusive growth" relies on targets regarding employment (rising the overall employment rate from 69% to 75%), education (reducing early school leaving and increasing tertiary education rates) and social exclusion (20 million less people in or at the risk of poverty and social exclusion) (European Commission 2010a:5). I now focus on "inclusive growth" because this priority most applies to labour market policy. Two flagship initiatives belong to it: "An agenda for new skills and jobs" and the "European platform against poverty and social exclusion".

The "agenda for new skills and jobs" is supposed to be a "European contribution towards full employment" (European Commission 2010b:2). It adopts the 'Common Principles of Flexicurity' described in an earlier document (European Commission 2007) intending to give this concept a new momentum. Flexicurity is a neologism created through the combination of the words flexibility and security. It aims at making labour markets more flexible without destroying social security systems. The common principles of flexicurity urge member states to act on four objectives: flexible and reliable employment contracts (reducing labour market segmentation and promoting internal flexibility of firms), comprehensive lifelong learning, active labour market policies and social security systems reform (European Commission 2010b:5-6). Besides flexicurity, the agenda includes three more key priorities: first, producing a more skilled workforce and attaining the education targets (reducing early school drop-outs to 10% or less and increasing completion of tertiary or equivalent education to 40% of the population); second, improving the quality of work and working conditions and making a strong argument in favour of the conviction that "high quality of work goes hand in hand with high employment participation" (European Commission 2010b:14); third, supporting job creation through "selective reductions of non-wage labour costs" and "well-targeted employment subsidies" to companies as well as promotion of entrepreneurship and self-employment (European Commission 2010b:3).

The "European platform against poverty and social exclusion" is closely connected to the European Commission's employment policies. Poverty and social exclusion must be addressed not only for moral reasons, that is, because they are "unacceptable in 21st Century Europe" (European Commission 2010c:6) but also because they are in line with the creation of an inclusive high-employment economy: "Achieving by 2020 the 75% employment rate target for both women and men set for the Union would represent the single biggest contribution to lifting 20 million Europeans out of poverty" (ibid.:6). Increasing employment and fighting poverty are seen as mutually reinforcing goals. Therefore, the Commission promotes the "active inclusion [into employment] of people furthest from the labour market" (ibid.:6) and focuses its attention on population groups displaying relatively low employment rates or particularly high unemployment rates: young people, (older) women, migrants, people with disabilities, homeless people and especially vulnerable ethnic minorities such as Romani people. The Commission urges the member states to better target their policies in order to meet the specific needs of these groups. The platform's objectives are resumed in the 2013 social investment strategy, which is completely saturated by human capital theory. For example, "investing in children" pays off amongst other things because "the adequacy of future pensions depends on the human capital of those who today are children" (European Commission 2013a:13). In a brochure about "Investing in Social Europe" the Commissioner for Employment, Social Affairs and Inclusion holds the following statement: "We can restore and maintain prosperity in Europe if we invest in our human capital, from cradle to old age" (European Commission 2013b:3).

5 Full Employment and Antidiscrimination Policies

A large consensus exists among scholars that full employment belongs to the age of Fordism and is no longer part of today's politics. But a careful reading of European Commission papers reveals quite a strong commitment to full employment. "Article 3 of the Treaty establishes full employment and social cohesion as EU objectives. These objectives remain the core concerns of EU citizens and are at the heart of Europe 2020" (European Commission 2012: 2). Of course, current full employment policies do not rely anymore on Keynesian deficit spending and job creation by the state. In the age of post-Fordism employment policy shifts its focus from the demand side to the supply side of labour markets. Thus full employment is now targeted through measures aimed at the mobilization of all potential members of the workforce. At the same time, labour markets must function better than up to now, offering maximum opportunities to all people and excluding nobody. Fordist full employment came along with the (relative or absolute) exclusion of large population groups from labour markets: married women (especially mothers), older persons (beyond the retirement age), people with disabilities and so forth. These groups were deemed to need special protection. In addition, the state protected the national workforce from competition by migrant workers. Today we can observe a shift away from social protection to inclusion, activation and social investment.

At the age of Fordism, selective de-commodification (Esping-Andersen 1990) was seen as the best way to foster social rights of specific population groups: older persons or people with disabilities had obtained the right to a decent income without selling their working capacity anymore and mothers were supposed to meet the needs of their families through the income of their husbands in the male breadwinner model. Today, empowerment and emancipation of these groups is supposed to be achieved through re-commodification, that is, by means of a stronger integration into the labour market. In this new conception of full employment there is no more trade-off between economic and social objectives: maximum employment and competitiveness of the economy on one side, social inclusion and anti-discrimination policies on the other side, are seen as mutually reinforcing in a virtual cycle describing the best of all possible worlds. The social protection function of the welfare state is not completely abandoned but it must not be an obstacle to the flexibilisation of labour markets (flexicurity) nor to an all-encompassing workforce mobilization (social investment).

At first sight this commitment of governments and companies to inclusion and anti-discrimination is puzzling. Does it mean that the social movements fighting inequality and social injustice belonging to the Fordist regime have won the battle? That would be too optimistic a conclusion. At the same time, this new political rationale certainly is not only about manipulating progressive ideas in order to round up a merciless machine of power and subordination. Rather we can detect real transformations of capitalism responding to, and tackling the demands of social movements fighting discrimination under Fordism. In an inspiring, albeit somewhat one-sided contribution, Fraser (2009:117) writes on how neoliberalism "instrumentalize[d] our best ideas". She concedes that second-wave feminism has unintentionally contributed to neoliberal transformation of capitalism. In a way, feminist movements neither have won nor have lost their battles. Today they should "think big" (ibid.) instead of simply to go on repeating the same demands as in the age of Fordism. Likewise, Purtschert (2007) asks what feminists can do when companies use the very concepts elaborated by feminist critique of capitalism. Sauer (2007) holds that diversity politics reflects a transformation of the capitalist state responding to social problems caused by globalization. Boltanski and Chiapello (2007) analyze the means by which the very critique of capitalism contributed to the formation of a new capitalist spirit relying on concepts like innovation, project, network and autonomy. Every one of these contributions help us avoid an all too simplistic view, either overestimating the success of social movements or reducing current policy changes to a mere strategy of manipulation.

Looking at antidiscrimination policies of the European Commission, we can see that the economic approach has become very influential. Today it goes hand in hand with ethical and legal considerations. Diversity management is a key concept. In 2005 the Commission published a brochure making the 'business case for diversity', presenting results of two surveys carried out among companies in the member states of the Union. Half of the companies responding were already actively engaged in diversity management. The executive summary begins as follows:

> "An increasing number of European companies are adopting diversity and equality strategies, not only for ethical and legal reasons but also for the business benefits they are expected to deliver. Among the most important of these benefits are enhanced employee recruitment and retention from a wider pool of high quality workers, improved corporate image and reputation, greater innovation and enhanced marketing opportunities." (European Commission 2005:5)

The brochure presents a list of good practice cases in 19 firms like Adecco, Bertelsmann, Deutsche Bank, IBM, Royal Dutch Shell and others. Among the specific grounds of discrimination tackled by diversity management in responding companies, gender (42.3%) and age (39.1%) are on top, followed by nationality (32.6%), disability (31.1%), racial or ethnic origin (30.4%), religion or belief (25.3%), language (19.2%) and sexual orientation (18.7%) (ibid.:53).

Amongst these specific grounds of discrimination, gender, age and disability are tackled within the Europe 2020 framework. Gender mainstreaming is considered to be fully implemented in all EU policies since the 1997 Amsterdam treaty. In its 'Strategy for equality between women and men 2010-2015' the Commission focuses on five priority areas (equal economic independence; equal pay for equal work; equality in decision-making; dignity, integrity and an end to gender-based violence; and gender equality in external actions) as well as on horizontal issues (gender roles; legislation; governance and tools of gender equality). The economic argument for equality is strongly advocated:

> "Getting more women on to the labour market helps counterbalance the effects of a shrinking working-age population, thereby reducing the strain on public finances and social protection systems, widening the human capital base and raising competitiveness. To reach the Europe 2020 objective of a 75% employment rate for women and men, particular attention needs to be given to the labour market participation of older women, single parents, women with a disability, migrant women and women from ethnic minorities. The employment rates of these groups are still relatively low and remaining gender gaps need to be reduced in both quantitative and qualitative terms" (European Commission 2011:12).

Reading these lines, one might believe the Commission has learned its lesson on 'intersectionality' (even if social class, contrary to ethnicity, is hardly mentioned in the context of gender equality). But there is somehow a more profound element to be considered in line with the economic approach:

> "Economic independence is a prerequisite for enabling both women and men to exercise control over their lives and to make genuine choices. Earning one's own living is the main way to achieve this and there has been progress in the participation of women on the labour market during the last decade, with the female employment rate rising to 62.5%" (European Commission 2011:12).

If economics is the science of rational human behavior under conditions of scarcity and alternative uses of resources, it follows that people must be able to 'make genuine choices'. Otherwise they cannot really be thought of as economic subjects. Therefore, tackling discrimination is more than a 'nice-to-have' to economists. Basic assumptions of economic theory are at stake. Women subordinated to their husbands or suffering from gender-based violence are hardly able to 'make genuine choices' regarding labour market participation and investment in their human capital. Discrimination, for the economist, is not only a case of market distortion, but also a menace to the very existence of economic subjects in the full meaning of this term.

Tackling discrimination of persons with disabilities has more recently become a matter of concern for the European Commission. The application of the United Nations Convention on the Rights of Persons with Disabilities, entering into force on 22 January 2011, has generated a dialogue between the EU and the UN Committee on the Rights of Persons with Disabilities. In the meantime, disability has been included in the social investment package mentioned above. The "Disability Strategy 2010-2020" addresses eight areas for action: accessibility, participation, equality, employment, education and training, social protection, health and external action. As with gender equality, the "business case" is strongly advocated:

> "Full economic and social participation of people with disabilities is essential if the EU's Europe 2020 strategy is to succeed in creating smart, sustainable and inclusive growth. Building a society that includes everyone also brings market opportunities and fosters innovation. There is a strong business case for making services and products accessible to all, given the demand from a growing number of ageing consumers." (European Commission 2010d:4)

Given that one in six persons (80 million) in the European Union have a disability and that the actual employment rate of the disabled is only around 50%, this population group represents a vast potential in order to attain the objective of full employment. Therefore, active labour market policies must reach out to persons with disabilities and the EU will "fight those disability benefit cultures and traps that discourage them from entering the labour market" (ibid.:7).

Age is very present in the Europe 2020 framework. Whereas young people are given a flagship of their own ("Youth on the move"), "Active ageing" is a key component of the social investment package. Given the challenges through demographic trends, the Commission resolutely promotes labour market participation of the elderly. In order to achieve this goal, they must be in good health. At the end of the "European Year for Active Ageing and Solidarity between Generations 2012" the 'Active Ageing Index' (UNECE/ European Commission 2015) has been launched in cooperation with the UN Economic Commission for Europe (UNECE). This index comprises indicators in four domains: employment; participation in society; independent, healthy and secure living; capacity and enabling environment for active and healthy ageing. Whereas employment indicators measure employment rates of four age groups (55-59; 60-64; 65-69; 70-74), participation in society comprises indicators about voluntary activities, care to children and grandchildren, care to older adults and political participation. Thus the elderly are invited not only to be active on the labour market, but also to accomplish more unpaid work (volunteering and care). The third domain (independent, healthy and secure living) consists of eight indicators quite heterogeneous in nature, ranging from physical exercise about poverty risk and feeling safe to walk after dark up to lifelong learning. The last domain (capacity and enabling environment for active and healthy ageing) is rather miscellaneous, its six indicators embracing health dimensions as well as the use of information and communication technologies, social embeddedness and educational attainment.

Of course, the reform of pension systems is of paramount importance to 'Active ageing' too. This is a policy area where the European Commission makes use of its Open Method of Coordination (OMC) in social policy. In the following section, I will address such issues of governance und discuss to what extent they are in line with the economic approach.

6 The European Semester: a sort of economic tribunal

In policy areas where member states' sovereignty remains fully intact, the European Commission cannot impose any decision on national governments. Therefore, the power of ideas is all the more important. More exactly, we are talking about the power of evidence-based ideas. The Commission, in order to influence member states' policies, leans on a vast machine of knowledge production (analysis, reports, indicators, benchmarks and recommendations) by its own experts as well as by scholars from OECD, Eurostat, university departments, mission oriented research services and so forth. A good deal of this knowledge emanates from economic analysis. This economic knowledge production is closely related to political debate and bargaining: bodies like the Social Protection Committee created by the 2003 Nice Treaty to foster OMC are authorized to define the indicators permitting to measure political performance of every member state, single out best practice examples and formulate policy recommendations. So in order to let markets 'tell the truth' about government performance, experts must 'make them speak'. Considering the crucial importance of knowledge production, it would make sense to investigate the European Commission not only as political, but also as an 'intellectual actor', likewise Stern & Ferreira (1997) analyzed the World Bank and its vast research units.

In the Europe 2020 policy framework, an economic governance mechanism quite evocative of Foucault's 'economic tribunal' has been created: the European Semester. Given that all member states have committed to achieving the common targets and have translated them into national targets, the Commission has the right and the duty to supervise and coordinate the policy performance of every single country. The European Semester works on an annual basis. In its '2015 Annual Growth Survey' the Commission proposed to streamline the process as follows: in October, member states submit their draft budgetary plan for the following year. The Commission issues an opinion on each of them in November. In February, the Commission publishes a single economic assessment report per member state analyzing their economic situation, their reform agenda and possible imbalances on the basis of the Alert Mechanism Report, a paper supposed to identify countries with major macroeconomic imbalances for which a closer analysis (in-depth review) is deemed necessary. The spring meeting of the European Council in March takes stock of these reports and provides general policy orientations covering fiscal, macroeconomic and structural reforms. In April, member states present their plans for sound finances and policy reforms. In May, the Commission proposes country-specific recommendations, being endorsed by the Council by the end of June or in early July. In the last years, public attention has been mainly attracted to the supervision of budgetary discipline, financial markets' imbalances and the banking sector. But the European Semester governance also applies to social policy and labour markets. For instance, as a result of the 2015 procedure 19 member states got recommendations concerning the labour market and 14 regarding the pension system.

This is called 'soft law'[1]. In the domain of labour market policy the Commission has no means to sanction member states. It can influence governments through incentives, for example by setting conditions for the use of European Social Fund resources. But soft law is mainly expected to work by means of 'mutual learning' as well as 'naming and shaming'. There is controversial debate about the effectiveness of OMC. I do not address this question here but describe some examples of policy coordination and recommendation. On its website the Commission releases plenty of information to citizens about member states' performance ('Europe 2020 in your country'). For key policy areas 'European Semester Thematic Fiches' have been issued. The Commission is ready to accept that each country must find specific measures appropriate to its economic situation and policy challenges. But targets must be met. In the 2007 paper on 'Common Principles of Flexicurity', the Commission describes four different 'pathways' member states might follow (tackling contractual segmentation; developing flexicurity within the enterprise and offering transition security; tackling skills and opportunity gaps among the workforce; improving opportunities for benefit recipients and informally employed workers) and describes the goal of coordination as follows:

> "While flexicurity is not about one single labour market model or a single policy strategy, best practices from throughout the Union provide ample opportunities for Member States to learn from each other by analyzing what works best in their national situations" (European Commission 2007:10).

The thematic fiche on active labour market policies takes over the OECD definition:

---

1 See the chapter by Ahrens & van der Vleuten in this book.

> "Active labour market programmes include all social expenditure (other than education) which is aimed at the improvement of the beneficiaries' prospect of finding gainful employment or to otherwise increase their earnings' capacity. This category includes spending on public employment services and administration, labour market training, special programmes for youth when in transition from school to work, labour market programmes to provide or promote employment for unemployed or other persons (excluding youth and disabled persons) and special programmes for the disabled." (European Commission 2015a:1)

This paper focuses on long-term unemployment and participation in labour market programmes. Long-term unemployment as a percentage of total unemployment is shown to be strongly different in member states: in the last quarter in 2013, whereas Sweden, Finland, Denmark and Austria performed best (20% to 25%), big member states like the UK (36.4%), France (42%) and Germany (46.6%) displayed a less inspiring picture. Greece (70.4%) ranked almost worst, but Slovakia (72%) even worse (ibid.:11). Here is an example of what the economic tribunal says:

> "Some Member States with high unemployment spend relatively small shares of their GDP on labour market services and active measures (notably Bulgaria, Slovakia, Lithuania, Latvia, Croatia and Greece). At the same time they can have comparatively high spending on passive measures such as unemployment benefits (notably in Ireland and Spain, and Portugal to a somewhat lesser extent). For these countries it may be worthwhile to shift some spending to labour market services and activation measures in order to decrease unemployment" (ibid.:5).

Regarding unemployment benefits, the thematic fiche states that their design

> "... needs to strike a balance between sustaining household incomes and preserving work incentives. How 'generous' such systems are relates both to their level (in particular relative to previous earnings), and to their duration. The level of benefits ought to be high enough to ensure an adequate standard of living, and long enough to give the unemployed enough time to find a 'suitable' job that matches their skills. However, the gap between the income from unemployment benefit and the potential income from work must be large enough to make returning to work financially attractive. Specific features can be part of the unemployment benefit system to help ensure incentives to return to work without affecting directly the level of benefits. These features include job-search and availability requirements, compulsory participation in active labour market programmes, and sanctions such as suspension of benefits in case of non-compliance." (European Commission 2015b:1)

Thus particular attention is given to specific 'traps', that is, financial disincentives supposed to prevent the unemployed ('unemployment trap') or people not receiving unemployment benefits but potentially benefitting from social assistance and other means tested out-of-work benefits ('inactivity trap') from returning to work. Looking at the big member states, Germany shows unemployment and inactivity traps clearly above EU28 average; in Italy, unemployment trap is high but inactivity trap is very weak; France is more or less in the average whereas UK is shown to have low unemployment trap and average inactivity trap. Quite interestingly Denmark, a country often depicted to be a flexicurity champion, displays very strong unemployment and inactivity traps, whereas in Greece and Romania returning to work seems to pay most (ibid.:4).

Another thematic fiche tackles the problem of all too strict employment protection legislation (EPL).

> "Economic theory and empirical evidence show that strict EPL reduces the likelihood that jobs are destroyed in the presence of shocks and thus diminishes labour turnover. At the same time, by raising the effective cost of employment, it also dampens job creation. By increasing the firing cost borne by firms, EPL would thus tend to reduce both job terminations but also hiring rates. While this may have little or no effect on overall unemployment, it does affect the process of job creation and destruction, the duration and the age composition of unemployment, as well as efficient labour reallocations across firms and industries. It is likely to translate into longer unemployment spells or into higher labour market segmentation resulting from a high share of fixed-term offers. It has been estimated that reforms passed between 2008 and 2011 in a number of Member States to make EPL less strict have entailed an increase in labour turnover between 13% and 50% relative to the pre-crisis historical average". (European Commission 2015c:5)

Tackling the segmentation of labour markets between a core sector of workers with permanent contracts and disadvantaged groups (youth, women, migrants and others) is a key concern of the Commission. Slovakia, Hungary, Greece, Italy and Bulgaria display the lowest rates of labour turnover (2007-2014 averages); Germany and France do not perform very well either, whereas the UK ranks clearly above the EU average and the Nordic countries (Finland, Denmark, Sweden) stay on top (ibid.:5). In the labour markets of France, the Netherlands, Spain and Poland, the share of temporary contracts is high but the transitions from temporary to permanent contracts is very low, so temporary contracts appear to be "dead ends" instead of "stepping stones" to the labour market (ibid.:6-7). This fiche also contains a table indicating the overall strictness of employment protection according to OECD data (ibid.: 14). It shows that the UK and the United States have markedly lower levels of protection than almost every other EU member state. For instance, the protection of permanent workers against (individual) dismissal index is 0.49 for the U.S., 1.12 for the UK, 2.04 for the unweighted OECD average, 2.41 for Italy, 2.60 for France and 2.72 for Germany. The index for regulation on temporary forms of employment offers quite a similar picture (even if Germany's score compared to Italy and France is striking): 0.33 for the U.S., 0.54 for the UK, 1.75 for Germany, 2.08 for the OECD average, 2.71 for Italy and 3.75 for France.

Labour market participation of women is among the Commission's key objectives. With a female employment rate under 60%, Greece, Italy, Malta, Croatia, Spain, Romania, Slovakia and Poland appear to be 'problem children'. In other countries like the Netherlands, Germany, Austria, UK and Belgium, female employment rate is high but a high share of part-time employment reduces women's overall employment participation. The thematic fiche singles out two main barriers: lack of childcare facilities on the one hand and financial disincentives resulting from gender pay gaps, tax levels and benefit systems on the other. As to the first problem, Hungary, Slovakia and the Czech Republic are the member states with the strongest negative employment impact of parenthood but Finland, Germany and the UK do not perform very well either in this regard (European Commission 2015d: 3). In the Czech Republic, Slovakia, Poland and Romania less than 10% of the children younger than three years are enrolled in formal care, whereas in the UK and Ireland childcare costs are too high (more than 23% of the net family income) (ibid.:10). As to gender pay gaps, they are particularly high in Estonia, Austria, Germany, Czech Republic, Slovakia and the UK. Finally, like the thematic fiche on unemployment benefits, this one displays charts and figures about specific traps to female labour market participation resulting from tax and benefit systems.

> "Due to an increase in effective tax rates when moving from inactivity to employment (inactivity trap), or when wages increase (low wage trap and part-time trap), the participation of women in the labour market may be discouraged. The contribution to the inactivity trap from labour tax is highest in Belgium, Germany, the Netherlands, and Latvia, and, to a somewhat lesser extent, in France and Italy. The low-wage trap is highest in Belgium, Italy and Germany." (ibid.:6)

Hence the Commission's repeated plea to reduce labour tax, respectively to shift tax burdens from labour to consumption or energy.

7 Emancipation Through Employment? Concluding remarks

Reading European Commission's papers about Europe 2020, it seems obvious that the bulk of it must have been written by economists rather than, say, by members of the legal profession or social science scholars. But such a claim deserves empirical verification because economic thinking has begun to cross disciplinary borders a long time ago. Of course, not every argument made by the Commission rests upon economic theory and analysis. Rather, the economic approach goes hand in hand with legal, ethical and social considerations. Surprisingly enough, economists have become today's anti-discrimination champions. And everybody honestly concerned by discrimination problems must admit that they address real problems calling for resolute action. In any case it would be wrong to retrospectively glorify the age of Fordism. Fordist discrimination of women and migrant workers was a very serious problem which, by the way, has not at all withered away. No doubt the elderly as well as persons with disabilities gained crucial social rights under Fordism but these achievements went hand in hand with social exclusion and spatial separation.

Nevertheless, the Commission's anti-discrimination policies are ambivalent and persons belonging to one or several diversity management target groups may feel like 'out of the frying pan into the fire'. Because if Europe 2020 aims at maximizing labour market opportunities for all, it may at the same time seriously restrict the diversity of legitimate biographical choices for many people. Let us take one example: family. Fordism assigned very different rights and duties to men and women. The overall picture clearly was in men's favour. It was a legitimate claim of women's movements to challenge these social constraints forcing people to adapt to one single legitimate family model. But are we not confronted today with just another single legitimate model people are urged to conform to? In the Commission's papers obviously the best family model happens to be a situation where both parents maximize labour market participation and childcare gets largely 'outsourced' to formal care institutions or grandparents. The experts raise an alarm because

> "... more than 20% of the potential female workforce in 2012 is inactive or work part-time because of personal and family responsibilities in Malta, the Netherlands, Luxembourg, the United Kingdom, Austria, Ireland and Germany." (European Commission 2015d:10)

Still, we may ask ourselves: do we want to live in a society where people becoming parents do not at all reduce their labour market participation? Is childcare outsourcing really the one best way to achieve an equitable division of rights and duties between women and men? Fraser (1994) argues that forced female labour market participation does not eliminate gender-based inequalities. Moreover, it carries the risk of deepening inequalities amongst women. In her eyes men bringing their lives more in line with those of women, so that both can appropriately participate in care work, would be more promising. And what about children's needs and rights? With all the talk about 'family-friendly policies' (translate: 'policies permitting parents to maximize labour market participation') are politicians not completely 'missing the child'? (Ostner 2002).

The economic approach always presumes the rational actor. It wants to maximize opportunities for the economic subject. At the same moment, it asks everyone to behave as an economic subject. For most persons to form up as an economic subject means to transform themselves as a human being into workforce. If children begin this process earlier than at the age of Fordism, it's all the better. If the unemployed or persons with disabilities do not seize labour market opportunities voluntarily, the state has a right to force them and to sanction their behavior. Thus if politics and society have a duty to maximize everyone's opportunities, it implies a duty for everyone to do his or her best in order to contribute to the well-being of society (translate: to the 'competitiveness of the economy' or to 'avoid Europe's decline'). Between the lines of the European Commission papers we therefore discover traces of what Lessenich (2008) calls the reinvention of the social: in the great transformation from Fordism to post-Fordism, society's responsibility for the well-being of its members is somehow displaced by every single individual's responsibility for the well-being of society. However, this is not a matter of more or less state. Rather we observe that new forms of statehood and state intervention emerge hand in hand with a great transformation in the world of ideas. The European Commission is a case in point.

Discussion Questions

1. What is a labour market? What is labour market policy all about?
2. What are the differences between Fordist and post-Fordist conceptions of full employment?
3. Why do economists fight discrimination?
4. What are the main proposals of the European Commission to raise female employment?
5. What do you think about the ambivalence of anti-discrimination policies based on the economic approach?

References

Boltanski, Luc/Chiapello, Ève (2007): The New Spirit of Capitalism. London: Verso Books.

Boyer, Robert (1990): The Regulation School. A Critical Introduction. New York: Columbia University Press.

Castel, Robert (2011): Die Krise der Arbeit. Neue Unsicherheiten und die Zukunft des Individuums. Hamburg: Hamburger Edition, p. 9.

Esping-Andersen, Gøsta (1990): The three Worlds of Welfare Capitalism. Princeton: Princeton University Press.

European Commission (2015a): Active Labour Market Policies. European Semester Thematic Fiche.

http://ec.europa.eu/europe2020/pdf/themes/2015/active_labour_market_policies.pdf (11.9.2015), pp. 1, 5, 11.
European Commission (2015b): Unemployment Benefits. European Semester Thematic Fiche.
http://ec.europa.eu/europe2020/pdf/themes/2015/unemployment-benefits.pdf (11.9.2015), pp. 1, 4.
European Commission (2015c): Employment Protection Legislation. European Semester Thematic Fiche.
http://ec.europa.eu/europe2020/pdf/themes/2015/employment_protection_legislation.pdf (11.9.2015), pp. 5-7, 14.
European Commission (2015d): Labour Market Participation of Women. European Semester Thematic Fiche.
http://ec.europa.eu/europe2020/pdf/themes/2015/labour_market_participation_of_women.pdf (11.9.2015), pp. 3, 6, 10.
European Commission (2013a): Towards Social Investment for Growth and Cohesion – including implementing the European Social Fund 2014-2020. Brussels: 20.2.2013, COM (2013) 83 final, p. 13.
European Commission (2013b): Investing in Social Europe. Luxembourg: Publications Office of the European Union, p. 3.
European Commission (2012): Towards a job-rich Recovery. Strasbourg: 18.4.2012, COM (2012) 173 final, pp. 2, 12.
European Commission (2011): Strategy for Equality between Women and Men 2010-2015. Luxembourg: Publications Office of the European Union.
European Commission (2010a): Europe 2020. A strategy for Smart, Sustainable and Inclusive Growth. Brussels: 3.3.2010, COM (2010) 2020 final, pp. 5, 7-8.
European Commission (2010b): An Agenda for New Skills and Jobs: A European Contribution towards Full Employment. Strasbourg: 23.11.2010, COM (2010) 682 final, pp. 2-3, 5-6, 14.
European Commission (2010c): The European Platform against Poverty and Social Exclusion. A European framework for Social and Territorial Cohesion. Brussels: 16.12.2010, COM (2010) 758 final, p. 6.
European Commission (2010d): European Disability Strategy 2010-2020: A Renewed Commitment to a Barrier-Free Europe. Brussels: 15.11.2010, COM (2010) 636 final, pp. 4, 7.
European Commission (2007): Towards Common Principles of Flexicurity. More and better Jobs through Flexibility and Security. Brussels: 27.6.2007, COM (2007) 359 final, p. 10.
European Commission (2005): The Business Case for Diversity. Good Practices in the Workplace. Luxembourg: Office for Official Publications of the European Communities, pp. 5, 53.
Foucault, Michel (2008): The Birth of Biopolitics. Lectures at the Collège de France, 1978-1979. Basingstoke: Palgrave Macmillan, pp. 215-260.
Fourcade, Marion (2009): Economists and Societies. Discipline and Profession in the United States, Great Britain, and France, 1890s to 1990s. Princeton: Princeton University Press, p. 1.
Fraser, Nancy (2009): Feminism, Capitalism, and the Cunning of History. In: New Left Review, 56, pp. 97-117.

Fraser, Nancy (1994): After the Family Wage. Gender Equity and the Welfare State. In: Political Theory 22, 4, pp. 591-618.
Friedman, Milton (1975): There's no such Thing as a Free Lunch. LaSalle: Open Court Publishers.
Lazear, Edward P. (1999): Economic Imperialism. Cambridge: National Bureau of Economic Research (NBER).
Lessenich, Stephan (2008): Die Neuerfindung des Sozialen. Der Sozialstaat im flexiblen Kapitalismus. Bielefeld: transcript.
Marx, Karl (1990): Capital. A Critical Analysis of Capitalist Production (London 1887). MEGA Vol. 9. Berlin: Dietz, pp. 146-147, 619- 643.
Milonakis, Dimitris/Fine, Ben (2009): From Political Economy to Economics. Method, the Social, and the Historical in the Evolution of Economic Theory. London: Routledge.
Ostner, Ilona (2002): Am Kind vorbei. Ideen und Interessen der jüngeren Familienpolitik. In: ZSE. Zeitschrift für Soziologie der Erziehung und Sozialisation, 22, 3, pp. 249-266.
Polanyi, Karl (2001): The Great Transformation. The Political and Economic Origins of our Time. Boston: Beacon Press, pp. 71-80.
Purtschert, Patricia (2007): Diversity Management. Mehr Gewinn durch weniger Diskriminierung? In: Femina Politica. Zeitschrift für politische Wissenschaft, 1/2007, pp. 88-96.
Sauer, Birgit (2007): Diversity. Eine staats- und hegemonietheoretische Reflexion. In: Femina Politica. Zeitschrift für politische Wissenschaft, 1/2007, pp. 33-44.
Radnitzky, Gerard/Bernholz, Peter (eds.) (1987): Economic Imperialism. The Economic Approach applied outside the Field of Economics. New York: Paragon House Publishers.
Scherschel, Karin/Streckeisen, Peter/Krenn, Manfred (2012): Neue Prekarität. Die Folgen aktivierender Arbeitsmarktpolitik – europäische Länder im Vergleich. Frankfurt/M.: Campus.
Stern, Nicholas/Ferreira, Francisco (1997): The World Bank as ‹intellectual actor›. In: Kapur, Devesh/Lewis, J.P/Webb, Richard (1997): The World Bank. Its first half century (Vol. 2): Perspectives. Washington: Brooking Institution, pp. 523-609.
UNECE/European Commission (2015): Active Ageing Index 2014: Analytical Report. Report prepared by Asghar Zaidi of Centre for Research on Ageing, University of Southampton and David Stanton, under contract with UNECE (Geneva), co-funded by the European Commission's Directorate for Employment, Social Affairs and Inclusion (Brussels).

Work and Organizations

Ingrid Jungwirth

Boundaries that Matter: workforce diversity in the STEM field in Germany

1 Introduction

In this chapter research about highly qualified migrant women's participation in the field of science, technology, engineering and mathematics (STEM) in Germany is presented discussing how it can contribute to Diversity Studies.[1] Diversity studies have been developed as an interdisciplinary field accommodating different disciplines, mainly in the social sciences, as well as different theoretical approaches. Within this context, a theoretical approach will be sketched as one possible theoretical frame for research in diversity studies. More generally, a 'middle-range theory' (Merton) is seen to be more appropriate as distinguished from an all encompassing theory. Consequently, one principle of diversity studies can be formulated as determining the theoretical concept for each research project and its aims specifically. Moreover, it is argued that the sociology of social inequalities as well as gender studies provide relevant approaches for the research of social realities characterized by diversity. Following this, diversity is understood as social structures and the societal processes through which they are reproduced, going beyond an understanding of diversity in the sense of individual differences. The research of the STEM-field – being highly gender segregated, can give insight in how gender inequalities are reproduced and, moreover, how they are interrelated with other processes of the reproduction of different forms of social inequali-

---

1 This chapter is a shortened and revised version of the previously published article (Jungwirth 2017b), and has been translated into English.

ties. In this sense, diversity studies can work as a frame for the research of multidimensional inequalities, taking up the claims for an intersectional research perspective that have been made in gender studies.

Diversity studies can already refer to a certain basis that has been developed particularly on objectives of diversity management and as such are located in organization studies. For the research that is presented here, Bourdieu's approach of the social field is taken up. The concept of the social field goes beyond specific organizations, including different organizations that together make up a social field like the STEM-field in Germany. Focusing on the experiences of highly qualified migrant women in this field, additional insights in its working and conditions of exchange can be arrived at. Since these women were not part of this field in the beginning of their career, they have a more clear-sighted vision of it. The concept of the social field enables us, additionally, to include a relational perspective on the career of highly qualified migrant women instead of limiting the analysis to the individual migrant woman and the promotion within her career. Social actors belonging to the dominant groups are focused on, too, instead of only the members of a dominated group. The interrelations of their actions are analyzed and how these lead to acquiring a certain position within the field and an organization, respectively.

The analysis of highly qualified migrant women's access to the labour market in the STEM field in Germany was carried out in three part projects in which different groups of highly qualified migrant women's career paths were focused.[2] In this chapter findings on the career of highly qualified migrant women who immigrated without work permission as highly qualified migrants but via other immigration paths, such as family related migration, are presented. 36 qualitative interviews were conducted, including 30 narra-

2 In this chapter the findings of the research project „Careers of highly qualified migrant women who immigrated without work permission to Germany" are presented, a sub project in the joint research project „Highly qualified migrant women's integration into the German labour market – effects of migration on highly qualified migrant women's careers in the technical sector", funded by the German Ministry for Education and Research and the European Social Fund, funding code 01FP0903. The sample included highly qualified migrant women who were graduates in a STEM subject and who had immigrated from a post-socialist state to Germany, some of them having acquired work experience prior to immigration. The research was carried through from 2009 to 2012 at the Institute for Social Sciences, Humboldt-Universität zu Berlin, project leaders were Ingrid Jungwirth and Hildegard Maria Nickel. Additionally to the study based on qualitative data, an analysis of quantitative, representative and longitudinal data of the SOEP (*Sozioökonomisches Panel*, 1995-2008) as well as cross-sectional-data of the Mikrozensus was carried through revealing insight in highly qualified migrant women's and men's integration in the labour market in Germany (Jungwirth 2017a). The analysis of quantitative data included all nationalities and specializations, while the qualitative study was specifically about highly qualified migrant women in the STEM field, having immigrated from a post-socialist state to Germany.

tive in-depth interviews, six expert interviews and numerous informal interviews in the field. The theoretical frame for the analysis is based on the concept of the technical field as a social field (Bourdieu 1984/2010) allowing more encompassing insights into barriers they face during their career after migration. Moreover, the concept of a 'culture of engineering' (Robinson/ McIlwee 1991) in the technical field is central, based on which the existing rules and dominant ideals in the technical field are examined. The chapter will, first, give an overview on the STEM-field in Germany and, second, the theoretical approach will be sketched. The analysis of the qualitative interview data includes, third, normative constructions in the technical field in Germany which emerge particularly clear from the 'external' perspective of migrant women in the field. Fourth, mechanisms of exclusion based on constructions of gender and the status of the migrant as well as constructions of ethnicity are presented. They determine boundaries which seem to be central for the functioning of the technical field – boundaries that matter.

2 The Technical Field and Masculine Domination

Women continue to be underrepresented in engineering in Germany, although there have been some changes during the last decades. Looking at students in engineering, women's share among the new students has more than doubled from 1983 to 2013, when it made up 23%.[3] Women's share among the graduates is 23%. In disciplines like electrical engineering (13%) and mechanical engineering (19%) women's share among the new students is even lower.

In the labour market women have greater difficulties to find a job and the opportunities for promotion are less. Particularly for the highly qualified women in the STEM-field the relation between the share of women among the unemployed in 2015 (26%; BA 2016:12) and the employed (18%; BA 2016:7) is unfavourable, if compared to non-academic women workers (14% among the employed and 11% among the unemployed; BA 2016:7ff.).[4]

Moreover, almost half of the women engineers and IT-specialists were overqualified (44%) in their jobs in 2000, compared to 22% of men (Schreyer 2008:46). According to an analysis by Schreyer based on the *Mikrozensus*, the yearly representative national survey, women's share in management positions in technology industries is so low that no statement can be made about

3 Source: VDI-monitorING data bank, retrieved Frebruary 28, 2019. The data before 1993 refer to the former West German states.

4 Similarly, the ratio between highly qualified men's share among the employed (82%) and the share among the unemployed (74%) is clearly more favourable than for highly qualified women in the STEM-field.

it (ibid.). She found a marked difference between women's presence in the labour market in West- and East-Germany, where almost a fifth of the employed persons in jobs in civil engineering/architecture, mechanical engineering, electrical engineering and information technologies were women in 2004, while accounting for only 12% in West-Germany (ibid.).

If we include citizenship in this analysis, it is the increase of women engineers without German citizenship that has contributed to the raise of engineers without German citizenship in Germany in the last years (John and Koppel 2012:23).

The STEM-field in Germany seems to be less accessible for women, compared to several other countries in the European Union. For example, the *She Figures* (European Commission 2016), which are based on Eurostat *S&T* data, show the substandard representation of women in the disciplines in the STEM-field in Germany. Compared to the average proportion of women PhD-graduates in the EU-28 states, the proportion of women PhD-graduates is clearly below average in Germany in engineering, manufacturing and construction (18% compared to 28% in the EU-28 states) and below average in science, mathematics and computing (40% compared to 42% in the EU-28 states) in 2012 (European Commission 2016:27). In several post-socialist EU-states women's share is above average in both fields of study. For example, the proportion of women PhD-graduates in engineering, manufacturing and construction makes up 32% in Bulgaria, 38% in Lithuania and 43% in Romania. Similarly, for science, mathematics and computing, the proportion of women PhD-graduates is 53% in Bulgaria, 53% in Lithuania and 57% in Romania. In several South-European states women's share among the PhD-graduates is higher, if compared to the EU-average. For example, in Italy, women's share among the PhD-graduates in science, mathematics and computing (53%) and in Engineering, manufacturing and construction (35%) lies clearly above EU-average (42% and 28%) (ibid.).[5]

A specific professional set of norms and ideals in the STEM-field has been analyzed to be decisive for the mechanisms leading to a gender segregated work place. According to Robinson and McIlwee (1992:405), within a "culture of engineering" an "ideology" is created that "emphasizes the centrality of technology and of engineers as producers of technology". The acquisition of "organizational power" is an ideal in this 'culture of engineering'

5 Other Southern-European countries with a share of women PhD-graduates above average of the EU-28 states are Portugal (58% women's share in Science, mathematics and computing and 41% women's share in Engineering, manufacturing and construction) (European Commission 2016:27) and Spain (47% women's share in Science, mathematics and computing and 30% in Engineering, manufacturing and construction). In Turkey and Morokko the share of women PhD-graduates is also clearly above the average in the EU-28 states (ibid.).

which is expected to be presented in an "appropriate form" being "closely tied to the male gender role" (ibid.). Technical competence is central for this "professional ideology" (ibid.:404) which values innovation and creativity (ibid.:405). Moreover, a "craft ethic" is presented in the technical workplace, "a fascination with tools, machinery and gadgets" in the manner of being "obsessed", not just "competent on hands-on skills" (ibid.). These norms and ideals are "strongly" linked to a male gender role, "emphasizing aggressive displays of technical competence" (ibid.:406) equating "professional competence with masculinity" (ibid.).

Boundary making has been identified as highly relevant in the technical workplace. For example, it has been analyzed to be characteristic for the STEM-field to delimit the technical workplace from the external (Ihsen 2006: 105), being based on the separation of "emotionality and factual pragmatism" (ibid.:104f.; translation IJ). A further significant opposition between the technical and the social has been pointed out by Lohan and Faulkner (2004), drawing on constructivist studies of technology which emphasize the interrelatedness of technological developments and social action as 'heterogeneous engineering' (Law 1986). An essential premise of feminist science and technology studies are that technology and gender are "mutually shaping" each other (Lohan and Faulkner 2004:322). For the German context, studies showed how historical masculinity constructions of the engineer were the basis for the marginalization of women, playing a role also in the context of the GDR (German Democratic Republic), while the image of the engineer as 'man of action' (Zachman 2004; translation IJ) was created. Additionally, Paulitz analyzed how masculinity constructions and ethnocentric constructions were intertwined in the development of technology studies at the beginning of the 20th century. Images of the engineer as "spearhead of Europe's scientific technological culture" (Paulitz 2012:55; translation IJ) and the idea of "national leadership responsibility" (ibid.:59; translation IJ) were shaped.

To which extent a culture of engineering and technology are associated with masculine behavior and behavioral expectations has been shown in many studies (Cockburn 1988; Wajcman 2010; Erlemann 2002; Neusel 2005). For the German context several studies showed how these norms lead to the marginalization of women already at the university (Walter 1998; Roloff 1999; Münst 2002; Wolffram, Derboven and Winker 2009; Ulich, Schraudner and Leicht-Scholten 2017). In their research of women engineering students' workplace experiences Powell, Bagilhole, and Dainty (2009) argued that the association of tasks with masculinity lead to a 'double-bind' situation for women. To the extent that female gender was associated with deviance from the norm as well as a lack of professional skills, they had the choice between two similarly unfavourable options: achieve acceptance through distancing themselves from female gender or refrain from being fully accepted in the work place (Powell, Bagilhole, and Dainty 2009:423). Further mechanisms that were analyzed in this regard are men emphasizing gender differences, while women would rather downplay gender differences in gender segregated work places (Heintz et al. 1997:36). Consequently, the presentation of masculine behavior would be used to exclude women from access to the field. Cockburn (1988) analyzed how men managed to use the definition of tasks as 'technical' and to achieve an advantage in income through this.

In this study Bourdieu's theoretical concepts for the analysis of social inequality are taken up to analyze the experiences of highly qualified migrant women in the STEM-field in Germany. Bourdieu's concept of the 'social field' (1984/2010) can give further insights into the mechanisms working in the technical workplace. This links well with Robinson and McIlwee's approach of a 'culture of engineering' that is similarly understood as a relational approach identifying social positions in the workplace and how they relate to each other. According to Mooraj (2002:119f.), in Germany the following actors as representatives of social groups can be identified to be involved in confrontations and the struggle for dominance in the technical field: engineers with polytechnic and with university degree, entrepreneurs and engineers who ideally would supplement each other's interests and, finally, older and younger engineers. In this context women are marginalized through excluding them from informal networks as well as questioning their technical competence (ibid.). In order to understand women's struggle even for visibility in the technical field, Bourdieu's analysis of women's position in "the economy of symbolic goods" (2001:48), can shed further light on these antagonistic contestations. Bourdieu's analysis of *Masculine Domination* is essentially founded on "games of honour" between men (2001:49), excluding women as such from these games, since it requires the "principle of equality in honour" (ibid.). The case study Bourdieu used for his analysis of 'masculine domination' in general was his research on the Kabyle communities in the 1960s in which the "priniciple of equality of honour" existed only between men, and men "of honour" particularly (ibid.:49). Interestingly, it can be seen as exemplary for competition between men also in other contexts, such as the technical field, this kind of competition being constitutive for defining their position, while excluding women as such who are not seen as 'equals' in these contestations. According to Bourdieu's theory of the 'economy of the symbolic goods', women are 'objects' not 'subjects' in this. Understanding the technical field as a social field entails analyzing the struggles between social actors inhabiting social positions in it, contributing through this to the reproduction of societal power – the technical field working as a 'Machinery of dominance' as Cockburn (1988) put it.

A more differentiated concept of 'masculine domination' has been developed by Connell (1987)[6] who distinguished between 'hegemonic masculinity' as dominant norms and ideals of masculinity and other forms of masculinity that are excluded from these just as behavior associated with femininity. These practices are not hegemonial, since they are not based on societal power. Examples are practices and ideals linked to dominated or marginalized social positions such as the working class or ethnic minorities.

In the following analysis of exclusion mechanisms in the technical field Bourdieu's concept of 'distinction' is applied (1984), referring to the practices of the dominant classes distinguishing themselves from dominated classes through consumption habits as well as the use of cultural goods in everyday life showing in certain lifestyles. Bourdieu's finding is that particularly that social group which is oriented towards upward mobility, the *petite bourgeoisie*, would entail these practices, "the striving for distinction" (Bourdieu 1984/2010:58), defining its lifestyle "against the 'aesthetics' of the working classes" (ibid.). He describes their orientation also as 'pretentious' (ibid.:63), as ambitious and determined by the will to approach the dominant classes through becoming like them. This kind of relation exists particulary with regard to groups that are close and between which a relation of competition is prevailing (ibid.). When analyzing the work place, these concepts enable further insights in the struggles women – and, for the purpose of this research, migrant women – are involved in.

Based on this theoretical foundation the experiences of highly qualified migrant women in the technical field will be examined. The objective is to find out to which extent migrant women experience exclusionary mechanisms and to which these are similar or different to experiences of women without migration background. One central question is how migrant women experience the technical field in Germany, based on their additional experience of a societal context in which women were seen to be acceptable in the technical sector to a higher extent as in Germany. Starting point are the experiences of strangeness that migrant women had in the labour market, particularly in the technical field.

6 Research in this context has been done by Scholz (2012), Heilmann (2011) as well as Meuser (2003).

3 A View From Outside: normative constructions of gender in the technical field

Migrant women's perspective on the technical field in Germany can shed further light on the prevalent conventions and ideals in the technical sector, since migrant women do not experience these as self-evident. To put it in the terms of Schütz, they are 'strangers' since their "thinking as usual" (Schütz 1944:501), the "recipes" (ibid.) they acquired in a different context of socialization do not entirely fit in the society of the aim of migration. The relative distance to the prevailing conventions enables them a conscious perception thereof and the construction of legitimate images of gender become visible. At the same time, the construction of gender in the sending region of migration becomes evident as well from their distant position.

The sample for this analysis consists of highly qualified migrant women who were graduates in a STEM subject and had immigrated from a post-socialist state to Germany on other immigration paths than regulated work migration, such as family-related migration, as German ethnic migrant or Jewish migrant as well as their spouses or for humanitarian reasons. The most pervasive experience of strangeness which highly qualified migrant women in our sample articulated was the experience that *the technical field was relatively exclusionary for women* in Germany. This stands in contrast to their experiences in the technical field in their countries of origin of migration. For example, they reported how the idea was promoted at school that subjects such as mathematics or natural sciences were important for girls and boys alike.

> "Different to Germany, in the Soviet Union it was like that we were interested in mathematics, chemistry or physics, boys and girls alike. Here it is entirely different. Here it is like that: boys learn this and that and girls prefer business administration, history, this direction. But with us it was totally different and mathematics and chemistry were always my favourite subjects." (Ivanna B., l. 33)[7]

This goes along with a high level of requirements at school which was brought up frequently in the interviews and was expected of pupils in every subject. The women in our sample showed how an *orientation towards high performance requirements* had become their own attitude.

> "If I am interested in literature and full of enthusiasm, and I am good in writing, that doesn't mean that I can't have the same enthusiasm for biology [...] And this is what I experienced about school. Because, if I was good in one subject, it didn't make a difference to me, if one of these was maths." (Lara D., l. 125f.)

7 All quotations from the interview transcripts were translated by the author, the indicated lines refer to the transcript in the original.

Moreover, in the socialist states in which the women in our sample had their school education, good performance was rewarded with an easier access to higher education or participation in a summer camp. Several women in our sample regarded high performance as a means to compensate discrimination because of ethnicity or antisemitism (see also Jungwirth and Wolffram 2017). Performance was associated with a high value and was not linked to gender. The narrations of the highly qualified women reveal, apart from that, that the construction of gender in the technical field in the sending societies was not exclusionary for women.

> "In Russia it was really quite normal, quite usual, that women were trained in these technical professions because one could find a job in these professions, it didn't matter if you were a woman or a man. It was quite normal to do these jobs, to get educated in these jobs, really, it was quite normal. [...] As a profession, that is, every human can learn something if he wants to. [...] But if engineering or something else, humanities or natural sciences, they are for both." (Sofia T., l. 41ff.)

When explaining *the process of their professional choice*, the narrations of the highly qualified migrant women revealed that professions in the science and technology sector were not associated with hegemonic masculinity, i.e. through the exclusion of female gender. The reasons for their decisions about a study program, that are cited, are often pragmatic, such as Sofia T.'s. Other women who varied between professional orientations towards technology and towards a creative occupation, such as journalism, referred to pragmatic reasons like employment chances which were decisive for them.

> "[...] women are expected to have a secure occupation, such as an accountant or manager or engineer. There is no question about that, it was important [to my parents] that I have a secure place, where I can work, or a secure position that I can count on to get by." (Lara D., l. 12f.)

Apparently in the Soviet Union and other socialist states, the profession of an engineer was connected to the prospect of employment in the planned economy as the following quote shows. In parts this seemed to be the case even in the post-Soviet era of Perestroika that was characterized by encompassing changes and to which Lara D. is referring in the quote above.

> "When deciding about a profession, there were several factors, and since I was very good at maths, and at that time cybernetics was very popular, I studied at a university [...] for statistics and economics, at the faculty for financial mathematics and graduated as financial mathematician. That was at times fun, at times less fun, I always had this interest for journalism, I published during this time some pieces, also poetry that I had written, but I could see that this life of a bohemain was very difficult for a woman. And with pain and misery, but still with summa cum laude, I graduated and some time later a job was assigned to me in a computer center at a ministry." (Tatjana F., l. 7ff.)

The quotations indicate that, when deciding about a professional career, professions in science and technology were connected to security in the sense of employment opportunities that were also attractive and accesible for women. The interviews suggest that these were seen to be even particularly suited for women protecting them not only from economic insecurity, but also possible sexual assaults are alluded to, when occupations such as a journalist or writer and their 'bohemian' life are described as not well suited 'for a woman'.

The pragmatic attitude and argumentation that is brought up with regard to the process of occupational orientation is remarkable from the perspective of societies in which individualism is a strong value such as (West)Germany. The pragmatic attitude contrasts with orientations towards self-realization that are not decisive or even disregarded when the highly qualified women in our sample report about their decisions for a career in the technological field. All in all, this pragmatic attitude shows to which extent the STEM-field in the post-socialist societies is not exclusionary to women and as such not determined by hegemonic masculinity which is based on the exclusion of women, even though women make up a minority in this field in some of these countries.[8]

A further experience of 'strangeness' the women in our sample expressed was associated with the issue of compatibility of employment and family caring tasks in the technical field in Germany. Although this ideal is perpetuated in the public discourse in Germany, the empirical reality for West-Germany at the beginning of the 21st century is a cultural model based on the "marriage of a male breadwinner and a female part-time career" (Pfau-Effinger 2005:29) or a "modernized male breadwinner model" (Oechsle 2002:XI; translation by the author) including, additionally, the sole male breadwinner family as well as dual earner couples (ibid.). According to Pfau-Effinger (2005:29), this cultural model accounts for an ideal of women being integrated in the labour market, on the one hand, while being expected to interrupt their employment for child care, on the other. Going along with this model is a lower participation of women in the labour market as well as a continuous considerable lower income compared to men. In fact, this model is based on the *assumption that, particularly for women, employment is not compatible with caring tasks.*

8 Still, in several post-socialist states women's share as PhD graduates is above the average of the EU states in science, mathematics and computing (24%) as well as engineering, manufacturing and construction (28%) (European Commission 2016:27). For example, in some countries women even outnumber men making up the majority among PhD graduates in science, mathematics and computing (Bulgaria 53%, Lithuania 54% and Romania 57%), in Slovakia there is an equal share of men and women (50%). In these countries women's share among PhD graduates in engineering, manufacturing and construction lies also clearly above the EU average (Bulgaria 32%, Lithuania 38%, Romania 43%, Slovakia 35%) (ibid.).

The interviews with highly qualified migrant women reveal to which extent this is a prevailing ideal in (West-) Germany because it deviates from their 'thinking as usual' and causes conflicts for them in the process of accessing the labour market. From the perspective of the migrant women in our sample, they did experience previously that employment can be combined with caring tasks because the employer took account of mothers with caring tasks. The engineer for electrical communications, Sofia T. explains how she stopped going on business trips after the birth of her daughter, while she used to do these before for up to four weeks and longer.

> "Yes, and after having given birth I worked again and that worked out alright. I didn't do business trips, I was in town, I worked in several work places, that was normal." (Sofia T., l. 55)

In the technical field in Germany part-time work is not widely spread (Minks 2001; Solga and Pfahls 2009) which makes it difficult for persons with caring tasks to be employed. The interview partners in our study experienced this prevailing norm of full-time employment. Several interview partners reported of the expectation to work, additionally to full-time, extra hours on a regular basis. For example, one mechanical engineer described how she was confronted with the requirement to be employed full-time after maternal leave. An electrical engineer experienced that she was downgraded in the organizational hierarchy after she had reduced her working time to 75% because of caring tasks. At the same time, this ideal of full-time employment in the technical field coincides with and is supported by the cultural model of the 'male breadwinner and female part-time carer'.

This model in combination with the norm of full-time employment made it difficult for some highly qualified migrant women who pursued a different care model to get access to a job because the employer was not able to even perceive these different ideas. This was the experience of a process engineer, Maria M., who was not employed after an internship, although she received positive feedback regarding her professional expertise, because the employer assumed that, as a mother of young children, she would not be sufficiently available for the job. But Maria M. and her husband had arranged a different division of work in their family, Maria M. would be the sole breadwinner and her husband the sole caretaker, an arrangement that was outside the employer's horizon. Instead, he gave her the advice to come back, when the children were older. He acted according to an *either-or norm* that seems to apply for women against this cultural background in Germany: *either* employment (plus extra hours on a regular basis) – *or* care work in the domestic sphere in the sense of two options that are exclusionary to each other. Although Maria M. was determined to work full-time and to be the breadwinner in the family, this attitude did not fit with the employer's expectations.

A further description of this *either-or norm* for women in employment gave the biologist Lara D. who encountered this during a period seeking access to the German labour market via a training programme for highly qualified migrant women. In this programme a role play to 'solve' or deal with a 'conflict of compatibilty', that was assumed to be usual for employed women, was enacted. Lara D.'s solution, to combine employment and family requirements by reducing the expectations on both sides to a certain extent, was assessed to be 'wrong'. Apparently, it was expected of the participating women to fullfill *either* the employment requirements and disregard the family plans *or* to fulfill the family plans and assert themselves towards the employer. In this narration, too, Lara D.'s attitude would not fit with the educational institution teachers' expectations. What becomes visible through this conflict, is a norm (for women) to be engaged *either* in employment *or* in care work in the domestic sphere in a mutually exclusionary manner: an *either-or norm* for women.

To sum up, from the perspective of highly qualified migrant women in the STEM-field in Germany, who perceived it in the sense of a 'stranger' not being socialized in this context, what became visible as norms is, *first*, the gendered construction of subjects and disciplines, mathematics, natural sciences and technology being exclusionary for women. Different from that, the highly qualified migrant women in our sample expressed a conception of performance and high performance orientation to be independent of gender. Going along with this, the narration about the process of occupational orientation was guided by pragmatic reasoning, contrasting with a norm of self-realization through the choice of occupation. *Second*, prevailing norms about employment and care arrangements in Germany emerged from the narrations of the highly qualified migrant women in our sample. Their experiences in the labour market revealed an ideal of full-time employment in the technical field and how this coincides with and is supported by the cultural model of the 'male breadwinner and female part-time carer'. This goes along with an *either-or norm* which seems to exist for women particularly: it is expected of women to be, *either*, available for the work place without any restrictions, *or*, to be mainly responsible for caring tasks in the domestic sphere. This conflicted with the women's previous experiences of being employed, while taking care of children or other relatives to a certain extent, too, which was enabled by employers' measures to take account of caring responsibilities. These findings raise questions about gendered constructions of employment and care which seem to be founded in the norms of the prevailing model of the 'male breadwinner and female part-time carer'.

4 Distinctions in the Technical Field: gender and migration status

Migrant women had experiences of exclusion in all stages of their career after migration. When accessing the labour market in the technical field they were facing barriers connected to gender and their status as migrants, both becoming signs of distinction through which the migrant women's qualification was assessed as 'not quite' sufficient and 'not quite' right. Taking up Bourdieu's theory of the social field, these experiences can be analyzed as results of mechanisms in a professional field through which the established defend their dominant position and their power to define the rules. Male gender is used as a sign of distinction conveying that women were not legitimate actors in the technical field. Apart from that, the migrant women experienced that the migrant status was made significant in interactions. By this, the highly qualified migrant women were relegated to lower positions in the field, others would get no or only limited access to the field. Gender and migrant status are superimposed on each other and contribute to the further devaluation of a position in the field. This logic is according to the mechanism of intersectionality, described by Crenshaw. Belonging to a minority group – such as migrants – can deteriorate women's relatively lower social position additionally (Crenshaw 1991:1249f.). In this chapter I will illustrate how these distinctions work together and have the effect for migrant women to exclude, marginalize or assign them to a lower position in the technical field compared to men.

It should be emphasized that the positions determined through these contestations between actors in the technical field are not only professionally defined. In a study on the scientific field Bourdieu identified opposing positions in the field that are confronted with each other in defining its subject as well as valid rules, the 'orthodox' and the 'heretics' (Bourdieu 1993:72ff.; 1988). If male gender and German origin, more specifically, having graduated from a university in Germany, are used as signs of distinction in the technical field in Germany, this is only on the surface about the ‚right school' or the maintenance of certain standards of orthodoxy. Instead, the narrations of the highly qualified migrant women show how they are not admitted as fellow players in the technical field or are relegated to marginal positions in it.

The following mechanisms of devaluation of qualifications while attempting to get access to the technical field were experienced by the highly qualified migrant women in our sample. A *form of direct devaluation of qualifications* is being classified in a wrong income group, exploiting the migrant women's lack of knowledge of the German labour market and specificities of the technical field. For example, the migrant women reported of being employed as a technical tracer, while doing the job of an engineer, to a lower or higher extent, or entirely. More frequent were *indirect forms of devaluation of qualifications* through the ascription of female gender and the status of a migrant. The highly qualified migrant women's experience of 'not sufficing' meant exactly the requirement of having to produce additional qualifications compared to other actors in the field with male gender and having undergone a qualification in Germany.

For example, the engineer for electrical communications Sofia T. reported how she got one specific job in the beginning of her career after migration to Germany because she had additional expertise in a certain software.

> "Because of that, for foreigners it is important, you need to have more, you need to be better than Germans. He only is given a job, if this is the case." (Sofia T., l. 78)

With regard to gender, the textile engineer, Ivanna B. expressed that being an average engineer would not suffice:

> "You have to do it, not somehow in the middle, but really good, in my perception. And if I can't do that I feel under pressure." (Ivanna B., l. 82)

When talking about her internship, she arrived at a perception of the technical field in Germany, at the same time, to be exclusionary to women:

> "First of all, in my department there was no woman except of laboratory assistants. So, all engineers were men. And that was a large company, we have a canteen and there were also almost only men. And it was clear to me, in this job in Germany it is like that. As a woman, you need to be better than a man. [...] To have a chance. And that's my opinion. I don't know but ... Okay, that was never expressed directly or something, no, of course not. But, I don't know. I had the feeling they thought a woman can't be good in this job." (Ivanna B., l. 100ff.)

These elaborations show how, for migrants and for women, they encountered expectations to have additional expertise, to be above average performance, in order to have access to the field in the first place. At the same time, this leads to the conclusion that the highly qualified migrant women's qualifications were devaluated because they were ascribed to female gender and to the status of a migrant.

Other forms of indirect devaluation of qualifications are exclusion from professional exchange through the sexualization of migrant women and assigning them repeatedly jobs of an interpreter or an intern, only, while exploiting their additional knowledge as an engineer, without remunerating this engagement. If we take up the concept of distinction to analyze these experiences, we can understand how the production of a boundary based on distinctions of gender and the status of a migrant leads to the maintenance and reproduction of a dominant position in the technical field.

Several highly qualified migrant women in our sample were successful in their career after migration. For these women obstacles in arriving at a position that was perceived to be appropriate to their skills was an issue. In the literature, the experience of women in organizations, not to succeed in moving beyond a certain function in the hierarchy, regardless of their acknowledged skills, is analyzed as 'glass ceiling'.[9] I will analyze this kind of experience of highly qualified migrant women, additionally, by taking up Bourdieu's conception of the social field. This analytical perspective allows us to identify power relations in the organization and the social field which have an impact on women's career, instead of focusing on the individual woman, only. In this regard, *distinctions of gender and migrant status* were applied also in more advanced stages of the career after migration.

The experience of exclusion from informal networks between men was pervasive in the interviews. Characteristics that are referred to are the presentation of a ‚passion for technology', struggling with the rules in the field, exclusion of higher positions because of taking over caring responsibilities, and German language skills. Based on Bourdieu's theory of social inequality, these experiences in interactions can be analyzed as forms of distinction. Members of the social group of the established attempt, through this behavior of boundary making towards the newcomers, to maintain and reproduce a dominant position in the field.

The demonstration of a 'passion for technology' through men was described by the highly qualified migrant women as contrasting their own 'pragmatic', solely professionally determined relation to technology. For example, the electrical engineer, Paula M., describes being excluded from interactions with men at the workplace because of her different attitude towards technology.

> "Of course, when they talk about the newest technology or something, what they have seen or heard of lately or so, I cannot participate in these conversations. I mean, again, some of them do it out of passion, this brings me back to that, yes, that they create a digital network in their homes etc." (Paula M., l. 118)

In other words, in these conversations, a passion for technology is presented by men that refers to a space external to the work place. At the same time, this kind of behaviour results for Paula M. in a situation of not being part of the exchange – although the conversation is not relevant for doing her job, the ideal of an engineer being generally passionate about technology is created through which the male colleagues distinguish themselves in the sense of

9 The term of the 'glass ceiling' was challenged by Baxter and Writght (2000). Taking up this critical stance, a more encompassing concept would entail "cummulative disadvantages" for women in organizations which add up to a lower representation of women in higher positions (Marx Ferree and Purkayastha 2000:809). Disadvantages are a lower representation of women already in the middle management, lower income opportunities as well as better qualifications compared to men.

Bourdieu's sociology of social inequality. They demonstrate through this who is and who is not part of the game. Other reasons for not being part of a conversation, referred to in the interviews, were caring duties, a topic that was apparently of low interest to the male colleagues, power struggles between men that women clearly identified from the outside and, at the same time, explicitly refrained from contributing to. In one interview, female gender itself was experienced to be a reason for exclusion from a conversation:

> "Well, you realize, even if you contribute information or so, but they prefer to talk to each other, the men. You are somewhat excluded [...] So, you realize, independent of how much you do or how many skills you have, it's men's stuff. You can't take that away from them. I think that doesn't have to do too much with migrant women, or something, but with women in general." (Regina M., l. 355ff.)

It is not surprising that, based on these presuppositions, women were often not seen to be a candidate for promotion but promotion was often enough explicitly connected to male gender. This was the experience of the mechanical engineer Regina M.

> "He said: Well, you know, we had these new employees, two young guys, he says, 'that cost something and they are not bad, either.' [...] In the end, he said, and what should I have done with this colleague?' whom he had made deputy group leader, what should I have done with him?' and so. Like, if he had given me the position, what should he have done with that guy?" (Regina M., l. 99f.)

The experiences above are referring to *distinctions of gender* through which women are addressed in a manner that they do not become 'part of the game' on an informal level and, consequently, are not considered for promotion, thus, not becoming 'part of the game' in higher ranks of the company formally either.

Apart from that, particularly *German language skills on a high level were used as a sign of distinction* towards highly qualified migrant women in the work place. Labour market integration on the level of academics is linked to the requirement of excellent language proficiency in general, the ability to engage in a conversation using the required specialist terminology and, moreover, to present a high level of education. This was also the experience of the highly qualified migrant women in our sample. One finding of our research is that, moreover, independent of the achieved position in a company, highly qualified migrant women experienced practices of distinction linked to language proficiency.

At the beginning of their career after migration to Germany, highly qualified migrant women experienced barriers in getting access to a job based on perceived insufficient German language skills. For example, one engineer for oil production received positive feedback on her technical skills but was not given the job after an internship because of lacking German language skills. One mechanical engineer experienced bullying because of the way she expressed herself. But also highly qualified migrant women who were very successful in their career after migration experienced situations in which they were addressed by pointing out that they had an accent when speaking German or had made a grammatical error like the IT-specialist Nicoletta D. describes.

> "And sometimes, I have to say, the colleagues do laugh, when they hear something. The article is different than you said it ..." (Nicoletta D., l. 104)

This practice of emphasizing the specificities of language use of the highly qualified migrant women in the work place can be analyzed as a form of distinction, engaged by actors in the field who attempt to reproduce an existing dominant position through producing German language use without any accent or grammatical flaw as a sign of distinction. Of course, one may ask if language skills are not central in the work place on the level of university qualifications. But the examples show how, on the level of the intern, who had apparently sufficient language skills that her specialist skills can be understood and used in the work process, as well as on the level of the successful IT-specialist, language skills are used, in order to determine who becomes 'part of the game' and on which level they are allowed to participate. For the established migrant women language can become, additionally to female gender, a sign of distinction relegating them to a lower position in the interaction and through this possibly adding up to a lower position in the organization, in the long run.

Our research showed how distinctions of gender and of migrant status are engaged in the work place in the STEM field reinforcing each other. Taking up the concept of distinction and the concept of the social field, allows us to focus not only on the individual migrant woman and her struggle during her career but to include also a relational perspective and power relations in the organization, as well as the more encompassing STEM field, in order to understand better the barriers, they face in their career. From this analytical perspective, the practices of actors in the dominant position, emerge as contributing to their reproduction by devaluating the position of migrant women, and women in general, one can add for the STEM field. They draw boundaries that matter in a way that they are not determined by professional skills but, rather, specialized skills are superimposed by the ascription of gender and migrant status and highly qualified migrant women are excluded or marginalized on the grounds of this.

5 Conclusion

The objective of the research, of which findings are presented in this chapter, was to examine the conditions of access of highly qualified migrant women from post-socialist states to Germany who were graduates in a STEM subject. Different from the image that is produced in the public discourse on highly qualified migration, the technical field is not particularly open for the transfer of qualifications across the borders of the nation state. In order to get further insights on the mechanisms working in the technical sector, and how a diverse work force fares, theoretical approaches from gender studies and the sociology of social inequality were taken up. It is argued that a relational analytical perspective, conveyed by the sociology of social inequality can lead to a better understanding of barriers that highly qualified migrant women encounter aiming at participating in thc labour market according to their qualifications. Findings of this research include that distinctions of gender and migrant status are used by men who are in a dominant position in the STEM field in Germany. This kind of behaviour is according to mechanisms of 'hegemonic masculinity', reproducing the dominant position of those men who fulfill the prevailing norms of masculinity. For the STEM field, these norms have been described as 'culture of engineering' which have been found to be prevailing also in the STEM field in Germany. A broad scope of research in gender studies, particularly approaches from feminist science and technology studies, have revealed specificities of the STEM field in Germany. I have argued that diversity studies can offer a frame for the research of the multidimensionality or intersectionality of inequalities. In the case of research on highly qualified migrant women's participation in the STEM field in Germany, this referred to examining the interrelatedness of exclusionary mechanisms founded on distinctions of gender and the migrant status.

Further research in this regard could address the changes in the world of labour and how competitive behaviour which has been analyzed as a feature and norm in the 'culture of engineering' is impacted through an increasing requirement for flexibility and mobility in the work place which, equally, includes orientations towards competitiveness. Further insights about different forms of masculinity constructions against the background of globalization and an ensueing interrelatedness between economies and nation states, leading to a higher level of diversity in the work force, would be highly desirable. Finally, the question to which extent migrant women and men influence norms and ideals in the work place, and professional fields beyond that, are equally most interesting. A result which the research about the highly qualified migrant women's experiences in the STEM field in Germany conveys is that participation in the technical field is not necessarily connected to constructions of hegemonic masculinity which justifies the assumptions that changes are possible.

Disucssion Questions

1. Describe the relational approach determined in this study for the analysis of exclusionary mechanisms experienced by migrant women in the technical field in Germany.
2. How does this approach go beyond the concept of the 'glass ceiling'?
3. Which 'distinctions' were practiced in the work place, as they were experienced by highly qualified migrant women in the STEM field? Give some examples.

References

Baxter, Janeen/Wright, Erik Olin (2000): The glass ceiling hypothesis. A comparative study of the United States, Sweden and Australia. In: Gender & Society 14, 2, April, pp. 275-294.

Bourdieu, Pierre (1984/2010): Distinctions. A social critique of the judgement of taste. London: Routledge.

Bourdieu, Pierre (1988): Homo Academicus. Stanford: Stanford University Press.

Bourdieu, Pierre (1993): Some properties of fields. In: Bourdieu, Pierre: Sociology in question. London: Sage Publications, pp. 72-77.

Bourdieu, Pierre (2001): Masculine domination. Stanford: Stanford University Press.

Bundesagentur für Arbeit (BA) (2016): Der Arbeitsmarkt in Deutschland – MINT-Berufe. Nürnberg. https://statistik.arbeitsagentur.de/Navigation/Statistik/Arbeitsmarktberichte/Branchen-Berufe/Branchen-Berufe-Nav.html (Retrieved September 17, 2017)

Cockburn, Cynthia (1988): Machinery of dominance: Women, men and technological know-how. London: Pluto Press.

Connell, Robert (1987): Gender and Power. Society, the Person and Sexual Politics. Cambridge: Polity Press.

Crenshaw, Kimberly (1991): Mapping the margins. Intersectionality, Identity Politics and Violence against women of color. In: Stanford Law Review 43, 6, pp. 1241-99.

Erlemann, Christiane (2002): Ich trauer meinem Ingenieurdasein nicht mehr nach: warum Ingenieurinnen den Beruf wechseln – eine qualitative Studie. Bielefeld: Kleine.

European Commission (2016): She Figures 2015. Statistics and indicators on gender equality in science. Brussels.

Heilmann, Andreas (2011): Normalität auf Bewährung. Outings in der Politik und die Konstruktion homosexueller Männlichkeit. Bielefeld: transcript.

Heintz, Bettina/Nadai, Eva/Fischer, Regula/Ummel Hannes (1997): Ungleich unter Gleichen. Studien zur geschlechtsspezifischen Segregation des Arbeitsmarkts. Frankfurt/M.: Campus Verlag.

Ihsen, Susanne (2006): Technische Fachkultur und Frauenbilder – warum sich die Technik mit den Fachfrauen so schwer tut. In: Buhr, Regina (ed.): Innovationen – Technikwelten, Frauenwelten. Chancen für einen geschlechtergerechten Wandel des Innovationssystems in Deutschland, pp. 103-113.

John, Pia S./Koppel, Oliver (2012): Erwerbstätigkeit von Ingenieuren im Spiegel des Mikrozensus. Köln: Institut der deutschen Wirtschaft Köln.

Jungwirth, Ingrid (2017): Geschlecht und Migration in der Lebenslaufanalyse – Berufsverläufe hochqualifizierter Migrantinnen im technischen Feld und darüber hinaus. In: Jungwirth, Ingrid/Wolffram, Andrea (eds.): Hochqualifizierte Migrantinnen – Teilhabe an Arbeit und Gesellschaft. Opladen: Barbara Budrich Publishers, pp. 33-82.

Jungwirth, Ingrid (2017b): Boundaries that matter: Hochqualifizierte Migrantinnen im technischen Feld. In: Jungwirth, Ingrid/Wolffram, Andrea (eds.): Hochqualifizierte Migrantinnen – Teilhabe an Arbeit und Gesellschaft. Opladen: Barbara Budrich Publishers, pp. 83-115.

Jungwirth, Ingrid/Wolffram, Andrea (2017): Zuwanderungswege und Migrationsmotivationen in Wirtschaft und Wissenschaft. In: Jungwirth, Ingrid/Wolffram, Andrea (eds.): Hochqualifizierte Migrantinnen – Teilhabe an Arbeit und Gesellschaft. Opladen: Barbara Budrich Publishers, pp. 197-224.

Law, John (1986): On the Methods of Long Distance Control: vessels, navigation and the Portuguese route to India. In: Law, Lohn (ed.): Power, Action and Belief. London: Routledge and Kegan.

Lohan, Maria/Faulkner, Wendy (2004): Maculinities and Technologies. Some Introductory Remarks. In: Men & Masculinities 6, 4, April, pp. 319-329.

Marx-Ferree, Myra/Purkayastha, Bandana (2000): Equality and Cumulative Disadvantage. Response to Baxter and Wright. In: Gender & Society 14, 6, December, pp. 809-813.

Meuser, Michael (2003): Modernized Masculinities? Continuities, Challenges and Changes in Men's Lives. In: Ervø, Søren/Johansson, Thomas (eds.): Moulding Masculinities, Vol. 1. Aldershot Hants: Ashgate, pp. 127-148.

Minks, Karl-Heinz (2001): Ingenieurinnen und Naturwissenschaftlerinnen – neue Chancen zwischen Industrie und Dienstleistungsgesellschaft. Ergebnisse einer Längsschnittuntersuchung zur beruflichen Integration von Frauen aus technischen und naturwissenschaftlichen Studiengängen. Hannover: Hochschul-Informationssystem.

Mooraj, Margrit (2002): Frauen, Männer und Technik: Ingenieurinnen in einem männlich besetzten Berufsfeld. Frankfurt/M: Lang.

Münst, Agnes Senganata (2002): Wissensvermittlung und Geschlechterkonstruktionen in der Hochschullehre. Ein ethnographischer Blick auf natur- und ingenieurwissenschaftliche Studienfächer. Weinheim: Deutscher Studien Verlag.

Neusel, Aylâ (2005): Technik und Gender. Ingenieurwissenschaften als Studium und Wissenschaft von Frauen. In: Spellerberg, Annette (ed.): Die Hälfte des Hörsaals. Frauen in Hochschule, Wissenschaft und Technik. Berlin: edition sigma, pp. 75-96.

Oechsle, Mechthild (2002): Keine Zeit – (k-)ein deutsches Problem?. In: Hochschild, Arlie Russel: Keine Zeit – Wenn die Firma zum Zuhause wird und zu Hause nur Arbeit wartet. Opladen: Leske + Budrich, pp. VII-XIV.

Paulitz, Tanja (2012): ‚Hegemoniale Männlichkeiten' als narrative Distinktionspraxis im Wissenschaftsspiel. Wissenschaftssoziologische Perspektiven auf historische, technikwissenschaftliche Erzählungen. In: Österreichische Zeitschrift für Soziologie, 37, pp. 45-64.

Pfau-Effinger, Birgit (2005): Development paths of care arrangements in the framework of family values and welfare values. In: Pfau-Effinger, Birgit/Geissler, Birgit (eds.): Care and Social Integration in European Societies. Bristol: Palgrave Macmillan, pp. 21-45.

Powell, Abigail/Bagilhole, Barbara/Dainty, Andrew (2009): How Women Engineers Do and Undo Gender: Consequences for Gender Equality. In: Gender, Work and Organization 16, 4, July, pp. 411-428.

Robinson, Gregg/McIlwee, Judith (1991): Men, Women, and the Culture of Engineering. In: The Sociological Quarterly 32, 3, pp. 403-421.

Roloff, Christine (1999): Geschlechterverhältnis und Studium in Naturwissenschaft und Technik. In: Neusel, Aylâ/Wetterer, Angelika (eds.): Vielfältige Verschiedenheiten. Geschlechterverhältnisse in Studium, Hochschule und Beruf. Frankfurt/M, pp. 63-86.

Scholz, Sylka (2012): Männlichkeitssoziologie: Studien aus den sozialen Feldern Arbeit, Politik und Militär. Münster: Westfälisches Dampfboot.

Schreyer, Franziska (2008): Unter Männern: Der Arbeitsmarkt von Akademikerinnen im technischen Feld. In: Haffner, Yvonne/Krais, Beate (eds.): Arbeit als Lebensform? Beruflicher Erfolg, private Lebensführung und Chancengleichheit in akademischen Berufsfeldern. Frankfurt/M: Campus Verlag, pp. 19-46.

Schütz, Alfred (1944): The stranger. In: American Journal of Sociology 49, 6, pp. 499-507.

Solga, Heike/Pfahls, Lisa (2009): Wer mehr Ingenieurinnen will, muss bessere Karrierechancen für Frauen in Technikberufen schaffen. WZBrief Bildung 07, April.

Ulich, Annika/Schraudner, Martina/Leicht-Scholten, Carmen (2017): "*Should I stay or should I go*?" – Studierende in MINT-Fächern. In: Jungwirth, Ingrid/Wolffram, Andrea (eds.): Hochqualifizierte Migrantinnen – Teilhabe an Arbeit und Gesellschaft. Opladen: Barbara Budrich Publishers, pp. 225-246.

Wajcman, Judy (2010): Feminist theories of technology. In: Cambridge Journal of Economics 34, pp. 143-152.

Walter, Christel (1998): Technik, Studium und Geschlecht – Was verändert sich im Technik und Selbstkonzept der Geschlechter? Opladen: Leske + Budrich.

Wolffram, Andrea/Derboven, Wibke/Winker, Gabriele (2009): Konflikte und Bindungserlebnisse von Studienabbrecherinnen in den Ingenieurwissenschaften. In: Thaler, Anita/Wächter, Christine (eds.): Geschlechtergerechtigkeit in Technischen Hochschulen. Theoretische Implikationen und Erfahrungen aus Deutschland, Österreich und Schweiz. München: Profil-Verlag, pp. 139-147.

Zachmann, Karin (2004): Mobilisierung der Frauen. Technik, Geschlecht und Kalter Krieg in der DDR. Frankfurt/M.: Campus.

Sarah Vader

Female Physicians in the Medical Profession: a case study in a German hospital

1 Introduction

Although nursing and care work have traditionally always been designated as feminine work, this has not been the case in the profession of physician. Until the early 90s, the medical profession was mainly male dominated and masculine connoted. This changed during the 1990s when more women participated in medical training. In Germany, currently almost 60 percent of physicians under the age of 35 are females and almost 70 percent of medical students are women, possibly leading to a further increase of female doctors in the future (Bundesärztekammer [1]2016) Besides undergoing a so-called feminization of medicine, Germany is also experiencing a shortage of physicians (Bundesärztekammer [2]2016; „Marburger Bund fordert mehr Studienplätze in NRW" 2017), resulting in a deficiency of personnel in hospitals as well as in practices (Roland Berger Strategy Consultants 2013; „Zahl der Ärzte steigt" 2015; „Marburger Bund fordert ausreichende Personalausstattung in den Krankenhäusern" 2017). This chain of events has not only brought more women to work in the medical profession, but also launched a discussion on how the increased participation of women might have an impact on medicine as a profession. Due to a shortage of physicians, it is expected that not only more women will enter the medical profession, but will also have more room to express and instigate their ideas and wishes concerning part-time work and family-friendly work structures. As medical journals in Germany explain, ever more women set these kinds of structures as a precondition for taking on a job position, which in turn could result in changes in the profession (Meyer-Radtke 2009; Von Eiff, Groth, Hindersmann 2013; „Feminisierung der Medizin" 2014). Furthermore, Gender Mainstreaming policies directed toward equal opportunities and the reconciliation of private and professional life[1] (Commission of the European Communities 2006) have incited debates

1 The reconciliation of private and professional life is one of the areas for the EU action plan for gender equality and presented in the EU Roadmap for Equality between Women and Men for 2006-2010.

on work-life balance in the medical profession in Germany, with more and more physicians pointing out the need for gender equality measures in medical organizational development in order to deal with the shortage of physicians and secure the provision of care (Kuhlmann 2014).

Besides foreseen changes in the organization of work, the discourse on the feminization of medicine also predicts qualitative changes in the practice of medicine and the content of care. These arguments are based on the idea that a majority in female doctors will give rise to a more humane and patient-centered medical practice, because women are perceived as being essentially different from men and therefore naturally more caring and empathic, and as bringing these skills with them in the practice of medicine (Ulstad 1993; Gray, Fabre, Brown, Des Spence 2004; Riska 2001; Heru 2005; Riska 2008). As Riska points out in her analysis of the feminization discourse, these discussions do not critically reflect on how gender is constructed. Furthermore, the medical organization is portrayed as being gender-neutral, and it is women as practitioners who bring in the gender component (Riska 2001). When critically analyzing the effects of the feminization process on medicine, it is important to move away from essentialist notions on gender and look at how gender differences are produced and linked to ideas of work, the provision of care, professionalism and male and female qualities.

Within the field of Gender Studies, scholars have argued for a social constructivist view focusing on the processes of reproducing gender and gender differences. As opposed to an essentialist definition of sex as well as biological differences between the sexes, the concept of gender refers to "the many and complex ways in which social differences between the sexes acquire a meaning and become structural factors in the organization of social life" (Braidotti 2002:286).

Gender studies is a trans- or multidisciplinary field of research that engages with different academic disciplines and research areas (ibid.). This study is set out as an interdisciplinary research project between medicine and gender studies. Coming from a gender studies background, and doing research in a hospital, I was able to use insights from the field of gender studies to contribute to the ongoing medical debate on the feminization process. The aim of this study is to use theories on gender to deconstruct the essentialist idea that women will change medicine because they are naturally different from men, and rather look at how gender differences are constructed within medical organizations.

Although some sociological research on feminization points to ongoing segregation along gender lines in the work field (Riska 2001; Boulis and Jacobs 2008), no in-depth qualitative research has been done on the effects of the feminization process on medical institutions like hospitals. I therefore conducted a case study in a German hospital to investigate the effects of the feminization of medicine on the organization and practice of the profession, not by taking essentialist notions on men and women as a starting point, but by looking at how gender is constructed, what qualities are ascribed to men and women and how these are linked to understandings of work and care.

In the first section of this paper I will outline the methodology used in this study, and then elaborate the concepts of feminization, constructions of gender and gendered organizations. In the second part of the paper, the outcomes of the case study will be presented and discussed. The paper ends with concluding remarks.

2 Methodology

In order to analyze the manifestation of the feminization of medicine in medical institutions, I conducted a case study in a hospital in the Ruhr area in Germany. The hospital was established in 1995 when two already-renowned hospitals consolidated into one clinic. The hospital has 696 beds distributed over twelve specialist departments. The study took place in three of these units: the department of Internal and Integrative Medicine, the Breast Center and the department of Surgery. When investigating the influence of feminization, it is impossible to speak of medicine or the hospital as a homogenous field since the effects will differ with regard to different organizational contexts. Therefore, I chose to study three hospital departments that were likely to differ in their organizational structure and culture and as such investigate the distinct effects of the feminization process on medical institutions.

Conducting a case study allowed me to get a detailed description of situations and events related to feminization in the hospital and an in-depth understanding of the actors involved in these events. More precisely, "the case method is said to be appropriate for describing, explaining, predicting or controlling processes associated with a variety of phenomena at the individual, group or organizational level" (Woodside and Wilson as cited in Gagnon 2010:2). I completed twenty-one interviews with male and female doctors holding distinct positions, ranging from assistant to chief physician in order to cover a broad spectrum of job positions. Physicians who were still in their preliminary medical examination phase or their practical year were excluded from this sample, as was the non-medical staff working in the department. The assistant physicians interviewed for this study were still in training to become medical specialists. The specialist physicians had already finished this training and were qualified as full specialist physicians. All the senior and chief physicians that participated in the interviews had management positions in their respective departments.

In addition to qualitative interviews, I carried out research into stereotypes, which enabled me to analyze which gender stereotypes play a role in each department and how these are linked to concepts of the good physician and feminization. Over the past years, a lot of research has been done on the workings of gender stereotypes in organizations (Bem 1974; Gmür 2006; Heilman 2012). For this study I used a tool developed by Gmür (2006). In his research on gender and managers, he used a list of thirty attributes compiled from various sources and categorized them as masculine, feminine or gender-neutral. He then asked his sample to identify the traits as either more masculine or more feminine (ibid.). In this study, I used ten characteristics from Gmür's list of attributes which were significant for the medical profession, and asked my interviewees to categorize these characteristics as male, female or gender-neutral and if they considered these characteristics important for a physician and a chief physician. Research shows that stereotype judgements are made relatively automatically and much quicker than non-stereotype judgements. Using attribute lists as a tool in my research enabled me to go beyond thought-out answers and gain insight on what kind of stereotypic images prevail in each hospital department, and how these influence ideas about men and women and the feminization process.

3 The feminization of medicine

The word feminization is generally used in reference to the increase of women in areas that have previously been male dominated (Fondas 1997). With regard to the feminization of a profession, the term points to "women's disproportionate entry into customarily male professions" (ibid.: 258). The discussion on the feminization of medicine, though, shows that the terminology refers to much more than an augmentation in numbers alone. It contains predictions about the qualitative changes that come as a result of the increase of female physicians in the medical profession. In the medical discourse on the topic, it is suggested that the feminization process will harm the future of medicine because women are not efficient enough in treating their patients (McKinstry 2008), are not taking on demanding jobs such as surgery (Black in Khan 2012) and that due to women's high demand for part-time work, the good quality of care can no longer be guaranteed (Black in Khan 2012; Von Eiff, Groth, Hindersmann 2013). Brian McKinstry, in an article in the British Medical Journal, expressed his concern regarding the increase in female physicians, stating that too many female physicians are bad for medicine because women are more likely than men to work part-time (McKinstry 2008).

As such, having too many female doctors will, according to McKinstry, lead to a shortfall in the provision of care in the future. Furthermore he states that men and women bring different skills to medicine, and while women engage in more patient-centered communication, they are also less efficient than their male colleagues (ibid.).

Carol Black, during her years as president of the UK Royal College of Physicians, also stated that there are simply too many women doctors ("More doctors needed" 2004). In her opinion, the feminization of medicine will result in a decline in the status and wages of the job. She compares medicine with the profession of teaching, which she claims also lost its status once women were a majority of the workforce ("Women Docs 'Weakening' Medicine" 2004). Black's concern in part stems from the fact that more women than men aim to work part-time. But she also feels that women have a less professional standing than men. She states that women avoid demanding jobs such as cardiology and are not likely to take top jobs (ibid.; Meirion Thomas 2014). Black hereby links professionalism to masculinity, and femininity to powerlessness, weakness and decline.

There are also doctors who welcome an increase in female physicians and see it as an incentive to change work structures within the profession ("More Doctors Needed" 2004; Dacre 2008). As Dacre states in a British Medical Journal article: "This change to a more flexible way of working will be more acceptable to colleagues with domestic and other commitments and is likely to result in more women taking on leadership positions" (Dacre 2008:749).

Besides the above mentioned structural changes, it has been suggested that the increase in female physicians will influence the provision of care. In the medical discourse, it is argued that women will 'humanize' the medical profession and that a majority in female doctors will give rise to a more caring and patient-centered medicine (Heru 2005; Gray, Fabre, Brown, Des Spence 2004; Riska 2001). These arguments are based on the essentialist assumption that women are naturally more caring and empathic than men are and bring these skills with them in the practice of medicine (Riska 2008; Heru 2005; Gray, Fabre, Brown, Des Spence 2004; Riska 2001; Ulstad 1993).

The discussion on the feminization of medicine in Germany also entails some the above-elaborated arguments, including the argument that the increase in female physicians will lead to problems concerning the quality and status of medicine, because women work less hours and demand family-friendly work structures ("Die Medizin Wird Weiblich" 2008; Von Eiff, Groth, Hindersmann 2013; Freyschmidt 2017).

As the discourse on the feminization of medicine shows, it is expected that an increase in female physicians will lead to structural changes in the profession. It is also suggested that women will influence the provision of care because they are perceived to have different qualities than men. It does not reflect, however, on how gender is constructed and what role organizations play in this construction. In the next section, I will elaborate on theories of the social and cultural construction of gender and gendered organizations.

4 Gendered organizations

In her book *Gender Trouble* (2010), Judith Butler introduces the philosophy of performativity to elaborate the construction of gender. She argues that gender is performatively produced and constituted. There is no ontological gender reality except for the one that is constituted through its various acts. Furthermore, the interior essence that is fabricated is an effect of public and social discourse (ibid.). This means that gender has no fixed ontology, but is rather a product of expressions that constitute its reality.

West and Zimmerman (1987), in their paper on *Doing Gender,* also argue for gender as a social construct instead of an innate quality of individuals. They do not see gender as an internal part of an individual but rather as an achieved property of situated conduct; individuals *do* gender. Thereby, it is not only a property of individuals but also of social situations and institutions (ibid.). Through various activities and interactions with other individuals, ideologies and institutions, men and women reflect or express gender. Doing gender, consequently, is situated action; men and women act in relation to their social context (ibid.).

As the above theories elaborate, gender is not something that naturally shows itself in males and females but rather is created in relation with, and mediated by, society. Gender as a category is also constructed by and in work life through the division of labour and in the workplace. As Joan Acker explains in her work on gendered organizations, gender identities are formed and changed as men and women participate in work processes, resulting in ideas about typical masculine and feminine traits that in turn become linked to jobs (Acker 2012).

In her work on gendered organizations, Acker (1990) elaborates how organizations are an arena in which widely disseminated cultural images of gender are invented and reproduced, and how individual gender identities are partly created through processes inside and outside the workplace (ibid.: 140). It is therefore important to look at the organization as a social context in which gender identities and gender behavior are constructed and reproduced, an aspect that is often neglected in the discussion on the feminization of medicine. Women doctors do not enter a (gender)neutral profession. It is more likely that they come into organizations with clear structures and an already existing organizational culture. So when women enter the medical organization, what is expected of them? And how do they interact with organizational structures and cultures?

Acker also argues that organizations are not gender neutral phenomena, but that gender is an integral and constitutive part of it. According to Acker, gendering occurs in five interacting processes: organizational structure, organizational culture, interaction on the job, individual identity and organizational logic. These five processes construct what she calls the gendered substructure of an organization (Acker 1990; Benschop and Doorewaard 2012).

The first of this set of processes is the construction of divisions along gender lines: "divisions of labour, of allowed behavior, of locations in physical space, of power, including the institutionalized means of maintaining the divisions in the structures of labour markets, the family, the state" (Acker 1990:146). Acker refers to these as organizing processes where inequalities between men and women emerge because of how jobs are designed, wages are determined and decision-making is distributed (ibid.). Organizing processes are based on the division of labour – the separation of family and work life. Traditionally, women stay at home to provide care work whereas men work in the public sphere. Since care work in the private sphere is not rewarded like work in the public domain, this division leads to inequalities between men and women. In the ideal of the bureaucratic organization, private matters like social reproduction and care work should not interfere with core workplace processes, automatically making women less favorable for jobs than men (Lewis and Humbert 2010). The division of labour not only occurs between the private and the public sphere, it also emerges within the organization itself, with men and women having different occupations and positions. Typical women's jobs such as teaching and caring are often valued less than men's occupations like finance and business, and men often hold high rank positions whereas women remain in the lower ranks. This distribution of jobs along gender lines is referred to as horizontal and vertical segregation, with horizontal segregation referring to women's specific jobs and vertical segregation to gender differences in high and low rank positions (Wilz 2001; 2004; Durbin and Fleetwood 2010; Leinonen 2012).

The second process is what Acker calls organizational culture. It is the construction of "symbols and images that explain, express, reinforce or sometimes oppose those divisions" (Acker 1990:146). These symbols and images not only reflect but also construct beliefs about gender difference. Additionally, organizational culture defines accepted and thereby unacceptable gender behavior. It dictates and legitimizes how men and women are supposed to behave (Acker 2012). The culture of an organization is placed in the larger cultural terrain of the surrounding society. Images of men and women in society are reflected in the organization and the other way around (ibid.). Stereotypic images of women and men play an important role in the construction of gender difference. Stereotypes are a set of subjective and often overgeneralized beliefs about personal characteristics, attributes and behavior of a group of people (Gardner, Macintyre and Lalonde 1995; Ganter 1997). Stereotypic images in the organization are not only a reflection of these beliefs, but also become internalized, dictating the actions of individuals (Durbin and Fleetwood 2010). Part of medical organizational culture is the image of a *good doctor* who is supposed to have certain attributes and characteristics, and behave in a particular manner in order to fit the picture.

The third process that composes the gendered substructure of the organization is interaction between individuals in the workplace. Through both formal and informal interactions on the job, the gendered substructure is being reproduced. The fourth point that Acker mentions is the gendered components of individual identity. Gendered identities are brought into the organization by individuals, but are also formed and changed in work processes. How people perceive themselves is influenced by the other three processes mentioned above (Acker 1990:2012). As discussed earlier in this paper, gendered individual identities are not a natural and static internal essence, but constructed by and through the interaction between an individual and its environment. Organizational structure and culture and the interaction between people thus influence the construction of individual identity and therewith the actions of men and women in the workplace.

The fifth set of processes that Acker mentions is the constitutional part that gender plays in the framing of assumptions and practices that underlie organizational structures. She calls this *organizational logic*; assumptions and practices that construct most work organizations (ibid.). Organizational logic contains rules and expectations that come with jobs. You need to be at work at a specific time, for a certain amount of hours and work needs to have your undivided attention. These rules seem to be gender neutral, but they are not; "they are implicitly built on the image of a gender neutral, abstract worker who has no body and no obligations outside the workplace; this worker is unencumbered" (ibid.:218). The abstract worker needs to be work oriented and thus available full-time. This worker is presented as gender neutral, but in fact resembles characteristics traditionally associated with workers who are men (Benschop and Doorewaard 2012). As a result, masculine characteristics are necessary to become an ideal worker, "making it difficult for women's achievements to be recognized unless women work in masculine ways" (Lewis and Humbert 2010:242). Men are the norm, and as such, the concept of the neutral worker "excludes and marginalizes women who cannot, almost by definition, achieve the qualities of a real worker because to do so is to become like a man" (Acker 1990:150). In the ideal form of an organization, individuals should not have too many obligations outside the workplace. Commitment to the job is required and defined in terms of behavior that indicates the primacy of work over the demands of private life (Lewis and Humbert 2010). Men are more likely to fit this image than women, since women are in many cases still the ones who take care of the family. Employers might be reluctant to hire women for jobs in which the worker is expected to be unencumbered. Hierarchies are often gendered because "those who are committed to paid employment are 'naturally' more suited to responsibility and authority; those who must divide their commitments are in the lower ranks" (Acker 1990:149-150). Organizational logic takes material form in job descriptions, work rules and policies such as work hours, overtime, paid hours, guidelines etc. (Britton 1997). Workers comply with these rules and principles because they view them as natural (Williams 2012).

Although Acker's theory of gendered organizations is very helpful when studying the link between gender and organizations, using it as a tool for empirical research brings some difficulties with it. Not all organizations are gendered in the same fashion and neither does the gendering of one level of the organization mean that other levels are gendered as well (Britton 2000). Britton calls for strong contextualization when studying the gendered nature of organizations (ibid.). Therefore, in this study, each different hospital department is considered as an organization in itself, with distinct structures and cultures.

5 Results

5.1 The Feminization of Medicine and the Division of Labour

All three investigated departments within the hospital experienced an increase in female physicians over the previous years. Just as in the discussion on the feminization of medicine, the physicians in the hospital strongly connect this feminization process to part-time work, stating that with more women entering the workforce, the demand for part-time work will increase. But although the general opinion is that feminization will lead to more part-time jobs and many female and male doctors wish for a better work-life balance, they see this as impossible to realize within current organizational structures. In the Internal and Integrative medicine department for example, the chief physician states that a ward cannot be taken care of with a part-time job. The same goes for the Surgery department, where the physicians do not see any possibility for part-time work. As Dr. Toman, a specialist physician explains:

> "Well, work is the top priority, right? Like, automatically, because most of the time you are just here. So, even if you were to try, then well, today you have an appointment, today you have to do this and that. But sometimes it just does not work, because I cannot just leave, because then you think, somehow they are also people, right, that are in your care, they are not some machines you can turn off, or office work, where you can say 'come on, leave it, go!'"[2]
> (Dr. Toman, female Specialist Physician, Surgery Department)

According to Dr. Toman, sometimes private appointments cannot be met because work needs to be finished first. She clearly distinguishes medical care work from other jobs where you can leave the work to be done the next day. It is the doctors' responsibility to provide good care for patients. Work is placed above private matters; personal necessities cannot obstruct the provision of care. Although this is partly due to organizational structures, there is another element that sustains this culture of long work hours: the image of a good doctor. In order to be perceived as good doctors, the physicians have to be unencumbered and available full-time. An exemplary case of the influence of this image on the physician's work life is that of Dr. Gras, a female specialist physician working in the department of Internal and Integrative Medicine, who experienced difficulties with her part-time employment. Although there is some room for private matters such as attending yoga classes or leaving work earlier due to family responsibilities, part-time jobs are difficult to sustain and not without consequences for the physicians' position and status. Dr. Gras started her work in the department with a part-time job. But after experiencing discrimination, information deprivation and extra work hours, she decided to work full-time again. Although Dr. Gras increased her work hours to 100 percent again because working reduced hours appeared incompatible with the department's structure, there is also a more personal side to the matter. As the next excerpt shows, now that she is working full-time again, she has the feeling of 'being somebody'.

> "Well, I have the feeling, that due to working 100% again, I am somebody. Well, before I had that... As soon as you reduce, you are 'part-time mummy', even if it is 80%, so minimally less than the others, then you are... Straightaway you are somehow, 'Yeah, yeah, she just can't do everything' or something like that. It is a little bit discriminatory. And you are indeed aware of less. It is like when you are on holiday for two weeks, then information is missing. And that is bad, it has an effect."
> (Dr. Gras, female Specialist Physician, Department of Internal and Integrative Medicine)

---

2 The author translated all quotes from the interviews from German into English

This statement illustrates how Dr. Gras has incorporated the image of a good doctor as unencumbered, and feels useful now that she lives up to this standard. She continues to explain how for her personally it would be better to work part-time, but for the job and for the patients it is better to be available full-time:

> "I also have the feeling that I take better care of my patients when I am there. But that, I think, depends on your personality. Well. Well, I think, for me personally it would be better not to work so much. But I think that for the patients it is good" (laughs).

The case of Dr. Gras is an interesting example of the difficulty many female physicians face when trying to reconcile their ideas on motherhood and part-time work with their image of what it takes to be a good doctor. Dr. Gras feels forced to fully inhabit an occupation and believes it is also better for her now that she is a full member of the team again, instead of the part-time mum who is not taken seriously by her colleagues. In order to be a 'real' doctor, you need to be available full-time. The image of a good doctor has many similarities with Acker's abstract worker. This image is internalized by many physicians and regarded as the norm. As Dr. Persch states, being a doctor is not simply an occupation:

> "Well, like the amount of time, that this somehow… Being a doctor is not just a job, but a calling".
> (Dr. Persch, female Senior Physician, Breast Center)

Not only are work life and private life clearly segregated, as in the division of labour, but work also dictates private life, not the other way around. With almost all doctors doing extra hours, one can hardly speak of a work-life balance. But instead of trying to alter this, the physicians seem to accept it as an inevitable part of their profession. Over time this has become a taken-for-granted aspect of being a doctor. Acker (1990) refers to this phenomenon as organizational logic; the implicit rule that you do not go home when your shift ends, but that you stay until work is finished and the patients are taken care of. Herewith, the image of a good doctor resembles Acker's unencumbered neutral worker that has no life outside the workplace. Dr. Vogel, a male senior physician in the Breast Center, underlines this picture when he says: "[…] you are after all a doctor, you cannot make allowances for private stuff or anything else." Being a physician is a calling and thus your work needs your undivided attention. Every other aspect of your life has to come second. Not serving this standard means not sufficing the image of a good doctor.

As the above statements show, the increase in female physicians has not straightforwardly led to an increase in part-time work. Although the feminization of medicine has engendered a discussion on family-friendly work structures, and most of the physicians wish for a better work-life balance, actual changes have hardly been achieved yet. Most of the doctors simply do

Not see a possibility for change and as such adapt to pre-existing norms and structures. "I think you have to decide, because the… I don't know how you would change the structures," Dr. Ott, a female senior physician from the Surgery department, says. This statement is exemplary for the general attitude of the physicians when it comes to organizational transformation as a result of the feminization process. The doctors talk about how the feminization of medicine will change medical institutions and lead to more family-friendly work structures, but they do not see themselves as actors who engender these changes. As such, their statements remain part of the larger discourse on the feminization of medicine, but do not become concrete.

5.2 The Division of Allowed Behaviour and the Practice of Medicine

As elaborated in the discussion on the feminization of medicine, it is assumed that the increase in female physicians will not only change the organization of medicine but will also alter the content and provision of care. How are gender differences produced in medical departments and how are these distinctions linked to ideas on work, professionalism and care? I started exploring these questions by asking the physicians about their ideas on gender differences in practice style. Their responses differed according to the type of work they were referring to. In the department of Internal and Integrative Medicine, the physicians referred to their specialization as a feminine type of medicine, thereby finding it difficult to establish the effects of the feminization on their medical performances. In the Breast Center and the Surgery department, both the male and female physicians often talked about women as the better communicators and caretakers.

> "Well, I would say, this typical caring aspect, this I look after, this caring, that you accompany patients, this might be more likely to suggest a feminization".
> (Dr. Peper, male Senior Physician, Surgery Department)

With regard to surgical operations or therapeutic decisions, however, gender differences are not recognised.

> "[…] whether women or men, the tasks in many areas must simply remain the same, like, like practical tasks also like operating or something. And that is not allowed to be influenced by whether it is a woman or a man. I don't believe that".
> (Dr. Adler, female Assistant Physician, Surgery Department)

Dr. Adler states that gender is not allowed to influence surgical operations. By arguing that regardless of being a man or a woman, the tasks remain the same, she does not deny the existence of possible gender differences, but these clearly should not interfere with surgical practices.

When it comes to gender differences, the physicians in both the Breast Center and the department of Surgery differentiate between medical procedures and general caretaking. Whereas in the former possible gender differences are neutralized, they are explicated in the latter. Women are therefore expected to show distinct behavior with regard to ward work and patient care, but when it comes to surgical operations or other medical procedures, gender differences are neutralized. When asking Dr. Vogel about his ideas on the effects of feminization on the practice of care, and if the feminization process has influenced the practice of care, he answered that guidelines decide the content and quality of care, not gender.

> "In the practice? (considers) Yes, I mean, concerning any therapy decisions etc. that cannot have an influence, that would be completely crazy. Because the therapies und such things… that would be fatal, if that were to change through feminization, that would just be crazy. That is not allowed to be. Facts must decide how the patient is treated".
> (Dr. Vogel, male Senior Physician, Breast Center)

Dr. Vogel argues that gender can and should never influence medical therapies. Doctors have to be completely objective and their decisions and actions should be structured by pre-given facts and guidelines, not by personal choices. In this case, gender is seen as a personal matter that should not interfere with professional medical practices. This sketches an image of the ideal doctor as an abstract phenomenon that, like Acker's abstract worker, follows bureaucratic rules, medical guidelines and objective standards.

Stereotype research in each department has revealed that characteristics like caring, communication skills and compassion are designated as typically feminine and that traits such as analytical competence, assertiveness and goal-oriented behavior are thought of as being more masculine. With regard to the expression of these traits and characteristics, a distinction in the ascription of gender typical behavior is made between ward work and surgical operations. Women are expected to show gender typical behavior in ward work because it is generally expected of them to be caring, understanding and communicative. But when it comes to medical practices, these perceived gender differences are neutralized and gender specific behavior is no longer accepted. Gender differences are thus only allowed and even welcomed in ward work and patient care because it matches the general stereotypes about men and women. Hereby, general stereotypes are reproduced in the department, and expected gender behavior is regulated by prescriptive stereotypes and normative ideas on masculinity, femininity, care and medicine.

6 Discussion

Organizations are not gender neutral phenomena but build upon gender divisions that are based on the separation of work and family life. Personal matters and care work are to be handled in the private sphere and should not interfere with core workplace processes. This division of labour is also visible in hospital departments where a clear separation of work and private life is existent. Physicians have long work hours and only go home when the job is finished and the patients are taken care of. Overtime is a normalized component of the job, leaving little room for a good work-life balance. Work is placed above private life and personal necessities have to be pushed aside during worktime. This division of labour is sustained by an image of the good doctor who, like Acker's abstract worker, is unencumbered and available full-time. This image is internalized by many male and female physicians and set as the normative standard. The division of labour also emerges within the organization itself, with men and women having different occupations and positions. Although all the participants in this study are physicians, a segregation of work fields and tasks along gender lines is clearly visible. Typical care work is still connoted as feminine, whereas medical operations and analytical tasks are neutralized or masculine-connoted. This strongly influences the second gendered division; that of allowed behavior. Women are allowed and expected to show gender distinct behavior in typical feminine areas such as care work and patient communication. But when it comes to other medical practices, gender distinct behavior is not accepted. In her theory on organizations, Acker discusses how ideas and images reflect and construct beliefs about gender differences. Images of men and women in different hospital departments clearly reflect general gender stereotypes about care work and the more technical and analytical skills. Through informal prescriptions of accepted and unaccepted gendered behavior in the departments, these stereotypes are reproduced.

What does this mean for the manifestation and the influence of feminization? Although all the departments investigated experienced an increase in female physicians, this has not automatically caused qualitative changes to take place. The physicians in each department talk about how the feminization process will engender more family-friendly work structures and better patient care, but actual changes have mostly remained absent. Transformation in the organization of the profession is only allowed as long as it does not interfere with a department's long work-hours and core work processes. Gender differences in the practice of medicine are expected in those areas that are traditionally connoted as feminine, such as communication and care work. What has changed is that with more women entering medicine, they are no longer a rarity in the profession. Even in masculine connoted specializations such as surgery, in which only 19.71 percent of physicians are female (Bundesärztekammer 2016), women have become a more common sight. The feminization process has also instigated a discussion about the high work load and family-(un)friendly work structures in medicine. Still, part-time jobs are often not accepted and if so, it is mostly women who want to and are expected to reduce their work hours. Feminization has thus not automatically led to transformations in the profession, and divisions along gender lines are reproduced – in the organization as well as in the practice of medicine.

7 Conclusion

Over the past several years, Germany has experienced a significant increase in female physicians. Discussions about this so-called feminization of medicine suggest that the gender demographic shift will cause changes in both the organization and the practice of medicine. These arguments are based on essentialist notions of men and women. How gender is constructed in organizations is not reflected upon in current discussions. This case study in a German hospital investigates how gender is constructed within the organization and how the feminization process is linked to certain ideas and practices concerning work and the provision of care. Although both male and female physicians wish for more family-friendly work structures and a better work-life balance, these changes are difficult to accomplish within the departments' current structures. Overtime, long-work hours and a strong separation of work and private life make it difficult for physicians to reduce their hours or take on part-time work. This work ethos is underlined by the internalized image of a good doctor as unencumbered and available full-time for patients. With regard to the practice of medicine, physicians link feminization to practices such as communication, ward work and patient-caretaking, areas where female physicians are expected to show gender specific behavior. But when it comes to surgery or decisions on patient treatment, gender differences are clearly distinguished from professionalism and gender specific traits are not allowed. As this case study shows, the increase of female physicians has not straightforwardly led to qualitative changes in the organization of medical work and the provision of care. Rather, when analyzing the effects of feminization, it is important to consider how gender is constructed in medical organizations and what is expected of men and women with regard to work, medical practices and caregiving. This determines how and where the feminization process affects the profession of medicine.

Discussion Questions

1. Which characteristics of feminization are proposed in the medical discourse on the feminization of medicine?
2. Name the five interacting processes that, according to Acker, constitute the gendered substructure of an organization.
3. Explain how thc division of labour is connected to gender segregation in the organization of work and in the medical profession itself.
4. What role do stereotypes play in the manifestation of the feminization process in hospital departments?

References

Acker, Joan (1990): Hierarchies, Jobs, Bodies: A Theory of Gendered Organizations. In: Gender and Society, 4, 2, pp. 139-158.

Acker, Joan (2012) Gendered Organizations and Intersectionality: problems and possibilities. In: Equality, Diversity and Inclusion: An International Journal, 3, 3, pp. 214-224.

Bem, Sandra (1974): The Measurement of Psychological Androgyny. In: Journal of Consulting and Clinical Psychology 42, 2, pp. 155-162.

Benschop, Yvonne and Hans Doorewaard (2012): Gender Subtext Revisited. In: Equality, Diversity and Inclusion: an International Journal 31, 3, pp. 225-235.

Boulis, Ann and Jerry Jacobs (2008): The Changing Face of Medicine. Ithaca: Cornell University Press.

Braidotti, Rosi (2002): The Uses and Abuses of the Sex/Gender Distinction in European Feminist Practices. In: Griffin, Gabriele and Rosi Braidotti (Eds.): Thinking Differently; A reader in European Women's Studies. London, New York: Zed Books Ltd, pp. 285-237.

Britton, Dana (1997): Organizational Logic; Policy and Practice in Men's and Women's Prisons. In: Gender and Society11, 6, pp. 796-818.

Britton, Dana (2000): The Epistemology of the Gendered Organization. In: Gender and Society14, 3, pp. 418-434.

Butler, Judith (2010 [1990]): Gender Trouble. London, New York: Routledge.

Bundesärztekammer [1] (2016): Ärztestatistik 2016. Retrieved Dezember 21, 2017 (http://www.bundesaerztekammer.de/fileadmin/user_upload/downloads/pdf-Ordner/Statistik2016/Stat16AbbTab.pdf).

Bundesärztekammer [2](2016). Ärztestatistik 2016: Die Schere zwischen Behandlungsbedarf und Behandlungskapazitäten öffnet sich. Retrieved Dezember 21, 2017 (http://www.bundesaerztekammer.de/ueber-uns/aerztestatistik/aerztestatistik-2016/).

Commission of the European Communities (2006): A Roadmap for equality between women and men 2006-2010. COM (2006) 92 final.

Dacre, Jane (2008): Are There Too Many Female Medical Graduates? In: BMJ 336, pp. 748-749 (Head to Head discussion with Brian McKinstry).

Die Medizin Wird Weiblich. (2008): In: Deutsches Ärzteblatt 105, 12, pp. 609-612.

Durbin, Susan and Steve Fleetwood (2010): Gender Inequality in Employment: Editors' Introduction. In: Equality, Diversity and Inclusion: An International Journal 29, 3, pp. 221-238.

Eiff, von Wilfried, Alexandra Groth and Yvonne Hindersmann (2013): Feminisierung der Medizin: Die große Herausforderung. In: Healthand Care Management 4, 5, pp. 36-39.

Feminisierung der Medizin: Kliniken befürchten Kostenschub. (2014): In: Ärzteblatt. Retrieved September 26, 2017 (http://www.aerzteblatt.de/nachrichten/57365/Feminisierung-der-Medizin-Kliniken-befuerchten-Kostenschub).

Fondas, Nanette (1997): Feminization Unveiled: Management Qualities in Contemporary Writings. In: The Academy of Management Review 22, 1, pp. 257-282.

Freyschmidt, Jürgen (2017): Wir brauchen eine Männerquote für Ärzte! In: Frankfurter Allgemeine Zeitung. Retrieved 21 December, 2017. (http://www.faz.net/aktuell/beruf-chance/campus/zuviel-feminismus-brauchen-aerzte-eine-maennerquote-14906675.html)

Gagnon, Yves-Chantal (2010). The Case Study as Research Method: A practical handbook. Canada: Presses de l'Université de Québec.

Ganter, Stephan (1997): Stereotype und Vorurteile: Konzeptualisierung, Operationalisierungund Messung. Mannheimer Zentrum für Europäische Sozialforschung (MZES), Mannheim.

Gardner, Robert, Peter Macintyre and Richard Lalonde (1995): The Effects of Multiple Social Categories on Stereotyping. In: Canadian Journal of Behavioural Science 27, 4, pp. 466-483.

Gmür, Markus (2006): The Gendered Stereotype of the 'Good Manager': Sex Role Expectations towards Male and Female Managers. In: Management Revue 17, 2, 104-121.

Gray, Selena, Clarissa Fabre, Kingsley Browne and Des Spence (2014): Women in Medicine. In: The BMJ 329, 7468, pp. 742-743.

Heilman, Madeline (2012): Gender Stereotypes and Workplace Bias. In: Research in Organizational Behavior 32, pp. 113-135.

Heru, Alison (2005): Pink-collar Medicine: Women and the Future of Medicine. In: Gender Issues 22, 1, pp. 20-34.

Khan, Maham (2012): Medicine – A Woman's World? In: BMJ Careers. Retrieved September 26, 2017 (http://careers.bmj.com/careers/advice/view-article.html?id=20006082#).

Kuhlmann, Ellen (2014). Arbeits- und Karrierebedingungen im Krankenhaus: Warum Fachkräftesicherung ohne geschlechtergerechte Organisationsentwicklung nicht zu haben ist. In: Hessisches Ärzteblatt 12/2014, pp. 698-699.

Leinonen, Minna (2012): Challenging and Reinforcing Gender Boundaries at Work. In: Equality, Diversity and Inclusion: An International Journal 31, 7, pp. 633-645.

Lewis, Suzan and Laure Humbert (2010): Discourse or Reality? „Work-life Balance", Flexible Working Policies and the Gendered Organization. In: Equality, Diversity and Inclusion: An International Journal 29, 3, 239-254.

Marburger Bund fordert mehr Studienplätze in NRW. (2017): In: Ärzteblatt. Retrieved December 21, 2017 (https://www.aerzteblatt.de/dossiers/aerztemangel?nid=76671).

Marburger Bund fordert ausreichende Personalausstattung in den Krankenhäusern. (2017): In: Ärzteblatt. Retrieved December 21, 2017 (https://www.aerzteblatt.de/dossiers/aerztemangel?nid=83260)

McKinstry, Brian (2008): Are There Too Many Female Graduates? In: The BMJ 336, pp. 748-749 (Head to Head Discussion with Jane Dacre).

Meirion Thomas, Joseph (2014): Why having so many women doctors is hurting the NHS: A provocative but powerful argument from a leading surgeon. In: Daily Mail UK. Retrieved December 21, 2017 (http://www.dailymail.co.uk/debate/article-2532461/Why-having-women-doctors-hurting-NHS-A-provovcative-powerful-argument-leading-surgeon.html#ixzz34KRK9laN).

Meyer-Radtke, Marion (2009): Aus Herr Doktor Wird Frau Doktor. In: Zeit Online. Retrieved September 9, 2017 (http://www.zeit.de/karriere/beruf/2009-12/feminisierung-medizin).

More Doctors Needed, Without Discrimination. (2004): In: The Lancet 364, 9434, pp. 555-556

Riska, Elianne (2001): Towards Gender Balance: But will women physicians have an impact on medicine? In: Social Science and Medicine 52, 2, pp. 179-187.

Riska, Elianne (2008): The Feminization Thesis: Discourses on Gender and Medicine. In: NORA – Nordic Journal of Feminist and Gender Research 16, 1, pp. 3-18.

Roland Berger Strategy Consultants (2013): Fachkräftemangel im Gesundheitswesen: Medizinische Berufe verlieren in Deutschland an Attraktivität. Retrieved September 9, 2017 (http://www.rolandberger.de/pressemitteilungen/Medizinische_Berufe_verlieren_an_Attraktivitaet.html).

Ulstad, Valerie (1993) How Women are Changing Medicine. In: Journal of the American Medical Women's Association 48, 3, pp. 75-78.

West, Candace and Don Zimmerman (1987): Doing Gender. In: Gender and Society 1, 2, pp. 125-151.

Williams, Christine, Chandra Muller and Kristine Kilanski (2012): Gendered Organizations in the New Economy. In: Gender and Society 26, 4, pp. 549-573.

Wilz, Sylvia (2001): Rethinking Gender, Work and Organization – Thinking About Organization. Paper presented to the Gender, Work and Organization Conference 2001, Keele University, Staffordshire, England, 27-29th June 2001.

Women Docs 'Weakening' Medicine. (2004): In: BBC News. Retrieved September 26, 2017 (http://news.bbc.co.uk/2/hi/health/3527184.stm).

Woodside, Arch and Elizabeth Wilson (2003): Case Study Research Method for Theory Building. In: Journal of Business & Industrial Marketing 18, 6/7, pp. 493-508.

Zahl der Ärzte steigt, doch Ärztemangel bleibt bestehen. (2015): In: Ärzteblatt. Retrieved September 9, 2017 (http://www.aerzteblatt.de/nachrichten/62466/Zahl-der-Aerzte-steigt-doch-Aerztemangel-bleibt-bestehen).

Victoria Showunmi

Leadership and Cultural Identity

1 Introduction

Leadership in Context: identity and culture

> *"Leaders come in many forms, with many styles and diverse qualities. There are quiet leaders and leaders one can hear in the next country. Some find strength in eloquence, some in judgement, some in courage."* (Gardner 1961:5)

Leadership theory has traditionally neutralised 'difference', including gender and racial/ethnic dimensions (Parker 2004). The defining group has been white middle-class men (Nkomo, 1992). Osler (2006) points out that textbooks aimed at aspiring school leaders published in the 1980s and 1990s in Britain rarely made references to equity even though minority ethnic communities were well-established. This was mirrored in academic journals and educational management courses. As researchers began to study women in management, the focus was still on white middle–class women. Existing leadership literature (Eagly and Johnson, 1990; Appelbaum, Audet and Miller 2003; Sinclair 2004; Coleman 2011) focuses on white men and women, is presented as race-neutral, and is assumed to be generalizable to all people. In general, masculine and feminine models of leadership based on Western (White middle- and upper-class) gendered identities exclude the experiences of other groups and render them non-legitimate or unimportant in the production of knowledge.

In the 21st Century, a diverse workforce has become a reality. Organisations would benefit by re-envisioning leadership from the multicultural perspectives of the workforce. With diversity come fresh perspectives on traditional organisational communication issues (Allen 1995). This research brings attention to one under-represented leadership perspective, that of Black Minority Ethnic (BME) women leaders.

Today, Western management research appears more committed to addressing issues of diversity. However, while some progress has been made, there remains work to be done to achieve gender equality at the top of organisations (Doldor et al., 2012). While women academics have written extensively on women's position within the gender division of labour, ethnic minority women are rarely included.

We are unaware of research that advances our understanding of BME women's experiences in leadership positions. Reviews such as Alvesson and Billing (1997) and Powell (2012) do not directly challenge assumptions of ethno-racial homogeneity in women. Devine (1989) suggests that many of the common stereotypes of Black people are transferred into leadership perceptions held of this group. For instance, whereas White leaders would be described as "working well under pressure" (Rudman and Glick 2001:751), "Black leaders are perceived as more incompetent than white leaders". Cook. S.G' (2013) recent study supports the claim that Black women are finding it hard in being taken serious in leadership roles. The study confirms that Black women reported feeling different and unappreciated. They were tired of defending themselves against being labeled angry, loud, aggressive, rude and obnoxious. One of the interviewees from the research study stated the following: "they think we are condescending, mean, unprofessional and harsh. Sometimes I feel that a majority of Black women feel that they are unable to be their real selves at work because they will be judged." Discrimination and dissimilatory stereotyping is something that many women faced on a daily basis. They experienced having to explain and justify their existence added to the feeling of being isolated othered in their role as a leader.

This Chapter will present findings of an ongoing research project about leadership and constructions of identity, focusing on Bangladeshi, Pakistani and African-Caribbean women in leadership positions in England. The women leaders came from a range of organisations spanning across public, corporate and voluntary sector. It will begin with an introduction to the literature, moving onto the research design and then takes up a discussion on the initial findings, highlighting core themes emerging from the data. An examination of existing literature shows that the question to what extent the construction of race is determining the concept of leadership or how constructions of Whiteness determine the concept of leadership needs further exploration.

2 Black Minority Ethnic Women in Leadership: the research design

The presented research has been developed within the context of the Institute of Education, University of London, and was commissioned by the campaign 'Race for Opportunity' to carry out research into Black Minority Ethnic (BME) Women. The study is building on the results from the research 'Race to Progress: Breaking down Barriers' (2011) published by 'Race for Opportunity' which is the race equality campaign at Business in the Community

(BiC), the Prince's Responsible Business Network.[1] 'Race for Opportunity' stands for diverse leadership on boards and at senior level, diverse representation and progression in the workplace, and the reduction of ethnic minority youth unemployment. This research study focused on leadership and identity among BME women with a particular emphasis on Bangladeshi and Pakistani women living and working in the UK. As part of the research project, a group of White women leaders were interviewed to include their views so as to ascertain and better understand whether the construction of race has an impact on one's individual leadership style. If we are to make some sense of the notion and concept of race perhaps making use of Omi and Winant (1994:198) definition "race as a concept which signifies and symbolizes social conflicts and interests by referring to different types of human bodies". Exploring race in the context of this study could suggest it is simultaneously an interpretation, representation, and/or an explanation of racial dynamics which adds to the challenge in the reorganizing of one's thinking along particular racial lines. This study presents 'race' as a particular discursive practice, in a way in which social structures and everyday experiences are racially organized, based on their meaning.

The research was not a comparative study, the focus was on BME women and an invited number of white women as part of the discussion which assisted with the research design. BME women are seen as an 'invisible' group within organisations, often not represented in any significant way on employer management programmes or bespoke development and leadership initiatives. The research is not the first to explore BME women (Parker 1996; Grimes 2005; Chin et al. 2008) experiences of leadership, however, it is the first piece of research seeking to add insights into leadership and the way in which cultural identity influences perceptions and experiences within the UK context. The women participating in the study were asked a range of questions which included questions on exploring the notion of leadership, how they define themselves as leaders, and what their experiences as a leader are, coming from a BME background. Questions surrounding identity and leadership, such as their leadership style being challenged by colleagues who may not have experienced being led by a BME leader, assisted with the development of the research study. Another question referred to their perceived impact of identity on their leadership style, this question generated a lot of discussion. The research design built on the methodological concept of 'Grounded Theory' which will be sketched in the following subchapter.

1 The purpose of BiC is to encourage the members to work together to tackle a wide range of issues that are essential to creating a fairer society and a more sustainable future.

Methodology

The research design applied Grounded Theory to develop the methodological and conceptual framework for the study. The research design emerged through a series of conversations, discussions and thoughts which took place with range of different people and organizations. The author's autobiographical account of her leadership experiences became the basis and reasoning for the research. The research materialized through the lens of the author who wanted to find answers to her recent leadership experience. The research design interchanges with the blurring of definition for autobiography and autoethnography. Ellis and Bochner (2000:742) define autoethnography as "autobiographies that self-consciously explore the interplay of the introspective, personally engaged self with cultural descriptions mediated through language, history, and ethnographic explanation". Similar to ethnography, autoethnography pursues the ultimate goal of cultural understanding underlying autobiographical experiences. The following steps were taken in designing the methodology for the research.

Step one – The autobiographical account

Step two – Discussion on lived leadership experience with other BME leaders

Step three – Recognition that the real lived experience connects with both personal and professional and the implications this may have with others perception in what leadership and a leader is.

Step four – Reflect on own autobiographical account

Step five – Review literature on identity and leadership and develop the key question: To what extent does the self-ascription and ascription by others to cultural identity and gender identity have an impact on how the women managers perceive themselves as leaders and their leadership style? To which extent is the construction of race and ethnicity as well as the construction of gender interrelated with the women managers' perception of leadership?

Step six – Present initial idea to an organization that develops leadership in Higher Education.

Step seven – Present a more fully developed idea to the director of 'Race for Opportunity' and initiate further and deepening research.

The semi-structured interview guide comprised a set of 12 open questions which examined constructions of leadership, barriers to leadership, exploration of personal identity, perceived impact of identity on leadership style, and perceived differences between minority and majority ethnic women as leaders.

Semi-structured focus group interview guides were used to examine notions of identity and leadership. The guides comprised a set of open questions based on the areas of theoretical interest. Specifically, participants were asked questions around three key areas: (1) their personal definitions of leadership, (2) the relationship between their social (i.e. gender/ethnic) and leader identities, and (3) their career journey to leadership, including when they first saw themselves as leaders, and factors that may have hindered this journey.

The prevailing aim of this type of study is to provide rich contextualised knowledge of the sample (Maracek 2003). In keeping with the study's exploratory nature and its constructivist-interpretivist approach, questions were used to initiate discussions and followed up with extensive probing. This elicited diverse responses rather than a systematic, reproducible list. Ethics were considered by adhering to the British Educational Research Association guidance. Pseudonyms were employed as a means to provide anonymity to the participants. All participants were given the option of opting out of the study during and after their interview.

The women were approached through the 'Race for Opportunity' (RfO) Champion Network, who funded the research. The Race for Opportunity campaign is led by 'Business in the Community' (BITC), a UK corporate-led charity focusing on responsible business. Invitations for participants in a study on 'Identity and Leadership' were distributed via email to network members. Women who indicated interest were informed about voluntary participation and assured about response anonymity. Additionally, 30 participants were recruited through snowball sampling, having heard about the study through friends or colleagues.

An RfO Administrator allocated respondents to focus group sessions across the country. Three sessions were conducted in London and six sessions conducted across North and Central England in Nottingham, Birmingham, Manchester, Bradford and Sheffield. Only minority ethnic women participated in focus group sessions. There were 28 women in the three London groups (4, 14 and 10 respectively); and 100 women in the North and Central England groups (8, 14, 18, 18, 16 and 26 respectively).

There were some differences in demographic composition across the regions. In London most participants (80%) were in senior management roles in public and private sector employment, comprising Asian and Black women between 28 and 60 years old. Outside London, leadership experiences were gleaned from wider contexts including the local community and independent businesses. Additionally, participants were mostly between 30 and 40 years old, of which 80% were Asian women. These demographics reflect the ethnic distribution in the UK, with larger populations of Asians living outside London, compared to other ethnicities. For the purposes of this paper, no further comparative analysis across regions was conducted.

Each focus group session lasted one and a half to two hours, during which refreshments were served. Considering the limited time and the size of some of the sessions, the author 'was sensitive to the risk of group dynamics restricting some participants' contributions. To mitigate against this, responses were collected on 'sticky notes' and incorporated into the data analysis, in addition to verbal data. Additionally, the author employed group facilitation skills and open, probing questionings to ensure all participants were engaged and fully participated in the discussion. Finally, all respondents were encouraged to contact the author if they felt they had more to share after the session.

Sixty follow-on interviews were conducted with minority ethnic female focus group participants for additional in-depth exploration and validation of initial findings. Interviews were also conducted with twenty White women. The white women were approached via the Business in the Community Women's Network. As with the BME women it was explained to them that a research study was being conducted on identity and leadership. Interviews were conducted face-to-face in private offices or via telephone. The semi-structured interview guide comprised of a set of 12 open questions which examined constructions of leadership, barriers to leadership, exploration of personal identity, perceived impact of identity on leadership style, and perceived differences between minority and majority ethnic women as leaders. The interviews lasted about 30 minutes.

3 Black Minority Ethnic Women in Leadership Positions: first findings

Focus group and individual interview responses were recorded and fully transcribed. Data were then analysed thematically, as the researchers sought to make explicit the structures and meanings the participants embodied in their responses (Gavin 2004). Although it might be expected that minority ethnic women would report particular challenges enacting leadership behaviours, in accordance with the constructivist and exploratory approach, no hypotheses were proposed. Rather, the aim was to ground findings in the data (Glaser and Strauss 1967). The question guiding the enquiry was 'How do ethnicity, gender (and other identities) influence majority and minority ethnic women's leadership?'

Coding and analysis were conducted in an iterative, constant comparative process between focus group and interview responses. The author began with open coding (breaking down and categorising). Here, salient and meaningful descriptions regarding the intersection of leadership and other social identities were coded directly from the data. This was followed by the author engaging in axial and selective coding for the purpose of this paper. Here, relationships between codes were considered and categorised into higher order themes. During analysis, the author adopted 'intersectional sensibilities' (Crenshaw 1991; Bowleg 2008). This meant paying attention to when and how gender, ethnic and any other identities became salient in respondents' experiences of leadership.

In the following sections, discussion on some of the emerging themes taken from interviews are presented. The themes discussed for this paper are: the women's own definition of leadership, challenges in asserting the role as a leader from a minority background, the impact of one's personal identity and leadership and cultural stereotyping in leadership.

3.1 Leadership Definition

The social identity group to which a leader belongs is considered a significant factor in a leader's potential leadership practice as well as the extent to which a leader may feel able to enact that identity (Knippenberg et al. 2004). As Lumby et al. (2014:2) states, 'Leaders in education construct identities in relation to their own predilections and to the expectations of others of what it is to be women/men and to be leaders. Fuller (2010) suggests that a leader's multiple identities are shaped by what it means to belong to a group. Belonging to a group may suggest the acceptance of values and ideologies – culture – that distinguish one group of people from another (Hofstede, 1991). As Dimmock and Walker (2002:71) claim, 'there are fundamental qualitative differences between societal and organisational culture[s]', where 'school leaders influence, and in turn are influenced by, the organisational culture'.

> "I think the way women define leadership is totally different from a man. We still have this way of thinking that is defined by a man and actually a women's way of leading is so different to the way that a man does." (Senior Asian Woman Leader)

The above quote is taken from an Asian woman leader who suggests that leadership is defined differently for women and men. Exploring the quote further it could be argued that the participant is essentializing femininity, as her perception of the world is rather narrow. The participant's perception of leadership will be shaped by her individual knowledge and experience of leadership development. Recognizing that women leaders are not a homogeneous group is integral to this research. Acknowledging the intersectional connections raises crucial questions: What makes the participant think that all women and men are the same? What sources are being used to support such claims?

According to Bhopa and Danaher (2013:21), 'Issues of identity have been examined in relation to intersectionalities of difference, such as 'race', class and gender', while examining identity requires an understanding of the notion of culture and ethnicity. Additionally, they argue that '[e]thnicity [...] is a mechanism for boundary formation and boundary maintenance. It is clear who belongs and who *does not'* (Bhopa and Danaher 2013:23-24). This leads to an emerging exploration of intersectionalities of difference. The term 'intersectionality' is often attributed to Kimberlé Crenshaw (1991), who drew attention to the invisibility of Black women's experiences in research that privileged White women's voices in gender studies and Black men's voices in race studies.

When the women were asked to provide a workable definition for leadership the answers that they gave were not clear-cut. Instead, there was a mixture of culturally related answers that would not fit the discussions regularly raised on leadership. Some of the women used familiar words such as "supervise, inspirational, provide aspirations for others" to describe leadership.

Many of the women viewed being in their leadership positions as a way to give back to the community in which they were connected. Many successful leaders feel the need engage in the process of giving something 'back to the community' in return for the help you previously got from the community.

Many of the women spoke about leading diverse groups of women and how that impacted on what they saw as leadership. Interestingly, some of the BME women were at odds with defining themselves as leaders and referred to the Western concept of leadership to assist with denying that they were already leaders. When the BME women were asked if they were in leadership positions, hesitation surrounded some of their answers, as reflected in the following quotes:

> "I am not sure of the specific characteristics, but I am responsible for managing some staff, I am responsible for delivering a program and moving them on – I am a Government officer – so I am responsible for moving part of the policy area forward and to bring about change." (Senior Asian Woman Manager)

> "It was not leadership in the sense that I wasn't managing people, I wasn't the figurehead if you like, but my role was to facilitate change. So in that sense I would say, yes it is a much more subtle kind of leadership. It is taking people with you when you don't have direct responsibility for them." (Senior Asian Woman Manager)

Others had a clearer understanding of what they considered leadership to be.

> "I think 'leadership' you have to lead people and management is managing systems and that's the way I have simplified it for myself. Trying to manage people is a total different concept than trying to lead people. Leadership is hard to define but you know when you have got it right." (Senior Asian Woman Leader)

> "You have to make people respect you and it is a lot involved, its time, you have to have that time to make people respect you, and your own black people as well." (Senior African Caribbean /African Woman Leader)

An occurring point that emerged from the findings is the need to receive respect and be valued. Many of the BME women spoke about this constant battle within and outside of the team to be respected as the leader in charge. They find that the need to affirm to everybody why they have the right to be in the leadership position and the right to be considered the expert in the field. Challenges such as these obstructed and interfered with their daily life as a leader.

There were other women who viewed leadership as the opportunities that you are given through both the external and internal factors of socialization – in other words the 'nature/nurture' debate of whether you are born as a natural leader or can be developed as a leader.

> "I think it is the opportunities that you get in life and I think leadership to me is helping, it is not someone physically giving you a helping hand, but not having too many obstacles that are insurmountable really, to help you get on and I think that leadership is having the passion to make things better." (African Caribbean Woman Leader)

The above quotes from the BME women implies that racial identity is playing a role in the way they are defined as leaders. Being seen and not heard contributes to the isolation that many of these women discussed during the interviews and focus groups.

In contrast, among the White women leaders, there was no mention of racial or ethnic identity playing any role in the notion of leadership. The White women leaders who were interviewed spoke about the need for vision, good teams making decisions and being able to inspire others.

> "The person who sets direction that sets the strategy, which makes sure the people are pulling together and actually also sets the way of working." (Senior White Woman Leader)

> "As a kind of series of inter-linked behaviors, ...being clear about vision and goal setting, aims and objectives, ...I think that leadership is an ongoing dialogue, visibility I think is key." (Senior White Woman Leader)

> "...a personal characteristic and being unafraid to take decisions, unafraid to take unpopular decisions and to inspire individuals so as to take them with you." (Senior White Woman Leader)

There was, however an agreement amongst the women that leadership was defined by the culture of the organization – which in most cases was the Western model of leadership, White, male and lacking in cultural recognition.

3.2 *Challenges in Asserting the Role as a Leader from a Minority Background*

When being asked to elaborate on barriers in their career to becoming a leader, many of the BME women roared with laughter and asked in return where to start with these experiences. All of the women interviewed, or who attended the focus groups, referred to challenges as a minority leader. Some of the women felt that their leadership style was being questioned in the eyes of others who hold stereotypical and prejudiced views on how they perceived women from a BME background should lead. Some of the women expressed concern that high level leadership positions were indirectly not being made available if leaders had childcare responsibility. It was perceived that BME women would not have the childcare arrangements in place, as their perception was that minority women were heading up single parent households.

> "Just because you are from a BME background and you have got children the perception is that you will not work as hard as somebody else and you won't have any commitment." (Public Sector, Senior African Caribbean Woman Leader)

The BME women also commented on having to face doubts on their ability to lead.

> "First of all, I think there is ..., sometimes there is an assumption about their [BME women leaders'; added by the author] capacity to lead and whether people would actually follow them." (Public Sector, Senior Asian Woman Leader)

> "I think that there is an issue around, and sometimes people who don't think that ethnic minority women can lead because they may appear to have less confidence or assertiveness because of coming across quieter, they may not speak up, perhaps not expressing their views as forcefully as maybe their white counterparts." (Private Sector, Senior Asian Woman Leader)

> "I think that I would have to say the challenges come daily, minutely in so many contexts." (Senior African Caribbean Woman Leader)

Some Asian women who attended one of the focus groups believed that they were being discriminated against by White and Asian people in their organizations. This meant that they were being pulled by their own cultural beliefs along with attempting to fit the company culture. The use of culture in this context relates to culture fit which is a concept that can be hard to define. Battling, with such challenges potentially has a direct impact on the leaders and their well-being.

Concerning barriers to leadership, the following quotes made by two Senior White women (with approximately 25 years difference in age) outline the difficulties that they have as White female leaders grappling with leadership because of their working class background. To ensure that organisations do not fall into the trap of attracting people that are similar to what they are used to, organisations need to define and articulate the organisation's culture – its values, goals, and practices.

> "I have never found an absolute barrier but my class and my lack of contacts and the fact that my parents didn't have contacts meant that when I did eventually get a job it was at the lowest level in the organization. Nobody has plotted my career. My parents thought it would be really good if I became a (Personal Assistant) to a businessman." (Public Sector White woman Senior Manager)

> "I think those barriers probably came more from within myself than when I look around and think about coming up against individuals or processes and procedures that perhaps are blockers to me. And I think that comes with coming from a very working class background, being the first in my family ever to go to university, the first in my family – you know you are breaking so many sorts of barriers by being the first I guess; so for me personally where I come from and I think there comes a point where you realize that your own insecurities and your own identity issues are just the things that hold you back more, you know sometimes feeling like an imposter. I just think 'how have I got let into this' and you sometimes step out of yourself and look down at what is happening and think, someone is going to tap me on the shoulder in a minute and ask me to leave." (Private Sector Senior White Woman Leader)

When White women were asked to which extent they had experienced to be responded to differently as a leader than, let's say, a BME woman, most of the White women felt it was rather a difficult question and until now something that they had not thought about before. However, they thought that it was an important question that needed to be asked. The following quotes reflect this.

> "It depends on the circumstances but a quick answer would be yes, I think probably yes and that is to do with difference – certainly in my leadership world there are more White men and then more White women and then as you say BME so in degrees is a man going to be ... I don't know this; I mean I have never actually talked about it but is a man going to be just more uncomfortable because we are both women or not?"

> "[…] is he less comfortable because he is more drawn to me as a White woman than a BME woman ... this is hard as it is so subtle, you don't get overt bad behaviour nowadays, so it is difficult to know. I am applying the theory of the boys' club." (Private Sector, Senior Woman Leader)

The following quote from another White woman leader suggests that difference has been a notable factor throughout her school and working life.

> "I am sure that they do. I am sure that they do." (Voluntary Sector, Senior White Woman Leader)

> "I mean it depends on, who the people are. I think you know, in my experience even from school and my friends, hanging out with Indian friends, the way that people react to them and to me were different, and they would have a different assumptions and

> possibly different level of assumptions in terms of who I was and who they were, just by looking at them. It can be quite pervasive can't it ... the assumptions that we make every day and how they play out. I think particularly in the workplace, the kind of micro inequities of the sort of drip, drip, drip. I think can, I imagine, have a very detrimental effect. So yes I am sure there is a difference in terms of the way that I am treated." (Voluntary Sector, Senior White Woman Leader)

Another woman leader gave rather a hesitant response which acknowledges barriers, and how it is the responsibility of the individual to find a way through any potential challenges and barriers that stand in their way of progression.

> "Well I'm sure there will be barriers and I'm sure it can take longer, I'm absolutely sure about that, because that is the way society is and I can't equate obviously being a White woman, I can't equate with those barriers myself, but where I have found barriers I think if you just stick at it and you prove yourself, I do think people tend to accept you once you have proven yourself." (White Woman Senior Manager)

In general, the BME women that were still embarking on the journey in becoming Senior Leaders received little or no help from their line managers. In contrast to this, a majority from the study's sample of White women were able to state that their continued growth was because of either having a supervisor /champion and or a mentor /coach. Much of this support came from the organization believing that the person had real potential. Similar to White males within the organizations, the White women had the opportunity to belong to networks that would enhance their careers. The BME women's lack of access to the 'closed networks' led to frustration, and to have no hope in the organization's promotion system.

The following quote highlights this;

> "I am frustrated because I feel that I have got the vision and I can see where I need to be but because I have been suppressed in my organization I am unable to progress at the moment, so you know, I have got this vision and I know that it is a journey I am on, it is just to get there." (African Woman Manager)

Discrimination and inter-cultural discrimination from other minorities' perceived stereotypes was something that many of the public sector and some BME women leaders dealt with on a daily occurrence. A great many of the BME women spoke about being emotionally tired and drained from always having to over-achieve in the workplace. Many of the Asian women mentioned grappling with balancing work and family life' along with the perceptions from within their community being a further constraint to deal with. When some of the Asian women mentioned perceptions from their own community they were implying as Asian women there was the need to conform to inherent stereotypes of what is considered to be the norm for an Asian professional – which did not include leading and or challenging the status-quo.

3.3 Impact of Own Identity

Much of the research study intended to find out whether there was a difference in the way leaders may be accepted as leaders when they held leadership positions. When asked to elaborate on the question in how far their own identity had an impact on their leadership style, many read the idea of their identity as having a social responsibility for others coming up through the system. Many of the women believed that their own identity had impacted on the way they lead teams within their organizations. What emerges from the data is the way each of the women leaders are grappling with their own conscious of and standpoint regarding their individual identity. Is this a similar struggle that women leaders have when faced with teams that are used to white male leadership styles? The following quotes highlight the complexity of exploring identity in the context of leadership.

> "Yes, I'm sure it does and I'm sure that everyone's identity impacts on their leadership style and that there has been a huge move over the last years for everyone to be authentic leaders and I think that sort of almost puts forward the idea that your family is then coming to the in a way, because you are being authentic it is your own identity." (Public Sector, Senior Asian Woman Leader)

The above quote is about the theme of authenticity that is linked to family and your own personal identity.

> "I came here when I was two, so I grew up here and so cultural identity is probably a bit mixed actually. But the reason it impacts on how you are as an individual is because you are more sensitive to those issues. Whereas a lot of people don't have to deal with those sorts of issues, so in terms of how it impacts your leadership you are particularly sensitive to issues around race, around sex, around minority groups, so I think that does make a difference to the organization." (Private Sector, BME Senior Woman Leader)

Others grappled with the whole idea of identity and what it meant in their context.

> "As a Pakistani woman – then yes. I would say that my leadership skill is based more towards my ethnicity of my parents, which is the hard work ethic. In my view minorities' work harder than many white British people." (Private Sector, Senior Asian Woman Leader)

Another woman stated

> "Well I guess it would, yes I think it is inevitable. Part of my identity is also my experience of life, it makes me who I am, not just my color, not just my gender, and so I would put that on an equal par as being women, being Black and my experiences." (Public Sector, African Caribbean Woman Leader)

Interestingly enough, the women from BME backgrounds were able to identify with the question, whereas the White women leaders interviewed for the study were not as conscious of the impact identity had on their leadership style. Therefore, these women found the question on identity difficult to answer. White women in leadership do however belong to the majority in respect of their whiteness yet do not belong to the majority of leaders in respect of their gender.

Understanding one's own identity contributes to knowing who you are and where you belong. The women from BME backgrounds were used to being asked: "Where are you from?" meaning not geographically but where are their biological parents from. Other BME women would be told that you speak extremely nicely – "how did you learn English so well?" In contrast to this all of the White women that were interviewed for the study except for the ones that had an accent or a surname that was 'ethnically' sounding had never experienced such detailed questioning. Therefore, the White women identified more with personality traits than with cultural identity. The following quotes reflect this:

> "I guess I'm a very outgoing person, loud. People know when I am around, so I mean that would be me if we were to go into looking at it from a diversity point of view, yes I am female, probably seen as middle class, ...White but to me that does not mean anything at all, but I guess that is how people would see me if they were looking at a person who they did not know." (Private Sector Senior White Woman Leader)

What was particularly interesting about this person is that, after she gave the above comment, she was asked about identity and leadership again. And the following comment was made;

> "I would say that my personality impacted on my leadership, but I am not convinced that my background necessarily has an impact." (Private Sector Senior White Woman Leader)

Another quote from a BME woman suggests that the environment shapes the identity that you have at work.

> "You are brought up in that environment where you are used to switching in lots of different environments and so it is never a problem. Sometimes I go to places and people will say, 'do you realize you are the only Black person here?' And I think well I did not really notice because overtime, it has taken time, I have built up a strong sense of identity and who I am and how other people perceive me. I say always retain who you are." (Private Sector Asian Woman Leader)

The above quotation implies that her social environment has played a role in being able to switch and operate within different contexts. Her sense of identity is entwined in intentional switching to the extent she is does not notice that she is the only Black person in the room. It raises the question of assimilation and whether through a conscious or unconscious understanding of not wanting to be noticed. Many of the BME women saw the need to leave their culture behind to move forward in the organization. Furthermore, recognizing the need to 'bleach' your identity is the only option that some women believed was available. Some of the Asian women reported that the clothes they wore for religious reasons sometimes blocked the way in which they were seen and assumptions are made. They felt that the higher up you get, the more culture you lose and change to the organizational identity. Therefore, the only way to progress is adopt the organisational culture. Some leaders struggle with mixing with other BME people if they have not had exposure to them outside work.

3.4 Workplace and Organisational Culture

The women were asked to which extent they would recommend their workplace /employer to women with ethnic minority background. Many of the women that worked for the public sector would recommend their organization to other BME women for security and flexibility. However, some of the BME women did not view the organisation as a place for progression for BME staff. Interestingly enough, others held the view that they would recommend their organization, as 'change' needs to happen – and this only happens from the outside, when new employees enter the organization. Many of the women held the view that the recruitment of new and diverse employees by organizations would ensure that change actually takes place.

> "I would recommend the job for the benefits, but if they want career progression then no." (Public Sector, Senior Asian Woman Leader)

The following quotes highlight the need firstly for the organization to be transparent about its culture when selecting potential staff for various roles. Secondly, the focus is placed on the actual person doing their homework and being aware of the type of organization they are wanting to join or progress in.

> "In some instances you are only given an opportunity because you fit into the culture of the organization and the team likes you ... and see you are the 'same' as them." (Senior Asian Woman Leader)

> "You need to understand the environment you are placed in and to grasp the concept of self-awareness ... overcoming hurdles can be achieved with the right support." (Senior African Caribbean Woman leader)

Concerning the general organizational culture, one BME women said:

> "...promoting White male colleagues and softening their fall or managing their mistakes, which is completely different scenario for BME, colleagues gathering round to mitigate and also providing mentoring/coaching to promote White males, forms part of the organizational culture." (Private Sector, Senior Asian Woman Leader)

The realization that the company is not equal in the treatment of White males and BME women is distressing for this participant. Watching the White male colleagues gaining access to mentoring /coaching as part of the normality of the organization creates disbelief and then well it's expected.

Many of the women believed that the climate was very much about who spoke the loudest, who knew the right people, and which determines who has the most influence. They felt that, to survive, you needed to be an effective net-worker. In addition to this, some of the women saw that breaking through the 'silent wall of knowledge' was seen as a real challenge for women and particularly for BME women, who felt they were often not made aware of the 'unwritten rules' of an organisation.

3.5 Cultural Stereotyping in Leadership

As previously mentioned, there are two competing models of leadership that have been fully advanced: masculine instrumentality versus feminine collaboration – based almost exclusively on studies of White women and men but presented as racially and culturally neutral (Parker & Ogilvie, 1996). In general, masculine and feminine models of leadership based on Western (White-middle and upper-class) gendered identities excludes the experiences of other groups and renders them non-legitimate or unimportant in the production of knowledge. Many of the women that took part in the study commented on the way in which they were perceived as leaders across the many organizations that they represented. When some of the senior women were appointed to their current position the challenge was breaking down the preconceived stereotype that their team members held onto. Instead of thinking that the team should have been developed in understanding diversity, the issues that arose focused on the BME leader and not the team. Therefore, the BME leader was not seen as competent for the position. The following quotes highlight some of the BME women's experiences.

> "I mean I think being an Asian woman, plus I wear a headscarf, I think some people do find it difficult to relate to that. It is their problem not mine, but they do make you feel uncomfortable and I think once you know what you are talking about, and you have to try hard to gain that respect, but once you have got it, then people will come to you and say, 'well she knows what she's doing'. But it is breaking through that barrier and the challenges." (Public Sector, Senior Asian Woman Leader)

> "I think you are prepared, as a Black person, if you are managing White people to come across a couple of issues. I think what made it really interesting was the fact that Black people weren't receptive to me leading them as well. That came as a bit of a surprise." (Public Sector, Senior African Caribbean Woman Leader)

The following quote shows the complex results of the selection of BME leaders. The speaker points out the way in which stereotypes are projected onto BME leaders. The perception of what a leader is and how that is then played out in an organization, contributes to the positive or negative experiences of female leaders.

> "When you are in leadership roles they still want to stereotype you. Usually your own communities or whatever, they want to stereotype you, you must be like this because you are Muslim, or you must be like this if you are African Caribbean woman, or you must be like this whatever ... it is internalized racism which people project onto you."

This Senior Asian Woman Leader continues her thoughts on the way she believes BME leaders are stigmatized.

> "People try to box you in and if you are a white leader, I would imagine, I don't know I'm not one, or if you are a male leader, you don't have to be defined by this very strict box you can be whoever you want to be. You are allowed to be diverse and yet ironically we are the people who are supposed to be the diverse leadership." (Senior Asian Woman Leader)

This section has highlighted the hidden complexities leaders have to embark whilst leading each of their individual teams. Something which came up time and time again was respect and the need to be valued. This was not explored in-depth as the author will discuss this in another paper. The section engages with the participants in the difficult conversation focuses on the need for a diverse workforce whilst attempting to understand what this means within the differing context where the women are leaders.

4 Conclusion and Recommendations

This paper provides an empirical examination into the leadership activity of women who are leaders in public, private and voluntary sector organizations. Overall, disappointment relating to achievement came across throughout the BME interviews. Many of the women expected to be much further on in their career; being held back due to discrimination featured in many of the interviews. The research has identified the common features which are found among successful women leaders. They include:

- Valuing of an Inclusive Leader and the importance of identity on women's leadership style
- The lack of cultural awareness of many White women and in some cases Black leaders
- There was a feeling amongst BME women that the organizational culture was not conducive to their culture as BME women. Most thought that they were dealing with a hidden challenge – white privilege which formed part of the company culture.
- BME leaders felt culturally and racially stereotyped
- Lack of confidence of some BME leaders shown in their hesitancy to acknowledge themselves as leaders
- BME women believed that they faced barriers and challenges including both gender and racial discrimination on their journey to becoming leaders.
- Line managers not being culturally sensitive to the needs of a diverse team

The research shows that some of the factors enabling women leaders to build successful careers are found within their organizations, while others are external. The organizational structure, working environment, mentoring activities and leadership style are all factors which can promote success, according to the women participants in the study. The examples given in this paper demonstrate that in order for women leaders to fulfill their full potential it is crucial the culture of the organization is 'female friendly'. The study indicates the need for further work to be carried out in organizations to unlock the barriers that potentially stop the women leaders moving ahead as fast as their male counterparts.

Informal and formal networks in the workplace open up opportunities and there is a growing awareness for the importance of networks. Integration and exclusion factors like opportunities to meet, communication skills, experiences of being accepted and respected determine a woman's' integration in networks and, last but not least, having something to offer for network partners is also required. Networks are essential for working, but often women are excluded or exclude themselves.

In the main, all of the women that took part in the research really did enjoy working at their organizations. However, throughout the interviews and focus groups the reoccurring theme of gender /racial stereotypes was being voiced and that organisations needed to firstly recognise that there is a problem and secondly take on the responsibility as the employer and not leave it for the individual. Based on these findings, the following recommendations for the public and private sector can be given.

Recommendations

1. Individuals and Line Managers should consider engaging in culturally sensitive training to build confidence and enable them to maximize the potential that their uniqueness brings to organizations.
2. Employers should use workplace data to identify demographic information on BME women at different levels within their organizations and identify where development and interventions are needed to map progression rates and to create inclusive action plans.
3. Employers should actively review all of their gender programmes and initiatives for inclusion of women from diverse Black and Minority ethnic (BME) heritages and backgrounds and put action plans in place to address zero or low representation and inclusion.
4. Employers with cultural and race diversity employee network groups should actively include volunteering and promoting work inclusion support as part of their commitment to Responsible Business and personal employee development.
5. Individuals and employers should consider introducing mentoring circle networks to encourage BME women to network and have a forum to discuss particular issues and challenges they face in the workplace.
6. Further research is needed to explore the leadership positions of BME leaders.

Discussion Questions

1. Which definitions of leadership are referred to in this chapter?
2. Which important values of a leader are presented?
3. What is the most challenging aspect of being a leader for the women in the study?
4. In your own experiences with group collaborations as a student at university, which leadership styles did get to know – your own or others'?

References

Allen, Brenda. J. (1995): Diversity and organisational communication. In: Journal of Applied Communication Research 23, pp. 143-155.

Alvesson, Mats/Billing, Yvonne Due (1997): Understanding gender and organisations. London: Sage Publications.

Appelbaum, Steven H./Audet, Lynda/Miller, Joanne C. (2003): Gender and leadership? Leadership and gender? A journey through the landscape of theories. In: Leadership & Organization Development Journal 24, 1, pp. 43-51.

Atewologun, Doyin/Sealy, Ruth (2011): Advancing racio-ethnic and diversity theorising through 'intersectional identity work'. In: Toombs, Leslie A. (ed.): Proceedings of the Seventieth Annual Meeting of the Academy of Management (CD).

Avolio, Bruce/Walumbwa, Fred/Weber, Todd J. (2009): Leadership: Current Theories, Research, and Future Directions. In: Management Department Faculty Publications. Paper 37. http://digitalcommons.unl.edu/managementfacpub/37 (Accessed April, 2012).

Bhopal, Kalwant/Danaher, Patrick (2013): Identity and pedagogy in higher education: International comparisons. London: Bloomsbury.

Bowleg, Lisa (2008): When Black+ lesbian+ woman≠ Black lesbian woman: The methodological challenges of qualitative and quantitative intersectionality research. In: Sex roles 59, 5-6, pp. 312-325.

Chin, Jean Lau/Lott, Bernice/Rice, Joy K./Sanchez-Hucles, Janis (eds.) (2008): Women and leadership: Transforming visions and diverse voices. Oxford: Blackwell Publishing.

Cockburn, Cynthia (1991): In the way of women: Men's resistance to sex equality in organizations. London: Macmillan.

Coleman, Andrew (2011): Towards a blended model of leadership for school-based collaborations. In: Educational Management Administration & Leadership 39, 3, pp. 296-316.

Coleman, Marianne and Fitzgerald, Tanya (2008): Gender and leadership development. In: Lumby, Jacky/Crow, Gary/Pashiardis, Petros (eds.): International handbook on the preparation and development of school leaders. New York: Routledge, pp. 119-135.

Cook, S. G. (2013). Black women's dilemma: Be real or be ignored. *Women in Higher Education*, *22*(4), 19-20.

Crenshaw, Kimberle (1991): Mapping the margins: Intersectionality, identity politics, and violence against women of color. In: Stanford law review 43, 6, pp. 1241-1299.

Cross, William E. (1991): Shades of Black: Diversity in African-American identity. Philadelphia: Temple University Press.

Davidson, Marilyn (1997): The Black and Ethnic Minority Woman Manager: Cracking the Concrete Ceiling. Sage Publications.

Devine, P. G. (1989). Stereotypes and prejudice: Their automatic and controlled components. *Journal of personality and social psychology*, *56*(1), 5.

Doldor, Elena/Vinnicombe, Susan/Gaughan, Mary/Sealy, Ruth (2012): Gender diversity on boards: The appointment process and the role of executive search firms. Equality and human rights commission research report, 85.

Due Billing, Yvonne/Alvesson, Mats (2000): Questioning the notion of feminine leadership: A critical perspective on the gender labelling of leadership. In: Gender, Work & Organization 7, 3, pp. 144-157.

Eagly, Alice H./Johnson, Blair T. (1990): Gender and leadership style: A meta- analysis. In: Psychological Bulletin 108, 2, pp. 233-256.

Ellis, Carolyn/Bochner, Arthur P. (2000): Autoethnography, Personal Narrative, Reflexivity: researcher as subject. In: Denzin, Norman K./Lincoln, Yvonna S. (eds.): Handbook of Qualitative Research. Thousand Oaks, CA: Sage, pp. 733-768.

Equality Challenge Unit (2008): Gender, Ethnicity and Degree Attainment Project: Final Report. London: Equality Challenge Unit.

Equality Challenge Unit (2011): Equality in higher education: statistical report 2011. Part 2: students. London: Equality Challenge Unit.

Essers, Caroline/Benschop, Yvonne (2009): Muslim businesswomen doing boundary work: The negotiation of Islam, gender and ethnicity within entrepreneurial contexts. In: Human Relations 62, 3, pp. 403-423.

Fuller, Kay (2010): Talking about gendered headship: how do women and men working in schools conceive and articulate notions of gender? In: Journal of educational administration and history 42, 4, pp. 363-382.

John W. Gardner Quotes. (n.d.): BrainyQuote.com. Retrieved September 16, 2017, from BrainyQuote.com Web site: https://www.brainyquote.com/quotes/quotes/j/johnwgard163160.html

Gavin, J. H., & Mason, R. O. (2004). The Virtuous Organization:: The Value of Happiness in the Workplace. *Organizational dynamics*, *33*(4), 379-392.

Grimes, Mary L. (2005): Re-constructing the leadership model of social justice for African-American women in education. In: Advancing Women in Leadership Online Journal 19. Retrieved October 7, 2017 from http://www.advancingwomen.com/awl/fall2005/index.html.

Gee, Gilbert C./Ro, Annie./Gavin, Amelia/Takeuchi, David T. (2008): Disentangling the effects of racial and weight discrimination on body mass index and obesity among Asian Americans. In: American journal of public health 98, 3, pp. 493-500.

Glaser, Barney/Strauss, Anselm (1967): Grounded theory: The discovery of grounded theory. In: Sociology: The Journal of the British Sociological Association 12, pp. 27-49.

Helgesen, Sally (1990): The female advantage: Women's ways of leadership. New York: Doubleday Currency.

Hofstede, Geert (1991): Empirical models of cultural differences.Psycnet.apa.org.

Holvino, Evangelina (2010): Intersections: the simultaneity of race, gender and class in organization studies. In: Gender, Work & Organization 17, 3, pp. 248-277.

James, K./Vinnicombe, S. (2002): Acknowledging the Individual in the Researcher. In: Partington, David (ed.): Essential Skills for Management Research. Thousand Oaks, CA: Publications Ltd., London, pp. 84-98.

Lumby, Jacky/Coleman, Marianne (2007): Leadership and Diversity: Challenging Theory and Practice in Education. London: Sage.

Lumby, Jacky/Azaola, Marta Cristina (2014): Women principals in South Africa: Gender, mothering and leadership. In: British educational research journal 40, 1, pp. 30-44.

Marecek, Jeanne (2003): Mad Housewives, Double Shifts, Mommy Tracks and Other Invented Realities. In: Feminism & Psychology 13, 2, pp. 259-264.

Maylor, Uvanney/Showunmi, Victoria (unpublished): Intersectionality: A reflective account of higher education challenges from two Black British academics in UK higher education.

McIntosh, Peggy (1992): White Privilege and Male Privilege: A personal account of coming to see correspondences through work in women's studies. In: Andersen, Margaret/Collins, Patricia Hill (eds): Race, Class, and Gender: an anthology. Belnt, CA: Wadsworth Publishing.

Nkomo, Stella M. (1992): The emperor has no clothes: Rewriting "race in organizations". In: Academy of Management Review 17, 3, pp. 487-513.

Omi, Michael/Winant, Howard (1994): Racial formations. In: Racial Formation in the United States. New York: Routledge.

Osler, Audrey (2006): Changing Leadership in Contexts of Diversity: visibility, invisibility and democratic ideals. In: Policy Futures in Education 4, pp. 128-144.

Stone, Howard/Parker, James D./Wood, Laura M. (2005): Report on the Ontario principals' council leadership study. In: Methodology 12, pp. 3-1.
Parker, Patricia S. (1996): Gender, culture, and leadership: Toward a culturally distinct model of African-American women executives' leadership strategies. In: The Leadership Quarterly 7, 2, pp.189-214.
Parker, Patricia S./Ogilvie, D.T. (1996): Gender, culture, and leadership: Toward a culturally distinct model of African women executives' leadership strategies. In: Leadership Quarterly 7, 2, pp. 189-214
Parker, P. S. (2004). *Race, gender, and leadership: Re-envisioning organizational leadership from the perspectives of African American women executives.* Psychology Press.
Powell, Gary N. (2012): Six ways of seeing the elephant: the intersection of sex, gender, and leadership. In: Gender in Management: An International Journal 27, 2, pp. 119-141.
Race for Opportunity (2010): Race into higher education. Today's diverse generation into tomorrow's workforce. London: Race for Opportunity, Business in the Community.
Rees, Teresa (1992): Women and the Labour Market. London: Routledge.
Rudman, Laurie A./Glick, Peter (2001): Prescriptive gender stereotypes and backlash towards agentic women. In: Journal of Social Issues 57, pp. 743-762.
Rush, M. C., Phillips, J. S., & Lord, R. G. (1981). Effects of a temporal delay in rating on leader
behavior descriptions: A laboratory investigation. *Journal of Applied Psychology, 66*(4), 442.
Sagebiel, Felizitas/Showunmi, Victoria (2012): Organisational culture and successful women leadership. Set WEPAN publication USA.
Scott, Elaine S. and Miles, Jane (2013): Advancing leadership capacity in nursing. Nursing administration quarterly 37, 1, pp. 77-82.
Sinclair, Amanda (2004): Journey around leadership. In: Discourse: studies in the cultural politics of education 25, 1, pp. 7-19.
Showunmi, Victoria/Atewologun, Doyin/Bebbington, Denise: (2015). Ethnic, gender and class intersections in British women's leadership experiences. In: Educational Management Administration & Leadership 40, 5, pp. 592-609.
Walker, Allan/Dimmock, Clive (2002): Moving school leadership beyond its narrow boundaries: Developing a cross-cultural approach. In: Leithwood, Kenneth and Halinger, Philip (eds.): Second international handbook of educational leadership and administration. Dordrecht: Springer, pp. 167-202.
Van Knippenberg, Daan/De Dreu, Carsten K. W./Homan, Astri C. (2004): Work group diversity and group performance: an integrative model and research agenda. In: Journal of applied psychology 89, 6, pp. 1008.

Contributors

Petra Ahrens, Dr. phil., is Senior Researcher at the University of Tampere, Finland, in the ERC-funded research project "Gender, Party Politics and Democracy in Europe: A Study of the European Parliament's Political Groups". She is also guest professor for Comparative Politics at the University Antwerp, Belgium. Her research focuses on European integration, gender equality policies, public policy and transnational civil society organisations. She is the author of Actors, Institutions, and the Making of EU Gender Equality Programs (2018, Palgrave Macmillan) and co-editor of the European Journal of Politics and Gender and the German feminist journal Femina Politica.

Carola Bauschke-Urban, Dr. phil., is professor of sociology, gender and diversity studies at Fulda University of Applied Sciences, Department of Social- and Cultural Sciences, Fulda, Germany. She is speaker of the Fulda Graduate Center of Social Sciences and co-editor of the peer reviewed journal GENDER. *Zeitschrift für Geschlecht, Kultur, Gesellschaft.*

Hazel Conley, Prof. Dr. phil., is Professor of Human Resource Management with focus on Equality in the Faculty of Business and Law at the University of the West of England, Bristol, UK. Her research interests include the implementation of equality legislation, particularly in relation to gender and equal pay. She has worked on the implementation of equality legislation in the UK and Northern Ireland and the Gender Pay Gap in UK, Italy and Poland. She is author (with Margaret Page) of Gender Equality in Public Services: Chasing the Dream published by Routledge in 2015 and is an editor of The Gower Handbook of Discrimination at Work published by Gower in 2011 and The Gender Pay Gap and Social Partnership in Europe: Findings from the Close the Deal, Fill the Gap Project to be published in 2018 by Routledge.

Amel Grami, Prof. Dr., is Professor of Gender Studies and Islamic Studies at The University of Manouba, Tunisia, a writer, and a human rights advocate. Her research focuses on culture, society, religion and politics in MENA and the Middle East: Islamist movements, gender relations, culture expressions, media and social movements. She is author of The Debate on Religion, Law and Gender in Post-Revolution Tunisia. Toward New Democratic Imaginaries – İstanbul Seminars on Islam, Culture and Politics, pp. 301-313. (Part of the Philosophy and Politics – Critical Explorations book series (PPCE, volume 2) https://link.springer.com/chapter/10.1007%2F978-3-319-41821-6_29

Ingrid Jungwirth, Prof. Dr. phil., is Professor of Social Sciences with focus on Diversity and Inclusion at Rhine-Waal University of Applied Sciences, Faculty of Society and Economics, Kleve, Germany. She is head of the study programme Gender and Diversity, B.A. Her research fields are gender and diversity studies, mobility and migration, sociology of work and organizations, sociology of the life course and social inequality and social theories. She is editor (2017, with Andrea Wolffram) and author of Hochqualifizierte Migrantinnen – Teilhabe an Arbeit und Gesellschaft. Opladen: Barbara Budrich. [Highly Qualified Migrant Women: participation in work and society] and author of Gendered configurations: transborder professional careers of migrant women. Migration and Ethnic Themes, 2011, Vol. 27, No. 1, pp. 105-121.

Doris Liebscher, LL.M. Eur, Ass. jur., is a legal scholar and activist with focus on anti-discrimination law and law and social justice. She is a member of the Humboldt Law Clinic for Fundamental and Human Rights at the Department of Public Law and Gender Studies at the Humboldt University in Berlin, partner of the Office of Legal Affairs and Science Berlin and board director of the Anti-Discrimination Office Saxony. Her research interests include legal gender studies and racism and the law. She is author of Handbuch Rechtlicher Diskriminierungsschutz Antidiskriminierungsstelle des Bundes (Legal Protection against Discrimination, 2014). She co-edited Antidiskriminierungspädagogik. Konzepte und Methoden für die Bildungsarbeit mit Jugendlichen, VS-Verlag 2010; Den NSU-Komplex analysieren. Aktuelle Perspektiven aus der Wissenschaft, transcript 2017.

Zeynep Oya Usal, PhD, is a lawyer at the Council of Europe (CoE)[1] in Strasbourg, France. Prior joining CoE in 2015, Dr. Usal worked as an assistant professor in human rights law at Koç University in Istanbul, Turkey. Her research interests are international human rights law and gender equality law. She is author of Usal–Kanzler, Zeynep Oya (2016): Special Compensation Regimes for Violations of Human Rights in Turkish Law: A Fast Track Remedy or No Remedy at All?. In: Bagińska E. (eds) Damages for Violations of Human Rights. Ius Comparatum – Global Studies in Comparative Law, vol 9, Springer.

Victoria Showunmi, Dr., is a Lecturer of Education with a focus on gender and equality at University College London, Department of Education and Policy Studies, United Kingdom. She is Module Leader for Minority, Migrant and Refugee MA course. Her research fields are gender, class, race and identity in the context of leadership and experiences of young girls and women. The following articles reflect her work; Showunmi, V., & Fox, A. (2018). Exploring Research Methods for Educational Leadership. *Management in Education, Volume 32 (1),* (pp. 3-5). Showunmi, V. (2017). The Role of the "Black Girls' Club": Challenging the Status Quo. In Martin, J.L., Nickels, A.E., & Sharp-Grier, M. (Eds.), *Feminist Pedagogy, Practice, and Activism: Improving Lives for Girls and Women* (pp. 229-246). New York: Routledge.

Constanze Schwärzer-Dutta is a political scientist, anti-bias-facilitator and counselor. She trains and coaches mainly university staff, social workers and counselors on diversity and antidiscrimination, unconscious/implicit bias in recruitment, internationalization

1 The views and opinions expressed in this article are her personal views. They do not bind the Council of Europe. Dr. Usal would like to thank the Raoul Wallenberg Institute of Human Rights and Humanitarian Law for providing a generous research grant that enabled her to conduct research for this article during September 1-October 15, 2014 at Max Planck Institute for Comparative Public Law and International Law.

at home and transcultural counseling. Her clients also include federal authorities, chambers of commerce and NGOs. She also teaches the anti-bias approach to students of the Social Sciences with a specialisation in Intercultural Relations at Fulda University of Applied Sciences. She is a member of ZSIMT (Centre for Social Inclusion, Migration and Participation, www.zsimt.com) and founding member of ZSIMT Berlin (www.zsimt-berlin.de).

Hülya Şimga, Prof. Dr., is Professor at Maltepe University Philosophy Department and Human Rights Center. Her research interests are gender studies, ethics and women's human rights. She is author of A Question for Humanity: Sexism, Oppression and Human Rights (2019, Lit Verlag).

Peter Streckeisen, PD Dr. phil., is teacher and researcher at Zurich University of Applied Sciences, and senior lecturer at University of Basel, Switzerland. His research interests include welfare states, labour markets, education and inequality, community development, neoliberalism, and sociological theory. He is author of Soziologische Kapitaltheorie. Marx, Bourdieu und der ökonomische Imperialismus (2014, Bielefeld: transcript) and editor of (together with Karin Scherschel and Manfred Krenn) Neue Prekarität. Die Folgen aktivierender Arbeitsmarktpolitik – europäische Länder im Vergleich (2012, Frankfurt/M.: Campus).

Anna Temkina, Ph.D., is the Chair in Public Health and Gender, co-director of the gender programme at the European University at St. Petersburg. Her research in gender studies and feminism began in 1990es. She has worked on reproductive health, sexuality, and gender relations in Soviet and Post-Soviet societies. She is the author of (together with Elena Zdravomyslova, 2015): 12 Lectures in Gender Sociology, St. Petersburg EUSPB (in Russian).

Martina Tißberger, Prof. Dr. phil., is Professor for Social Work with the focus on Interculturality in the Faculty of Medical Engineering and Applied Social Sciences at the University of Applied Sciences Upper Austria, Linz. Her research focuses on Subjectivation, the Critical Studies of Whiteness, Gender, Cultural Studies, Postcolonial Theory, Intersectionality and Diversity. Apart from Social Work she worked in departments of Psychology, Education, Gender Studies and Early Child Education. She is author of Critical Whiteness. Zur Psychologie hegemonialer Selbstreflexion an der Intersektion von Rassismus und Gender (2017, Springer VS).

Sarah Vader, Dr. rer. med., is a research associate at the Rhine-Waal University of Applied Sciences, Faculty of Society and Economics, Kleve, Germany. Her research interests include gender and organizations, women in care work and gender and diversity in academia. She has worked on the topic of the feminization of medicine and care at the University of Duisburg-Essen and the Kliniken Essen-Mitte in Essen, Germany. She is the author of 'How Women Change Medicine; A Case Study in a German Hospital'.

Dagmar Vinz, Dr. phil., is a political scientist (Diploma) who works freelance with her 'Büro Vinz Berlin'. She works at the edge of observation, research, creative writing and training for transformation. Her special interests include the conversion of space and time in the context of globalisation processes. She has worked extensively on the intersection (and polarisation) of gender and diversity. She is the author of Gender and Sustainable Consumption. A German Environmental Perspective. In: European Journal of Women's Studies 16, 2, 2009, pp. 159-179. She is editor (2011, together with Sandra Smykalla) and author of Intersektionalität zwischen Gender und Diversity: Theorien, Methoden und Politiken der Chancengleichheit [Intersectionality between Gender and Diversity: theories, methodologies, and policies of equal opportunities]. Münster: Westf. Dampfboot.

Anna van der Vleuten, Prof. Dr., is Professor Contesting Europeanization at the Institute for Management Research, Radboud University, Nijmegen, The Netherlands. Her research interests include EU gender equality policies, LGBT rights and the ECJ, and comparative regionalism. With Anouka van Eerdewijk and Conny Roggeband she has edited Gender Equality Norms in Regional Governance: Transnational Dynamics in Europe, South America and Southern Africa (2014, Palgrave).

Heike Helen Weinbach, Prof. Dr. phil., is Professor of Education with focus on Didactics of Early Childhood Education at Rhine-Waal-University of Applied Sciences, Kleve, Germany. She is Gestalt Pedagogue, mediator and counsellor. Her research and teaching focus: transformative didactics, gender and diversity education, cultural literacy, ethics and philosophy, trauma pedagogy and counselling.

Elena Zdravomyslova, Dr., is Professor in the Department of Political Scince and Sociology European University at St. Petersburg, Russia. Her research interests include paid domestic work im postSoviet tranformations, elderly care, civic initiatives and gender. Her recent publications include Zdravomyslova, Elena (co-authored with Temkina, Anna, 2015): 12 Lectures in Gender Sociology, St. Petersburg EUSPB, in Russian.

Index

Gabriele Wilde et al. (eds.)

Civil Society and Gender Relations in Authoritarian and Hybrid Regimes

New Theoretical Approaches and Empirical Case Studies

2018 • 269 pp. • Pb. • 33,00 € (D) • 34,00 € (A)
ISBN 978-3-8474-0729-4 • eISBN 978-3-8474-0874-1

Is civil society's influence favorable to the evolvement of democratic structures and democratic gender relations? While traditional approaches would answer in the affirmative, the authors highlight the ambivalences. Focusing on women's organizations in authoritarian and hybrid regimes, they cover the full spectrum of civil society's possible performance: from its important role in the overcoming of power relations to its reinforcement as backers of government structures or the distribution of antifeminist ideas.

The Editors:
Prof. Gabriele Wilde, Prof. Annette Zimmer, Dr. Katharina Obuch, Dr. Isabelle-Christine Panreck, all: Westfälische Wilhelms-Universität Münster, Germany